A NEW ORDER OF THE AGES

A NEW ORDER OF THE AGES

A Metaphysical Blueprint of Reality and an Exposé on Powerful Reptilian/Aryan Bloodlines

VOLUME 1

Collin Robert Bowling

iUniverse, Inc.
Bloomington

A NEW ORDER OF THE AGES
A Metaphysical Blueprint of Reality and an Exposé on Powerful Reptilian/Aryan Bloodlines VOLUME 1

Copyright © 2011 by Collin Robert Bowling.

All rights reserved. No part of this book may be used or reproduced by any means, graphic, electronic, or mechanical, including photocopying, recording, taping or by any information storage retrieval system without the written permission of the publisher except in the case of brief quotations embodied in critical articles and reviews.

The views expressed in this work are solely those of the author and do not necessarily reflect the views of the publisher, and the publisher hereby disclaims any responsibility for them.

iUniverse books may be ordered through booksellers or by contacting:

iUniverse
1663 Liberty Drive
Bloomington, IN 47403
www.iuniverse.com
1-800-Authors (1-800-288-4677)

Because of the dynamic nature of the Internet, any web addresses or links contained in this book may have changed since publication and may no longer be valid.

Any people depicted in stock imagery provided by Thinkstock are models, and such images are being used for illustrative purposes only.
Certain stock imagery © Thinkstock.

ISBN: 978-1-4620-3715-5 (sc)
ISBN: 978-1-4620-3716-2 (hc)
ISBN: 978-1-4620-3717-9 (ebk)

Library of Congress Control Number: 2011912104

Printed in the United States of America

iUniverse rev. date: 11/07/2011

Table of Contents

Dedication vii

Epigraph ix

Introduction xi

IN THE BEGINNING xv

Part 1: Thy Brethren, Us All 1

    I.   Structure of Reality 3
    II. The Nature of Time and Soul 24
    III. Universal History Part 1 41
    IV. Universal History Part 2 70
    V. Lemuria, Atlantis, and the Ancient Mystery Schools 81

Part 2: The Virus of Life 113

    I.   The World's Religions and Secret Societies 115
    II. Columbus and the New World 245
    III. Freedom From Oppression 262
    IV. Thank-you, Mr. Tesla 287
    V. Make Love, Not War 294

Bibliography 321

Index 337

Dedication

This book is for Mother Earth. Our individual electronic circles are likened to the great central neuron of the planet, and as we ascend, Lady Gaia holds us in her arms. For many years she has waned at the feat of mammon, and finally she is shedding that negative weight through hurricanes, volcano eruptions, earthquakes, and tsunamis. She has always been there for us, and now as we undergo the transformation process we will finally be reunited with the great spirit of our mother, a rose by any other name.

Epigraph

"This world is indeed a living being endowed with a soul and intelligence . . . a single visible living entity containing all other living entities, which by their nature are all related . . . [furthermore] . . . the cosmos is a single living creature which contains all living creatures within it."

-Plato: Dialogues

Introduction

Over thousands of years a gulf has been made between the far-seeing elite and the simple-minded peasants, and like a blind man without his stick, both are hopelessly lost without the other. These elite, who allege to be "illuminated," have corroborated/interbred with powerful Reptilian/Aryan bloodlines coming out of Sumer, Babylon, and the northern Caucasus mountains. Secret societies are the backbone of the takeover of planet Earth through these powerful bloodlines, which were accouched by demonic reptilian and human extraterrestrials many thousands of years ago. Many major players in the fields of politics, religion, and entertainment today share the D.N.A. of reptilian "gods" who came down to Earth before the deluge and upgraded the primitive humanoid species to a more advanced biological form. Within our human species on Earth exists a combination of D.N.A. from 22 extraterrestrial races. Of these extraterrestrials who visited the pre-diluvian Earth, several reptilian factions have conspired with a group in the Universe known as the "Dark Lords" to erect a compartmentalized state of control and suppression on this planet so they could eventually take over. An arduous task like this one could not be completed from the outside alone, as 13 primary Reptilian/Aryan bloodlines have perpetuated a series of mystical orders throughout the centuries in order to have fully commandeered the most powerful agencies of religion and politics by the year 2012 when major vibrational shifts are expected to occur.

The Illuminati, the nucleus of these interbreeding alien-demonic families, plans for the takeover of Earth and the instigation of the reign of the Antichrist as prophesized by their supreme manual, known as the "Protocols of the Learned Elders of Zion." This is a Jewish conspiracy, and the Learned Elders of Zion are rich Jewish rabbis, yet the word 'Jewish' doesn't relate to any race in particular. There were many Semitic peoples who migrated into Mesopotamia, Anatolia, Great Britain, and China from the northern European mountains, these traveling clans emerging as the Indo-Europeans (Aryans), Akkadians, Babylonians, Amorites, Hittites, and Elamites. There was no specific Jewish race, though, and the only group that could have been likened to it was the Khazarian people. Abraham, Moses, King Solomon, and King David are depicted falsely in the Bible, which is an allegory of the truth. In reality, it was composed by closely-guarded bloodlines who to this day claim to be seeded on this planet from the aliens. In the course of very meticulous interbreeding in antiquity, ancient bloodlines who claim to be seeded from the "Star Gods" have infiltrated powerful mystical orders and secret societies (in some cases started them) and have erected the nation-state of Israel to act as a worldwide headquarters for establishing a New World Order based on the worship of the false god Lucifer. It was not Moses who established the "home of the Jews" but in fact agents of the Rothschild family acting in direct accordance with these Reptilian/Aryan bloodlines. Israel was bombed into existence in 1948, and today, it serves as a headquarters for the so-called "Jewish conspiracy" and as you will see, a "New Order of the Ages" (New World Order).

These interbreeding bloodlines, throughout the course of the last two thousand years, created religion, politics, and banks to control massive populations of people and establish a constricted state of awareness among individuals. They have effectively created a hierarchical pyramid of control and suppression so that information is improperly disseminated down the ranks, ensuring power to only the select few. At the top is Lucifer who heads an organization in the universe known as the Dark Lords. Below him, the Grand Druid Council and the Committee of 300 work in conjunction to perpetuate the continual consolidation of power and decision-making into a few evil hands. In the United States, the Council on Foreign Relations and the Trilateral Commission labor tirelessly to ensure the alien-demonic stranglehold over the post-diluvian Earth (10,000 B.C.E. to present). The invaders are evil and they have a diabolical plan for the future, but the original creators of Earth are back to secure a future of love and prosperity for all. Lucifer is the false god of light; that is, he is light without love. The real God embodies the concept of unconditional love. When the Age of Light commences in 2012 and the Earth rises next to the constellation of Aquarius, the planet will ascend to the fifth dimension. The Dark Lords wish to prevent this as they see a future where everyone is a slave to the New World Order.

The cohorts of the New World Order are under the control of so-called "Big Brother," who is nothing more than a subliminal propaganda campaign orchestrated to make you feel small. Liberty is a guise worn

by these men who masquerade around as disillusioned sorcerers
end up seeing only two distinctions of man, a man of mature mind
a man of immature mind. Assuming these two leagues are far apart
could conjecture that the proponents of Zionism are diplomatic
professional, but yet again, we must consider the fact that they w
masks. For these men, the socio-political circumstance of a country
nothing to do with the moral, and anticipating a society on the brink
extinction I ascertain the fact that the clever division is only a ruse.
power is the ultimate aphrodisiac of man. It is quite ironic, howev
that the people whom the Elders see as fodder now have the possibil
within them to reach a new state of ecstasy, metamorphosing them in
the divine. So, in the end, when all the moves have been made, which w
usurp the throne of objective reality? Power . . . . . or Spirituality?

IN THE BEGINNING . . .

In pure unbounded awareness, there is no beginning, middle, or end. For our purpose however, let us say that the beginning, duration, and end of creation are all one act. This act of creation is vibrating at different frequencies in an infinite number of dimensions and exists indefinitely, meaning it is transcendent. We will also say that this act of creation was manifested by a being known to extraterrestrials from the star system of the Pleiades as "Prime Creator." This being is called many names by races all over the universe and other universes existing within the cyclical omniverse of creation. On Earth, we call it (him and/or her) "God." The word 'God' though carries negative monotheistic connotations and we will instead use 'Prime Creator.' In the beginning/middle/end is, was, and always will be CONSCIOUSNESS. Creation is consciousness suspended in a blissful state of pure ecstasy, that which we on Earth call "love." Love has no cause except that which is bestowed by Prime Creator. Like consciousness, love is infinite, unbounded, and eternal. In individualized states, both love and consciousness are mirrored reflections of the larger scope of their manifestation. Like a hologram, every piece is a perfect replica of the whole image.

Moving along, we will now say that love and consciousness are intertwined into one being. This being is non-local, meaning it does not exist in space and time. All the souls in this universe and other universes are individual sparks of this one being subsisting within the one being. These souls inhabit universes, galaxies, stars, planets, humanoid bodies, non-humanoid bodies, animal bodies, insect bodies, and plants. The analogy of Russian Dolls works nicely here: creation manifests as universes, galaxies, stars, planets, people, animals, insects, and plants, each stratum of creation residing within the larger one. On Earth, people, plants, etc. are spirit beings inhabiting a planet containing a spirit being, which is inhabiting a star system containing a spirit being, and so on. Our bodies as well as the bodies of our ancestors and the other life forms on this planet are physical representations of consciousness while our souls are non-physical representations of consciousness. The body of the Earth is the physical representation of her spirit being, which was referred to as "Lady Gaia" by the ancients. As a soul raises its vibration and level of consciousness/love, it can inhabit larger bodies (like a planet, star, or galaxy). In the end, however, we are all one soul (the one being) existing as a matrix of infinite possibilities for creation. On Earth, we are experiencing ourselves as individual states of consciousness in a low vibrational density. Creation is not solid and the space-time continuum is an illusion. We are a hologram of higher consciousness/love. When one awakens to this higher reality, one can ascend to a higher vibrational density.

PART 1

Thy Brethren, Us All

I
STRUCTURE OF REALITY

If you have ever read *Prometheus Rising* by Robert Anton Wilson you might refer to that work on numerous occasions throughout the reading of this book as you sift through the layers of reality I present to you. In chapter one of that great work, which is entitled "The Thinker & The Prover," Wilson suggests from his own theoretical influences that both the 'thinker' and the 'prover' can have it their way, the only difference between the two being that the prover has to work harder in order to satisfy the dilemma of proving something, even if it is based on fallacious thinking. The thinker has the freedom to wander wherever he or she wants in the mind, the mechanism for spirit to experience a physical body. In this book, however, I make it simpler. There are two aspects of yourself: the 'thinker' and the 'knower.' In this case, the thinker uses the brain to analyze a present situation and the knower feels what the right response would be based on a sensation in consciousness. Both work, but the knower has a direct advantage over the thinker—the knower doesn't have to think. Can this really be? Does ultimate objective reality transcend thought? It all comes down to knowing what "reality" is.

What do I mean by 'reality?' Based on the writing preceding this section I suggest that reality is a panorama of infinite possibilities projecting out from a center of pure consciousness and love. Consciousness and love create realities, and they do it on different vibrational frequencies in many dimensions. If I were to ask you to imagine a beautiful red rose you could do it, but where would that rose be? You are the wizard who conjures up the rose, but if I opened up your brain all I would see is a network of tiny neurons carrying electromagnetic currents.[1] These currents merge at nexus points, which are really gaps between neurons called synapses. In the synapse, a release of chemicals takes

---

[1] Electromagnetic currents are called "virtual photons" because photons are the smallest units of energy and information.

place. We can see a variety of chemicals, but there are two predominate ones: gamma amino butyric acid and glutamate (the former depresses and the latter stimulates). The electrical activity is due to an electrical action potential, which is basically the exchange of ions across cell membranes. In your brain, however, there is no rose. Your brain was merely a mechanism for creating the reality of the rose, which actually existed in your consciousness (soul/sprit).

The same applies for the outside world. When you look at an orange flower, an invisible electromagnetic beam (photons) hits your eyes causing your retinas to produce chemical reactions which in turn send electrical currents to your brain. Your brain interprets those signals as a picture of an orange flower, but those signals are not orange in color and they do not represent a flower. The experience of the flower as a whole occurs in your consciousness. When you hear a sound, your eardrums vibrate and this causes the cilia in your ear canal to send electrical impulses to your brain. Your brain interprets those signals as sound, but those signals do not make a sound. The experience of sound occurs in your consciousness. In the outside world, the only reality is energy vibrating at different frequencies and changing form. The experience of a three-dimensional holographic reality complete with sounds, colors, pictures, smells, and textures takes place in only one place, and that is your spirit, that which I refer to as consciousness. Although you experience a continuous stream of information, reality is actually flickering on and off. This is happening at such a tremendous rate, however, that you cannot experience that resonance. You don't experience the world as vibrations, you experience it as a solid, physical reality.

Let me explain further by calling to attention an experiment done in the early part of the 20th century where scientists shot beams of particles through slits in a metal frame.[2] They wanted to understand the nature of matter and so the particles (electrons) in this experiment represented microscopic bundles of "matter." When the scientists projected beams

---

[2] Thomas Young and Augustin-Jean Fresnel performed double-slit experiments in the early 19th century to prove the wave nature of light while others corroborated the particle nature of light proposed by Isaac Newton. In the 20th century, Werner Heisenberg reconciled the two views by formulating his uncertainty principle which stated that light (matter) is both a wave and a particle simultaneously, but both a particle's position and linear momentum cannot be calculated at the same time.

of electrons through two upright slits in the metal frame the waves interfered with each other after passing through the slits, creating columns of imprints on a fluorescent screen. The spots on the screen where the waves from the two slits arrived in phase showed up bright and the spots where the waves arrived out of phase and canceled each other out showed up dark. Hence, there was a pattern of alternating light and dark spots revealing a wave interference pattern. The scientists then decided to make the beam very weak and only shoot one electron at a time. What happened was unexpected as the single electron passed through both slits at the same time as a wave function and interfered with itself when re-emerging, causing the same interference pattern on the fluorescent screen. The scientists were baffled so they placed a measuring device by the slits to see how the single electron could possibly go through both slits at the same time. When they observed this the electron behaved like a particle, going through only one slit and not causing an interference pattern on the screen.

The conclusion was made. The very act of perceiving the electron turned it from a field of possibilities (a wave) into a singularity (a particle). Consciousness (the measuring device) created the reality. Similarly, when physicists studied the atom they found a nucleus orbited by a field of electrons. When they tried to pinpoint individual electrons the task became impossible because the electrons only existed as a field of wave functions. Both the momentum and position of a single electron could not be calculated at the same time; the areas hypothesized to reveal the electron only existed as a probability field. It was like the electrons existed in this dimension but also other dimensions as well because they would pop in and out of the electromagnetic field. When the scientists tuned their microscopes deeper into the field of electrons they found nothing. Nothing? No, they did not find nothing. They found a field of infinite possibilities that looked like nothing because it was really everything. So what is matter? Matter is an infinite field of consciousness condensed down into a singularity. When this field is open matter acts like a wave, but when it is condensed down into a singularity it is a particle. Matter is a particle and a wave simultaneously. When you are viewing it matter appears as a particle but when you aren't it appears as a wave function, hence the paradox of quantum mechanics.

So you see, you really are a god. Your consciousness is your divine power. Everything you give consciousness to becomes a reality. To view this topic from a higher perspective you must think of everything in terms of energy. Everything is energy. The cause of everything is energy. Everything that you see around you is a condensed vibration of energy. God is not a person, it is an infinite field of spiritual energy. Everything vibrates, so the lower the frequency of vibration the more it appears as a solid. When something vibrates at higher and higher frequencies it appears as light or it is invisible to you. The physical manifest world that you see with your eyes is actually only a fraction of what really exists because you cannot see vibrational frequencies existing above and below the spectrum of the rainbow. Your eyes cannot pick up infrared or ultraviolet color frequencies, although these emanations are evident to many animals and insects.

In pure consciousness (objective reality), only love and light can subsist. If light is what you see, then love is what you feel. Love is the force which sustains all of life. Everything was created using love. It is the most powerful force there is. It is through the infinite matrix of love that information is brought out through light in tiny light-encoded filaments. When our brains receive information it is through light, and the encoded filaments are sent through a decoding process performed by neurons, our brain cells that process and transmit electrical and chemical signaling. Together they form a network which structures our entire reality based on how we decode the light that enters our eyes. The reality that most people perceive is a highly condensed version of the ultimate reality that exists around them all the time. Through belief systems, people create for themselves a critical factoring unit that acts as a filtration device for what they perceive.

The five sense realm is the reality that most people on Earth are stuck in now. They only believe what they can see, hear, taste, touch, and smell. In other words, they are trapped in their own bodies. They are limited to the frequencies of light and sound that their bodies can handle. Since everything vibrates, that means our bodies vibrate. If a frequency spectrum of sound and color is outside the range that our bodies can detect, then we believe that it does not exist. Many people do not believe in ghosts because they cannot see them, but there are realities beyond physical sight. Electromagnetic plasma light entities vibrate at frequencies above the spectrum of the rainbow, so that is why we cannot see them. Millions of people will encounter ghosts, poltergeists, and manifestations of discarnate entities every year, but those experiences will remain a mystery until the collective consciousness of our planet expands its mode of perception.

The Seven Planes of Existence

Much like the Kabbalah,[3] the higher we move up the ladder of existence, the farther we travel away from human experience and the closer we come to the Source from which all other planes emanate. We have a "body" on each of these planes which acts as a vehicle for our consciousness (soul). The seven planes are listed henceforth:

PHYSICAL PLANE: The first plane is dense and solid. It is the material world and all things measured by the material senses. The Matrix anchors itself into this plane as it is the plane of space, time, solid form and causality. Our body on this plane is the physical body.

ETHERIC PLANE: The second plane is an energetic spiritual template upon which the physical world is based. The etheric realm is the blueprint for the physical world. Our body on this plane is the etheric body; it is a blue/grey mist emanating 1 to 2 inches from our physical body.

ASTRAL PLANE: The third plane is the realm of idealized form. The astral plane is the idealized template for the etheric plane as the etheric plane is the mold for the physical plane. Astral forms are affected by energy, intention, and emotions and the astral plane is the first realm of spirits, from benevolent spirit guides to ghosts to discarnate entities. It is also the dream plane and the collective consciousness of our planet. Our body on this plane is the astral body, the vehicle we use for astral projection and remote viewing.

---

[3] According to the Zohar, the foundational text for Kabbalism, the *Sod* is the most esoteric interpretation of mystical Judaism which is expressed in the Kabbalah. The Kabbalah purports that there are many emanations from the Divine Source and the goal of humans is to ascend through the various levels which rise in frequency and consciousness the closer one gets to God.

EMOTIONAL PLANE: The fourth plane is somewhat of an extension of the astral plane and is where our highest emotions reside, such as love. The Ascended Masters can aide us on our journey from this realm. Our body on this plane is our emotional body and it emanates about 2 to 3 inches from our physical body.

MENTAL PLANE: The fifth plane is the realm of ideas, thoughts, and concepts. In order to create something, one must first conceive a thought and then give it emotional energy so it can manifest form on the astral plane and then eventually onto the etheric and physical planes. The mental plane is the realm of information, abstract concepts and communication; our body on this level is our mental body, which radiates 5 inches to 3 feet from our physical body.

PSYCHIC PLANE: The sixth plane is the connective plane where seers and psychics have visions of the past and future. When you remember something or when you project an image, you are enacting your consciousness on the psychic plane. Our body on this plane is the crystal light body, which is activated by the Merkabah vehicle, the three-dimensional star tetrahedron of light that is contained within our electronic circles. It interpenetrates all other bodies.

DIVINE PLANE: The seventh plane is the home of our Divine Monad, our connection to Prime Creator. This field of energy surrounds the other six planes and is the container and source for all of creation. This is where the higher self resides. Our body in this plane is the nirvanic body, which emanates 3 to 5 feet from our physical body on the highest octave of the 12th dimension.

According to metaphysicians, each of the seven planes can be subdivided into seven dimensions, so together, forty-nine planes of existence are manifested through the will of Prime Creator.[4] Each plane has one of each of the aspects (physical, etheric, astral, emotional, mental, psychic, and divine) since we can use these abilities and call down this energy from the third dimension.

---

[4] This only accounts for the universe in which we reside. There are many universes existing within the omniverse.

The Holographic Universe and the Dimensions of Light

Our universe is a hologram. It is not real in the sense that everyone thinks it is real, that being a solid structure. Rather, our universe is malleable and manifest on many dimensional levels outside the range our bodies can detect. This particular hologram contains 11 creational densities, or 11 frequency spectrums of sound and color with each spectrum containing 11 additional levels.[5] In this model of creation, the frequency of light and its counterpart, sound, are recorded on different density levels (this does not directly relate to the 49 planes of existence discussed above as it is more concrete, although it fits the overall scale). Color relates to the wavelength of light, so the spectrum of the rainbow is just light vibrating along a certain spectrum radiating from blue to red. That is only what we can see from 3rd density (our physical universe), however, since there are an infinite number of colors ranging from black to white. Black is the absence of color and white is all the colors combined, so if you want to picture Creation just imagine an infinite field of love that perpetuates a color and sound frequency from zero to infinity. Zero is the gap, the point of creation, and 3rd density is the first vibrational level of existence since it carries the lowest vibration. The 11 creational densities range from 3rd density, which is the observable universe (Physical Plane), to 13th density, which is the beginning of the Cosmic Center of Consciousness (Divine Plane). This density is never ending and stretches on to infinity. Third density is our perspective of creation, although it is severely limited.

There is another dimensional model that is very much relative to and intertwined with the previous models and it was given to us by the Plejarens (Pleiadians).[6] This is the model of "Manifestation of Nine Dimensions," where dimension is not a synonym of frequency. Instead, dimension in this sense refers to a realm of awareness and manifestation. The creational densities model of the universe shows us layers of sound

---

[5] Alex Collier, "Awake and Aware," September 2009: http://www.youtube.com/watch?v=uR46QjXjLH0.

[6] According to Billy Meier, who was contacted by the Pleiadians in the 1970's in Switzerland, this group of extraterrestrials are advanced humans who have come back in time to help Earth avoid impending catastrophe. They also worked with Barbara Hand Clow in the 1980's, helping her compose several books, one of which outlines the model of Manifestation of Nine Dimensions.

and color vibrating at higher and higher frequencies. This model is the basic understanding of the composition of the universe and is the concrete version of the Seven Planes model. The model of "Manifestation of Nine Dimensions" is the most practical for our understanding since it can be considered as the process by which thought manifests from higher dimensions down to lower dimensions (9th dimension down into the 1st dimension according to the Pleiadians). Thought is the origin of everything. In the Bible it says, "In the beginning was the word," however this is a mistranslation among numerous mistranslations. In the beginning was thought. That is why understanding this model is crucial in manifesting whatever reality you desire.

    I will explain this model from the perspective of Earth, as to make it easier to understand.[7] The first of Earth's nine dimensions of consciousness is the iron core crystal at the center of the planet. This center is the most solid of the nine dimensions and is like an anchoring point for the higher dimensions. This iron core at the center of the planet radiates out electromagnetic waves, which are then triggered by electromagnetic frequency waves in the atmosphere that are the result of higher light frequencies traveling from the Sun and passing through the Earth's atmosphere. We are connected to the iron core crystal at the center of the Earth because there is iron in our blood, which pulses to the rhythm of the iron core. The iron molecules in the iron core crystal pulse because as the Earth spins on its axis it vibrates to all the planets, moons, and asteroids in our solar system, including the Sun itself. All these bodies in turn vibrate due to the forward motion of the galaxy as it spins around the central black hole. The entire galaxy pulses to the quasars, supernovas, and other stars and planets in the galaxy, and also to the sister galaxy of Andromeda.

    When the Earth spins to the tune of the solar system it creates movement, which in turn transforms particles into waves contriving moving energy. This is how the iron core crystal at the center of Earth pulses out electromagnetic radiation; it is because of the energy produced by the spin of the Earth on its axis and the movement of its revolution around the Sun. Just as the iron core crystal is the one dimensional point of Earth, the black hole at the center of the galaxy is the one dimensional point of the Milky Way. The frequency of vibration determines the qualities of matter, light, and consciousness, and as

---

[7]   I will use this model most often throughout this dissertation as it is the easiest to relate to.

the pulses of the Earth's iron core radiate out into the universe they become more and more refined until they turn into light in the center of the galaxy. The first dimension likewise is the source of gravity. It holds the Earth and everyone on it together, and as it reaches the higher dimensions it becomes less and less noticeable (in other words weaker). Just as on the Earth, all one-dimensional centers in the universe are gravity, and this force holds all the dimensions together on the vertical plane of ascending dimensions rising out of the black hole in the center of each galaxy.

The second dimension is the realm of the elementals. The minerals, radioactive materials, viruses, and bacteria are all forms of intelligence subsisting between the iron core crystal at the center of the Earth and the surface of the planet. This area is known as the "Telluric" realm and it is the source for surface life. These minerals exist in the third dimension, but have as their foundation a dense, powerful vibrating structure rooted in the second dimension. Trillions of workers maintain the structure of life and provide sources of nourishment for higher intelligences such as animal and human life, forms of consciousness who owe their very existence to the second dimensional life forms that form roots to the tree of life. Vitamins and minerals keep our physical bodies in good working condition while crystals like opal, pearl, amethyst, topaz, and sapphire work to heal and harmonize our energetic bodies.

A roman poet named Ovid wrote a series of stories call the *Metamorphoses*, and in one of these stories the goddess Themis rises out of the water and tells a man and a woman—Deucalion and Phyrra—to throw their mother's bones behind them in order to populate the Earth with children. The two realize that the Earth is their mother and the source of all life, so they throw stones behind them and the stones grow and become people. Ovid's tale is a myth, but it is also grounded in truth. The Earth is our mother and the Telluric realm is the source of life. Geomancy is an ancient art form dealing with the divination of nature spirits to harvest the Earth's energy gridlines, and it was practiced many times over by the ancient peoples. They learned how to meditate and align with the consciousness of the second dimension, thereby gaining a foothold into the Earth. From there they could control the weather, seasons, and rain cycles. Another ancient science, alchemy, deals with the ability to change base metals into gold, which was then used to build palaces, temples, and places of worship. A more practical aspect of alchemy can be viewed as disporting inorganic chemistry to work as empirical magic. We often think of the ground as just a place to walk on, but it is so much more than that. It contains the biological, chemical, mineral, and crystalline life forms that structure our entire ecosystem.

The third dimension is the realm of linear space and time and is the place where the physical and non-physical dimensions intersect. The realms of the first dimension through the third dimension are measurable, while the realms of the fourth dimension and beyond are subtle frequencies existing within the third dimension. They are non-linear and non-physical, but sometimes they seem more real than some things that exist in the third dimension. For example, sometimes you will walk into a room where two people are fighting and you will instantly feel a rush of intense emotional energy that frightens you and sends you back to where you came. This emotional energy feels very palpable. In some cases, a person will throw an insult at you and you feel like you have been struck by a blow to the stomach. That person didn't really hit you, but it felt like it because of the enacting subtle frequencies that are non-physical but exist within space and time. Time is just an instrument we use to accomplish certain tasks. One might realize the past is just a data bank of information which can be tapped into at any time to the extent of grounding oneself into the present moment, the present moment being a platform that one can then spring forward into a future possibility. The science of the third dimension is Newtonian physics, which becomes obsolete in the higher dimensions. One of Newton's laws, however, holds the key to everything. This law states that every action has an equal and opposite reaction, and you will see how this law is the premise for everything as we dive further into this book. In effect, the third dimension is just a space where the material and spiritual realms can become accustomed to one another.

The fourth dimension is the realm of the collective mind of humanity. It is the thoughts and emotions that run our society day in and day out. The entire history of humankind on this planet is contained within the fourth dimension. All thoughts and feelings are vibrational codes embedded within the fabric of the fourth dimension where they remain in eternity, because there is no time in the fourth dimension. When you dream, you are allowing your subconscious and superconscious minds to communicate with one another in a symbolic fashion in a timeless realm. Dreams aren't random, they are messages. Telepathy, channeling, and mind control are practices utilizing the secrets of the fourth dimension to control and manipulate people into killing themselves, others, and the environment. The gods of antiquity are not really gods, they are just fourth dimensional archetypes which manifest themselves in the third dimension using conduits. These conduits can be political leaders, religious leaders, or just some demented kid who shoots up a school. These archetypes are just ideas and thoughts, but they could also be aliens who visited Earth in the past.

When messages from higher intelligences reach the canopy of the fourth dimension they split into two polarities, those being light and dark. You could say that there are good plans and evil plans, but good and evil are just paradigms based on the principles of light and dark. The electromagnetic fields that travel through the fourth dimension meet the second-dimensional magnetic fields rising out from the Earth in the third dimension, where physical realities are established. When poets write or musicians compose music they anchor in higher dimensional thought forms and use them as ideas to create. When someone assassinates a famous politician or activist they are usually unaware of the fact that they are enacting someone else's thoughts and impulses. The science of the fourth dimension is quantum mechanics, which deals with the properties of light. Light can be viewed as a particle or a wave, depending on the point of observation. In ultimate reality it is both, and the means by which it manifests in physical reality is through consciousness.

The fifth dimension is the realm of light, which is centered in the heart chakra of the planet. As the heart chakra of each individual person centers the seven-chakra system, so the heart is the center of the Earth chakra system. The Earth is now passing through the photon belt radiating out from the center of the galaxy. The result is that it is transmuting the atmosphere. Photons are particles of light vibrating to the full spectrum of electromagnetic radiation. They usually range from low frequency waves to gamma rays. Gamma rays hold much more energy than low frequency rays, so the effect of the Earth passing through the photon belt is an expansion of consciousness. Gamma ray bursts cause humans to be conscious in nine dimensions simultaneously. 225 million years ago the Earth was in a similar position it is now when it was picked to be a laboratory for biological life forms, those forms after evolution, mutation, and recombination then in turn being able to seed the rest of the galaxy. We are now reaching the end of a cycle and on December

21, 2012 this culmination of biology will be disseminated into the Milky Way as the planet makes its transition into the fifth dimension. The fifth dimension is centered in the heart. In the fourth dimension light appears as either a particle or a wave, but in the fifth dimension it appears as both simultaneously. The science of the fifth dimension is creativity, which is the checkpoint for all creations manifesting in multiple dimensions synchronously.

The sixth dimension is the realm of geometric forms that hold buildings and people together in the third dimension. It is the home of our spirit bodies, the vehicles which allow us to measure the vibrational patterns of the four body system.[8] Long ago, ancient civilizations found that buildings lasted longer when they were reflective of sacred, sixth-dimensional geometries. Why do you think that structures like the Great Pyramids, the Sphinx, and the Greek acropolis last for thousands of years? It is because those structures were built with powerful energies of the sixth dimension, energies which clairvoyantly gifted people can see. Objects last longer when they are venerated by people. The sixth dimension is analogous to Plato's Theory of Forms. Everything you see in the third dimension is a copy of a perfect paradigm in the sixth dimension. In the third dimension cows are just animals that eat grass and produce milk, but in the sixth dimension a cow is a geometric pattern contained within a vibrating morphogenetic field. Most of our bodies are actually empty space, so why do we appear so solid? It is because our individual morphogenetic fields hold our form together through the vibration of our four bodies. Scientists today are discovering that when they beam into a frog embryo the morphogenetic field information of a salamander, a salamander is created. This might sound like fantasy but it isn't. A cow looks like a cow because its morphogenetic field generates that image at all times, otherwise the cow would look like something totally different and change its appearance every day. The science of the sixth dimension is the five Platonic solids. These are the tetrahedron, hexahedron, octahedron, dodecahedron, and icosahedron. The universe is structured in a logical way according to these archetypal patterns, which influence structure in the material realm. If it wasn't for the geometry of the sixth dimension everything would be chaotic.

---

[8] Our being is typically referred to by extraterrestrials as a four body system because it is composed of four frequencies of consciousness: body, emotions, thoughts, and spirit.

The seventh dimension is the realm of cosmic sound that generates the sixth-dimensional geometric forms by vibrational resonance. As planets spin on their axes and revolve around solar bodies they create sound, the music of the universe. Within the photon bands in the galaxy, eighth-dimensional waves of light create seventh-dimensional sound waves, whose unique vibrational tendencies structure geometric patterns. Just as everything in the third dimension is held together by geometric forms in the sixth dimension, geometric patterns in the sixth dimension are held together by sound patterns in the seventh dimension. The science of the seventh dimension is music. Octaves are sequences of eight notes and are grouped together into sound vibrations. Each octave is a scale of notes that appears henceforth: C-D-E-F-G-A-B-C. Each subsequent, higher octave is a doubling of the hertz (pulses per second) of the one below it, so lower A is 220 hertz and middle A is 440 hertz. The vibration of air molecules creates sound, which then creates solidity. Cymatics is the study of this process.

The eighth dimension is the realm of the mind of Prime Creator. This realm is light. As vibrational frequencies rise they go from lower audible (deep hums) to higher audible (high pitch sounds) to inaudible. The inaudible range and above is where the visible spectrum of light exists. When we look at a color we are seeing a frequency that is vibrating at millions of pulses per second. When the earth moves into the fifth dimension light will take on a whole new meaning as new colors will be discovered, colors which exist above the spectrum of the rainbow.

The ninth dimension is the black hole at the center of the Milky Way. All black holes are stars that have imploded upon themselves and collapsed into a singularity. This condensing of an immense energy field into a single point creates an event horizon which surrounds the singularity in a spherical fashion. Light (and anything) that reaches this "horizon" gets sucked into the black hole and reemerges from a white hole in a brand new universe. In essence, the black holes in the center of each galaxy are portals into "no-time" zones where creation happens. The ninth dimension is a vertical axis that extends above and below the plane of the galaxy, and the black hole at the center is a spinning, gravitational nucleus which manifests itself in time-waves. These waves of created "time" influence events in the galaxy like storylines in a book. The galactic center is constantly receiving ninth-dimensional synchronization beams from other galaxies, which elicits events in this galaxy.

On August 16, 1987 our galaxy received a synchronization beam, causing the cycle of the Harmonic Convergence to extend into the year 2012 when all of our crown chakras will be activated and we will awaken to the higher dimensions.[9] When the Milky Way received this beam, its liquid darkness essence pulsated, forcing photon bands to become nuclear clearing zones for the whole galaxy. Every star and planetary system in the galaxy sooner or later undergoes this ninth-dimensional galactic pulsation by means of the seventh-dimensional photon bands. This is all orchestrated by eighth-dimensional galactic sound tones. The ninth-dimensional galactic center is a state of eternal bliss where no time exists. This is where manifestations of the galactic center of consciousness take form and create galactic systems based on the flux and flow of matter. In ultimate reality, time does not move. Matter moves, creating the illusion of time.

The tenth dimension is the vertical axis that aligns the other nine dimensions into a single gravitational point—the iron core crystal at the center of Earth. When one's consciousness is simultaneously aware in all nine dimensions equally, it is in the tenth dimension. The eleventh dimension is the all-encompassing energy field that manifests and contains the other ten dimensions. This is the first realm of universal consciousness. The twelfth dimension is the Great Central Sun of our universe and it is the source form which all the galaxies in our universe emanate and around which they all revolve. In religious texts, it is the Universal Logos, the "first word of God," but we know that thought comes first. The thirteenth dimension is the gateway to the universes beyond our own universe and is the center of divine emanation, the "first thought," so to speak. This dimensional model works in even and odd numbering, at least for the first nine dimensions. The odd-numbered dimensions have a more intuitive and emotional composition (feminine) and the even-numbered dimensions have a more analytical and intellectual (masculine) flair. Also, the even-numbered dimensions of the alchemical tree of life create structural laws for the galaxy and the odd-numbered dimensions live out those laws by exploring free fill. Here is an illustration of the Pleiadian model for the structure of the primary nine dimensions; notice how they are split down the middle by the vertical axis of the tenth dimension into even and odd dimensions residing on opposite sides:

---

[9] Barbara Hand Clow, *Alchemy of Nine Dimensions* (Charlottesville, VA: Hampton Roads, 2004), 57.

10th –Dimensional Gravitational Axis

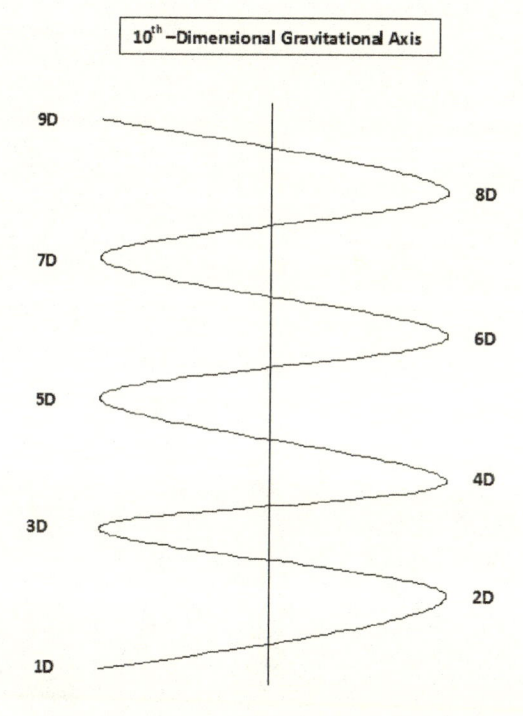

**Representation of dimensional model
based upon vertical gravitational plane**

All the universes are structured according to wavelength, so it should be no surprise this chart looks like a sine wave. The Annunaki, Orion, and Sirius extraterrestrials are more masculine in nature (4th, 6th, and 8th dimensions, respectively) while the Pleiadians, Arcturians, and Andromedans (5th, 5th, and 7th dimensions, respectively) are more feminine in nature.[10]

If one were to envision this dimensional model from the perspective of the third dimension, this picture would illustrate it nicely:

---

[10] The extraterrestrials who are more masculine in nature have created a patriarchal system of control on Earth while the extraterrestrials who are more feminine in nature are here to help us evolve spiritually. The even-numbered dimensions represent male consciousness while the odd-numbered dimensions represent female consciousness. The former has controlled Earth since at least 10,000 B.C.E.

```
              7D
        6D     |     8D
          \    |    /
    5D     \   |   /    9D
       \    \  |  /    /
        \    \ | /    /
         _____/
              4D


              3D
          /       \
         /         \
        /           \
   2D  /             \
      /               \
     /                 \
    /_____\
              1D
```

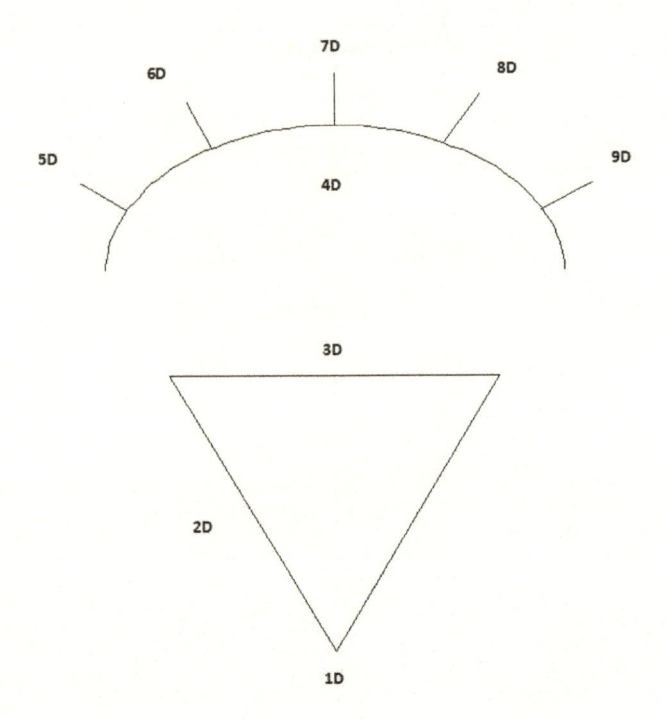

Model of Manifestation of Nine Dimensions

The center chakra of the Earth is your grounding point while you lay on a table in three-dimensional time and space. The 4th dimension is like a canopy (collective mind) hanging over you. This dimension encompasses the other three dimensions and provides an interface for the higher dimensions.

    From a big picture standpoint, light is information. The higher the frequency of light the more information it can hold. Information is pure consciousness. The frequency of creation is love. Love sustains this information in perpetual suspension. In ultimate reality the past, present, and future exist simultaneously in the highest dimension of the mind of Prime Creator, but in a lower density (like 3rd density), time appears linear. If someone were to go back in time they could change the future, but when they did this they would create a separate fabric of time-space extending out from the original timeline into a parallel timeline.

Our reality, ranging from the most distant galaxy to subatomic particles, is what we constitute as our universe, even though all the universes that have ever been created are right here in this space and are all interlinked. You can't see or experience them because they are all operating on different wavelengths. In quantum physics, every object can either be looked upon as particles (atoms) or sounds (wavelength), and every particle or piece of matter has its own sine wave signature. If you look at all the viewable objects (those which reflect light) in this universe and averaged them by wave length, you will find that this average is 7.23 centimeters. Dimensions are separated from each other by wavelength exactly the same way notes are separated on a musical scale. There is a void between dimensions like the void between two notes on a piano, and there is a greater void between octaves. Each dimension is also separated from the others by a ninety degree rotation. In a sense, if you could change your wavelength (vibration) and rotate ninety degrees you would disappear from this dimension and reappear in whatever dimension you were tuned to.

The key to understanding how to move from one dimensional level to another starts with locating and merging with an electromagnetic field around your body shaped like a star tetrahedron. There is a tube which runs through the body and connects the apexes of this star tetrahedral field, and this tube is essentially the funnel of energy that connects your seven primary chakras. As we have a physical body, an emotional body, an intellectual body, and a spiritual body, each has its own tetrahedral shape and each higher body (in frequency) is superimposed onto the lower bodies. The word "Mer" denotes counter-rotating fields of light, "Ka" means spirit and "Ba" is body (or reality). Essentially, the Merkabah is a counter-rotating field of light encompassing both spirit and body. It is a time/space vehicle which transports one (mind/body/spirit) to higher planes of consciousness, or in other words, other dimensions of reality. One can align all aspects of oneself—those being spirit (consciousness), mind (attention, intention), and body (cellular intelligence)—and activate the Merkabah vehicle.

Everything seems so solid and yet it is only a three-dimensional hologram. Our brains decode energy fields (packets of waves of energy and information) into touch, sight, taste, smell, and sound from electrical impulses sent to the brain by every nerve in the body. If you could see the world as it truly is you would see that it's mostly empty space. It is the process of third-dimensional perception that entraps one into experiencing a solid, physical experience. In the higher dimensions, however, the outside world is only energy, and consciousness shapes energy into reality. You can go to the store and buy a hologram machine and see for yourself how this concept applies. The device works by directing two parts of the same laser onto photographic film. One part, called the "reference beam," is directed at the film through a semi-transparent mirror, while the other half, called the "working beam" is deflected away to strike the object you wish to be holographically photographed. The working beam is then directed back onto the photographic film where it collides with the reference beam. This creates an interference pattern on the film, and hence, the object is reconstructed in perfect three-dimensional holographic form. It looks totally real, but you can put your hand through it. This process is depicted in the following figure:

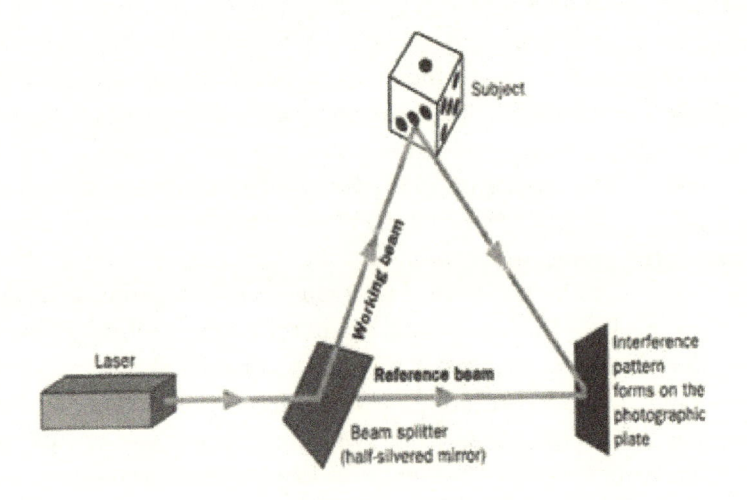

Diagram of a hologram machine

The physical world seems solid because our senses hem us in to the third-dimensional world. The body is an electro-chemical computer, and when we operate from the level of our body computer, we lose touch with infinite awareness and other dimensions of consciousness.

If we could see the world before our brains decode the information (electrical, chemical, magnetic, and spiritual information), it would be a sea of wave patterns vibrating at different frequencies and clashing with each other. If you were to open up a television set, you would not see the pictures you see on the screen. Rather, you would see electrical circuit boards. The circuit boards convert electromagnetic information into pictures, sounds, and landscapes, and that is projected onto the screen. The world you see is not outside of you, rather, it is your central processing unit (your brain) converting raw data and waveforms into a holographic reality in your head imprinted onto your visual cortex. The world you experience happens inside of you, not outside.

Moreover, every partition of a projected hologram (whether it be your body, an object, or the visible universe) is a microscopic version of the whole. Every piece mirrors the whole hologram. If you are dealing with the hologram pictured above (the dice) and you cut the interference patterns into four pieces and point the laser at each one, you will not see four different pieces of the dice. You will see quarter-sized depictions of the whole image. The body is the same. Each cell is a smaller version of the whole body, which is why a body can be grown from a single cell. Palm reading and acupuncture work because of this principle. Every part of the body is a representation of the whole.

D.N.A. is a crystalline substance with a shape that makes it a perfect receiver/transmitter. It receives, transmits, and amplifies frequencies of light that connect to the cosmic internet, the "broadcast" of Creation. Earth is nothing more than a complex computer program our body-computers are wired to. Each cell is part of the body's hard drive, the official memory source. When conditions in the environment change, the D.N.A. mutates so the body-computer can compensate for survival. When we drug our bodies with pollutants, the information processing unit (the brain) and the hard drive (the cells) become corrupted, much like a computer that has been affected with a virus program. The virus slows down the flow of information and energy, and when this happens, disease occurs. In order to stay healthy, one must keep the meridian channels (acupuncture channels) clear so the chi/prana (love) energy can flow unobstructed. One must also keep the chakras clear so that the body-computer can connect to other dimensions of reality and higher frequencies of information. When fear is the prevailing paradigm, the body-computer (the droplet) is shut off from infinite consciousness (the ocean). Fear constricts consciousness and love expands it.

The Divine Matrix is a sea of consciousness which propels itself from the 13th dimension down through the 5th dimension and projects out into a fifth-dimensional hologram:

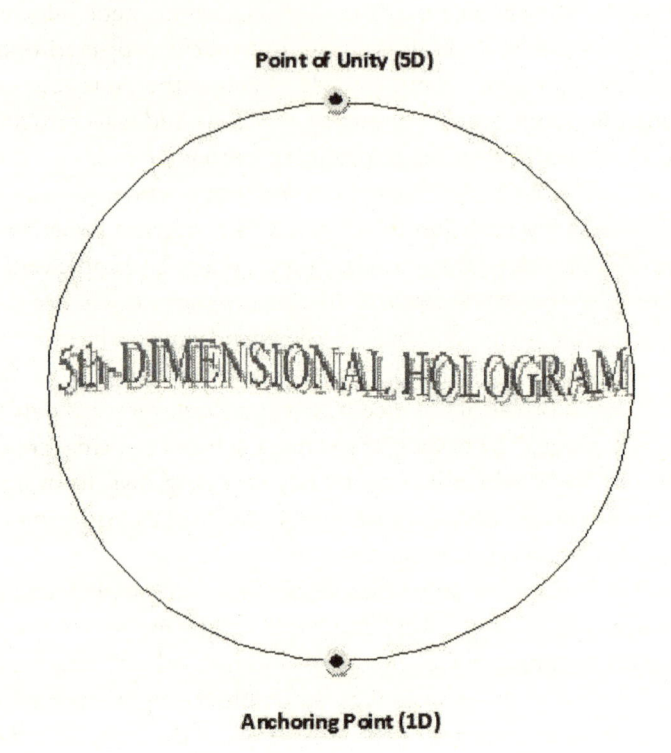

Point of Unity (5D)

5th-DIMENSIONAL HOLOGRAM

Anchoring Point (1D)

Earth as a 5th-dimensional hologram

A New Order of the Ages

Ever since the advent of quantum physics, scientists have started to realize that this hologram follows very basic rules. These are:

1. There is a field of energy (consciousness) that connects all of creation.
2. This field plays the role of a container, a bridge, and a mirror for the beliefs within us.
3. The field is nonlocal and holographic. Every part of it is connected to every other, and each piece mirrors the whole on a smaller scale.
4. We communicate with the field through the language of emotion.

When one (soul) awakens to the higher reality of being connected to this source of energy and awareness, a window is opened to a more universal field of infinite possibilities.[11]

---

[11] For supplementary reading to help understand the rules of this hologram, I suggest *The Divine Matrix* by Gregg Braden.

II

The Nature of Time and Soul

The nature of time can be confusing, where time travel seems like a paradox. In reality, time is malleable and likened unto a tapestry or quilt of time-space realities interwoven into one another. The tapestry is a panorama representing dimensions beyond time and space, with the threads of the fabric being time-space continuums. Consciousness creates reality, so timelines are created by souls who render upon the tapestry thoughts and feelings. When an individual soul creates a timeline, that timeline resembles a fiber optic wire lit up with electricity in front of a dark background. When millions of souls create a collective timeline it creates a greater imprint upon the tapestry and illuminates with a greater intensity. Some might say that these collective timelines are more "real" then the individual timelines, although this is not entirely true since all thoughts create reality. There are an infinite number of possible timelines and a finite number of probable timelines, which are given more consciousness. At any given moment a collective consciousness of souls will be creating along a particular timeline when they run into a crossroads where multiple futures are possible. The timelines that are given more conscious thought are the more probable realities with the other future timelines existing as less probable realities. Every thought, emotion, and action in a timeline is imprinted upon the Akashic medium, which records all thoughts, actions, and emotions from all the dimensional realities; it is a snapshot camera. At any time the Akashic records can be accessed on the non-physical plane of existence using astral projection (enacting consciousness on the astral plane using deep meditation).

Every moment you are creating new possible and probable timelines within the greater scope of planet Earth, which proceeds along a collective timeline. There are an infinite number of possibilities for the future, but you are restricted not only in your daily life with your job and family but also in regard to the rest of the souls on this planet. Even though there are an infinite number of possible futures, you will progress along one of the predicable timelines because of your restrictions. This predictability also affects the planet because the fate of the planet is intertwined with the fate of its inhabitants. How time is experienced on the planet is also related to the collective consciousness of the inhabiting souls. We all know what it's like to languish in a dentist's waiting room and have time drag or to experience a dream that seemed like it only lasted a few seconds when really it lasted for three hours. So it's really not time that moves but energy, and consciousness controls energy.

Burt Goldman, an avant-garde researcher of quantum physics and parallel realities, speaks to audiences all over the world concerning the nature of time and consciousness. He opines that all the universes/parallel realities exist right here and now, but we cannot experience them because we are not "tuned" into them, so to speak.[1] Every time you make a decision, a universal split occurs and a parallel universe is created. In the universe you live in currently, you experience daily all the decisions you have ever made. In parallel universes, however, there are an inconceivable number of versions of yourself which made different decisions. There is a way to communicate with those other aspects of yourself living in trans-dimensional realms by what Goldman calls "thought transference." Since thoughts are energy, one can alter the frequency of his/her thoughts in order to manifest consciousness in another dimensional realm (parallel universe) through deep trance and meditation. This makes more sense when you ponder that you are pure consciousness. Your physical body is an illusion, living in an illusory world. When you raise your vibrational frequency to 4th density and above, you begin to merge with all those other aspects of yourself. At 5th density, you become a field of pure potential (consciousness subsisting on the fifth dimension and above) and you can view all your past/present/future/parallel lives.[2] This is the realm souls travel to when their physical bodies wither away and die.

---

[1] Being "tuned" into a dimension is likened to watching television. When you are watching a channel, you are only seeing one broadcast although all the channels exist in the room with you. When you tune into another dimension or parallel timeline, you are switching channels in your consciousness; of course, this takes much practice.

[2] When you are in the 5th dimension you are a spirit, so you do not live in time or space and you can see all your lives (past, parallel, and future).

In a higher vibration time is flexible, so from the perspective of 3rd density, someone operating in 5th density will appear as moving at lightning speed and accomplishing tasks in the blink of an eye. From the perspective of the person in 5th density, the person in the lower density will appear to be in slow motion or at a standstill. That is how highly evolved beings can work with millions of souls at the same moment. It is because they are not affected by time or space. Ascended masters and angels live in the higher dimensions where time does not exist, so they can experience a million years in a few seconds or a few seconds that seem like a million years. All time intersects what is called the "eternal now," so when one reaches a certain state of mind and vibration he or she can ride the 'eternal now' up like an elevator into the realms where time does not exist. The eternal now is a vertical plane which intersects an infinite number of possible horizontal planes representing linear timelines. These timelines are not really linear though, they are circular. They circle around the vertical line of the eternal now, and when a civilization reaches 5th density its incumbents are accelerated in time to a higher realm where there is not time or space. From a lower perspective, the future is like a partially completed picture on a canvas. When the picture is altered the past and present are also altered because everything is happening "now."

As was explained earlier, everything that you see around you is created by thought. All thoughts are electrical impulses surrounded by an electromagnetic field of radiation.[3] All thought, when generated, travels out from the sender in a spherical fashion radiating out in equal direction with equal force. The higher the density the being the more energy (or cosmic energy that is really spiritual energy condensed down into various frequencies) will be there to manifest the reality. In 3rd density, the thoughtforms carry a low vibration, especially when emotional levels surrender to the grades of fear and guilt. The mindset of 3rd density is that of survival to the primitive soul, for peace to the advanced soul, and enlightenment for the ascended soul. The ascended masters manifest thoughts and emotions which carry a high enough frequency to be dexterous and manifest on higher planes of consciousness. Ascension is the process of the physical form and all its primitive, ego-based emotions collapsing back into the mind, which in turn surrenders to

---

[3] Jasmuheen, "UHP—Telepathy & the Arcturians," http://www.youtube.com/watch?v=DwG3AL7XdJ0.

the soul. This process propels a person into 5th density.[4] The fifth dimension can only be entered through the heart chakra, which sits at the center of your chest. It carries a green vibration and holds the qualities of unconditional love and compassion. When this state of mind is reached, love is activated in the heart chakra and this stimulates a raise in vibrational frequency. One is brought into a higher state of consciousness. In this state of consciousness, connection to the soul is pure and one can access knowledge from the Akashic medium, which is like an historical almanac. Your oversoul stands above this medium. The oversoul is your higher self. It is the "you" that is forever connected to the Cosmic Center of Consciousness and which has traveled back in time billions of years to help your lower self progress on your journey through the physical incarnations in space-time continuums.

The Harmonic Convergence is what the Mayans were referring to when they created their calendar which supposedly ends on December 21st, 2012.[5] What they were referring to was the transition from one vibrational density to another, from 3rd density to 5th density. The Harmonic Convergence is the gateway, or portal, into your Christed Selves (all the aspects of your oversoul which live in other dimensions). As the Earth travels through the photon belt it aligns with the black hole at the center of the galaxy, a void which emits higher frequencies of consciousness through light. The root and heart chakras are unity points for the void (the gap between creation points as it manifests on multiple frequency levels and on many dimensional levels) as it manifests in the first and fifth dimensions. The 13th dimension is the conception point from which all other thought creations manifest. The Sun in our solar system is not just a source of energy, it is a portal into a higher dimensional frequency that expands your consciousness via the merging of the conscious, the subconscious, and the superconscious minds. In effect, this portal leads one into the 13th dimension, or the "Cosmic Center of Consciousness."[6]

---

[4] How long this takes is highly dependent on an individual's vibrational frequency and level of consciousness.

[5] The Harmonic Convergence is discussed by metaphysician David Wilcock in his lectures. He proposes the Mayans ascended to the fifth dimension which is why their civilization vanished without a trace. The Harmonic Convergence can be viewed as the souls on Earth reuniting with the Christ energy (unconditional love) in 2012 as the Earth aligns with the galactic photon band emanating from the central black hole.

[6] This is what the Pleiadians refer to as "God."

The chakra system, likewise, is not just an energy source, it is a gateway to higher consciousness. The first chakra vibrates to red and holds the qualities of power, anger, and sexuality. The second chakra vibrates to orange and holds the qualities of the emotions, the muscles, fury, sensuality, and healing. The third chakra vibrates to yellow and controls intellect, immunity, protection, patience, and fear. The fourth chakra is the middle of the planetary chakra system and it vibrates to green. It embodies the qualities of love, transformation, healing, frustration, and loss. The fifth chakra vibrates to blue and holds the qualities of communication, spiritual knowledge, mourning, and separation. The sixth chakra vibrates to indigo and represents spiritual power, telepathy, and victimization. The seventh and final chakra of the planetary chakra system vibrates to violet and represents spiritual certainty, release, and religious confusion.

In the transformation process, the heart chakra is activated and higher spiritual awareness floods the aura. Your ninth chakra is within a few feet of your body and once the ten helixes in your D.N.A. are formed this chakra will move into the atmosphere of the Earth in order to serve as a link to it. Your tenth chakra is connected to the solar system. Your eleventh chakra is held interchangeable by the twelfth chakra, which is guarded by the Arcturians. When connected and receiving information from the eleventh chakra one can receive messages from Sirius, the Pleiades, Arcturus, and Andromeda. The twelfth chakra connects to the universe and interfaces with the ascended masters and angels. The thirteenth chakra is also connected with the ascended masters and is inter-galactic. This is where the Galactic Federation of Light works from. During ascension the Earth will go through a transformation process in which the negative energy will be cleansed and higher vibrational energies will be in a position to beam in. After this process our galaxy will be closer to the Stargate of Andromeda, procuring light beings from other galaxies.[7]

Before I progress further I feel I must explain the concept of soul fragmentation in order that the reader will understand the information that will be presented later in this chapter and in other chapters. The nature of reality is twofold in that you are an individual as well as a part of the whole. When understanding the nature of creation, you must

---

[7] Atlantean Academy of Knowledge, *We the Arcturians*, http://www.ingridwhitecloud.co.nz/index_files/acturians.htm (1998).

realize that you are a cell in a planet, which is a cell in a galaxy, which is a cell in a universe. At the end of the day, creation is one being with numerous smaller beings living within the greater being. A star is a living organism living within a larger organism called a galaxy, living within a larger being called a universe. If your brain was the galactic center, then your individual fingers are just extensions of that consciousness that perceive the surrounding environment from their own unique points of view. Every day your brain receives billions of electrical impulses from your external sensory organs which give it information regarding their perception of reality. The brain's reality is the totality of all the impulses it receives from the extensions of itself. This concept can be applied to soul fragmentation. When God wishes to experience itself as individualized fragments, it creates souls that are just newborn sparks of pure consciousness. All of the souls that God creates are parts of the whole, even when those souls (operating from the perspective of individual consciousness) become disillusioned into thinking that this is not so. In other words, you and God are one and the same whether you believe it or not.

When the original sparks of consciousness are created they can fragment themselves into further individualizations. When they do this they fragment into twelve pieces and further into 6 male-female pares. Souls are really androgynous, so when I say male and female I mean two particular aspects. God is both male and female, so when a soul becomes individualized it can take one of either two polarities (male: logical, rational; female: emotional, compassionate). These twelve fragmentations are represented as pairs of the two aspects of consciousness, which does not mean that souls are either male or female because this is not true. You might hear someone tell you that they have found their soul mate, but really what they're saying is that they have found their twin flame, a soul who resonates with them and represents the other aspect of that particular male-female pair. After the first set of integrated souls fragment into 6 male-female pairs, each of these pairs then fragment into more and more pairs until you have many souls living in a respective universe. What I have explained thus far are fully integrated souls. There are souls who become non-integrated. This happens when pieces of soul energy become detached from a soul and annex to other souls. They can manifest as poltergeists, apparitions, ghosts, or discarnate entities. These pieces of soul matrix attach to the auras of other souls, usually when the emotional or mental body of an individual soul becomes traumatized. Some people who are raped, tortured, involved in unhealthy relationships, or victims of a crime have non-integrated soul fragments living in their aura and sucking the energy out of them. They become weak and need a lot of sleep.

The body is ultimately an illusion. It is an instrument, like a car. The person who drives the car is only using the car to get from point A to point B. The driver is not the car. Rather, the driver is the cognizance who uses the car to achieve a certain result, and sometimes, who trades the car in for another car when the old one breaks down. When a soul enters a body it uses that body to interact with the third-dimensional reality. The soul is the driver and the body is the car, and when the body dies the soul leaves to inhabit another, healthier body. The body is a biological intelligence and you can communicate with it. When you have a cramp or when you are hungry your body will tell you, but when there is no user to receive that input it becomes null, or discontinued. The body has no life apart from the life that the soul gives it, so in other words you could say that a body is neutral (neither good nor bad). A body is just a biological spacesuit that can be programmed in any way, so it is up to the user regarding how he or she uses that body.

The body can be a prison, but only when it is reflecting that state of mind of the user. Some people think that pain is punishment from God and pleasure is reward from God, but that is a total misconception. Pain and pleasure are merely stimuli, responses from the body when it feels something. The body is a gift, and when it is hurt it will feel pain, not because pain is bad but because that is the body's way of distinguishing pain from pleasure. Most people become trapped in the duality of pain and pleasure and seek drugs, vanity, money, and perversities until they realize that all suffering stems from attachment. They will wake up one day, forthwith, and become cognizant of the fact that soon they will get old, become sick, lose their loved one, and die. Most people when they reach this point will become very religious and search for a new meaning to life. Isn't it obvious? The meaning to life is not the body. It is the fact that you are alive in the first place and will never die. I could tell you that the body is an illusion, but that is not entirely true. In ultimate reality the body is an illusion, but while you're in it you experience it as a reality. The body is 99.9999% empty space. It is composed of tiny atoms which whirl around huge empty spaces, and the atoms aren't even solid objects. They are quite literally packets of waves of energy and information. The body is not entirely an illusion, but at least a very limited version of what is really happening. The key then, is to be in the body but not of it. Heaven and Hell are not afterlives. They are occurring now and can be created at any time or in any place.

The body seems so physical when vibrating at third density and so people become attached to the physical, material world. The body is not physical in the manner that most people think it is. Rather, it is an energy matrix or geometric pattern of electromagnetic flux that is controlled by the mind and emotions. Only when a soul has purified its emotional, mental, and spiritual bodies can the physical body be fashioned in any way, shape or form the user sees fit. Only then can the soul become aware of the higher perceptive mechanisms. These mechanisms allow one to become more in tune with the higher dimensional frequencies and therefore more in tune with the source of all consciousness. The body is the perceptive mechanism for the third dimension, the mind is the perceptive mechanism for the fourth dimension, and the heart and crystal light body are the perceptive mechanisms for the fifth dimension. Hopefully you can see clearly now that heaven and hell are merely states of mind, as the experience depends on the state of consciousness of the soul. When you traverse the higher dimensions the body becomes obsolete, because everything is governed by thought.

Just as the Earth has an electromagnetic field, so too does the human body. In fact, the primary trait of consciousness is the presence of an energetic field (energy and information) which governs physical and etheric characteristics (from 1st density through 12th density). In the sixth dimension, morphogenesis uses sacred geometry to structure life forms, the ancient Sanskrit languages paying tribute to this concept as they, when spoken, cause matter to vibrate in certain geometrical patterns. Swami Murgugeus, the creator of the Sri Lankatheeswara temple in Nuwara Eliya, once pronounced: "Certain sounds can affect our circulation and nervous system . . . Whatever change such vibrations cause, extends to the mind of a person and also to the surrounding atmosphere, causing warmth or coolness. All this can be known by study and shown by practice." Eighth-dimensional sound carries seventh-dimensional cosmic light which structures six-dimensional sacred patterns. Of course, all of this is achieved by consciousness. Consciousness commands the electricity which flows through parineural cells around every nerve in the body. These pathways are called energy meridians and the very practice of acupuncture deals with these meridians. This relates to Ley lines on the Earth's electromagnetic grid. Great stone monoliths erected in the past mark these planetary energy meridians.

Each planetary body has its own unique resonant frequency that is determined by its diameter and circumference as well as its rotational speed. Earth resonates from 7.8 hertz to 43.2 hertz, and this spectrum is divided into seven levels of vibration, each representing a chakra. Just as the human body is composed of seven primary chakras acting as interfaces between the physical dimension and etheric dimensions, so too does the Earth. Think of the planetary chakras as mediums through which the consciousness of Earth manifests on this physical dimension. These chakras are not lined up straight (up and down) like in the human body. Rather, they are spread out equidistant from each other on various vortexes around the planet which emit specific electromagnetic frequencies. The crown chakra sits at the vortex which emits the highest electromagnetic frequency and the root chakra sits at the vortex which emits the lowest electromagnetic frequency. Here is where all the Earth's chakras lay:[8]

1. Root chakra: Mount Shasta, California
2. Sacral chakra: Lake Titicaca, South America (Island of the Sun)
3. Solar Plexus chakra: Uluru Kata Tjuta, Australia
4. Heart chakra: Shaftesbury, England
5. Throat chakra: Great Pyramids of Giza, Egypt
6. Third Eye chakra: Kuh-e Malek Siah, Iran
7. Crown chakra: Mount Kailash, Tibet

The resonant frequencies of Earth converge through the human brain from both sides on the pineal gland. Consciousness is electromagnetic energy; when it is standing still it is potential energy and when it is moving it is kinetic energy. Kinetic energy propels the false ego while potential energy embodies the true Self (Christ Self). Thought is the partition of consciousness, so it is thought and intention which govern the resonance (frequency) and shape (information) of a planetary body as well as a human body.

---

[8] Ben Stewart, Director, *Esoteric Agenda*, 2008.

We must recognize the power of our thoughts. A universe is in effect a thought dimensional plane, or a realm of creation. Christopher Penczak, a highly regarded author and teacher in the area of metaphysics and spirituality, relates in his book *Asension Magick* that there are 352 dimensional planes of light outside of this universe which lead back to the source of creation through higher and higher universes. This particular dimensional plane is on the 45th plane, and it is on this plane that we as creators joined to create a physical and spiritual density. These souls numbered in the trillions and gathered at numerous black holes, or portals, with each portal pertaining to a specific path of evolution. Here our collective consciousness was divided into three groups: (1) those that were to remain in 4th density and evolve up; (2) those that were to be planets, moons, stars, suns, animals and other forms; and (3) those that were to be true carriers of the spirit in physical forms (3rd density).[9]

We, as sparks of consciousness emanating from Prime Creator, were vibrating at 4th density when we decided to create with our thoughts a lower vibration of density. Three immense pockets of creational light energy were manifested and discharged into the three-dimensional world that we can see now with our eyes vibrating at 3rd density. This is the "Big Bang" mainstream science says occurred 15 billion years ago, although time can take on a different meaning in higher dimensions. Mainstream science sees this universe as a closed universe because nothing has been created below 3rd density, and most people cannot perceive the fourth dimension and above. Black holes exist below the center of each galaxy and act as windows from which the big bang explosions came from.

Our journey into 3rd density began in the 9th density, the ninth dimension correlating to the black holes at the center of each galaxy. At 9th density you are pure consciousness. This is an interesting state of being, however you cannot directly experience life on a planet or in a galaxy since you have no physical form. The idea of soul fragmentation is important here because in 9th density we were all at one with our oversouls, or soul families. At 9th density we weren't very individualized, so many wanted to enter the lower dimensional frequencies to experience life at that level. At 8th density we had more individualization, but many wanted to go further into 7th density. The transition from 8th density to 7th density is that of pure energy to a physical structure, so in 7th

---

[9] Alex Collier, "Secret Earth History," http://www.youtube.com/watch?v=QRATOtRt6D4.

density there was more to experience with. Still, we wanted to go lower and at 5th density a difference of opinion started to arise, because at this level individualization was much more distinct; henceforth, factions erupted. At this level a thick membrane was created and many souls descended into 4th density. In this density a being could kill another being, which was the game that we all wanted to play. Duality became manifested and a soul called Lucifer took on the polarity of Dark while a soul called Michael took on the polarity of Light. Fourth density and below is considered the realm of the lower self since you are cut off from unconditional love and acceptance, those qualities being the nature of the higher self. Fifth density and higher is considered "heaven" since death is not possible and connection with the higher self is pure.[10]

What is happening on this planet and in this galaxy at this time is what is called a "Polarity Integration Game." The light and the dark are two opposites, but this doesn't mean that one is better than the other. They are both necessary for complete balance. Light can be looked upon as the reward of love, joy, and bliss, while the dark can be seen as the lesson of pain, fear, and anger. The upper three chakras represent the qualities of light while the lower three chakras represent the qualities of dark, but if one were to stay on either side too long one would in effect be polarized to that side. The heart chakra is stationed in the middle of the chakra system because it is the balance point. It represents love and compassion, the necessary tools for the integration of the light and the dark. When a state of compassion is reached a soul understands the benefits of both the light and the dark and does not judge either as being inherently good or bad. Finding the positives in the dark is challenging but necessary for spiritual growth, otherwise we would become spiritually stagnant. This happens when a soul becomes polarized to one side or the other and in which case loses it procreative abilities. The ability to procreate is lost because when one side is polarized the physical body is partially emotionally shut down. Procreating without difficulties is the result of balance between the light and the dark. Planets, likewise, are schools with varying degrees of free will. Earth is a school of total free will and is one of three that have existed in our universe. When souls incarnate into a planetary school they have the goal of achieving spiritual

---

[10] George Kavassilas, "Our Journey and the Grand Deception," http://www.youtube.com/watch?v=IZDcn-LJNlo (June 2, 2009).

evolvement, which makes Earth a popular place because of its polar extremes. It is a difficult school where souls can learn many lessons.

When apprehending the concept of soul, one must transcend the notions of polarity and move into unity. For most people, everything occurs in opposites. There is good and evil, up and down, left and right, smart and dumb, spirit and matter, and so on. However, there is a third component in every polarity consciousness, and that is the point of interface. There is a middle (between up and down), a mind (between spirit and matter), a straight (between left and right), a neutral (between good and evil), etc. In reality, this pattern is also fundamental. Between two "on's" there is an "off." The nature of reality is that it is discontinuous—there are gaps. In the space that we live, there is a microcosm and a macrocosm, a larger version and a smaller version, but what is large and small? If space is an illusion, then how could one comprehend this distinction? It is because large and small are comparative; they are relative. There cannot be a small unless there is a large from which to say, "ah, now that must be small!" That is why in every partition of relativity there is a middle, a point of unity. It is the gap between dimensions, the off between the on's, the place between the microcosm and the macrocosm. It is from this space where our entire reality is constructed from. It is the point where infinity is contained within no space and no time.

Infinite creativity operates in this area. It is the progenitor of everything. Information (light) is absorbed into every living organism and every material object via an infinite matrix of love (energy) in every moment, and that information is transmuted into color, smell, sight, taste, touch, solidity, time, space, etc. Once it is transmuted into a particular form, that information is sent back to the Cosmic Center of Consciousness (which operates from the "off") and that being is the totality of all of our spirits. It is male/female, love/hate, good/bad, conscious awareness/unconscious awareness . . . . everything. That is what we are. We are not physical bodies. We are a field of infinite consciousness experiencing itself subjectively, a perceptual event we experience consciously in the "on's" and unconsciously in the "off's."

This universe is a game and we are all players. Once a group of souls become evolved enough they can create universes of their own where other souls can come and participate in evolutionary lessons. I mentioned before that Earth was one of three planets which experienced or is experiencing total free will. For simplicity I will refer to these as the "Three Earths." Many extraterrestrial races call these planets the "Grand Experiments" because they are like laboratories where many diverse life forms incarnate and live with each other. Most of the planets in our Galaxy have only one or two primary life forms, but on Earth we have many. Many races have colonized our planet, bringing a myriad of plant and animal life and creating a complex ecosystem. Most of the humans living on Earth now, however, have manipulated D.N.A. This traps them in a vibrational prison where they are only able to perceive three dimensions. Naturally, the powers-that-be have sequestered this information so they can control you more efficiently.

Order of Manifestation

You must now erase all the bane energy that has caused your mind to fritter. You are not a slave controlled by the Illuminati. In the great game of creation, you are a wayshower. In this position, you are contracted by higher intelligences to manifest constituency. You are a conduit and a co-creator simultaneously, and in this way you create physical reality by being a vessel and a consciousness. An ultraviolet beam of energy will soon enter this planet through the Arcturian Stargate, invoking a massive increase in fifth-dimensional light transmission—this is the step toward ascension. The planet will pass through a highly charged membrane of photons which will expand, intensify, and increase all thoughts, feelings, emotions, perceptions, and actions on the physical plane (as the vibrational frequency raises everything is intensified—like turning up the volume). The ultraviolet fluorescent blue magenta beam radiating from the galactic heart chakra of our twin universe will clear the control patterns of old polarized beliefs. The high frequency energetic vibration streams out in spectral rays from the central universe's heart chakra creating energetic new soul codes and programs as it enters the crystal and sacred geometries of the incarnated souls on Earth in linear time. This is the activation point (zero point). I will talk more about zero point in *Part 2*.

The third dimension is analogous to the solar plexus chakra, where power is centered in negative space for the manifestation of positive creation. In order to manifest creation on the physical plane, the spiritual,

A New Order of the Ages

mental, emotional, and astral planes have to be segregated in order to install a program of intensity and focus within the extension of the third-dimensional experience. This relationship requires a regulator which filters out the higher multidimensional timeless and infinite awareness and induces a finite temporal spatial separation from wholeness that allows for the regeneration and intensification of seed generation. This means that the higher dimensional frequencies and energies are regulated in and out of the third dimension through the fourth dimension via mind and the fifth dimension via heart. Through energy deceleration from higher non-polarized timeless universal experience to physical duality and stabilized crystallization into manifested form, a three-dimensional seemingly physical world appears as an experience of consciousness. This process is the basis of astrological theory where stars are communicators of energy and measure managers for planetary bodies. Our sun is one of these beings referred to in metaphysical terms as the "Solar Logos." These energy fields vibrate with beings in resonance in the solar system, so it is wise to align yourself with this energy stream.

From the cosmic energetic perspective, the omnicentric root chakra is the basis of dark matter, the black holes, and the seed of all that comes into existence. The void is equated to the oneness of all that is. The "off" or "gap" of creation is the physical representation of the void as the void itself cannot be apprehended by logical thinking. From the void, or rather womb, existence expands into the atomic/mineral/elemental structures, which are the second-dimensional domain just as human beings are the third-dimensional domain. Upon the third dimension as held with the energy of the solar system and the solar plexus chakra does this energy stream become the power control and focus for manifestation. It is herein that existence arrives at a spatial temporal mirror and a reflection of what is communicated to be created from thought is exemplified by light and love. The fourth-dimensional matrix and the heart chakra work in the quantum field, where all probabilities operate upon the astral energies of the emotional desires, choices, and mental probabilities. Advancing acceleration from the void raises the level of conscious awareness and the disappearance of space-time continuums.

The fifth dimension operates under concepts of unified field theory in cooperation with string or membrane topological fields of creation.[11]

---

[11] This correlates with the diagram of the Earth as a fifth-dimensional hologram positioned at the end of "Structure of Reality." The fifth dimension is a point of unity which projects higher

The throat chakra operates to assimilate and sensitize the elemental energies of diversity within the second-dimensional field of the naval chakra through the communication and formulation of feelings into expression. With the acceptance of the sixth-dimensional energies and the higher mind, the focus of this single stream of light in the third eye chakra is connected and focused into the third dimension. The third and sixth chakras operate in harmony to empower creation with light energy. The sixth dimension holds the intrinsic mathematics of sacred geometric forms, which are the fundamental metamorphic paradigms containing the archetypes of all manifestation. Everything that appears in the third dimension has as its divine blueprint a precise mathematical formula in the sixth dimension. The light body (fifth dimension) is held in singularity within the pineal gland of the brain (third dimension) and the crown chakra of the mind (fourth dimension), and when the higher dimensional energy accrues the expansion of conscious awareness is fulfilled. At this point, ascension occurs. This is where spirit descends into form on behalf of the soul to experience, enlighten, and raise more matter into acceleration from polarized and crystallized potential energy. When seeing the reversal of this energy from the soul into matter, the deceleration of energy moves from the highest realms of recognizable energy through sound into creative action. This is the first creative principle of the seventh-dimensional sound that organizes the sacred geometrical archetypes of the sixth dimension.

The love and light energy of absolute eternal abundance and timelessness flows into existence through layers or dimensions to become form. From the sixth dimension where it is universal patterns of the infinite generic geometric design templates, it becomes a unified field of light energy in the fifth dimension. In this dimension, light spins through the photonic grid of superconductive waves were all is held in the eternal now moment. Each dimension connects with the closest layer to create reversal dissonants in the ascending harmonics in order to facilitate the flow of light and love energy. The filters and valves between dimensions are created by higher intelligences, which are aligned with eighth-dimensional agreements and ninth-dimensional higher intelligence. From the fifth dimension, the energies pass through the stargates into creation. These portals are celestial light bodies, stars,

---

consciousness out into a five-dimensional hologram; the five dimensions in this hologram are length, width, height, mind, and love.

and planetary beings which are assisting in the radiating of light and acceptance through love, beings who manifest the expansion of reality in the lower dimensions. Fourth-dimensional energy is lowered into contextual fields of content where it becomes emotionally and mentally charged particles. Duality exists in the fourth dimension and below, and polarization occurs upon the astral template of the quantum field when fifth-dimension love energy is activated in the heart chakra. Within the fourth-dimensional realm, duality is perceived to spin quantum particles, which become recognizable as electrons, protons, neutrons, and the subatomic groupings of localized space-time particles.

In the third dimension, the spin of matter locks into tiny space matrices where events are manifested into zonal realities of individual perception and creation. We as human beings have our own individual perception and at the same time a planetary, galactic, and universal awareness. Conceptual reality occurs when the collective agreement of perceptions of mutual participants in an active field of awareness has taken place. The solar plexus chakra controls the mood and temperament of the content of each resonance that contains a separated piece of cosmic conscious energy which appears in a spatial, temporal location as a charged material particle, event, or past experience (our physical bodies occupy these dimensions). The third dimension is always based upon time as a linear, separated past event that is measured empirically from the point of view of a relative or subjective observer. The past is regulative charged space which creates a vortex that sucks consciousness into unconsciousness and the lower vibratory rates of crystallized, internalized being (this refers to your subconscious mind). The third dimension rests on a platform of elements, which are established by the impersonal interaction of spirit into matter in order to create complete duality where the attractive energy between them empower the sacred essence of kundalini, chi, ka, sex, prana, love, and electromagnetism (this refers to your conscious mind).

The second dimension and naval chakra operate to promote positive attraction and creation from negative space. The second-dimensional consciousness is held deep within experience as gift of life while third-dimensional consciousness is experienced as a battle of two opposites. The fifth-dimensional awareness of the heart chakra stimulates a return to wholeness. The essence of being will always be spirit, which is anchored in the root chakra and the void. The spin and vibratory frequency of all energy rests within the root chakra where the will and the power of eternal potential becomes a pulsation of oneness where duality ceases and the seed of the universe is mirrored in the reflection of light by the contrast of dark. All the experiences you ever had or ever will have are mirrored reflections of consciousness and energy. Your chakras are the spiritual manifestations of these occurrences and are the key to unlocking the potential to create love, eternity and abundance.

Earth is a living library. Aeons ago this planet was chosen by high density beings to be a galactic exchange center since it is located on the outer fringes of the Milky Way and near many wormholes and dimensional portals.[12] There have been myriad forms of life on this planet, but space wars have lowered the consciousness and density of the planet causing it to be a prison. 300,000 years ago, evil reptilian overlords fought the benevolent creator gods in space and won the territory of Earth. Earth was made their domain and they went about rearranging the D.N.A. of the native human species so it would be manageable. Everything that was unnecessary for survival was disconnected. If you imagine the D.N.A. molecule to be a library housing genetic information for a particular organism, you can understand how the native human species has been partially shut down. When the invaders came in, they disconnected 10 strands of D.N.A. leaving only 2 (a double helix); it was like they took most the books off the shelves and tore out all the pages and threw them in a messy pile on the floor. The information was still there, but it was unorganized and hence unrecognizable. As a result, Earth humans became locked into the third dimension.

What is happening now is that the information that was trashed in the library is slowly recombining back into form. When the 12 strands of D.N.A. are realigned they will plug into the 12 chakras, which are vortexes of information (7 are in the body and 5 are outside the body). Humans on Earth must now learn to reintegrate this information into the collective consciousness so that it is available to everyone. Just as Earth is a library, so too is your body. Every cell holds the history of the universe, and when you learn to extract this information and decode it into understanding you will become a conscious co-creator of reality. Light is information, so the paradigm of the new age is light. We are entering the Age of Light.

---

[12] Barbara Marciniak, *Bringers of the Dawn* (Rochester, VT: Bear & Company, 1992).

III

Universal History Part 1

The progenitors of this universe are known as the "Founders." These nine souls had completed many universal games and decided to come together to create a new universe. In technical terminology I say they created this universe but what I really mean is that they created this GAME. Since what every soul desires is spiritual evolution the Founders decided to create a polarity integration game, which is one of many games involving the integration of the light and the dark. They set the stage and put out a call to all the souls in all the universes (omniverse) to come participate in this experience with them. The call was answered by ninety souls who were highly evolved and wished for a place in which to continue their spiritual evolution. This group of ninety was composed of forty-five Carians and forty-five Felines, souls who liked to take on physical characteristics of cats (the Felines) and birds (the Carians). They came into this universe and convened with the Founders. They selected from their group one named Devin to act as a liaison between this group of ninety and the Founders. Devin was the patriarch of the Feline race. The Felines were given a home planet in the Lyra constellation in the galaxy in which to incarnate on while the Carians were given a planet in the Orion constellation. In this game (our universe) the Felines represent the light and the Carians represent the dark.[1]

After a period of evolution both races had crossbred with other life forms, creating unique physical bodies (including humans) with which to incarnate in and had also established royal lines with respective hierarchies. One day the Carians colonized a planet in the Lyra constellation which is where the first Earth ("Grand Experiment") began. On a neighboring planet the Felines had fashioned advanced technology with which they could create worm holes and space travel, so they traveled back and forth between the planets in this galaxy and

---

[1] The Nibiruan Council, www.nibiruancouncil.com.

created alliances with many Carian nations. Myriad children were birthed and the two primary races (Carians and Felines) mixed their royal lines in order to create a caste system appearing as such: royalty → priests → scientists → military → workers. An afflictive lack of communication led to the "First Great Galactic War" in which the Carians launched an attack against the Felines. Much destruction ensued.

After the First Great Galactic War, Devin and several others fled on the star ship *Pelegai* to a star cluster known as the Pleiades (the Seven Sisters), where they established a colony on a blue planet and called their home Avyon. This was known as the second Earth (Grand Experiment). Life progressed on this planet and great human civilizations advanced their technology to the point of space travel. Central governments ruled while disease and disparity were all but eliminated. There was little individuality and the dark side was totally ignored. People did not use their lower three chakras and so became spiritually stagnant. A race then came who was their polar opposite. They were very masculine, and upon first viewing the planet attempted a peace treaty until they realized there was more to gain from taking over. When the humans became cognizant of this they pulled out all the stops in an attempt to drive the invading race away, but in so doing decimated their planet. The survivors fled to many places in the galaxy and established colonies on other planets.

The third Earth (Grand Experiment) is our Earth. The first two Earth's never made it through an ascension process because they never learned how to properly integrate both the light and the dark. Many souls on Earth today were on one or both of these planets and now are here to complete an ascension process. The Earth we live on now is highly conducive toward the learning of compassion because it is so diverse. In fact, the present Earth is the most diverse planet in this entire galaxy which is why many extraterrestrial races are here now observing what happens in the next several years. No matter how it happens, the ascension process will come to pass, as never before has there been so much assistance.

I will now give a brief overview of the original races in the universe:

The Felines:

    The Felines have a cat-like countenance and were one of the two primary races which fomented this universal polarity integration game. They range from 12 to 16 feet in height and are bipedal. They do not have fur, but they do have sot fuzz covering their bodies and manes. Both the males and females have long hair, and as they mature their body color changes from golden brown to white. The overall Feline temperament is intellectual, confident, and gentle. They are very fair and their nature is inquisitive. When the Feline form first appeared in the Lyra star system it was very etheric in nature, so over millions of years the Felines evolved for themselves physical bodies taking on the appearance of lions and cats. As many of the Felines began incarnating into these physical bodies, some stayed in etheric form to serve as guides and mentors, because just like on any 3rd density planet with free will a veil of amnesia is pulled over those incarnating souls. Through countless incarnational cycles the Felines evolved a form that walked upright and was capable of holding the higher Feline consciousness as a result of D.N.A. mixing from bipedal mammals (these lower order hominoids were naturally evolving at the same time). Eventually a physical form evolved that had a human-like body and a Feline face, and it was this form that was introduced to the Royal Line of Avyon.

    After further D.N.A. upgrading and evolution the Felines developed space travel and warp technology. Some groups became space travelers while others became master geneticists. They developed complex life forms and spread them to other planets in this galaxy and in other galaxies. After many genetic experiments they took the D.N.A. from bipedal mammals and upgraded it to produce humans. Originally, there were two types of humans—those with red hair and those with blonde hair. The red-headed humans were outgoing and energetic while the blonde-headed humans were gentle and introspective. Over time, human-feline crossbreeds were created which infiltrated the Royal House of Avyon. The Felines are and remain the guardians of their genetic offspring, the humans. Devin (Feline) is the reigning patriarch of the 9th dimensional Royal House of Avyon and Anu (human) is the reigning patriarch of the 5th dimensional Royal House of Avyon.

The Humans:

The humans are the youngest of the four primary races in this universe and were created by the Felines. They were given the gene of compassion as a gift from the Felines, who realized that the ultimate tool for integrating the light and the dark is indeed compassion. The humans were taught how to open the heart chakra and live in harmony with all races. When the humans began colonizing the Pleiadian star system they became heavily involved in the Royal House of Avyon.

The Carians:

The Carians are the other primary race that came to this universe when it was in its infancy. They are birdlike beings who resemble human-like eagles. When they arrived at their planet in the Orion constellation they found humid swamps, jungles, and tropical islands. Like the Felines, several Carian souls stayed in etheric form to serve as guides while the rest incarnated into genetically upgraded physical bodies. These incarnations took the form of birds illustrating luminous colors. The bodies took on a wide variety of forms ranging from a few inches in height to 12 feet. After many thousands of years they took on genetic engineering experiments and created a cross-breed between themselves and certain types of reptiles that were evolving in the swamps and other warm regions of the planet. These experiments led to the genesis of the Draconian race. The Royal House of Aln is the counterpart to the Royal House of Avyon, and at one time contained only purebred Cariáns until the Draconian crossbreed became abundant. The Draconian race had another genetic offshoot called the Flying Serpents, both races later emerging as the aggressors of human societies.

The Carian race exhibits the qualities of sharp, analytical thinking and organizational skills. They learned how to be master geneticists from the Felines and now they are controlling planet Earth. When I say Earth, I mean of course the planet we live on now. Over aeons of time there have been three Earth Grand Experiments. At the time of the first Earth Grand Experiment, the Royal House of Aln was headed by a winged serpent named Cobazar. Cobazar is the father of Jehowah. The Carians are good team players and therefore know how to achieve goals. They are not to be undermined as they are very distinguished at what they do. They make codes of conduct adhering to strict discipline, and that is why you will find many Carians involved in creating and maintaining stargates, dimensional grids, and magnetic fields throughout the Milky Way Galaxy and other galaxies in the universe. They possess strong militaristic capabilities and bear admirable fleets of starships which traverse the universe. During the first Earth Grand Experiment they held the position of guarding many military posts, and it is a Carian you will find that ruled over the massive fleet of star ships for the Lyran Galactic Federation during the First Great Galactic War. A Carian also ruled over the Royal Houses of Avyon and Aln for many thousands of years.

The Reptilians:

The reptilians are the creation of the Carians. On a planet in the Alpha Draconis star system in the Orion constellation was this form evolved. The royal line of reptilians is and always will remain the Draconians. The Draconians look like winged dragons and their royal line of beasts is called the Ciakar (pronounced 'Cee-kar'). They are white and have very long tales. The generals on the top chain of leadership have large horns on their head. The shapes of their faces take many forms but always remain in a reptilian fashion. The reptiles are divided into two sub races, the Winged Serpents and the Lizards. The reptilians have a highly refined knowledge of universal physics and were responsible for many of the mystery Schools on Earth, their teachings being the highly refined knowledge from their parent race. The reptilians were given by their parent race a creation myth which clashed with the creation myth of the humans. The creation myth of the reptilians stated they had the right to take over and colonize any planet they chose and to destroy any civilization they saw there, while the creation myth given to the humans taught them to live in harmony with their planets and develop agricultural civilizations. This is the reason why there has been so much conflict between reptilians and humans throughout the dimensions. It is the polarity integration game being acted out. The reptilians are much less emotional than their human counterparts, so that is how they can kill without feeling much. The reptilians represent the dark in the polarity integration game and the humans represent the light. If there was no conflict then soul evolution would cease and the universe would become stagnant. Through this game all souls have the opportunity to evolve back into Prime Creator.[2]

At this time Jehowah is the patriarch of the 9th dimensional House of Aln, and until recently Enki was the reigning patriarch of the 4th Dimensional House of Aln. Marduk, Enki's son, was the commander of the Federation Flagship Nibiru after he had wrestled control of it from his grandfather Anu. This story has been told on many ancient stone tablets found throughout what is known as ancient Mesopotamia, but many tablets have been distorted, fragmented, and stolen. Right now, Enki is the patriarch of the 5th dimensional House of Aln and also the head of the 5th dimensional Nibiruan Council representing the dark.

The Nommos:

The Nommos are a race of beings that take on the physical form of dolphins, whales, and mermaids/mermen. A planet in the Sirius star system full of warm, aqua blue water was given to them as their home planet. When they don't take the form of dolphins or whales many of the Nommos walk upright in physical human-like bodies. The Nommos are advanced in their use with sound. Many etheric Sirians are incarnated into dolphin and whale bodies on Earth at this time and they are overlooked by the Nommos, the guardians and guides to these souls. When the Earth ascends the Etheric Sirians are the soul group that will become the guardians. They were given Earth as their new home when their former home, a planet near the star of Sirius B, imploded. After 2013, many of the Etheric Sirians now in aquatic form will have the option of taking on a human form while serving as a land guardian. Many in the meantime are returning to the Nommos home world for training on how to live in a human body. Those humans walking the earth right now that are of the Etheric Sirian soul group are usually attracted to dolphins and whales, and many are in organizations which aim to heal the Earth's ecosystem and conserve its resources. Most of the Etheric Sirians incarnated right now on Earth are in black, red, and brown races.

---

[2] All channeled and spoken material given by the Arcturians, Andromedans and Pleiadians to contactees corroborates this last paragraph.

Orbs:

The simplest of sentient beings in the universe, orbs are dense groupings of charged particles called plasma that appear as glowing balls of any color. They are very innocent because they are polarized towards the light, meaning they are very fragile and cannot process feelings of anger, guilt, or unhappiness. They live in what is called a "collective consciousness," meaning they all live in a group mind where all thoughts, feelings, and experiences are shared. They exist to serve mankind and are called upon to provide windows into other dimensions and alternate timelines. They are time travelers of light and act as historians to society. In some cultures they are revered as gods because they can hold an immense amount of information. They can also be used as crystal balls.[3] Orbs have sent members of their society to represent them as starseeds on Earth, just like many other galactic races. Each soul that comes to Earth from the orb star system agrees to help the planet and evolve by helping others, this in turn benefiting itself. Orb starseeds on Earth are highly sensitive and psychic, very polite, private, shy, introverted, creative, and passionate about learning.

The Introduction of Life

I would like to divert for a moment now and talk about how life on planets gets introduced. It is important to remember that only a soul can give a body life. A physical body of any kind is just a dimensional spacesuit held in form by complex configurations of nucleobases strung along a D.N.A. structure.[4] D.N.A. is a nucleic acid that stores information about genetic coding in a particular species of organism and it can be tampered with by minds of higher intelligence. In the end though, it is spirit that gives life its true qualities.

---

[3] Many accounts from antiquity concerning wizards and warlocks using crystal balls to predict the future and speak to entities in other dimensions most likely come from the presence of orbs.

[4] It has been reported at national U.F.O. conferences that the human form on Earth only has two strands of D.N.A. molecules while forms in other sectors of the galaxy have more. Having more strands means being connected to higher consciousness.

In this universe the Founders, being 12th density beings, created a complex variety of energy patterns acting as precursors to the D.N.A. molecule. In essence, these energy patterns were literally packets of conscious light energy descended into 9th density, at which point they were transmuted into intricate configurations of light codes called "D.N.A. keys." These keys were then brought down to 7th density where the first level of "D.N.A. codes" was established. When they descended their consciousness down to 7th density, the Founders were able to experience life on evolving planets directly. These different D.N.A. codes were scattered throughout the universe. As galaxies formed from galactic clusters, life was seeded into several regions of each galaxy. The Milky Way Galaxy was seeded in several quadrants with our quadrant in the Vega/Lyra region of stars. Through the permutation of the D.N.A. codes, 7th density life forms were created, and then after many millions of years life forms were created through all the densities down to 3rd density. That is how life grows. The original hundred or so souls in this universe went through a process of differentiation where each 3rd density, 4th density, 5th density . . . (and so on) being that fragmented off from its parent Self (the 12th density core of the universe) became a sovereign being, or in other words, a complete soul. As each soul evolves it aligns more and more with its higher self until it merges into its higher self. We are all connected with the 12th dimensional core of the universe, which in turn is connected to the Godhead, the undifferentiated infinite source of light and love emanating from Prime Creator.[5]

Devolution is a process that results when an aspect of the Godhead extends itself into the lower densities and becomes differentiated. When the Founders extended parts of themselves down to 1st density consciousness they existed as pure elements, the simplest element being hydrogen.[6] The process of evolution begins when the hydrogen element is imbued with consciousness. Quantum mechanics is the science of this type of consciousness as it is the study of processes taking place

---

[5] Sal Rachele, "The Founders on Earth History Part 1," http://www.salrachele.com/webchannelings/foundersonearthhistorypart1.htm.

[6] It should be apparent now how the densities/dimensions of consciousness are used in varying but proper context. Dimensions from the Pleiadian model are used when speaking more generally as the dimensions of light model is less abstract and used more interchangeably with the densities model.

at the level of atoms. There are many types of life forms in this universe including carbon-based, silicon-based and lithium-based life forms.

All life forms that were created had a natural tendency to become more organized and complicated over time, giving them more self-awareness. The Darwinian evolutionary model of life forms is correct along its general premise. Intense growth and expansion of the simplest life forms creates mutations in the D.N.A., which in turn leads to a dramatic change in the form and structure of a living organism. As life evolves from 1st density consciousness up through the mineral and plant stages and on to the animal kingdom, a sophisticated level of awareness is brought forth. At the animal stage, it is possible for higher density souls to incarnate into these life forms because this level of awareness is strong enough to merge with the higher consciousness of the incarnating soul. When you are an animal, the tiny fragment of yourself that is the animal consciousness is united with the larger part of yourself that is your soul consciousness. The hominid form is the most sophisticated level of consciousness on a planet and was originally designed to be able to teleport itself from one place in the universe to another. The first hominid bodies were quasi-physical in that they could go from a solid form to a translucent form; they also carried the ability to align with the gravitational and electromagnetic fields of planets and shift density from 1st density to 7th density. When the Carians and Felines were given planets to evolve on they had to first evolve animal forms with which to incarnate in. As an animal consciousness is nowhere near the consciousness level of a soul, the etheric guides of each race stayed in the higher densities to guide the souls in the evolving physical bodies.

The Seeds of Life on Earth

The process of D.N.A. birthing discussed above is difficult for many to comprehend. One must understand that in the higher dimensions there is no "physicality" as we know it on Earth. Everything is a thought, or a template. Before you write a book what must happen? You must make a general outline in your head and do the necessary research. This analogy is like how life is created. Before the actual physical structure is created an energetic mold must be made acting as a precise blueprint for an organism's molecular structure. Geometric patterns taken from sixth-dimensional sacred geometry manifest in 6th density physical reality. Many times there is much experimentation done before a D.N.A. template is agreed upon by higher density beings. Many left-brained scientists on Earth are under the impression that all life on this planet came from an organic soup consisting of hydrogen, oxygen, nitrogen, and carbon that just mysteriously and accurately culminated and mutated into the complex life forms that we see today. In higher spiritual science, however, it is consciousness that creates life, and consciousness has an invisible quality to it as well as a physical quality.

All of life comes from spirit. Spirit is what animates the physical body, which is really just a dimensional spacesuit used for occupying the lower dimensions. During the time of Pangaea many millions of years ago, the Earth was like a genetic laboratory for high density beings and also for advanced extraterrestrial races. There are myths today about exotic life forms such as the Pegasus and the flying dragon which aren't really myths. On the continent of Pangaea there were many exotic creatures roaming the land, all of them carrying the genetic code called by the Founders the "inbreath of creation." This is Prime Creator's mark, so to speak, on all life forms following the typical path of evolution where intelligence and self-awareness increases on an upward spiral roadway. Each of these life forms on the primordial Earth contained the blueprint for ascension. No matter what life form exists or who created it, all of life merges back to Prime Creator in the end.

As these exotic life forms grew, they developed increasing levels of mental and emotional faculties until they realized they were spirits embedded into various physical and etheric bodies. They had a longing to return to the source of love and light. The tree of knowledge of good and evil is an allegory to this time period when the first exotic life forms on Earth realized they were all part of Prime Creator on its journey into physical embodiment and the lower dimensions. The realm of creation that was given to these life forms was the fourth dimension, the realm of mind and imagination. Under the law of free will,[7] all of these new life forms had the ability to create anything they wanted. As a result, they used their own D.N.A. to create malformed creatures.

With creation two processes are intimately entwined: evolution and devolution. Devolution is where sparks of spirit differentiate from

---

[7] Not all planets in this universe are a "free will" zone. Earth is very unique when it comes to diversity of life and free will.

the Godhead and form as 12th density beings of light where they drop their vibration down and incarnate, thereby allowing themselves the opportunity to experience all the levels of evolution from 1st density consciousness to the Source. Evolution is the process these beings take from inanimate objects like a grain of sand to trees, animals, and further on to more intelligent life forms, eventually making their way back to Prime Creator. As the continent of Pangaea existed when the Earth was a tropical jungle and still carried the firmament (the thick band of moisture suspended in its atmosphere), it was known as a "paradise."[8] This is where we get the stories from antiquity about the Garden of Eden and the Golden Age. Also at this time (300+ million years ago) Earth was being colonized by different races from all across the galaxy. In all there were 22 races: 17 human and the rest insectoid, botanical, and reptilian.[9] They set up numerous colonies on the planet. Many of these races were hyperborean, meaning they were scientific travelers collecting samples of D.N.A., life forms, plants, minerals, and just data in general about newly evolving planets. Later, there were small groups of hominoids seeded onto the Earth who lived in relatively remote areas of the world. They were 7th density beings with wings and strong psychic abilities who communicated with the exotic plant and animal life; they also extracted their food directly from sunlight.

During the time period of 200 million to 60 million B.C.E. there were dinosaurs and other large animals roaming the earth. They were genetic experiments of higher density beings and over the years grew to mammoth proportions. There were all types, but about 60 million years ago the comet Arunhatak came to close to the Earth and blocked out the Sun. There was an enormous cool down which destroyed much of the vegetation and animal life, so the hominids (roughly a few hundred thousand) retreated underground and dug a vast labyrinth of underground cities and tunnels with help from several Pleiadian factions. There are an incredible amount of stories today about the Earth being hollow with underground cities and caverns, and most certainly the myths of dragons and centaurs today are the result of the genetic experiments performed by the aforementioned high density beings. The

---

[8] Sal Rachele, "The Founders on Earth History Part 3." http://www.salrachele.com/webchannelings/foundersonearthhistorypart3.htm.

[9] Alex Collier, "An Andromedan Perspective on Galactic History," http://www.bibliotecapleyades.net/esp.

faerie kingdom also existed during this epoch. This was brought about by 7th density Pleiadians incarnating into hominoid bodies with wings. The faeries were etheric looking and were highly telepathic.[10]

Approximately 10 million years ago the end of the cosmic cycle commenced and the electromagnetic polarities of the Earth shifted, evoking huge storms and floods. Most of the Earth became covered in water and many species were wiped out. Also at this time there was life on two other planets in the solar system, Mars and Maldek, the fourth and fifth planets from the Sun. The weather on Mars and Maldek was colder and the environments were less hospitable than that of Earth, but there were forests laying along the equatorial regions and water in the polar regions. The civilizations on Mars and Maldek at this time were very diverse as these planets became a depository of bizarre and creative thought forms. These thoughtforms reside in the astral realm and influence the way life forms think and operate. Many of the souls that perished during the polar shift on Earth reincarnated on Mars and Maldek and joined civilizations from many different star systems. These civilizations existed mainly in 4th density, so you can see how they would be sensitive to the inception of the many diverse vibrations of souls coming from Earth.

As the life on Mars, Maldek, and Earth progressed and flourished to many unique levels, advanced races from all over the galaxy took notice and a group of reptilians from Alpha Draconis sent scout ships to investigate. A reptilian race from Orion also came here, but these races could not place a foothold, so to speak, in these planets because beings of 9th and 12th density were guarding the Earth experiment closely. There was a protective vibration around Earth, but Mars and Maldek were left out in the open resulting in the Orion and Draco races going and interbreeding there. After a period of this they became stuck in the astral fields of Mars and Maldek and began cycles of reincarnation. They had an aggressive mentality and never forgot their original reason for coming over, which was to mine minerals and dominate other races. As the Orions and Draconians traveled to and reincarnated on Mars and Maldek more and more, great stone cities and fortresses started to adorn the surface of the planet.

---

[10] Antiquity is replete with stories of faeries. A faerie is even one of the main characters in the Peter Pan story. In this chronicle, there is a land where children never grow old (the Fountain of Youth).

A New Order of the Ages

When the Maldekian people discovered neutron technology it became destructive. Several warring factions grew in opposition of each other and about three million years ago the neutron weapons were deployed. After several hundred thousand deaths a new bomb was made and fired at an underground military base. Unbeknownst to the launchers, the underground base contained a large supply of neutron bombs. The invasion of the bomb simultaneously ignited over 200 nuclear silos in the base and the explosions tore apart Maldek into what can be seen today as the asteroid belt between Mars and Jupiter. Many of the ten million souls that met their demise in the blast reincarnated on Mars. This event altered the orbits of Mars and Earth, and the electromagnetic disruption that swept through and out the solar system attracted the attention of many other extraterrestrial races. A council of high density beings convened in the Alcyone star system and it was decided that no more planetary destruction would be allowed anywhere else in the galaxy. This was the beginning of the Great White Brotherhood.

After the inception of the Great White Brotherhood, a civilization on Mars was in full bloom and the souls from Maldek set up incarnational cycles through breeding with the Pleiadian, Orion, and Draconian lineages. The Mars civilization took on an exponential growth process as many of the Maldekian souls fragmented themselves into more individual souls. The atmosphere of Mars was much thinner than Earth's and therefore could not sustain as large a population. Wars broke out over water rights and eventually uranium and plutonium bombs were created. The Great White Brotherhood saw this and warned the souls on Mars about nuclear warfare. They even helped to build extensive underground shelters and cities. Even so, many of the souls from Maldek had not learned their lessons and holes were subsequently blown in the atmosphere of Mars, disrupting the ecological balance necessary to house life. Most of the surface life became extinct and 10 million Martians went underground. The underground cities were then sealed off from the outside world and they still exist today on 4th density. The pyramids and the face on Mars are the few remnants of the lost civilizations. The 100 million souls that did not survive the destruction reincarnated on Earth into Pleiadian, Orion, Draconian, and other lineages which had resurfaced after the destruction of Pangaea. The Earth became a tropical jungle once again and had about 90% water cover.

During the period of 10 million to 1 million B.C.E., life on Earth evolved and became abundant once again. Once the vibration on Earth dropped below 5th density, the Orions and Draconians came in larger numbers and started to control the stargates and portals around the planet. As Earth attracted more and more souls from across the universe (most being 4th density) it became a melting pot of genetics. Most of the Orions who came were escaping the wars occurring between the Rigel and Betelguese star nations, and since their physical bodies were more adaptable to the Earth environment they proliferated more than the Draconians. There was much chaos because rival groups were once again fighting for control of resources.

Many archangels and ascended beings from the 8th and 9th density were watching the Earth at this time and a being called Lucifer came down to Earth with a group of souls to set up mystery schools teaching how to use intellectual faculties in order to control the emotions. As many souls on Earth were learning how to control the emotional body, these qualities were suppressed to the point where the vibration dropped to 3rd density. Archangel Michael saw this and brought a group of ascended beings down to Earth for the purpose of bringing those souls back into the light. When they arrived the vibration was so dense they became caught in the game of duality and saw the more regressive civilizations as an evil that needed to be destroyed. During this struggle Archangel Michael took the side of the light and members of the Councils of Rigel, including most of the Draconians, took the side of the dark. Lucifer and his band of followers saw this and became strategists, building up both sides to see which one would reign supreme. Lucifer taught the soldiers to suppress their emotions while Michael taught them to be passionate. When Lucifer saw what Michael was teaching the soldiers he waged war on Michael's forces and the "War in the Heavens" ensued, taking place in the astral and etheric realms above Earth.[11] The negatively polarized Orions and Draconians propagated rapidly after this incident since their foes were now fighting each other.

This immense struggle occurred in roughly 500,000 B.C.E., the period between 1,000,000 and 500,000 B.C.E. seeing the rise of the Earth population from 200 million to nearly 1 billion inhabitants. There were minor conflicts on the surface using conventional weapons but they

---

[11] The war in the astral world between Archangels Michael and Lucifer is a classic story told over and over again and it is referenced to in the Bible.

did not last long. After 1000 years of fighting Lucifer and Michael agreed upon a truce, with Lucifer agreeing not to promote over-aggression and Michael agreeing not to overcome the suppression of emotion by fighting. Both groups retreated into the celestial realms to integrate the lessons learned. Between 500,000 and 200,000 B.C.E., life evolved on Earth and a few souls reintegrated their 4th density awareness. Many more souls also came to Earth during this time, which deepened the melting pot of life even more. The Orions from Betelguese and Rigel were still the largest groups on the planet. During the War in the Heavens the factions from Betelguese sided with Michael while the factions from Rigel sided with Lucifer, and during the transition phase after the war both Orion groups maintained their polarities. The Betelguese factions continued to breed peaceful groups while the Rigel factions continued to breed aggressive groups of life forms. Around 200,000 B.C.E. the population of Earth was 1.5 billion.[12]

The War between Reptiles and Humans

I want to narrow the scope a bit now and focus on the dispute between the reptiles and humans in this galaxy since it is so pertinent to what is happening today on the third Earth Grand Experiment. The reptilians, when they were planted in this galaxy in the star system of Alpha Draconis, were given a creation myth that pronounced them the dominant life form and the rightful rulers over any civilization they chose to conquer. They have had space travel for over 4 billion years and their space fleets are highly sophisticated. The humans evolved in the Lyra star system and became very agricultural, abiding there for approximately 40 million years. One day a large reptilian spacecraft appeared in the sky near the planet Bila and a squad of Draconians came down to the planet. The Draconians wanted to control the humans, who misunderstood their intention and wanted to know more about them. The Draconians took this as a sign of refusal and destroyed three out of the fourteen planets in the Lyran system killing over 50 million Lyrans. The three planets that were destroyed were Bila, Teka, and Merck. Since this time the reptilians have seen the humans as a food source, and as a

---

[12] Sal Rachele, "The Founders on Earth History Part 7," http://www.salrachele.com/webchannelings/foundersonearthhistorypart7.htm.

result they are the force behind the repression of human populations in this galaxy, instilling fear-based belief systems and restrictive hierarchies on planets with human populations. The reptilians themselves live in a fear-based system containing specific hierarchies. They fear the humans because they see them as a threat.

The Draconians and their sub-races are populated mostly in the Orion star system in this galaxy and also in the Rigel and Capella star systems. They teach their children that they were in this universe first and therefore are the rightful heirs. They possess extremely advanced technology which they use to conquer star systems and genetically alter the life forms they find there. They live in a belief system proclaiming fear as the dominant factor over love and are always stuck in survival mode. They live in societies where it is survival of the fittest. This can be seen in many reptilian races where the mother, after giving birth, will abandon the offspring to fend for themselves. If they survive, they are brought up by a warrior class that uses them for combat games. Their mentality is opposite to that of the humans, who live in peace and are very family-oriented. It is programmed into their belief system never to trust a human because humans invaded their universe and forced them to struggle for survival. The reptilians are mostly "service-to-self," meaning they do what they please and care not for other races. I must emphasize here that not all reptilians are service-to-self. There are many humans who are service-to-self and fight for power and control over other races, so one should not get confused and think in terms of black and white.

In the Milky Way Galaxy there are two schools of thought, one being negative in vibration and the other being positive. The regressives want to control others and therefore live in a state of fear, meaning they constantly fight for survival. The top of the regressive hierarchy chain is the Ciakar. The other school of thought is "service-to-others." This school of thought teaches divine oneness and action for the good of the whole. The way the Draconians enslave a race is they reduce the number of D.N.A. strands in that race's biological blueprint, trapping it in a vibrational prison. This prison keeps the race in a low vibrational frequency wherein the thought patterns of the race are restricted. These reduced thought patterns keep the race in a fear-based system where each member of the race fights for survival with the other members and does not evolve its intellect and spirituality. This is a perfect example of what is happening on Earth now.

I would also like to clarify an issue concerning the Greys, the aliens that are the most commonly seen when reports of abductions flood the arena. Many millions of years ago, the Greys were more human-looking and had much more emotion. They were living in the star systems of Zeta Reticulum 1 and 2 when they decided to explore the rest of the galaxy. 900,000 years ago they were captured by group of reptilians from the Orion star system who were genetically altered and under the control of the Alpha Draconians. In order to control the birthing process of the captured Greys the Orions slaughtered almost all the females leaving only a few, and these few they then genetically altered so that all children born thereafter would also be genetically altered. The males were enslaved to mine metals for the reptilians. On Earth right now there are many factions of Greys that work for the Alpha Draconians. The Greys that aren't subject to the rule of the reptilians have come here attempting to warn us about the reptilians, although we did not heed that warning.

Most humanoid races in other parts of the galaxy live according to the Law of One and are in service to the light.[13] In this part of the galaxy there are 21 star systems under control of the Alpha Draconians. In ancient galactic wars the humans were able to steal Draconian records which stated that one day out of nowhere a race called the Paa Tal appeared and created a species of humans to war with the Draconians. This race is most notably the Founders, who were only acting out the polarity integration game. Alex Collier is an Andromedan contactee who lectures about the Draconians, Lyrans, and Paa Tal.

The Human Form

As was mentioned earlier, the human form originated in Lyra. The Lyrans were the original white (Aryan) race and were very agricultural. After the wars with the reptilians the human survivors fled to many other star systems in this galaxy where they became the Sirians, Arcturians, Antarians, Pleiadians, Andromedans, Cignus Alphans, Alpha Centaurians,

---

[13] Adherence to the "Law of One" was prevalent in Atlantis. See *The Children of The Law of One & The Lost Teachings of Atlantis* by Jon Peniel.

Cassiopians, and many others. The only two races now that have pure human D.N.A. from Lyra are the Pleiadians and Andromedans, both of which are here now assisting the Earth in its evolution. The Pleiadians are mostly fair skinned while the Andromedans have many different skin colors, as do other human races in the galaxy. Some of these races lost their human appearance through breeding programs as now there are numerous physical appearances among races in this galaxy, though the reptilians have kept their general appearance. As many human colonies were established on different planets after the First Great Galactic War, many root races were created with varying mental, emotional and spiritual aspects, which in effect led to an abundance of life in the universe. The nature of the reptiles is cheating and many Alpha Draconians have demonstrated their dominance over inferior races, but it is all part of the spiritual evolution of the universe.

As the Lyrans settled in different parts of the galaxy they learned to adapt to multitudes of planetary environments. As there was some minor conflict, peaceful solutions were always thought up. The human race is very creative and it has this advantage over the reptilian race. Obviously, the destruction of planet Earth now is not a result of Lyran belief because the Lyrans were experts at planetary evolvement as well as individual evolvement. The fact that millions of people on Earth starve everyday is due to reptilian hierarchical belief systems that have been imposed on this planet and not to Lyran philosophy. The Lyrans knew how to grow an abundance of food and live in harmony with nature. In early times the lifespan of the Lyrans was between 300 to 450 years, but this was to grow considerably over many aeons. Even the reptilians have learned to live for thousands of years.

The Lyrans knew how to live in large communities and held a belief system which stated the needs of the many outweighed the needs of the few. When the Lyrans were invaded by the reptilians many of them settled in the Pleiades star system. The Pleiadians developed effective weapons which aided them in wars with reptilians from Orion. They can be considered our ancient ancestors as their genetics were used in our creation. We are very similar to the Pleiadians, except for the fact that they are much more evolved emotionally, spiritually, and technologically. They are here now trying to teach us about their growing pains and how we are experiencing many of the same problems, but not enough Earthlings are listening. The Pleiades is a cluster of 254 stars located in the constellation of Taurus. The Pleiadians are concerned about our use of scientific knowledge and they state that we use this to hurt the planet and not help it, which is why Earth is dying now. The Pleiadians here now can speak all the Earth languages and they are trying to teach people that religion and politics are really two sides of the same coin, with both being used for the enslavement of humanity. All the Earth languages are derived from an ancient language called Tamil which was spoken in Lyra. The Pleiadians stress that we create our own future and they do not want to be responsible for us if they try to help and all goes wrong. They are linked karmically with Earth and what faces them now is somewhat of a conundrum. They are waiting for more Earthlings to wake up so we can take more responsibility for ourselves. The Pleiadians have a fear that if they try to help us and it fails we will just blame it on them. Pleiadian contactees Billy Meiers, Barbara Marciniak, and Barbara Hand Clow all talk about this.

The group of humans that settled in the Arcturus star system is known as the Arcturians. This race of humanity is very private and adept at healing. Their technology is highly advanced, but is only used for education, travel, and healing. It is used not at all for warfare, although they do have the ability to protect themselves when need be. The Arcturians have intervened in the past on Earth in order to resolve conflicts. They were involved with the Hebrews (Hibiru) and Moses (Tuthmoses) on Mount Sinai.

Space Travel

I would like to touch upon the subject of space travel now to satisfy any concerns the reader might have regarding how extraterrestrial races move around in the universe. Various methods are exerted on the fabric of space-time. Quantum flux is the flow of energy, and assuming the holographic nature of the universe there really is no such thing as "here" and "there" since everything exists everywhere at once. Time seems like a reality in the lower densities but in the higher dimensions it doesn't exist. All form of matter that you see around you is simply condensed vibrations of spiritual energy. Keeping this in mind, there are three modes of space travel utilized by extraterrestrials coming and going to

Earth right now. These are: (a) phase-shifting, (b) zero-point fields, and (c) thought transference.

The Greys from Zeta Reticulum 1 and 2 and other races from third and fourth density use phase-shifting, which utilizes the natural Ley and grid lines of planetary bodies and also wormholes that exist within the space-time fabric. The wormholes and warp holes in our universe are called "portals" and "stargates" by many spiritual teachers. This mode of travel likens to the analogy of drawing two points on a piece of paper connected by a straight line and calling these points A and B. If one were to ponder the fastest way of getting from point A to point B one might realize that it would be by folding the paper in on itself so the two points met with each other. When phase-shifting occurs an electromagnetic field is spun around the craft that attunes itself to the Ley line or vortex in question.

Zero-point fields employ the use of zero-point propulsion. This dualistic reality we live in can actually be transcended and one can enter into a state of "oneness" where there is a balance of polarity in the electromagnetic null zone. This is the zone in which a spacecraft utilizing zero-point propulsion will enter into, the etheric field known as the "aether" in antiquity. A ship that enters into this field can then re-enter into third-dimensional or fourth-dimensional space by re-polarizing itself at the destination in question. The dimensional shift the ship and its occupants experience during zero-point propulsion transcends the laws of Newtonian and Einsteinian physics. When a ship enters into this null zone it is subject to an infinite amount of energy, which it could then potentially command.

The most advanced form of space travel is thought transference. This method is not employed by technology. Rather, it is the result of spiritual energy that is the source of everything. Ships using this method are aligned with the higher dimensional frequencies of light and can travel to any place in any of the universes in a second. They also can travel to any period of time in any dimensional reality. These lightships bring messages from the Cosmic Center of Consciousness which could help humanity in the ways of attaining spiritual growth. Every universe, galaxy, planet, and person has a unique energy signature, and when one wishes to travel among the stars one can just attune his/her consciousness to the desirable energy signature. In the higher dimensions everything exists in a point or singularity, so there is no here, there, or time. Everything is everywhere at once. When a soul evolves beyond 9th density, space travel becomes obsolete. A being of high density can appear to anyone and communicate with that entity by altering the molecular structure of the being's auric field. When beings channel, the channel itself is contained within an etheric field that has an energy signature matched as much as possible to the energy signature of the receiver. When the thought forms of an individual are scrutinized, that individual is communicated to by a being of higher vibration using terminology and language recognizable to the individual in reception of higher wisdom.[14]

The Arcturians

Now back to the Arcturians, who are one of the most advanced civilizations spiritually and technologically in the universe. The Arcturians originally settled in the Bootes star constellation where they evolved into a 5th density life form. Many humans when they die on Earth will pass through the Arcturian Stargate, the midway programming center for the physical brotherhoods of this universe. Many souls coming to Earth use this energy as a training course for life on the planet and pass through the stargate where they become accustomed to physicality. The Arcturians are very private and work to serve Prime Creator, a being they call the "Radiant One." They work as an energy healer for humanity on an emotional, mental, and spiritual level. They teach souls how to live in the fifth dimension, where the qualities of negativity, fear, and guilt are exchanged for love and light. The Arcturians are a highly advanced consciousness, and when they take on physical bodies they usually appear four feet tall with a slender, green body and large almond shaped eyes. The leaders of their race sometimes take on the appearance of horses. They are totally empathetic, telepathic and telekinetic. They serve as a protection team for many developing civilizations in this galaxy and have been protecting Earth from negative, regressive races since its inception. The Starship *Athena* (named after the Greek goddess) has been orbiting the Earth for thousands of years and now plays a crucial role in Earth's ascension, as many negative races wish to prevent this.

---

[14] Sal Rachele, "The Arcturians on Space Travel," http://www.salrachele.com/webchannelings/arcturiansonspacetravel.htm.

The Arcturians execute healing procedures on the energy bodies of humans by taking them in their dream state and aligning them with high frequencies. Many humans are taken in their dream state to the 5th density Arcturian starships where higher light vibrations are downloaded into the four body system. The Arcturians have given much information about Earth's history through channels (Dr. Norma J. Milanovich of the Athena Leadership Center and Jasmuheen of the Embassy of Peace are two of these contactees and channels), and they also have been charging the planet's energy matrix with high frequency beams, altering the consciousness of humanity. Many of these insertions of high vibrational energy into the chakras of the Earth and also our individual human bodies have helped raise the consciousness of our planet to a point where more people can access higher levels of knowing. The Arcturian civilization is like a sign post for the future Earth, and many here now from Arcturus are teaching humans how to let go of fear and allow their intuition to guide them along their chosen paths.

The Arcturians travel the universe in highly advanced starships which utilize fifth-dimensional crystals, energy grids which harvest the energy of the central suns of all the galaxies. They are currently holding the electromagnetic energies of Earth in balance and are preventing many negative catastrophes that have been predicted for centuries. The polar shift that many people are talking about will actually be on a spiritual level instead of a physical one. In the first part of Earth's history the Arcturians created a space of love and harmony for the creation of the blueprint for the human etheric body, and now we are re-learning how to transcend the dense, physical body for a body of light (a fifth—dimensional crystal light body). They teach us that love created everything, so it is unnecessary for us to constantly seek conditional love. When the negative energies are removed from Earth and from our physical bodies, the unconditional love will flow much easier and it will be easy to clear the negative lower-astral entities living in people's auras; they feed of lower human emotion and consume life energy.

On the home planet of Arcturus there is a governing hierarchy, but it is nothing like the controlling powers on Earth. On Arcturus, a group of wise elders with extremely high vibrational frequencies guide the planet and missions of love and peace away from Arcturus. Everyone on their planet works for the good of the whole, which in turn works for the good of every individual. Your profession on Arcturus is determined by the colors in your aura. The Arcturians here now assisting the Earth have no permission to remove the dark forces because it is all part of the experiment. When the year 2012 moves closer these beings will reveal themselves and assist Earth into the Golden Age of Aquarius.[15]

The Language of Light

Many people incarnated on Earth right now do not understand that the physical manifest world is truly an illusion. This illusion is called the "Maya" in Hinduism. In this illusion, one may wander endlessly, searching for answers that are never there. We are all victims of the Matrix, the world that has been pulled over our eyes to blind us from the truth. Everything that you experience on 3rd density Earth is an illusion of the mind, as your reality is mostly determined by electrical impulses interpreted by your brain. In reality, your brain is just the physical manifestation of your mind stemming for your third eye chakra. It manifests into two polarities—left brain: logic, deduction and induction; right brain: intuition, feeling, emotion, bigger picture mentality. Many on Earth are left brain prisoners, slaves to their hidden masters who manipulate the five sense reality from behind the scenes. In essence, we have been disconnected from our higher selves, the highest expression of ourselves being pure love. When you enter your body in the womb your soul (consciousness) attaches itself to the photon receptors in your brain and spinal cord, the central nervous system being the prime conductor of the body. We are consciousness experiencing the world through a human nervous system.

Science will mistake the central nervous system for conscious life, but this is not so. Your consciousness exists in your aura and your soul, that being an extension of your oversoul. There is a chakra that sits six inches above your head that serves as a connection to the oversoul. Most of the time, we are acting out divine blueprints of learning in three-dimensional physical reality without even realizing our lives are manifestations of incarnational learning cycles. We are now reaching the end of a cycle—the Age of Pisces—and breaking free from the Matrix will be as easy as it ever has been. Earth has been a Galactic Federation school

---

[15] For more information on the Arcturians I suggest reading *We, the Arcturians*, which was channeled by Norma J. Milanovich.

since 1987, and the souls in this school that choose love will graduate in 2012. Those who chose not to align with the higher frequencies of light will incarnate on another planet of their choosing which will serve as another opportunity to ascend. All is as it should be. The language of our planet is not English, Spanish, French, or German. It's the language of photons and electrons. Our brains are starved for light.

The Earth Conspiracy

It has recurrently been debated whether or not ancient astronauts visited the early civilizations of Earth, but now, with channels bringing forth higher spiritual knowledge and new information leaking out from inside the secret government, a higher state of awareness has assumed the position of authority over those who are perceptive enough to pick up on these higher thoughtforms. Closed minded science will never understand what happened in Egypt and Sumer, but New Age thinking and revolutionary archeological finds are finally starting to reveal the real story. In order to fully understand the early history of Earth, one must understand the nature of a "conspiracy," and how it maintains a low frequency of behavior.

The word "conspire" means to breathe together, so in actuality two people could create a conspiracy, however large, in order to advance a common desire. On Earth there are many micro-conspiracies, some intertwined within the larger alien conspiracies and some not, however it is the alien conspiracies that I wish to focus on. The secret world government controlled by the Illuminati (interbreeding Draconian bloodlines) seeks to maintain order out of chaos, or in other words "organized chaos." They have as their goal the complete destruction of organized society. Why would they do this? I realize it is hard to understand why any human would have this as their agenda, but in order to fully comprehend it the darkest of all conspiracies must be exposed. This organization calls itself the Dark Lords, and has been involved in numerous battles over Earth and on other planets throughout many aeons.

The Dark Lords work under the protection of the Dark Forces. These Dark Forces are souls (any soul who chooses this) who have organized together and conspired, attempting to seize light away from other souls.

A New Order of the Ages

I mentioned earlier that everything is light, so how can this occur? There is one way called an entropic energy exchange. When this occurs the darkness can take light and convert it into an array of distorted impulses, whereby the illusion of power and superiority is manifested as a sort of ego-dominion. This transfer of power cannot hold indefinitely, so after a while the illusion will disintegrate and the light will return to the Source. As the dark force believes it is separate from the Source, it is stuck in survival mode where it must take the energy drawn from the lower-ego desires of money, prestige, and power from others. Most souls will not consciously surrender their power, so the dark forces have to use trickery and deception in order to gain the victim's life force energy. When a person uses drugs it expends lots of hate energy, and negative astral beings controlled by the Dark Forces are attracted to that person's aura where they live and feast. Most people are unaware of this, because if they were it would not be occurring so much. On Earth at this time a transition period has been initiated whereby light energy is being directed into the dark, dense corners of the planet and many conspiracies are coming to the surface. The vibration of Earth is so low right now that this is taking time, time that is speeding up to the perception of many Earthlings who are finally sensing the truth.

The most ostentatious conspiracy on Earth right now concerns the reptilian factions. They originate in many 4th density worlds and are spread out though many sectors in the Orion, Sirius, and Alpha Draconis star systems. They even have bases in our neighboring galaxy of Andromeda. Not all Draconians are Dark Lords, so again I urge the reader to not think in terms of black and white. I laid out in discourse earlier the nature of the reptilians, so the reader can make his/her own conjectures about the Dark Lords and why they do what they do. Right now there are many Dark Lords on Earth who live in the astral plane in the fourth dimension. They siphon off the energy of people who live in states of anger and fear, and they use their puppets in the political and religious arenas to channel as much negative energy as possible to them so that they may increase their power and dominion over other sentient life forms. Most of the governments and police forces of the world have been penetrated by these forces, the ones who take fear and give fear in return. The military-industrial complex is one of the ways human herds are quelled with technology and war.

The Dark Forces will remain in power until a certain mass of people wake up to the greater reality of who their rulers really are. When enough people do wake up, it will be like the "100 Monkey Effect." When enough souls become aware and increase their light energy, this awareness will spread through the whole morphogenetic field of the planet and other souls will start to feel this energy and consciousness. This could happen in another form. When enough individuals demonstrate knowledge of a new idea or concept, it embeds itself within the overall consciousness of the population. This is beginning to happen on Earth, and when enough people focus their attention on love and higher consciousness, the rest of the population will have the benefit of a portal extending through the vibrational prison currently covering the planet. This electromagnetic prison has been called the "Net" by many channellers. When only one person out of seven billion people attempts this it is nearly impossible, but when enough people focus their energy and concentration, a hole of consciousness will be burned into the stratosphere of negative thoughtforms hanging over Earth like a garment. When this hole reaches a critical mass the entire population of people can access higher vibrational feelings and thoughtforms with ease instead of concentrated effort.

The Illuminati is another secret organization which will be exposed in this book. The Illuminati began as a series of secret mystical orders, but over time has been corrupted by power, greed, and the interbreeding bloodline families seeded by the "gods" of the Bible. The members of this faction originally called themselves the "Illuminated Ones" because of the higher spiritual knowledge they gained, but after a while many freedoms were taken away (the order of the Druids is an excellent example of this). As centuries passed it became harder and harder to gain entry into these organizations, which were prided on secrecy. Instead of schools they became cults that practiced demon worship and blood sacrifice. Today, the Illuminati is composed of international bankers and members of the power elite including presidents, prime ministers, Roman Catholic officials, and generals of war. They meet in secret and perform rituals designed to increase their hold over society, this hold of hypnotization perpetuated by the media and education systems of many nations. Their control of the entire monetary system also ensures them the capability of moving power influences anywhere on the planet. They control Hollywood and many professional actors who have surrendered themselves to Lucifer and the New World Order.

They also control the C.I.A. and organized crime, as well as the drug trade industry. Major big-name pharmaceutical companies are owned by these "elite" men and women who wish to destroy our youth with harmful opiates and chemicals that destroy our immune systems. That is why they release chemtrails in the sky and pollute our drinking water with sodium fluoride, a toxicity that reduces the abilities of our bodies to produce white blood cells. It is because Earth is overpopulated and they are losing their foothold in the entire infrastructure of the planet. They employ the advertising of fatty foods, harmful drugs and sex to corrupt the youth, and they pollute the air and water in order to reduce our health and life spans so we demand more healthcare. The healthcare is also controlled by the Illuminati as conventional medicine does not even come close to the healing potential of love, light and higher consciousness. There are, however, members of the Illuminati who work for the Galactic Federation of Light and who are "double agents," so to speak.

There is a group of Greys from Zeta Reticulum here on a mission to save their species from extinction. Since they have suppressed their emotional nature they chose humans (a species with powerful emotional energy) to breed with. This Grey faction has lost the ability to reproduce because they bred out their emotional nature in return for high intellect and technology. Many members of the Zeta race agreed to incarnate into human bodies to later be abducted and disseminated of genetic material. When these souls reach childbearing age they are brought to the ships. If they are female they are impregnated with Zeta embryos and if they are male their sperm is extracted. The females are brought back to the ships later where the fetus is extracted and grown. Many Grey nations have formed alliances with the governments of the world, where they have exchanged technology for anonymity. There are races of Greys who are slaves to the Reptilians and do their dirty work, and there are also species of Greys that have been bred by the reptilians. These genetic "offspring" wear a skin tight grey suit over their bodies, which actually look rough, sinewy, and pink. The large black eyes are goggles that cover their real eyes, which are large and have slit pupils.

The Nature of Karma

Thus far into our endeavor the reader might be a little confused. Those who have heard of karma might ask the question, "Why would these evil forces do what they do if it's all going to come back around and bite them?" Well, karma doesn't work like that. Karma is simply the result of a mental misconception of the need to atone for past mistakes. Those who do evil will not succeed not because they are evil, but because all things in the end must return to the Source. This Source is pure light. Evil is just an interpretation, and many times it comes in the form of a lesson that must be learned. If no lessons were learned there would be no evolution. The Illuminati does what it does because it can get away with it. Their secrecy is coming to an end though and soon their organization will bleed itself out from the inside. Their so-called "evil" actions do not result in evil being done upon them in the future, but rather result in the actions leading to a conflict resolution where the light and dark are fully integrated.

Karma can be defined as an energetic residue held within an incomplete expression of divinity. Our society on Earth right now is an incomplete expression of divinity because most people are polarized to either the light or the dark. Our karma resonates as a whole. The political and religious leaders of the world hurt us because we let them hurt us. We are our own worst enemy. If everyone stood up for themselves right now the Illuminati would not be able to exist anymore. Karma is accumulated when an unforgiving situation is stored into one's subconscious mind and precipitated by the belief that one must atone for past mistakes. An unresolved issue is an emotional charge held in the subconscious mind, and it cannot be released by simply forgetting about it. Forgetting is not releasing. Forgetting is storing that charge even further into the subconscious where it will be even harder to access for future healing. An individual who holds no karma experiences life fully and then releases it fully. Every situation is either a lesson or a reward, because all of life is learning. Those who hold regrets are operating under the assumption that they have done something wrong, although in reality doing something "wrong" is just an illusion. Since all of life is constantly evolving and merging into the Godhead, no experience should be perceived as regret. All experiences are life lessons that must be embraced fully.

Since everything is part of the Godhead, everything is connected to everything else. The reptilians are just as loved as the humans because everything is one at all times. Karma results when the illusion of separation enters one's awareness. Until now the Earth has not had sufficient enough energy levels to allow for the release of residual emotional energies contained within the collective consciousness of the planet, and also within groups of incarnating souls as well as individual souls. A karma-free existence is one where the present moment is fully realized at all times and one lives in harmony with spirit. There is no guilt or shame, and all souls learn lessons of humility and self-acceptance while embracing every emotion. Each emotion that is not totally embraced will sink down into the subconscious mind where it builds residual energy. Numerous people on Earth now repress their emotions, disabling them from feeling the full experience of life. They are afraid that they will not be taken seriously or that they are victims of bullies. Those who stay in the victim consciousness will never be free of karma because they aren't in tune with spirit. Being in harmony with spirit means one is self-empowered. At this time a wave of this self-empowerment is stretching over the Earth, waking people up to their true potential. Above all, the main ingredient for living a karma-free life is being able to live in the moment. Near the year 2012, much of the karma will be released on the Earth, freeing herself and her inhabitants to ascend into the fifth dimension.

IV

Universal History Part 2

In regards to our galactic and universal history, Nibiru has cropped up as the *raison d'être* for recent investigations into the history of the solar system. It is purported that when Nibiru came into our solar system in the past, it passed through the orbits of Mars and Jupiter and out past the Sun, hooking back around into its orbit, the duration of which was 3,600 years[1]. It used to be an outer planet of the Sirius A star system, but was damaged in battle and relocated to our solar system, where it orbited the two stars (the sun we know and its twin, which sits below the plane of the solar system) until it was fashioned into a battlestar. There are other small planets that orbit Nibiru as well as asteroids that have been converted to battleships. Nibiru does have rings around it, but they are not like the rings around Saturn. Instead, they act as an advanced propulsion system, meaning Nibiru can and does break its orbit occasionally. Currently Nibiru is a roaming field office for the Galactic Federation and a planetary ascension battlestar. It was involved in several wars transpiring in our galaxy and in our solar system in which its atmosphere was severely crippled. That is why gold dust is needed to repel the radiation from space. There are many civilizations on different dimensional levels living on Nibiru and on many of its orbiting bodies. They have technology that is aeons beyond ours.

Nibiru is encased in a metal-like substance while the protective force fields around the planet give it a bright hue. The reason why many ancient peoples thought it was a star is because it glows so brightly. The inhabitants of Nibiru live inside the planet instead of on the surface. Nibiru was created by the Galactic Federation as a battlestar when it was converted from a lifeless planet into a battleship after the explosion of the star Sirius B threw it completely out of orbit. It is now a peace-keeping ship which promotes harmony among the civilizations in the galaxy, and

---

[1] Sitchin, Zecharia, *The 12th Planet* (New York: HarperCollins, 1976), 274.

it has assumed an orbit around the two suns in our solar system. On the inside Nibiru houses many advanced civilizations on the many levels of its interior. It has a simulated night and day, mountains, lakes, forests and an abundance of plant life. It even has a night sky. In a sense it was made to resemble the planet Avyon. Since Nibiru is a battlestar it provided the feminine-polarized Pleiadian Royal Line of Avyon the opportunity to experience masculinity by protecting other planets and civilizations from negative forces. This has greatly helped them in their spiritual growth. The great Sirian/Egyptian god Anubis is the guide who currently holds Nibiru's orbit in form and he travels with the solar system through the Galactic Night, just has the Pleiadians hold the orbit of the solar system as it travels through the Photon Band. A great Sirian/Pleiadian alliance has allowed for Earth to become a repository for creative biological forms to coexist together; the invasion of the Annunaki from Nibiru has only helped foster learning experiences.

On its inception day Nibiru was crowned with the most advanced technology in the universe. Anu's forefather Niestda was the first commander of Nibiru and, seventeen generations later, it is now Anu's grandson Marduk. Anu began his rule over Nibiru long before it came to Earth 480,000 years ago, and it was Marduk, not Alalu, who wrestled away control of Nibiru. It has been transcribed on many stone tablets that Anu stole command of Nibiru from Alalu, his brother, but that was not so. After he took control in 2,200 B.C.E. Marduk had all the written records changed. Anu and the rest of his family live on a Pleiadian mothership managing an orbit near Saturn. There are many parents of starseeds on Earth also residing on this mothership, along with other races who are involved in the fulfillment of the divine plan for Earth.

It has been wrongly assumed that Anu is a dark reptilian here to enslave Earth. Anu is actually a Pleiadian of pure Lyran descent. He is 9 feet 11 inches tall with platinum blond hair who works to keep pure Human D.N.A. samples for future generations. Sananda, the oversoul of the man formerly known as Jesus, is one of the nine founders of the Universe and it was he who fragmented himself to create Amelius. His line became the Amelius line, the Royal House of Avyon. This royal house settled in the Pleiades after Avyon was destroyed millennia ago and it was Devin who was the family patriarch. Remember, Devin was one of the 45 Felines who came to set up this universe and game.

Nibiru was involved with Earth in the past, mainly as an aid. Members from Nibiru came to mine gold on Earth and realized that it was too hot, so they created a worker class of homo-sapiens to do it for them. That worker class became us. The manipulation of the D.N.A. and the interaction with the ancient Sumerians has been a hotbed of debate lately, and I hope to clear that subject up at this point in the discourse. I will offer a different take on universal history and Nibiru according to members from the Royal House of Avyon, which itself is from the Lyran planet of Avyon. When the twelfth-dimensional Council of Nine (Founders) finished creating this universe the Felines and the Carians chose the game of polarity integration. After this decision the original ninety Felines and Carians birthed into the Amelius Line (Felines) and Lucifer Line (Carians) on the ninth dimension. These ninety members became the Ninth-Dimensional Nibiruan Council when it was formed as part of the Galactic Federation. Council members below the ninth dimension are soul fragments of the original members. The primary members of the Royal House of Avyon are mentioned below as such:

9th Dimensional Royal House

Devin: 9th dimensional Patriarch of the House of Avyon. Oversoul of 6th dimensional aspect Anu.

Jelaila: 9th dimensional Matriarch of the House of Avyon. Oversoul of 6th dimensional aspect Ninhursag.

Satain: 9th dimensional son of Devin and Jelaila. Oversoul of 4th dimensional aspect Marduk (current ruler of Nibiru).

Kavantai: 9th dimensional brother of Devin. Oversoul of 4th dimensional aspect Nabu (son of Marduk and second in command of Nibiru).

Shalandrai: 9th dimensional sister of Devin. Oversoul of 6th dimensional aspect Enlil.

6th Dimensional Royal House

Anu: Head of Galactic Federation's 6th dimensional Nibiruan Council. Former commander of Nibiru. Father of Ninhursag, Enki and Enlil. Grandfather of Marduk.

Ninhursag: Daughter of Anu by consort Rayshondra. Chief Medical Officer of the Earth Mission. Co-creator of mankind along with Enki.

Enlil: Son of Anu by Anu's half sister Antu. Half brother of Enki and Ninhursag. Heir to the throne of Nibiru until Marduk took over.

Enki: Son of Anu by Dramin, the Dragon Queen of Earth. Husband/brother to Damkina (Ninki). Known also as Ptah, ruler of Egypt.

Ninurta: Son of Enlil by half sister Ninhursag. Grandson of Anu.

Adad: Son of Enlil by spouse Ninlil. Grandson of Anu.

Nannar: Son of Enlil by Ninlil. Grandson of Anu.

Inanna: Daughter of Nannar by spouse Ningal. Half sister of Ereshkigal. Great granddaughter of Anu.

Ningishzidda/Thoth: Son of Enki by consort Ereshkigal. Grandson of Anu. Also known as Quetzalcoatl.

Ereshkigal: Daughter of Nannar by Id, Snake Princess of Earth. Wife of Nergal. Half sister of Inanna.

Nergal: Son of Enki. Lord of the Underworld (African Mines). Husband of Ereshkigal.

Dumuzi: Son of Nannar. Brother/husband of Inanna.

4th Dimensional Royal House

Marduk: Son of Enki by Damkina (Ninki), Dragon Princess. Leader of the Dark Forces. Present commander of Nibiru and Earth.

Nabu: Son of Marduk. Great grandson of Anu.

I will rhapsodize now about the formation of this polarity integration game from another perspective. This one is outlined from Anu himself and is very intricate concerning the spiritual game set up and the leaders of the various dimensional realms. This material was taken from the book *We Are the Nibiruans, Return of the Twelfth Planet* by Jelaila Starr, who is a contactee of the Devin and the Federation Flagship Nibiru.[2]

Our universe is divided up into clusters of hierarchies, each larger one containing the others. There are spiritual hierarchies present that oversee the planets, galaxies, and star systems. The Great Spiritual Hierarchy oversees all of this and represents the cosmic hierarchy, which receives directions from Prime Creator. All the hierarchies are composed of souls who have chosen the angelic realms as their path. Sananda (Amelius) is in charge of the Earth Spiritual Hierarchy since he is the head of the Etheric Sirians. The Etheric Sirians are heirs to the Earth, this being discussed later on.

One hierarchy oversees the divine plan for the different soul groups, which are themselves divided into two groups—those that incarnate and those that do not, the latter being those who become angels. The beings that choose the role as angels evolve by serving on the spiritual hierarchies which minister to the incarnates. The incarnates evolve by learning to serve each other. In the end everyone serves everyone else through unconditional love, since that is what every soul wishes to achieve. The goal for the souls on Earth now is compassion.

Souls are also divided into groups according to their current stage of evolution and whether they are an incarnate or not. These groupings make it easier for them and their divine plans. Since some souls evolve faster than others they can move in and out of groups very rapidly. Soul clusters are larger groupings of souls who are working on a particular

---

[2] This is the first of Starr's books which exists in a trilogy of volumes. The second and third books in the trilogy are *The Mission Remembered* and *Bridge of Reunion*, respectively.

lesson, such as greed, obsessive compulsion, pain, etc. Guides of angels watch over each soul cluster and assist the souls in their incarnations. The incarnates have twelve dimensions in which to evolve and the angels have seven realms in which to advance. Right now the Earth Sirians are the main group on Earth. This is a large soul group in which the two stranded D.N.A. biological vehicles were created for. All the souls on Earth have these same vehicles now, however, they were originally designed for the Earth Sirians.

Every soul was once in complete oneness with Prime Creator. After a while Prime Creator fragmented into individual sparks of consciousness. These souls needed a way to evolve and so the game of polarity integration was created where different souls would take on roles of light and dark. Prime Creator also created a formula for the achievement of integration and this was called the "13th Dimensional Formula of Compassion." Prime Creator is pure love so every soul's task was to achieve unconditional love with every being, regardless of their roles in the light or the dark. At the end of the planetary ascension game on Earth this formula will be given to every soul who chooses to ascend and it will permanently release negative emotions and thoughtforms, thus lightening the planet to the 5th dimension. This shift into the 5th dimension will then move all the planets ahead to the next dimensional frequency, whether they be ahead of or behind Earth.

The creation of the divine plans came after the polarity integration game was created. Every galaxy, star system, planet, and universe has a divine plan, along with every individual soul. Our universal divine plan was created by the Council of Nine (Founders). They strived in cohesion with the Universal Spiritual Hierarchy and the ninety Felines and Carians, who act as the Game Engineers. In the universe from which they came the Felines represented the light and the Carians represented the dark. They came to this universe and became the Game Engineers—they constructed the universe, created the life forms and seeded the planets and stars. All the planets were created by the Universal Construction Engineers, and the Feline Genetic Engineers created the life forms. The Carian Magnetic Engineers created the stargates, dimensions, portals and grids. The primary races from which this game would commence became the humans, descended from the Felines, and the reptiles, descended from the Carians.

Forty-five of the Game Engineers birthed into the Lucifer Line of the Reptiles and forty-five birthed into the Amelius Line of the Humans on the ninth dimension. The Game Overseers remained abided on the tenth and eleventh dimensions as the Councils of 24 and 12, respectively. The Game Directors maintain the twelfth dimension as the Council of Nine. Devin was the one chosen to represent the Game Engineers on the Council of Nine and he resides as the ninth member. His part was to begin the game by birthing into and becoming the patriarch of the Amelius Line. After this was accomplished his job was to remain on the Council of Nine and arouse the other Game Engineers at preconceived times regarding their completion of the planetary and galactic games. Once all the souls in the universe achieve polarity integration the game will be finished and our universe will join with Prime Creator once again. When the polarity integration game on Earth comes to fruition the universe will be one step closer to reuniting with Prime Creator.

All the species of incarnates in our universe are offspring of the Felines and Carians. The D.N.A. blueprints were created by the Felines in conjunction with the Founders, and the Carians were assigned the role of protecting the infant races while they evolved. The goal of each soul was to experience roles on both sides and eventually move beyond the illusion of fear, hate, and prejudice, thereby establishing the 13th Dimensional Formula of Compassion within their cellular structure. The Earth Divine Plan calls for the completion of the Avyonian Divine Plan and the Etheric Sirian Divine Plan, the two going hand in hand. The Lyra humans who had moved to Sirus B became the Etheric Sirians, who were then given Earth as their home by the Founders.

The reptiles lived on Earth from its inception when it was known as Tiamat.[3] That was when the planet was much larger. When it was struck in half many of the reptiles went underground, our modern day snakes and lizards being the descendents of them. The reptiles on Earth now are more masculine and technologically advanced than they are feminine and spiritually advanced. In the beginning, the creation myth that was given to the humans by the Felines asserted they were to colonize any planet they wanted and if they saw a race there they would attempt a peace treaty. The reptilians were given orders to dominate and destroy. There are two pure strains of D.N.A. and they are the Royal Houses. The

---

[3] Zecharia Sitchin is a Mesopotamian scholar who asserted in the 1970's that Earth was once known as "Tiamat" when it was larger many thousands of years ago before the Annunaki came. Other researchers have since corroborated this claim.

Royal House of the Reptiles is the House of Aln and the Royal House of the Humans is the House of Avyon.

The Felines created the human seed in the ocean, and when the physical form evolved to an aquatic primate form they moved the seed onto land and upgraded it to the form of what anthropologists have termed "homo-erectus." The aquatic primate forms that stayed in the oceans on Avyon became the dolphins and whales, which were intended to maintain the biosphere. Once the humans evolved to space travel they colonized another planet in the Lyra star system called Avalon. They made it a femininely polarized colony. When the reptiles arrived they had advanced technology and were polarized toward the male side. They sowed the seeds of discord among the human population when they gave their technology to them, creating a rift among the denizens. Those that wanted to evolve spiritually and those that wanted technological advancement were strung into two divisions. When this occurred the reptiles took the side of the humans wanting technological advancement and the result was the near destruction of the planet. The reptiles saw the humans as a threat because they viewed them as a consumer of space and resources.

When the colony of Avalon nearly destroyed itself the Founders took the humans and placed them on a planet near Sirius B. They then continued their evolution without interference from the reptiles for a while. The Lyran humans then became the Sirian humans. Two groups developed from this movement, those being the Etheric Sirians, a non-physical group, and the Physical Sirians. The Etheric Sirians were headed by Amelius, the Physical Sirians choosing physical form and masculine polarity. The Etheric Sirians went on to culminate the spiritual knowledge of healing and the Lyran way of life. The Founders and the spiritual hierarchies moved the Physical Sirians to Aln, a planet near reptilian colonies, thus enabling them to develop their masculine side and better understand themselves. The reptiles did not like this and many wars ensued. The conflict ended when the reptiles enslaved the Orion humans and nearly destroyed Aln. A small band of Orion Humans formed a resistance movement against the reptiles called the Black League. Later, members from the Black League escaped Orion and traveled to Tiamat, the home given to the Etheric Sirians. The Etheric Sirians were to be the guardians of Tiamat, but they needed physical bodies in order to fulfill this role. The Felines seeded the planet and when the Etheric Sirians arrived the land guardians were in the aquatic primate stage. They decided to watch over their future physical vehicles until they were ready to inhabit them, although incidentally a few Etheric Sirians incarnated into these animals which worried the remaining group. Since thought creates reality there was a real concern about the incarnated Sirians forgetting who they were, so a portion of the Etheric Sirians formed the Christos Alliance as part of the Planetary Spiritual Hierarchy. This group was mandated the duty of overseeing the Sirians in animal bodies until they were evolved enough to rejoin the consciousness of their brothers and sisters.

When the reptiles heard about the newly formed planet Tiamat they set out to colonize it and found an evolving primate civilization being watched over by the Etheric Sirians. The Founders allowed the reptilians to pioneer the planet in hopes that it would serve as a chance for polarity integration. The Etheric Sirians began to send positive energy to the reptile clan in hopes that they would look beyond their creation myth and see the human primates as friends. After a while Amelius asked Devin to leave his home planet of Avyon and travel to Tiamat in order to provide D.N.A. upgrades for the primates. The Amelius line (Royal Line of Avyon) was the only pure line of Human D.N.A., so it was needed to advance the primate race into a human race. When this was accomplished the reptilians still had superior technology, but the human race was more spiritually evolved. Avyon was the home planet of the humans in Lyra, and it was also the name given to the human planet in the Pleiades. After the Pleiadian planet of Avyon was destroyed by the reptiles, an immense emotional barrier was erected between the humans and the reptiles. This pleased the Founders. This Avyonian emotional block was delegated over to Earth (formerly known as Tiamat) through the Royal House of Avyon on Nibiru. This was accomplished by a female from the House of Avyon marrying a Pleiadian male from another planet in the Pleides. Niestda, the first ruler of Nibiru, was born.

When Anu became commander of Nibiru he transferred the Amelius line of D.N.A. to Earth through his children. When Amelius incarnated as Adapa (Adam) he produced a son named Seth, and it was Seth who mated with the daughters and granddaughters of Anu, merging the two Amelius lines in the royal line of Sumer. A man named Terah was born from this royal priestly line and he became the father of the biblical Abraham, whose great grandson Judah became one of the twelve sons of Jacob. The royal house of Judah unfolded from the royal priestly Sumer line. Most the people on Earth today are descendents of one or both of the Amelius lines.

Over the course of time the humans living on Tiamat became friends of the reptiles, who lived on either side of the human colony bridging down Tiamat's middle. The reptilian snakes and the reptilian dragons had civilizations flanking the humans, but relations were harmonious as the humans offered the reptilians an abundance of food. When the Founders and Etheric Sirians saw this they became ecstatic, suspecting the prospect of polarity integration. Even so, a group of reptilians from the Orion Council came to Earth expressing a very displeased nature, due to the fact that they considered this peaceful union a direct breach of their creation myth. The council members from Orion spoke with the ruling families of the reptilian colonies, but they were unable to persuade them in destroying the humans. They then pulled out their usual tricks and convinced the reptilian colonies that the humans were covertly trying to destroy them. The Orion Black League of humans, having just arrived on Tiamat, increased the tension even more by telling the human colony to destroy the reptiles for the reason that they could not be trusted. After 10,000 years of growing unease the reptilians agreed to destroy the humans through biological warfare. After the Pleiadian Avyonians and the Etheric Sirians were consulted a plan was put into motion where the humans would leave Tiamat on the starship *Pegasus* and travel to another planet where they would continue evolving. The Etheric Sirians then became the guardians of the whales and dolphins, thereby maintaining the biosphere of Earth until a new race of human vehicles could be erected in which the Sirians could then fulfill their land guardian duties.

When Earth was larger and called Tiamat, there where fusion generators in the middle of the human colony which maintained the magnetic and electrical fields of the planet, and it was these generators that were destroyed, killing most of the reptilian inhabitants. Some would survive, however, just like a few of the Etheric Sirians stuck in animal bodies. They survived by moving underground, and after a long while moved back to the surface. When Anu became commander of Nibiru he was assigned the task of destroying Tiamat. Piloting the battlestar Nibiru he entered the solar system from the back, which is why the ancient tablets from Mesopotamia called Nibiru the "12th planet" (if you count Nibiru, the Sun, and the Moon, there are 12 planets). Nibiru (controlled by Anu) harnessed a satellite from Saturn and shot it into Tiamat with such velocity that it augmented her. A laser beam was projected into the fusion generators and the planet was split in two. Nibiru guided the upper half of Tiamat into a new orbit, which became Earth, and the lower half was disintegrated into the asteroid belt. The asteroid belt between Mars and Jupiter today is a combination of the upper half of Tiamat and the remnants of Maldek. The satellite used to upend Tiamat was thrown into an outermost orbit of the solar system and became Pluto. An outpost was built there by the Galactic Federation to monitor events thereafter occurring in the solar system. Only two percent of the reptiles survived by moving underground, and those that did not want to destroy the humans in the first place were brought aboard Nibiru and taken care of.

Anu's next assignment was to destroy the Reptilian Royal Planet Aln in the Orion constellation. Once this was accomplished the reptiles set before themselves the task of destroying the entire human population in the galaxy, seeing them now as a major threat. This was the beginning of the First Great Galactic War. The planet Maldek was forged as a military outpost for the reptilians, now untrusting of any human. The upper half of Tiamat, now called Earth, was reenergized and reseeded by the Felines and the Christos Sirians with all forms of plant and animal life. Once this came to pass, there stood three distinctions of Sirians—the Christos Sirians who worked with the Spiritual Hierarchy, the Aquatic Sirians who maintained the biosphere, and the Earth Sirians who watched over the newly evolving land guardian race. After a few million years a colony called Hybornea was fashioned together with many different human races living in conjunction within the feminine polarity. As usual, the reptile colony on Maldek took an aggressive stance and destroyed Hybornea, leading to the destruction of Maldek as well as the human colonies on Venus and Mars. This brought an end to the First Great Galactic War.

As a result of the atomic weapons utilized by the reptilians during their attack on Earth, Maldek was destroyed by a nuclear blast and Nibiru lost its force field. Nibiru was forced to find large quantities of gold or the planet would no longer be able to serve as a battlestar. This brings us to the epoch of roughly 500,000 B.C.E. when Nibiru came to Earth looking for gold. The Nibiruan gods were praised in the Sumerian tablets as the "Annunaki."

V

Lemuria, Atlantis, and the Ancient Mystery Schools

When the Annunaki arrived on Earth 480,000 years ago there were several races living there. These where the Lemurians, the Etheric Sirians in animal bodies, the reptiles (the descendents of those who went underground after Tiamat was destroyed), and the evolving human primates. The human primates were the ones seeded by the Felines after the destruction of Tiamat, and when the Annunaki came down they were at the stage of homo-erectus. They were telepathic, intelligent, and benevolent toward the other animals in the wild. The Lemurian civilization posed as the mother colony to Yu and Atlantis, two other civilizations coexisting at the time. These empires were started by Ashen (Yu) and Alta (Atlantis), two relatives of Anu who arrived on Earth after the destruction of Hybornea. Yu was a colony of Orientals and Atlantis was a colony of red skinned humans (Native Americans today). Each of these three civilizations (Lemuria, Atlantis, and Yu) started in Lyra as white skinned human colonies and each had their D.N.A. altered by the Felines in order for them to survive in the varying environmental conditions on Earth. The humans on Earth now with red, yellow, or brown skin are descendants from these three civilizations. The black race was brought here from another star nation. The white race on Earth was installed here by the Royal House of Avyon on Nibiru, which sent the Annunaki down for two reasons: (1) mine gold to be placed in the force field around Nibiru, and (2) create the two strand D.N.A. physical vehicles for the Earth Sirians. These two operations went hand in hand as the gold would end up being mined by the worker class created with the two stranded D.N.A. bodies, a cross between the primates and the Nibiruans.

Since there was a relatively large reptilian population on Earth at the time, the Nibiruans knew a truce had to be made before they could commence mining. To satisfy this pact, Anu married Dramin, the Dragon Queen of Tiamat who fled to Nibiru after the destruction. Enki was born to the pair, becoming a half-human/half-dragon. When it was all settled Enki was the first to land on Earth along with several other Annunaki, who set up mining operations. Enki built the city called Eridu, which was known as "Earth Station One," a place where space shuttles could land and retrieve the mined gold. Anu's daughter, Ninhursag, arrived on Earth next and accommodated the workers mining the gold with medical attention. Shortly after that Anu arrived with Enlil. Enlil was the heir to Nibiru at that time. If you are a scholar of ancient Sumer you might recognize this story from the *Enuma Elish*, the Sumerian epic of creation found transcribed on clay tablets.[1]

As tensions among the Annunaki escalated it became apparent that the gold was not being mined fast enough as members aboard Nibiru were dying due to exposure. Extensive gold mines were found in Africa but they were underground, meaning more tireless work was required from the miners. Pressure between Enki and Enlil sought to divide the Annunaki as well, since Enki felt he deserved command of Earth over Enlil as he had toiled relentlessly to build Eridu and extract the gold. From the point of view of the Earth reptilians, they felt Enki deserved the post as well because he was the son of Earth's Dragon Queen and was therefore viewed as the rightful heir. The rest of the reptilians residing on Earth claimed their own inheritance of the planet giving their creation myth as substantiation. By Pleiadian law, Enlil was the rightful heir to Nibiru and Earth since he was the son of Anu and Antu, a human. To settle the dispute both Enki and Enlil drew straws, metaphorically speaking. The continent of Africa was given to Enki as Enlil inherited the remainder of Earth. The Annunaki were moved to Africa to mine there, but there was another problem. Alalu's grandson, Kumarbi, was harboring some animosity toward Anu and his children since it was Anu who took control of Nibiru after Alalu stepped down and not Kumarbi.

---

[1] In his first work on Nibiru entitled *The 12th Planet*, Zecharia Sitchin lays out a detailed map depicting the layout of the various cities in Sumer erected by the Nibiruans. These cities were advanced spaceports and mining and medical facilities. This is far unlike conventional anthropological theories, as modern historians say Earth was never visited by extraterrestrials.

The Igigi, Kumarbi's followers, waged war against Anu's grandson Ninurta and many others and was subsequently defeated. Again, you might recognize the parallels to Mesopotamian stories, especially Hittite and Akkadian.

During this epoch of Earth, Mesopotamia was a beautiful, lush arcadia with several cities providing the needs of the Annunaki. Sippar was a spaceport, Nippur was a mission control center, Bad Tibira was a metallurgical center, and Shuruppak was a medical center. For approximately 200,000 years Mesopotamia provided Enki and Enlil ample amounts of gold, as well as a lush paradise in which to reside. Fruit trees of all kinds were brought to this Garden of Eden (or "E. Din" as the Annunaki called it). Around 250,000 B.C.E. the Annunaki mining in Africa revolted. They were unhappy because it was terribly hot in the mines and they were becoming exhausted, so when Enki informed his brother of the incident the workers took Enlil hostage. After some persuasion the workers released Enlil. Both Enki and Enlil went before the Nibiruan Council, which came upon an agreement. There existed the possibility to kill two birds with one stone as a worker class could be created to mine the gold, and they would also serve as land guardian vehicles for the Christos Sirians. Since Enki was the master geneticist, he and Ninhursag disappeared to the laboratory at Shuruppak to perform the duty.

The Felines gave assistance to the Nibiruan Council in creating the workers, this satisfying the Council's agreement with the Galactic Federation and the Christos Office of the Planetary Spiritual Hierarchy. Rayshondra, Anu's Feline wife and mother of Ninhursag, came to Shuruppak to oversee the assignment. She was the one who taught Enki and Ninhursag in the field of genetics. Being the descendents of Devin and the Royal House of Avyon, Anu and his family were karmically and genetically tied to Earth. The original humans of Tiamat were now evolving on a planet in the Pegasus star system, but with the creation of the primitive worker race the Nibiruans were a parent race for life on Earth once again. Part of the Nibiruan/Pleiadian Divine Plan was to complete polarity integration by mentoring and parenting this newly created race, and it is for spiritual reasons the occupants of Nibiru came to Earth, although this fact has been taken out of the historical records. To complete the job, Enki, Ninhursag, and Rayshondra accelerated the D.N.A. evolution of the workers, taking them from the stage of homo-erectus to homo-sapien. This gave the Earth Sirians time to relocate from the animal bodies they were occupying to the new human physical vehicles through incarnational cycles. This process took nearly 200,000 years to come to fruition.

So Zecharia Sitchin was correct, but not entirely. The Nibiruans garnered help from the Sirians in creating our race, that which we today call "homo-sapien-sapien."[2] After the D.N.A. was transmuted, the Halls of Amenti served as the fertilization ground. The Halls of Amenti is a very ancient place, built over six million years ago. It is a dimensional warp in our space-time continuum resembling a womb. There is only one way to get in, and once you do it is like being in infinite space. In our creation, preparation was being made on Sirius B. Sixteen males and sixteen females comprised a marriage family and then traveled to Earth going directly to the Halls of Amenti, which was like a temple on the surface of the planet. The thirty-two members went into one of the chambers and merged their minds with a trans-dimensional flame. Their conception period here (trans-semination) was two thousand years.[3] So it stands that several advanced races joined in creating us from naturally evolving primates.

D.N.A. upgrading gave the primates more efficient reasoning abilities as well as the capacity to learn reading and writing. They still retained their telepathic abilities, although they did not acquire any new psychic abilities. This was back when the glands associated with the sixth chakra in beings were fully activated; the pineal and pituitary glands of the primates were at full size and secreting pinoline and ambrita, respectively. These glands have atrophied over the years so they no longer produce these chemicals, and that is why people on Earth have not been able to communicate telepathically for quite some time. These abilities, along with all psychic abilities, lay dormant in humans today (meaning they can be brought back through practice and the raising of vibrational frequencies). Although various psychic abilities were needed for spiritual growth, the physical vehicles given to the Earth Sirians were not too complex, due to the fact that those inhabiting animal bodies had regressed for millions of years.

---

[2] Further genetic upgrades have produced the line of humans known today as homo-sapiens-sapiens, a more intellectual genetic line than homo-sapiens.

[3] Bob Frissell, *Nothing In This Book Is True, But It's Exactly How Things Are* (Berkeley, CA: Frog Books, 1994), 98.

I mentioned before that the Nibiruans were tied genetically to the Earth. This is how it is so: When Enki and Ninhursag had gathered tissue and blood samples from the primates, they acquired eggs from the primate women and used sperm from some of the Annunaki to fertilize those eggs, which were then embedded into the wombs of several female Annunaki. Twelve children were born with the abilities of the primates as well as the intellectual powers of a galactic human. In other words, the animal spirit had been replaced with a human spirit, although the soul still lacked. We, as physical incarnations on Earth, carry in our cells some of the Nibiruan D.N.A.

Since hybrids cannot procreate on their own the Nibiruan scientists had to do it for them, but the Annunaki women grew tired of being pregnant all the time. Enki and Ninhursag returned to the lab and gave the newly created race an upgrade, allowing them to reproduce on their own. This new race was referred to as Lulus, meaning "primitive workers." It was now difficult for the Nibiruans to persuade the Earth Sirians to transfer into the new human bodies since they were comfortable in the animal bodies only using animal instinct. The Lulus, containing only spirit, were like a smart pet. They communicated with the Earth Sirians in the animal bodies and cajoled them into accepting the new physical space suites. They catechized the Earth Sirians concerning the benefits of being in a human body. Unfortunately at this time, some of the Annunaki only saw the workers as free slave labor and so mistreated them. Ninhursag was like a mother to the newly created race and she appealed to Enlil, asking him to give the workers more rights. He accepted, and it was agreed upon to treat the Lulus more favorably.

The epoch of 150,000 B.C.E. saw a new glacial period, forcing the Lulus and other civilizations on Earth (Andromedan, Pleiadian, Sirian, and others) to halt their spiritual evolution in order to focus on survival. This was one of the reasons it took so long to transfer the Earth Sirians to their new human bodies, the other being that it was easier at the time to be an animal than a human. There were many large animal groups that roamed in packs and hunted humans. When the Earth was reseeded after the destruction of Tiamat, a mutation in the plant life caused animals to grow very large. This resulted in the dinosaurs and other large creatures creating a hazardous experience for the humans living on the planet. Many humans from the Lemurian colony retreated underground during this time to survive, and their descendents still occupy the inner Earth today. Starting in 100,000 B.C.E., the climate warmed back up and there was a return to spiritual evolution. At this time some of the Annunaki were marrying the Lulus who had Earth Sirian souls. This is why it says in the Bible in "Genesis" that the gods came down from heaven and married the daughters of men. The real translation should be: the Nibiruan and Sirian royal families came to Earth, created a hybrid race with primate D.N.A from Earth and human D.N.A from the genetic laboratory on Nibiru, and interbred with the new biological creation.

Another Ice Age hit Earth around 75,000 B.C.E. and spiritual evolution became stagnant once again. One group of beings, called by archaeologists today "cro-magnon man," had achieved a greater degree of evolutionary progress and had survived during this time, so other tribes that died off began incarnating into this group. Around 50,000 B.C.E. Ninhursag and Enki were given orders by the Christos Sirians and the Planetary Spiritual Hierarchy to upgrade the human bodies to the next level, giving them the opportunity for spiritual growth instead of physical and mental development. At this time, representatives from the civilizations of Yu, Rama, Lemuria, Egypt, and Maya were sent to Atlantis to ascertain a way of getting rid of the carnivorous large animals. This agreement, which saw the end of the animal threat, resonated in conjunction with Earth's divine plan. The remaining Earth Sirians residing in animal bodies were also freed during this time. This was an important step, as the next stage of the spiritual evolution of humanity came with the introduction of the Christos seed. The Earth Sirians now had roughly 52,000 years to evolve into land guardians capable of overseeing the planet. This period of time was divided into ten 5,200 year cycles, and during each cycle the Planetary Spiritual Hierarchy, the Christos Sirians, the Galactic Federation, the Sirian A Council, and the Nibiruan Council would meet to discuss the progress and necessary adjustments for the continued evolution of the Lulus.

When the transfer of Earth Sirian souls from animal bodies to human bodies was complete the Christos upgrade was given to the Lulus by Amelius, the head of the Etheric Sirians. In the Bible, the story of Adam and Eve is really the apologue of Adapa and Lilith, the first two humans with the Christos upgrade. This was brought about by Ninhursag contributing an egg to be fertilized by Enki, which was then placed in Ninhursag's womb. Adapa was born, and it is he (Amelius) who is the integration point between the reptiles and humans. Adapa carried D.N.A. that was reptilian and human, and it was the added Feline and Carian D.N.A. which gave the created race the gene of compassion. Adapa was cared for by Enki and Ninhursag, and later sperm was taken from him and fertilized by Ninhursag, creating Lilith. In real life, Eve was not born from her counterpart's rib like it says in the erroneous and fallacious biblical teaching. These new physical bodies (called "adams" by Anu) were given to the red, yellow and brown races, which were then placed in various locations on the planet as directed by the Planetary Spiritual Hierarchy. Adapa and Lilith stayed in the Garden of Eden with Enki and Ninhursag where they grew up together and eventually married in accordance with Pleiadian law. In the biblical Garden of Eden the Lord can be replaced with Enlil and the snake can be replaced with Enki.

The Tree of Good and Evil in the Bible relates to the school Enki formed to teach Adapa and Lilith ancient universal knowledge. It can be replaced with the Brotherhood of the Snake, the first mystery school of the epoch.[4] The fruit of the tree was symbolic of the wisdom taught to the Adapa line in the school. It states in Genesis that the Lord was mad at Adam and Eve for eating from the tree, but this is a lie. Enlil was angry with Enki for giving Adapa and Lilith too much knowledge when they lacked spiritual maturity, which is the literal version of events. Enlil feared the future generations would destroy themselves, thereby ruining the chance for polarity integration. It was Marduk who constructed the story about the serpent deceiving Eve, tricking her into eating the apple and sharing it with Adam. Marduk is behind many of the poisons instilled by modern religion, another one being the true nature of Jesus. Contemporary Christianity preaches that the only way to absolve sin is through Jesus, which is a total lie. There really is no sin. Sin is used by the churches as a scare tactic. The insertion of the snake deceiving Eve was Marduk's way of planting the seed that would eventually grow into a patriarchal society. Today, we are a patriarchal society in total, where a very few men make all the decisions and control all the money. The

---

[4] Lucifer had created another mystery school in the epoch before when the "War in the Heavens" transpired and it is not to be confused with the Mesopotamian schools. The Brotherhood of the Snake was really the first mystery school commandeered by the Draconian bloodlines, the other mystery school being the Babylonian Brotherhood. The demonic secret societies today that vie for the erection of the New World Order stem from both of these mystery schools.

reinsertion of the Divine Feminine is necessary for polarity integration and planetary ascension.

The Brotherhood of the Snake is the precursor to the mystery schools of the post-diluvian era and the Masonic Lodges. You will see very shortly how Freemasonry has taken over the world and suppressed the knowledge granted by the original mystery schools. It was Enki who formed the Brotherhood of the Snake to teach Adapa and his descendants spiritual wisdom, and it was Enlil who disapproved of this. In Enlil's mind, mankind must always stay spiritually one step ahead over technology, and he feared that Enki was giving Adapa and Lilith too much knowledge about sacred geometry and energy manipulation. Finally, after some quarrelling, the Galactic Federation and Spiritual Hierarchy (including Enki and Enlil) agreed to move Adapa, Lilith, and their children outside of the E. Din complex. This would ensure their race would have to fight for survival, slowing down technological advancement. The Brotherhood of the Snake continued, but it became corrupted. When power hungry members took over control of the school, the Priesthood officially began. This same Priesthood has been corrupting Earth for thousands of years, hiding the real history of the planet and replacing it with organized religion.[5]

In 11,000 B.C.E. Enlil turned out to be right. The Adapa race had degenerated to the point where it had to start over. It began in roughly 25,000 B.C.E. when Marduk and his reptilian allies arrogated Atlantis and began to harness powerful energy contained within the giant crystals. This technology was first used to power aircraft and underwater vehicles, but it served other purposes. Marduk, basically acting out the instincts of his predecessors, introduced advanced Nibiruan and Reptilian technology to the Atlanteans, slowly earning their trust. Delegates from Lemuria travelled to Atlantis and attempted to warn the rulers about the dangers of trying to take over the world, but the Atlanteans in power did not heed the warning. There was a great division stirring in Atlantis at that time, those who wanted to grow technologically and those who wanted to grow spiritually. Sound familiar? We are literally at that point today. Marduk felt that he should have the right to rule since he was the son of the Snake Princess and the grandson of the Dragon Queen.

---

[5] The Priesthood today is the Druidic Council, the 13 chairs given to the patriarch of each of the original Draconian bloodline families. They use the Jewish race as a scapegoat and they hide behind Israel and the Committee of 300.

The giant Atlantean crystal was Marduk's hidden card. He used it to project a tractor beam onto one of Earth's comets, harnessing it and threatening the other civilizations on the planet with total destruction if they did not surrender. When Nibiru returned to Earth on its yearly course it forced a discontinuity in the tractor beam holding the comet in place, and the result was the sinking of the entire continent of Atlantis when the comet fell and struck it. This occurred in 21,000 B.C.E.

The Great Deluge was also Marduk's doing. The band of moisture three miles around Earth at the time was called the "firmament." It was necessary to maintain the tropical environment by providing continual moisture and filtering the Sun's rays. The firmament was held in place by crystal temples located underground. Marduk had his son, Seth, utilize a laser weapon in the Great Pyramid to launch an attack on the temples, which caused the collapse of the firmament, casting down a rain storm lasting for over a month. This is the story of Noah's Flood in the Bible. The Nibiruan Council, the Planetary Spiritual Hierarchy, the Galactic Federation, and the Felines came to an agreement not to alert the human population concerning the impending disaster, mainly because they underestimated Marduk and his reptilian collaborators. With Marduk wreaking havoc they saw the destruction of mankind happening anyway.

When the Nibiruans left Earth and watched the flood from their space station they were unaware of the fact that Enki had warned Noah (his son, one of many children not mentioned) and told him to build a submarine in which he could safely transport him and his family. One of the Annunaki was sent to help build and pilot the underwater craft (it wasn't a boat). Anu and the Council was doleful when they saw 400,000 years of work destroyed, but ultimately grateful for what Enki did. It made it much easier to begin repopulation again. After the deluge, Enki and Enlil brought everything necessary to farm and practice husbandry to Noah and his family. Mount Ararat was indeed the place Noah's submarine landed when the flood was over and the waters receded. He began farming on the slopes as Ninurta and Nannar damned the surrounded land as Enki had taught them. It wasn't until 10,500 B.C.E. that mankind had proliferated once again in Mesopotamia and in other areas. The modern day Jerusalem was known as Mount Moriah in the days the Annunaki walked the Earth. This was where the spaceport was built anew. Eridu, Nippur, Shuruppak and the other cities were also rebuilt. The Great Pyramids remained intact but had to be dug out from many feet of sand and dirt.

In 9,000 B.C.E. Osiris and Seth, descendants of Enki, were now ruling Egypt. You will recognize Osiris of course as one of the main Egyptian gods. Nannar and Ninurta, descendants of Enlil, facilitated the ruling of Earth since Marduk was no longer trusted. Adad, Enlil's other son, went to South America to set up gold mining operations there. It was during this period that many of the younger generations of Nibiruans started to fight for power. The ancient Greek stories about the battles between the Titans and Olympians relate directly to this time when Ninurta, Nannar, Utu, Adad, Inanna, Seth, Osiris, Marduk, and other young descendants of Anu saw themselves as worthy rulers. A new conflict was soon to emerge that began the "Pyramid Wars." Seth and Osiris both wanted to rule Egypt, so Seth slew his brother. Horus, Osiris's son, pledged to avenge his father's death by instigating the First Pyramid War. It is important to insert here that the Great Pyramids back then were space facilities, among other things, such as initiation chambers and technology vats. The Second Pyramid War started 300 years after the first one, on this occurrence the descendants of Enlil battling the descendants of Enki. It ended on direct intervention from Ninhursag, who took control of the great pyramids and emptied them of their advanced equipment. Thoth, one of Enki's later born sons, was given rulership over Egypt in 8,600 B.C.E. From 8,500 BCE until 3,500 B.C.E. there was peace and harmony on Earth.

Egypt was an interesting place. It became the home of not only the Tat Brotherhood (a group of immortal beings headed by Tat, Thoth's son) but also many Atlantean survivors. With their memory erased by the pole shift, the Atlanteans reverted back to barbarism and had to wait a long time before they could even begin to evolve again. It was the Tat Brotherhood who established the Egyptian civilization and not the Sumerians like Sitchin says.[6] This brotherhood of ascended masters waited until the time was right and then sent members from their group dressed like Egyptians to re-seed the knowledge of Atlantis. They aided in the stair-step evolution of the Egyptians because they knew how civilization can grow or diminish overnight. Both the Egyptian and Sumerian civilizations seem to have not only risen but also fallen overnight, and the explanation for this lies in the precession of the

---

[6] This was taken from Frissell's research.

A New Order of the Ages

equinoxes. As the Earth moves away from the center of the galaxy, humanity falls asleep, and as the Earth moves closer to the plane of the Galaxy (to the Photon Band), humanity wakes up and becomes more conscious. After the last pole shift, the Earth was at the point in its precession where planetary consciousness fell asleep and thus, each time new information was given, the people almost immediately began to lose it until about 500 B.C.E. when the Egyptian civilization was almost totally gone.

Towards the end of their culture, the Egyptians were losing the knowledge about the one spirit and began to worship many gods. One can only conjecture that the Annunaki were some of these gods. The ascended masters decided to intervene once more and so sent a Christ consciousness being to be incarnated into a body in order to capture that notion and place it back into the Akashic Records. This being was the person we know now as Akhunaton, who was a soul from Sirius. Akhunaton disrupted all the religions, told everyone that priests were unnecessary and that God was in each person. He gave initiates a twelve-year advanced training and produced nearly three hundred Christ consciousness beings. In 1,350 B.C.E. these beings joined with the Tat Brotherhood and lived in the underground city beneath the Great Pyramid. Later, they migrated to Masada, Israel where they became known as the Essene Brotherhood (the group that Jesus joined). Mary (Jesus' mother) was one of these immortal beings. Although Akhunaton was disposed of after a seventeen year reign, everything in Egypt reverted back to old ways, but it didn't matter because the leader did his job. He placed the forgotten information back into the Akashic records and established the Essene Brotherhood, which accepted Christ and prepared the planet for the Age of Aquarius (the Age of Christ Consciousness), the Age of Pisces acting as the period of incubation.

In 3,700 B.C.E., kingship was officially lowered from Nibiru to Earth, the Nibiruans seeing that mankind had proved itself worthy of ruling itself. The new Priest-King line, as it was, consisted of half-Nibiruan/Pleiadian D.N.A. and half-Earth Human D.N.A. In Nippur, Enlil gave the humans the calendar, this corresponding to the period when time began to be documented on Earth. Alulim was the first demigod of the Neolithic period. He was the first half-Nibiruan/half-Earth human ruler of Earth, his predecessors all being extraterrestrial. Marduk was banned from many places but he was still ruler of Babylon.[7] He convinced the Babylonians to create their own spaceship and launching pad, later to be known as the Tower of Babel. As the Planetary Spiritual Hierarchy and Galactic Federation saw that Marduk used humans as pawns for his plans, they made a decision to confound the languages of mankind, thereby slowing them down and preventing Marduk from amassing an army. In order that humans could communicate with each other once again Marduk had to spend much time teaching them all the languages, but the Planetary Spiritual Hierarchy had further plans to thwart Marduk's designs for world and galactic domination. They decided to alter the humans' D.N.A. structure and suppress their psychic and telepathic abilities. Enki and Ninhursag retreated to the laboratory in Shuruppak once more and unraveled the humans' 12 D.N.A. strands. They then disconnected 10 strands from the endocrine system in the physical body,[8] and what this did was halt the production of the chemicals that activate the pineal, pituitary, and hypothalamus glands. Only a few humans retained this connection, and they served as a communications link between the Nibiruans and Earth humans for future generations. These humans were to become prophets, mystics, and shamans. Today they are known as "psychics," although everyone possesses this latent ability.

After this act of protection Marduk was enraged. He returned to Egypt and replaced Thoth as ruler, who in turn traveled to South America and started the civilizations that today compose the whole continent. Thoth was known to the ancient peoples there as Quetzalcoatl (the "White Plumed Serpent") in 3,113 B.C.E. The serpent, taking on the representation of the descendants of Enki, was carried around by Quetzalcoatl as a talisman. Conversely, the symbol carried by Enlil and his descendents was the cross, the emblem of Nibiru and the house of Anu. In his fight for command over Egypt, Marduk indiscriminately caused the death of Dumuzi, the husband of Inanna, throwing the widow into inflammation. She demanded justice and Marduk was almost killed, however, intervention from Ninhursag constituted Marduk to be a prisoner in the Great Pyramid of Giza instead. After he was released he went into exile. In 2,900 B.C.E. Inanna was granted rulership in the Indus Valley in what is now modern day India; she was also granted

---

[7] It was most likely Marduk who erected the Babylonian Brotherhood.
[8] The endocrine system is the physical connecting point for all the chakras and the D.N.A. structure.

A New Order of the Ages

the historical records concerning the Nibiruans' relationship with Earth, which she later wrote down. In 2,300 B.C.E. Inanna fell in love with Sargon and they formed a new empire called the Akkadian Empire. She and Marduk continued their altercation. They fought acrimoniously back and forth and these battles were recorded in the ancient records of India and Mesopotamia. In 2,200 B.C.E. Marduk finally succeeded in controlling all the knowledge-encoded crystals scattered throughout the Earth.[9] The possessor of the crystals gave him/her power over whatever the crystals controlled, so one crystal might have controlled the weather, another might have controlled the electromagnetic variations of the planet . . . . and so on. With these in his grasp Marduk assembled an army on Mars, which was deserted at the time. With things finally going his way Marduk dethroned Anu from command of Nibiru and Earth.

In 2,024 B.C.E. the Nibiruan Council made a decision to bomb the space facilities on Earth, lest Marduk were to gain control of these facilities and attempt to take over the Pleiades star system. If Marduk ever succeeded at this he would be only one step away from taking over the galaxy. The Council chose Abraham, born from a royal Nibiruan family, to carry a plutonium bomb from Sumer to the spaceport in southern Mesopotamia. From there, Uta (a son of Enlil) detonated the bomb, evoking the destruction of all the space facilities in the area along with Sodom and Gomorrah. The city was left at the bottom of the Dead Sea and the surrounding area was turned into a desert. The populations in the cities of Sumer were also wiped out due to the radiation from the bomb. It was this area that was given to Abraham as his heritage and labeled the "Land of Canaan." Another part of Abraham's mission was to deposit uranium into the Annunaki temples bordering Sumer so as to control the emotional bodies of future progeny. There is a symbiotic relationship between the breakdown of the emotional body through karma and the breakdown of radioactive elements via transmutation, so you can see how radioactive materials have been powerful devices on Earth (just ask the physicists who exploded the hydrogen atom). After 5,000 years, uranium is thoroughly polluted with emotional body detritus (human karma). In later years, more uranium was placed underground so Anu could monitor Earth when he left via the radiation. Naturally, Abraham became a patriarch of the Old Testament because

---

[9] This could relate to the legend of the crystal skulls. See *The Crystal Skulls: Astonishing Portal's to Man's Past* by David Childress.

the canon religions were set up by the Annunaki. Eventually, Abraham's descendants reclaimed the land of Canaan from scattered tribes with the help of Tuthmoses (Moses), another descendant of a priestly royal Nibiruan family.

In 1,500 B.C.E. Marduk is now fully in control. To secure his position he had to go about changing many things, which he did. He worked to demote women to a lower social status, he began the churches and he proclaimed himself to be God. In the *Enuma Elish* (the Sumerian Epic of Creation), Marduk is the god who defeats the goddess Tiamat and claims the throne of the heavens, having set before him fifty epithets by which he would be known. The religions that were set up discontinued Goddess worship and Pleiadian communal life. Women who were leaders were branded as witches and burned at the stake. Fear became the ultimate control factor and continues to be so even today. The global elite and popular icons today who masquerade around on television and in expensive cars worship Marduk and Lucifer, although many of them do not even know it.

The lizards who evolved naturally on Earth were worshipped as gods by the Annunaki because of their advanced technology and the kundalini energy surging in their spines. The Annunaki are a metallic biology, so to us they would look like robot lizards. The metallic electromagnetic force in their bodies resonated with the sacred fire of the Earth lizards, and as such they received electromagnetic kundalini energy from these Earth reptilians. In this way they were able to monitor all devices based on electromagnetism, but were unable to monitor silica-based technologies. That is why they are trying to stop the transmutation of our cells from carbon to silica-based because they would no longer be able to control us. When the Annunaki came to Earth they donned various biological costumes, and that is why they were depicted as great beings with cat, lion, and bird heads.

The system of control set up on Earth has utilized metallic forms of communication (the intelligence agencies of current use this type of communication), but it is unbeknownst to the general population that this current of information can be tapped into at anytime. So, just as the C.I.A. can monitor everything you are doing, so too can you monitor everything the C.I.A. does! It all has to do with holograms. A hologram is produced when a laser beam is split into two beams. The first beam is bounced off an image to be photographed while the second beam is mirrored back so it will collide with the reflected light of the image. This creates an interference pattern which is encoded on film, and if you shine another light into it the image that was photographed can be projected onto any space. The space we currently live in is filled with waves from numerous sources forming interference patterns, and images can be created out of them. The media has specific surface three-dimensional sounds and images that we can all hear and see, but there are also masked sounds and images. These subliminal communications are used to encode us with negative thoughtforms. Any one of us is capable of picking up these metallic vibrational communications because our own life forces generate electromagnetic fields. However, unless your vibration is raised beyond the access of the "World Management Team" (the Annunaki-imposed Earth management team), your electromagnetic fields can be penetrated and/or monitored.

According to researcher David Icke, a race of Nordic humans lived primarily in Atlantis before the firmament collapsed (the Deluge) and a reptilian race lived primarily in Lemuria (Mu). After the Great Flood, peoples who survived in the higher elevations returned to the lowlands. Survivors from Atlantis (mainly Nordic and Aryan bloodlines) and Lemuria/Mu (reptilian bloodlines) trekked to other lands and utilized advanced knowledge to found other cultures.

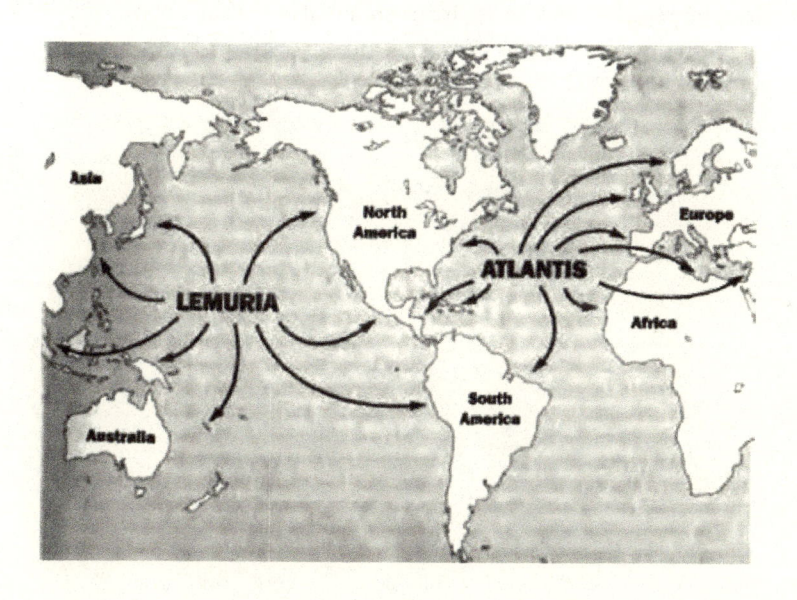

Migrations from Atlantis and Lemuria

Fernando Montesinos, an early Spanish chronicler, asserted that there were two distinct Inca empires, one before the deluge and one after. Survivors who had found shelter in the mountains, possibly Machu Picchu, returned to Cusco in the Andes to start their civilization over again. The most notable of these start-again civilizations was Sumer in Mesopotamia, the "Cradle of Civilization." Conventional historians and anthropologists maintain that other independent civilizations of great advancement also appeared suddenly in Egypt and the Indus Valley.

The "Golden Age" is typically referred as the time period circa 50,000 B.C.E. and before, when the Lulus and other primitive hominids lived among the alien gods. Many extraterrestrial races were visiting Earth at this time as the climate was much warmer and more tropical, hence a paradise-like vision conjured by the Bible. After the deluge, the gods returned to humans and bestowed upon them advanced knowledge that was passed on through initiation in the mystery schools, the forebears of modern secret societies. Dr. Arthur David Horn, former professor of Biological Anthropology at Colorado State University, corroborates this information in his book *Humanity's Extraterrestrial Origins*. Today's ruling families employ reptilian symbolism on a regular basis because their gods are literally reptiles who came from space. The caduceus double-snake image is the logo for today's medical profession, and it represents two snakes forming a D.N.A. double helix.

A New Order of the Ages

Caduceus

The wings at the top represent what happens when the kundalini energy shoots up the spine and out through the crown chakra. Kundalini is a Sanskrit word meaning "coiled up" (like a snake). In people who are spiritually asleep, the kundalini stays in the root chakra, but once the mind opens, the kundalini uncoils and one can fly, psychically and spiritually that is.

In Egypt, the Brotherhood of the Snake was known as the Royal Court of the Dragon, and it was erected to infiltrate the royal and religious centers of power, especially the mystery schools. Historian and 33° Mason Manly P. Hall recounts how the black magicians of Atlantis were reptilian arch-sorcerers from Lemuria who attempted to hijack the magical power of Atlantis from the Nordics using crystal energy and black magick.[10] Hall writes:

---

[10] 'Magick' differs from 'magic' in that the former is ritualistic, philosophic, and alchemic, while the latter is phony stage shows based on illusions.

While the elaborate ceremonial magic of antiquity was not necessarily evil, there arose from its perversion several false schools of sorcery, or black magic, [in Egypt] . . . the black magicians of Atlantis continued to exercise their superhuman powers until they had completely undermined and corrupted the morals of the primitive Mysteries . . . they usurped the position formerly occupied by the initiates, and seized the reigns of spiritual government. Thus black magic dictated the state religion and paralyzed the intellectual and spiritual activities of the individual by demanding his complete and unhesitating acquiescence in the dogma formulated by the priest craft. The Pharaoh became a puppet in the hands of the Scarlet Council—a committee of arch-sorcerers elevated to power by the priesthood.

The Priesthood was the most powerful ruling class, and it consisted of reptilian hybrids; today, it is the Druidic Council headed by Baron Guy de Rothschild.

There were numerous types of reptilian, reptilian-human hybrids, and etheric reptilians running amok on the Earth at this time, so it is wise to not compartmentalize who is who. A myriad of ancient tablets describe many types of gods and/or advanced beings. In northern India lays a secret vault housing ancient tablets. These tablets tell the story of how the Nagas/Naacals (reptilians) from Lemuria had traveled to India via Burma to establish a colony there. The Vedas detail that the earliest royal bloodlines of India, the priest-kings, arrived from a place across the sea (Lemuria). These bloodlines were descended from the Bhrigus, an order of adepts initiated into the ancient knowledge. In his book, *Gods, Sages, and Kings: Vedic Secrets of Ancient Civilization*, David Frawley relates that the monarchs of these bloodlines included the serpent king Nahusha and that they expanded into the five tribes which populated a large part of the Indian subcontinent. The Nagas also populated China, Tibet, and other parts of Asia. The *Mahauyutpatti*, an ancient Indian Buddhist text, lists eighty kings who descended from the Nagas. Hindu legend claims the Nagas can shift between human and reptilian form at will. This is what is called "shapeshifting" today and there are signs of it in positions of power.

Whomsoever has the proper D.N.A. split can focus his/her attention on specific genes and shapeshift via unlocking vibrational codes in the cellular structure. The serpent fish gods of Babylon and Sumer were also said to have this ability. Michael Mott, an ardent researcher into this topic, proclaims in his book, *Caverns, Cauldrons, and Concealed Creatures*:

> The Nagas are described as a very advanced race or species, with a highly-developed technology. They also harbor a disdain for human beings, whom they are said to abduct, torture, interbreed with, and even eat. The interbreeding has supposedly led to a wide variety of forms, ranging from completely reptilian to nearly-human in appearance. Among their many devices are 'death rays' and 'vimana,' or flying, disc-shaped aerial craft. These craft are described at length in many ancient Vedic texts, including the Bhagavad-Gita and the Ramayana. The Naga race is related to another underworld race, the Hindu demons, or Rakshasas. They also possess, as individuals, 'magical stones,' or a 'third eye' in the middle of their brows, known to many students of eastern mysticism today as the focal point for one of the higher chakras, or energy channel-points, of the humanoid nervous system—the chakra associated with inner visions, intuition, and other esoteric concepts.

Even the Chinese emperors claimed descent from serpent gods. They were known as the "Lung" and the earliest emperors were depicted with reptilian features. The priest-kings of the Peruvian Incas wore bracelets and anklets in the image of a snake, as the Greek kings during the Mycenaean age were regarded as being "snake-like." In fact, serpent symbolism abounds in almost every ancient culture.

Stewart Swerdlow is an American author who speaks out against the takeover of the planet by reptilian entities, who operate in between dimensions and from the lower astral realm. Stewart was kidnapped as a child at night (with his mother's full knowledge) and taken to Montauk, where he endured a mind-control program. Under government/military control, Stewart learned about the agenda for global domination and the trans-dimensional reptilians behind it all. He relates how he saw reptilian entities at Montauk who appeared to pop in and out of this dimensional frequency at will. Even Preston Nichols, and engineer who worked at Montauk, describes these reptilian entities, who worked alongside human scientists and also Grey aliens. In his book, *Blue Blood, True Blood*, Swerdlow announces how the reptilians who entered into this dimension long ago were borderline physical, that is to say they did not have a concrete physical form like we know our bodies to be. In order to satisfy this dilemma, the reptilians mixed their D.N.A. with the Nordics from Atlantis so that they could operate in this dimension. That is why they are so obsessed with blond-haired, blue-eyed people; they need their genetics to play in this dimensional reality.

Swerdlow also states that the reptilians are from numerous star systems, including Alpha Draconis, Orion, and Sirius. This could be why the picture below depicts how the Great Pyramid of Giza lined up with the star systems of Alpha Draconis, Sirius, Orion, Ursa Minor, and Ursa Major:

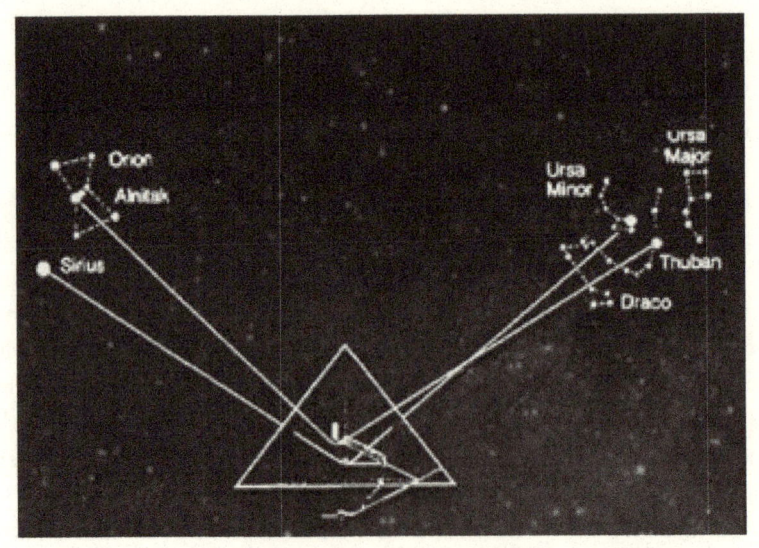

Great Pyramid in alignment with important constellations

The British and Roman Empires were the work of these reptilian bloodlines. Royal and aristocratic families have long been called "blue bloods" because the increased reptilian D.N.A. means their blood contains more copper. This copper-based blood turns blue-green when oxidizing, hence the blue blood color.

When Lemuria was destroyed, the survivors relocated to northern India and built a massive underground civilization, all the while re-launching their genetic takeover of the world. Sumer was just one of the places selected to continue this procedure. The Sumerians were known as the "Sum-Aryans" and they expanded into northern Africa, central Asia, northern India, and the steppes of Russia. According to Swerdlow, the "Aryan leaders, all bluebloods, became the Sultans and Rajas of legend" and the Sumer-Aryans infiltrated Egyptian society and implanted their reptilian bloodline into the royal families of the pharaohs, especially the Hyksos kings. The Egyptians were also known as the Phoenicians and were descendants of Atlantis. In Africa, the Sumer-Ayrans created a royal bloodline of black African kings and queens. The bloodline-computer network was just getting started.

When Atlantis and Lemuria were destroyed, Earth was thrown into a Dark Age where humans lost a lot of the secret knowledge gained in the epochs before the flood and the technology struggles which destroyed most the planet. Earth fell from the fourth and fifth dimensions into the third dimension and many survivors of this shift fled underground to live in the great caverns and cities erected there many thousands of years ago. There are still people today who accidentally stumble across secret passageways which lead them underground and into mystical cities and caves. Throughout recent history we can look back at different personas and see the perpetuation of the work of the Atlantean and Lemurian arch-sorcerers. Francis Bacon was one of the occultists ordered to work on the grand plan of the Atlantean Necromancers during his stay in the Renaissance. Even Shakespeare was aware of the plan of the Black Nobility (the European patriarchs and matriarchs of the interbreeding Reptilian/Aryan bloodline clans). He inserted alchemical anecdotes in his plays and died on a very symbolic date.

Agartha and the Hollow Earth

To most people's bewilderment, there is an extensive network of underground tunnels and cities right underneath our feet. It is home of the reptiles which control the planet and many other extraterrestrial civilizations that have been living on the planet for thousands of years. Some civilizations are the ancestors of Lemuria, Atlantis, the Mayan civilizations, and others. Many extraterrestrials who come to earth build bases underground and conduct biological and scientific operations there. There is one major underground civilization known as Agartha, and many of its inhabitants are giants. They have much more advanced technology and agricultural methods than that which is presented to the general population living above ground. Many of the underground cities share a common capital, that being Shamballa. Most of it resides on 5th density and souls can travel there during the dream state or during meditation.

There is a tunnel which connects Agartha to the Great Pyramid of Giza and there are also holes at both the poles which lead to it. These holes are wide enough that ships and planes can fly into them, but there is an energy field that camouflages the entrances. If one were to look hard enough one would find them. Many explorers and pilots have accidentally entered the inner Earth in past history. The structure of the planet is deceiving because the very top and bottom of the Earth are actually concave (most people think they are convex). That is why explorers unknowingly enter the inner Earth on their expeditions. They think they are travelling parallel to the surface of Earth when they really are travelling perpendicular. There are also entrances to the inner Earth in Africa, the Yucatan Peninsula, Tibet and Russia. There is a dimensional portal in the Bermuda Triangle that takes one to the inner Earth and has been the source for numerous disappearances in the area over the last 200 years. There is also a sun in the inner Earth, but it is not like the sun in the center of the solar system. It is very small and utilizes technology to produce light.

One case of a certain Admiral Richard Byrd recounts the story of how in 1947 a man (Byrd) and his crew accidentally flew into the inner Earth when they thought they were flying over the North Pole. When they were flying underground they saw mountains, lakes, exotic vegetation, and a diverse animal life. Animals with mammoth size grazed in fields and roamed areas that were like major parks. Byrd's plane was finally greeted by flying saucers of an unusual type who directed him to a safe landing area, where he met the queen and king of Agartha. They told Byrd they allowed him to enter because they gauged him to be of high moral standard. They expressed their concern for the above ground civilizations, especially after the United States dropped the atomic bomb on Hiroshima and Nagasaki. They were worried that the humans living above ground would destroy the planet and ultimately Agartha as well without even knowing it. The Agarthians taught Admiral Byrd and his crew many things and after a while led them back to their plane to be escorted back out, at the end expressing a great interest in Byrd to inform the rest of the Earth population about his discovery. In 1956 Byrd led another expedition to the South Pole, penetrating well over 2,000 miles to the center of Earth. The American Press released Byrd's discovery, but lo and behold, the secret government covered the story right up. Ray Palmer, the editor of the magazine *Flying Saucer*, published a detailed story about Admiral Byrd's journeys into the inner Earth. The secret government destroyed nearly every copy and even the plates at the printing press. This happened once more when *National Geographic* published a similar article.

Underground bases and cities have been erected all over the planet. Vedic lore tells us the Nagas dwelled in the two main underground cities of Patala and Bhogavati. It was there they battled with the Nordics living in underground kingdoms. This same type of struggle can be seen today with the Western powers of Atlantis (United States, Great Britain, and South America) working against the Eastern powers of Lemuria (China, Japan, and Russia). They work together to enslave the population, but at the top they struggle amongst themselves for ultimate control. Similar stories of underground cities and tunnels can be found in Tibet and China, and even in the Gilgamesh stories. In *Caverns, Cauldrons, and Concealed Creatures*, Mott writes that in England, Scotland, Wales and Ireland, there are many traditions of underground cultures.

Researcher Alan Walton has also written extensively concerning these underground fiefdoms. He writes:

> Underneath most major cities, especially in the U.S.A. in fact, there exist subterranean counterpart 'cities' controlled by the Masonic/hybrid/alien 'elite.' Often, surface/subsurface terminals exist beneath Masonic Lodges, police stations, airports and federal buildings of major cities . . . and even not so 'major' cities. The population ratio is probably close to 10 percent of the population (the hybrid military-industrial fraternity 'elite' living below ground as opposed to the 90 percent living above). This does not include the fullblood reptilian species who live in even deeper recesses of the Earth. Some of the major population centers were deliberately established by the Masonic/hybrid elite of the Old and New 'worlds' to afford easy access to already existing underground levels, some of which are thousands of years old. Considering that the Los Alamos Labs had a working prototype nuclear powered thermolbore drill that could literally melt

tunnels through the Earth at a rate of 8 mph forty years ago, you can imagine how extensive these underground systems have become.

These sub-cities also offer close access to organized criminal syndicates, which operate on the surface. They have developed a whole science of 'borg-onomics' through which they literally nickel-and-dime us into slavery via multi-levelled taxation, inflation, sublimation, manipulation, regulation, fines, fees, licenses . . . . and the entire debt-credit scam which is run by the Federal Reserve and Wall Street. New York City, I can confirm, is one of the largest Draconian nests in the world. Or rather the ancient underground 'Atlantean' systems that network beneath that area. They literally control the entire Wall Street pyramid from below . . . with more than a little help from reptilian bloodlines like the Rockefellers, etc. In fact, these reptilian genetic lines operate in a parasitic manner, the underground society acting as the 'parasite' society and the surface society operating as the 'host' society.

We must rid ourselves of these parasites.

The Emerald Tablets, which were discovered beneath a Mayan temple in Mexico, were supposedly written by Thoth and they relate the reptilians and their ability to shapeshift and possess people. Maurice Doreal discovered the tablets and completed the translation in 1925, but it was much later when he was given permission to publish part of the translations. Here is an excerpt and you can understand why they have been suppressed from the mainstream:

> Speak I of ancient Atlantis, speak of the days of the Kingdom of Shadows, speak of the coming of the children of shadows. Out of the great deep were they called by the wisdom of the Earth – man, called for the purpose of gaining great power.
>
> Far in the past before Atlantis existed, men there were who delved into darkness, using dark magic, calling up beings from the great deep below us. Forth came they into this cycle, formless were they, of another vibration, existing unseen by the children of Earth-men. Only through blood could they form being, only through man could they live in the world.

A New Order of the Ages

In ages past were they conquered by the Masters, driven below to the place whence they came. But some there were who remained, hidden in spaces and planes unknown to man. Live they in Atlantis as shadows, but at times they appeared among men. Aye, when the blood was offered, forth came they to dwell among men.

In the form of man moved they amongst us, but only to sight, were they as are men. Serpent-headed when the glamour was lifted, but appearing to man as men among men. Crept they into the councils, taking form and ruling o'er man. Only by magic could they be discovered, only by sound could their faces be seen. Sought they from the kingdom of shadows, to destroy man and rule in his place.

But, know ye, the Masters were mighty in magic, able to lift the veil from the face of the serpent, able to send him back to his place. Came they to man and taught him the secret, the Word that only a man can pronounce; swift then they lifted the veil from the serpent and cast him forth from place among men.

Yet, beware, the serpent still liveth in a place that is open, at times, to the world. Unseen they walk among thee in places where the rites have been said; again as time passes onward, shall they take the semblance of men.

Called, may they be, by the master who knows the white or the black, but only the white master may control and bind them while in the flesh. Seek not the kingdom of shadows, for evil will surely appear, for only the master of brightness shall conquer the shadow of fear.

Thoth speaks of the trans-dimensional reptilian entities and how they appear in this dimension etheric at first but then taking on a physical characteristic. They come from the "Kingdom of Shadows" (the space in between dimensions) and they rule over society via secret societies ("crept they into the councils, taking form and ruling o'er man"). Their bloodlines practice black magick and can shapeshift between human and reptilian forms ("in the form of man moved they amongst us, but only to sight, were they as are men").

The Ancient Mystery Schools and Initiation

The ancient mystery schools are teachings that were descended from the Brotherhood of the Snake. There are many derivatives of these ancient teachings that exist in other cultures, but for now I will focus on Egypt. After Atlantis was destroyed many of its inhabitants traveled to Egypt, one of them being Thoth (Hermes). Thoth was an incarnation of the Buddha and closely connected to the Great White Brotherhood. He taught the Egyptians many things about spirituality and soul evolution, these concepts originally being propagated by the Brotherhood of the Snake. He also aided in the construction of the pyramids and temples. In the movie *Raiders of the Lost Ark*, there was a device called the Ark of the Covenant. The Nazis had stolen it and were attempting to harness its power, although the audience was unaware of the specifics of the technology (you will see later on how Hollywood uses subliminal messages in movies to hint at certain factual events). The Ark of the Covenant in Ancient Egypt was a device that transmitted high-frequency energy beams. In effect, this device could nullify gravity. When this beam was shot at ten ton rocks they floated in the air like pebbles. It is interesting that many scholars believe the great pyramids were built with ropes and underfed slaves. I wonder if the history books left out the fact that those slaves were actually giants on steroids. If they were, I would consider for a moment believing mainstream archaeology.

Among the endless amount of suppressed history, there is much misconception regarding what the Great Pyramid of Giza was actually meant for. Again, mainstream archaeology incessantly tries to fool us. We are told that it was a burial chamber for the fourth dynasty Pharaoh Khufu. Really? It's just a tomb for one man? Allow me to clarify. The Great Pyramid was in reality a large antenna that pulled in cosmic energies as it was aligned perfectly with the cosmic current of this solar system and the central sun of the galaxy. When it was first built it was encased in white limestone which caused it to shine, and floating above the top in suspension was a large and powerful crystal sheathed in pure gold. Microwave generators were stationed in the shaft in the center of the pyramid traveling strait into the ground, and they were used to anchor the high frequency cosmic energies into the Earth. An ark of the covenant (there was more than one) was placed in the center of the capstone, and once charged by the strong mental powers of a spiritual master, the covenant could function on its own and distribute light and energy throughout Egypt. The Great Pyramid also acted as transmitting device for the Earth's kundalini.[11] The golden crystal capstone represented the third eye of the planet and acted as a communications device, making it easier for the Planetary Spiritual Hierarchy to communicate with inhabitants on Earth. Later in this dissertation it will become clear to you how the symbol of the pyramid and "all-seeing eye" on the back of the one dollar bill relates to this concept and how the global elite use this image to control mainstream society.

In and of itself, the Great Pyramid represents the spiritualization of matter as all physical matter you see around you is the condensed form of spiritual energy. The Great Pyramid was also an observatory used for charting the heavens. As the capstone represented the third eye chakra, other parts of the pyramid represented other chakras. The King's Chamber symbolized the heart chakra. The Chamber of Rebirth and the Well of Life symbolized other chakras. Above the aforementioned roles, the Great Pyramid was used as a place of initiation for the Great White Brotherhood. The very essence of initiation works to unite the conscious and subconscious minds with the superconscious mind (the soul). Initiates were taken into the Great Pyramid where they were put through a series of tests, in all there being seven stages of initiation. Each subsequent (or higher) stage drew the initiate closer and closer to self-realization. The early stages dealt with the development of psychic abilities such as channeling, telepathy, telekinesis, and communication with the nature spirits. During the early phases of initiation an initiate developed proficient clairvoyant, clairsentient, and clairaudient abilities and was severely tested in the release of negative emotions and tendencies. For example, many initiates were taught to balance the twelve sets of opposite characteristics. These opposing forces appear below:

> Keeping silent versus talking,
> Receptivity versus resistance to influence,
> Obeying versus ruling,
> Humility versus self-confidence,
> Lightning speed versus circumspection,
> Accepting everything versus being able to differentiate,

---

[11] Dr. Joshua David Stone compiled this information before he passed away in a book called *Hidden Mysteries*.

Fighting versus peace,
Caution versus courage,
Possessing nothing versus controlling everything,
Having no ties versus being loyal,
Contempt for death versus regard for life,
Indifference versus love.

Initiates were also often taught the seven octaves of vibration which are:

Physical .... Mineral and Plant
Emotion .... Animal
Mental .... Average Person
Intuitive .... Genius
Atmic .... Prophet
Monadic .... Divine Wisdom and Universal Love
Logoic .... God-Being.

These seven octaves also relate to the seven primary rays emanating from the Source.

Among many other things, initiates were educated about universal history and the importance of raising one's personal vibrational frequency. The process of initiation can be likened to lucid dreaming. In the higher levels of initiation an initiate is put into a trance, at which point he/she is traveling in his/her astral body. Spirit guides acted out scenes that the person experiencing astral body consciousness would react to. Often, in one of these scenes, an initiate will enter a room where many people are having sexual intercourse. That person would then be approached by an attractive member of the opposite sex and would have to refuse their advances. In another scene an initiate would be surrounded by men with daggers who would then threaten him/her. A priest would come to the initiate's aid and offer to sacrifice himself so the initiate could escape. To pass the test the initiate would have to refuse and offer to stand by the priest and fight the invaders to the death. There were many other tests. Many historical personages like Jesus, Earlyne Chaney, Elizabeth Haich, and others have gone through initiations in the Great Pyramid.

History Rewritten

In the 1990's, researcher David Icke traveled to Africa to corroborate the information I have presented thus far concerning the reptilian/extraterrestrial takeover of the post-diluvian Eearth. In Africa Icke met with a man named Credo Mutwa, one of the last two remaining Sanusis (shamans) of the South African Zulu Nation. He is an official keeper of ancient knowledge concerning the birth of our civilization and the reptilian "gods" which came down from the sky and interbred with the human females. These crossbreed bloodlines called the "Nephilim" have ruled for ages by maintaining positions of power all over the world. David Icke himself has uncovered an immense collection of knowledge and data from his worldly travels revealing this exact same story. He has interviewed an extensive network of mind controlled slaves, Illuminati, and Freemason whistle-blowers, and also those who have seen people in positions of power shapeshift into reptilian entities and then back again. David Icke has deduced that these people are members of the bloodline families stemming from the original Nephilim. In 1999 he released a video called "The Reptilian Agenda," an interview with Credo Mutwa in a small village just outside of Johannesburg. In this consultation much information was revealed which will now be disseminated.

Credo refers to the reptilian extraterrestrials as the "Chitauri," also known as the "Children of the Serpent." They came down in large golden bowl-like craft one day in ancient Africa thousands of years ago and appeared to the native tribe of black people. At that time, the people did not speak because they communicated telepathically. Their minds were so powerful that a hunter could crouch in a bush and mentally call for an animal to kneel before the hunter to be slain. Animals and humans respected each other and communicated with each other. The particular tribe in Africa in which Credo is speaking of was also androgynous, meaning both male and female qualities were intact in one body. The reptilian extraterrestrials told the people they were their gods, and therefore should be worshiped as such. They stated that they had evolved on the Earth long ago and had come back to make the people of Africa gods. First, they divided the Africans into male and female and taught them how to speak. After this was done the Africans realized they had been hoodwinked. They had lost their mental powers and they now were divided sexually. When the males and females had relationships together there arose the problem of those who "slept around," causing disharmonious relations between members of the tribe. The Africans were also forced to mine metals. The chief of the Chitauri was named Humbaba, and it is interesting to note that in the Sumerian *Epic of Gilgamesh* the king of the ancient city of Uruk, along with his friend Enkidu, slay a monstrous beast named Humbaba (guardian of the Cedar Forest). This Humbaba Credo speaks of could most likely be the same entity.

Credo also tells of how the Chitauri fought the real God (Prime Creator) in a war in the higher dimensions. They tried to usurp the throne of heaven and were banished to the lower frequencies (4th density and below). This is the "Fall of Lucifer" in Christian myth. God sowed their mouths shut so they could not eat, and that is why they must feed off of intense human emotion. Humans supply the needed energy for the Chitauri, most of them living underground. That is why they cause wars, famines, and epidemics. They feed off the negative human emotions emitted from these periods of time. The Greys who are the genetic offspring of these reptilian entities work for them controlling the human populations of Earth. There is also a group known as the "beasts of the blanket." They are involved in the selection of various African kings and also reconnaissance missions where they collect crashed U.F.O. disks and other technology. Credo also notes that when the Chitauri get sick they rub gold dust on themselves, which harmonizes their energetic bodies.

One fascinating story Credo recounts tells of how once, him a few friends ate the skin of what they called a "puwana" or a Grey alien. When they did this they became very ill, breaking out in intense rash and swelling. After a week all they all healed up and experienced a dramatic increase in their perception of reality. Their sense of smell, taste, and sight became radically sensitized. When Credo looked at a tree he saw 'colors beyond colors' and felt that he was 'one with the whole universe.' It is commonly believed that these heightened senses have been breed out of us, which is partly correct. It happened when our D.N.A. was reduced from 12 to 2 strands. Credo also noted that the richer people in this world become the more they act like the Chitauri, and I agree. People in positions of power who are rich and well connected are generally greedy and arrogant. They always want more. More control, more money, more power. They are also privy to a certain knowledge

A New Order of the Ages

which Credo says is incredibly more ancient than Einstein or any other famous mathematician or physician. The ancient Africans themselves were aware that space and time are really one and the same, and that it is possible to travel backward and forward in time.

In the possession of Credo is an ancient necklace he calls the "Necklace of the Mysteries" with carvings and depictions of the reptilian gods and various relatable symbols imbued onto its surface. Credo says it was forbidden to depict the reptilians as they really were, and that is why ancient drawings in caves and on stone tablets reveal human looking gods who are taller than everyone else. The size difference was the ancients' way of relating the difference of the gods when their real appearance could not be depicted. One of the symbols on the belt was the constellation of Orion, a place Credo concludes the Chitauri came from originally. The Chitauri themselves believe that women are lower than males, and that is why our society is based on a patriarchal nature. The symbol of the phallus is seen over and over again in ancient structures and monuments, and even today in popular culture. The cover of *The Little Mermaid* D.V.D. shows a hidden phallus posing as one of the pillars to the castle in the background. Phallic symbolism is literally everywhere in our present and past culture. Popular depictions of the devil also bear striking similarities to what the Chitauri were said to look like. In the movie *Star Wars episode I: The Phantom Menace*, the protagonist is named Darth Maul. He face is almost an exact representation of that of a Chitauri. Some Chitauri, according to Credo, had a third eye in the lower middle portion of their foreheads. This eye was psychic. It could penetrate into anyone's mind and was deemed the "all-seeing eye." Later this became the Eye of Horus.

There is another interesting story related by Credo which tells of how the ancient Africans used to kill the Chitauri by sharpening a poisonous type of wood called Rodasia Tick Wood into a stake. They would then pound these stakes into the hearts of the reptilians. Since the Chitauri also drank human blood, it becomes obvious that the stories of Dracula are descended from this time period. The relations to pictures of the Devil and the fact that the reptilians set up all the religions makes it clear that they were setting us up. In horror movies the victim often brandishes a cross to shield himself from the evil. You will see later how the cross is nothing more than a pagan adaptation of the cross of the Zodiac. It is also no wonder why the Egyptian Pharaohs all had long beards under their chins and whore python-looking hats. They were mimicking the reptilians.

There are also stories of African kings who could shapeshift. In one instance, the people of a certain village were afraid of their king because one day witnesses saw him turn into a lion in his home. Credo believes that there is a certain blind spot in our brains, a blind spot which the education system and the religions exploit. Most people will see something completely out of the ordinary and disregard it altogether as part of their reality. Vaccines given to children inhibit their abilities to see spiritual entities, and it is forcefully impressed upon the public to ridicule those who see U.F.O.'s or experience interactions with discarnate entities. It is no mystery all the ancient civilizations worshiped the python and why there are and uncountable number of references to extraterrestrial gods in religious texts and ancient historical documents. It is Credo's belief that the Chitauri will soon reveal themselves. We have all been so blind as to destroy the environment and ourselves, and now the reptilian "gods" will come and try to reappear as saviors. Most people who are bathed in ignorance will either accept it or be scared into submission, either way the might of the reptilians will be imposed on our society again unless human beings begin to stand up for themselves.

The reptilians, in Zulu lore, brought the Moon here many centuries ago. Two brothers, called by Credu "Wuwani" and "Umpenku," piloted the hollow craft. The reptilians that control the Earth live in inside the moon, just as they live inside the Earth. Wuwani and Umpenku were Enki and Enlil, the two sons of Anu, chief commander of Nibiru. Enki and Enlil were the chief patrons of the Annunaki described in the Sumerian tablets. According to the Zulu shamans, Wuwani and Umpenku were also known as the "water brothers" because they had scaly skin like a fish. This is where the legend of the fish god Dagon comes from and the concept in our economic system known as Maritime Admiralty Law. The Pope represents Dagon (he dons the mitre) and he is of a pure reptilian bloodline connected to the ancient bloodlines of Nimrod in Babylon and the Hyksos in Egypt.

It is perhaps time we re-wrote our own history?

PART 2

The Virus of Life

I

The World's Religions and Secret Societies

"Sexual suppression supports the power of the church, which has sunk very deep roots into the exploited masses by means of sexual anxiety and guilt. [It] engenders timidity towards authority and binds children to their parents. This results in adult subservience to state authority and to capitalistic exploitation. It analyzes the intellectual critical powers of the oppressed masses because it consumes the greatest part of biological energy. Finally, it paralyzes the resolute development of creative forces and renders impossible the achievement of all aspiration for human freedom. In this way the prevailing economic system (in which single individuals can easily rule entire masses) becomes rooted in the psychic structures of the oppressed themselves."

-Wilhelm Reich

Human civilization on Earth has always been teeming with ideology and mythology. To our ancestors, there was a spirit in everything, an invisible aspect of the self which permeating every life form. Even Shakespeare thought that every person, animal, object, event, and idea was a prop in the stage for God's play. Historically, we can look back and count innumerable religions which differed in patronage, identities of deities, devotional methods, etc., but there has always been one element that has never changed, and that is the meaning given to any observation. Meaning comes from the heart. The thing binding us all together is spirit, and that exists eternally. It is the eternal truth that drives us every day. If you think you will die one day you are only viewing things from the perspective of your self image, not your real self. Your real self does not think. It feels, it's from the heart. You feel this sensation in your heart chakra when you meditate. This hearkens back to the first paragraph of this book when I suggest that reality transcends thought. The highest form of perception to the ancient mystics and seers has always been a feeling of oneness with all, not intellectual calculation. The self image calculates and the self feels. This is a feeling of immortality.

All ancient scriptures point to the fact that there was a time when mankind was immortal, or at least close to immortality. In the Bible, Adam and Eve (Adapa and Lilith) were bequeathed an abode in the Garden of Edin (the E.DIN complex in Mesopotamia) by the Creator, but one day they were excommunicated after having eaten from the forbidden Tree of Knowledge (the Mystery Schools) and were forced to live elsewhere. Ever since that fateful day, great heroes like Herakles, Odysseus, Gilgamesh, and Alexander have traveled far and wide in search of this garden, which supposedly enclosed the elixir of life. We have been told the New World was discovered when explorers from Europe sought a new maritime route to India (of course knowledge of the New World was known beforehand), and that Christopher Columbus was the hero, but these are lies as I will detail later. When the New World was supposedly "discovered," Queen Isabel and King Ferdinand of Spain entreated Christopher Columbus to search for the "Fountain of Youth," the begotten water of the gods. When he arrived he questioned nearly every Native American, oftentimes under torture. Ponce de Leon, a man well trained in excursions, witnessed one interrogation and heard something which intrigued him. He reported to King Ferdinand that several Indians coming from the Bahamas and Lucayos islands spoke of an island which contained a "perennial spring of running water of such marvelous virtue that the waters thereof being drunk, perhaps with some diet, make old men young again." In March of 1513, de Leon set sail for the island of Bimini under the pretense of searching for gold and silver. The expedition traveled in vain, but more talk of the island was heard. Later, the king and queen of Spain sent de Leon to the coast of Florida. It was there where de Leon met the fate of an arrow.

Even so, tales of a "Fountain of Youth" and an "Elixir of Life" continued to echo throughout the ages. Have not the Greeks and Romans left behind tales of immortality? What about Herakles and his twelve labors? What about Apollo and the promise that if he brought back from Hesperides the divine golden apples he would receive immortality? What about the goddess Aphrodite granting a potion to Phaon, and whence drunk transforming the man into a beautiful youth? There was also the tale of Tantalus becoming immortal by eating at the table of the gods, feasting upon their nectar and ambrosia. In *The Odyssey*, the mighty Odysseus is offered a query by the nymph Calypso that if he stayed with her as her consort he would be made to live forever. Even Glaukos was transformed into a sea god by Okeanos and Tethys. Predating these tales are the stories from Sumer and Babylon. The manly Gilgamesh had the answer to immortality in his grasp before he was turned away. The general of Macedonia, Alexander, who conquered most of the ancient world in the 4th century B.C.E., quested for immortality as well. On one attempt, he battled demons in an underground passageway whereupon an angle came to him and proclaimed:

> I will tell thee something whereby thou mayest live and not die . . . .
> In the land of Arabia, God hath set the blackness of solid darkness, wherein is hidden a treasury of this knowledge. There too is the fountain of water which is called 'The Water of Life'; and whosoever drinketh therefrom, if it be but a single drop, shall never die.

In the end however, Alexander's toils went to naught. So where was this fountain of the gods? How did the Greeks and Romans know about it? How did the Native American's know about it? Or was it just a ruse, like a fantasy? Whether it was a fantasy or not though, it was indeed taken seriously. All the religions talk about it. If the search for the Fountain of Youth was not among the reasons for the First Crusade (1095), it was for the ensuing ones (1147 and 1189, respectively).

Probably the most detailed versions of questing for immortality and the afterlife have come from Egypt. The Pharaoh was believed by the people to be immortal by virtue of the fact that he had sat on the throne; the first Pharaohs were known to be gods who came down from heaven (space). Later, Pharaohs were more like demi-gods to be worshipped. Howsoever it took place, each successive Pharaoh claimed direct descent from the gods. Egyptian tradition held that in times immemorial, "Gods of Heaven" came down unto Earth via the Celestial Disk:

The winged celestial disk

This symbol has appeared many times throughout ancient history, and later you will see why. As legend has it, this immense celestial disk came down to Earth and raised Egypt from under the mud and water (because it had been submerged); that is why Egypt is nicknamed "The Raised Land." The god who piloted the disk was name Ptah and eventual he begot a son named Ra,[1] who was given the kingdom of Egypt. One should notice here where the word "amen" comes from. So effectively, when you pray in church, you are praying to the god Ra-Amen. Amen in Egypt also meant "the hidden one," so perhaps religion is hiding something from you? Ra-Amen divided his kingdom between Osiris (day) and Seth (night), and so begins the whole Egyptian pantheon.

It is clear immortality is misunderstood today on Earth, although in the past it might have been well known. We clearly have forgotten who we are and why we are here let alone where we are going. We think we are mortal, finite beings, and for some, religion serves as a means for attaining an afterlife, but for others, science prevails and there is no afterlife. If we are to ever find the real hidden truth, we must go beyond science and religion and reconcile the two. Obviously, there are valid elements in both perspectives. When Columbus sent sail from Spain in 1492, the Muslim occupation of the Iberian Peninsula concluded with the surrender of the Moors at Granada. The Muslims and Christians had bickered for centuries and contested the peninsula, but there was one thing the two ideologies had in common, and that was the tale in

---

[1] Ra-Amen, or Amen-Ra, was the Sun god in orthodox Egyptian religion. The popular "Eye of Horus" is the hawk's eye that is associated with Ra; it legates royal power and protection. Today, it is associated with the all-seeing eye of Lucifer in demonic secret societies.

the Koran concerning the fish and the fountain of life. Since this story was almost identical to the Greek legend of Glaukos, the Moors believed in the fountain as well. In the Bible, the fountain is more like a river (as in many Native American accounts) and it is described in the "Book of Revelation" as a: "pure river of water of Life, clear as crystal, proceeding out of the throne of God . . . In the midst of the street of it, and on either side of the river, was there the Tree of Life, with twelve manner of fruit." It is clear all religions share common themes and symbols, one of them being immortality. If we are to understand who we are we should start with this notion and try to figure out what the ancient peoples meant by the Fountain of Youth/Life.

Whatever it is, it does not dwell solely in science or religion; it is somewhere in between. Anton LaVey, High Priest of the Church of Satan, once proclaimed that there is a force between good and evil, and that is the force of creation. If we are to find it, we must expand the way we think and maybe even ourselves. One powerful occult image to higher level Satanism and Freemasonry is the androgynous devil goat Baphomet.[2]

---

[2] Baphomet is the demon supposedly worshiped by the Knights Templar.

Baphomet

In this picture of Baphomet, the hermaphrodite has one arm pointed towards the sky (Heaven) and one pointed toward the ground (Hell). The Freemasons believe that all opposites eventually unite (i.e. heaven is hell, good is bad, up is down) and that order is achieved only after chaos, the begetter of order.[3] For a more practical approach to this dilemma, however, we should consider the true nature of religion and how it counters real spirituality.

Let us move on to the next stage of suppression. First it was knowledge about who we are and where we have come from (as detailed in *Part 1*). Now, I will discourse on the religions of the world and how they evolved from the secret priesthoods and mystical orders of antiquity, who thought that real knowledge should be bestowed upon only the chosen few. Who are the heroes of the modern major religions and why are they

---

[3] The aphorism of powerful occult bloodlines has always been "order out of chaos" because they are in the business of creating power (order) out of fear and confusion (chaos).

powerful pagan gods? It is all about suppression of information. Light is information. Darkness is absence of information.

Come Unto Me

"Come unto me." This messianic expression is often attributed to Jesus Christ, the savior to many who border on the obscenities of organized religion, a type of exo-politics used by the global elite to induce the masses into a state of hyper-suggestibility. If one is seeking a moral, spiritual, and rewarding life, in can be obtained in many ways; religion is not the "end all." As it was once stated, "none are more hopelessly enslaved than those who falsely believe they are free," and this pertains to the three major orthodox monotheistic religions of the world: Christianity, Judaism, and Islam. For the victim consciousness to fully manifest in reality, an aggressor, as well as a victim, is needed to supply the invisible imprisonment. This aggressor has come to be the Church, but more specifically Draconian bloodlines who work through the Church. The parlance "come unto me" is a beckon toward enslavement. Although Moses and Muhammad, the main prophets/messengers of Judaism and Islam, are not viewed as gods like Jesus is, they have nevertheless been projected as beckoners toward a strict, prison-like religion.

I will now share the facts concerning the "god" Jesus I have extracted from my research into the occult and new age channeling:

The soul known today as Jesus was a fragment of the Sananda lineage, so Sananda is the name of the oversoul of Jesus (his higher self). Sananda is the head of the Great White Brotherhood in this sector of the galaxy, and after watching mankind freefall into ignorance, incarnated in 39 B.C.E. as the son of Joseph and Mary on March 31st. Jesus was not born from an immaculate conception as it is believed by the Nicene Creed. That was inserted later to give the illusion that Jesus was a god. Also, Mary and Joseph were not married when they had Jesus. Sananda is an 8th density being, and Jeshua (Jesus' real name) was born with many of his spiritual abilities intact. He was intelligent, psychic, and a gifted healer. His parents, Mary and Joseph, were opposed to the political situation at the time and saw the authorities as oppressive, so they migrated toward the Dead Sea. They met a spiritual order there called the Essenes and left Jeshua in their care, later returning to Galilee. Jeshua joined the Essene Order and for three years built temples and houses for his caretakers; this is where we get the notion that Jesus was a carpenter. While attending the sacred teachings of the Essenes, Jeshua learned much about having respect for Mother Earth and all other life forms. The Essenes were left alone by the governments of the region because they paid their taxes, although they were seen as anti-social and for the most part eccentric. Jeshua was an avatar because he could consciously rotate his Merkabah vehicle, thereby controlling space, time and matter. The miracles he performed—like walking on water, healing the sick and transmuting ordinary materials—were a result of two things: Jeshua's high density level and his ability to control his Merkabah vehicle.[4]

The inception of the Essene Order began in roughly 1,973 B.C.E. in Egypt with Melchizedek, a great spiritual master of the time.[5] It was the precursor to Judaism, representing a sort of Jewish mysticism that studied the Kabbalah. The Kabbalah taught reincarnation, astrology, channeling, prophecy, soul travel, and psychic development. The Essenes were very inclined toward the study of angelology (angels), beings that were invisible sources of power and energy in the universe. They were able to communicate with these entities and paid homage to them through daily meditational practices and rituals. A Tree of Life was designed by the Essenes incorporating the positive angelic forces. The roots of the tree represented the seven Earthly powers including the Earth Mother, the Angel of Earth, the Angle of Life, the Angel of Joy, the Angel of the Sun, the Angel of the Water, and the Angel of the Air. The seven branches of the tree represent the heavenly realm containing the Heavenly Father, the Angel of Eternal Life, the Angel of Creative Work, the Angel of Peace, the Angel of Power, the Angel of Love, and the Angel of Wisdom. Contact with these fourteen angelic forces on a daily basis was required of anyone joining the order to enhance his/her own lifestyle and spiritual development. In today's satanic world, the Tree of Life (containing the Ten Sephiroth) and the Kabbalah have become symbols of Luciferic occult power instead of mind-freeing spiritual revelations.

---

[4] This information on Jeshua and his life in the Middle East has been offered by recent channelings of the Founders, the Pleiadians, and the Arcturians.

[5] David Stone, *Hidden Mysteries* (Flagstaff, AZ: Light Technology Publishing, 1995), 287.

A New Order of the Ages

Jeshua, not any soul to proclaim himself god in any way, incarnated at what has been called "zero point" in order to evolve humanity into empathy, the highest vibration of the Age of Pisces. Zero point is defined in Barbara Hand Clow's book *The Pleiadian Agenda* as the official beginning of the Common Era (1 C.E.) when the Annunaki cast an electromagnetic net around the Earth, trapping everyone into 3rd density.[6] They orchestrated events through the Holy Roman Empire, and when Emperor Theodosius declared Christianity the official religion of the new Roman Empire, Jesus was portrayed as a god. Jesus was to be worshiped as a god so the people would not worship the god inside of themselves. On the opposite side of control and suppression lays empathy. Empathy opens humans to spiritual access, and when Jeshua incarnated he came as a model for the nine-dimensional human. He arose from a deep planetary lineage and carried the instrument of ultimate creativity that could transmute human violence. This was later called the "Eucharist." He also delivered his bloodline through Mary Magdalene, the priestess of Isis at the central Goddess temple of Jerusalem, and right now, the Christ Consciousness lives in the D.N.A. of all our bodies. Jeshua activated the mind of Gaia in the plants, and during the Age of Aquarius the Sun will awaken the Christ Consciousness in our bloodstream. This elixir, the Gaian alchemy Jeshua brought to Earth, contains the Dionysian/pagan memory codes that, when triggered, will quicken Gaia's spirit during the next Age.[7]

At the age of sixteen, Jeshua and several Essenes traveled to India where they met with gurus and saints. Jeshua studied with a guru for two years where he learned much about the mystical elements of life. When he returned to Galilee he met a dancer named Mary Magdalene, whom he fell in love with. In the Bible, Mary Magdalene is portrayed as a prostitute, but this is only to contradict the fact that she had a sexual relationship with Jesus. She bore a child to Jeshua, but because the two were not married they became social outcasts in regards to the governmental authorities. Mary was allowed to stay at the Essene Temples with Jeshua although this was against the rules, and when their son was old enough they all three traveled back to India. When

---

[6] It has been revealed by E.V.P. and reverse speaking expert Peggy Kane that the reptilians who control this planet have also cast trapping electromagnetic nets around Mars and the Moon.

[7] Barbara Hand Clow, *The Pleiadian Agenda* (Rochester, VT: Bear & Company, 1995), 157-160.

word spread that Mary had an illegitimate child both she and Jeshua feared for their son's survival, although nobody knew the identity of the father. The child was left in the care of an Indian saint while Mary and Jeshua returned to Galilee. They missed their son, so after two years they returned to India to see him. They spent only a short while with him but it was all they could afford. He was to remain under the wise guidance and watchful eye of the saint due to the political instability in Galilee. The social climate of the town was too harsh to raise a son in and Jeshua and Mary knew he would learn much more while staying in India. Their foresight proved valuable, and their son grew up and became a wise sage who taught in India.

During his education, Jeshua went through an initiation in the Great Pyramid of Giza. The first through seventh initiations passed by Jeshua included the tests of sincerity, justice, faith, philanthropy, heroism, divine love, and brotherhood. Later, Jeshua received intense visions from his soul family telling him to teach spiritual wisdom to anyone who would take the time to listen with sincerity. His ministry began in his late twenties and he gathered many disciples, more than the twelve mentioned in the Christian canon. He kept his relationship and fatherly status secret from even his closest friends, and being highly clairvoyant, saw that he would inevitably be killed by the authorities who saw his teachings as a threat to the law imposed upon the citizens of the region. Jeshua taught people how to influence the cosmic energies around them with their minds in order to manifest a desired result in the physical reality.[8] His learnings in the Essene Order cultured him well, and he showed ordinary peasants how to communicate with the spirit world and the angelic hierarchies. Several of Jeshua's disciples learned how develop their own spiritual and psychic gifts as well. Later in his life when Jeshua reached a certain level of consciousness he was reminded by his oversoul and cosmic family his position in the Melchizedek priesthood.

The "Book of Enoch," one of many discluded in the New Testament, relates the keys of Enoch and the descent of the Melchizedek Brotherhood and the many ascended masters to the Earth at the end of days for spiritual purification. Really, this should have been included in the book of Revelation although this was inserted instead: "And I looked, and behold a pale horse, and his name that sat upon him was Death, and

---

[8] "Pleiadian Message from the Galactic Federation," http://www.youtube.com/watch?v=thIN9yfS368.

Hell followed with him, and power was given unto them over the fourth part of the Earth."[9] I believe the fourth part of the Earth is reference to the fourth age, the one that will be triggered in 2012. Death is most notably a reference to the Luciferian Order. This passage notes the destructive tendencies of the global elite and how they look forward to mass depopulation over the next several years. It is my opinion that the beasts of the Earth refer to the reptilians that live under the surface and influence everyday politics and decision making. In conventional reality, I admire this passage's integrity as it has been the master plan of the ruling aristocracy for many centuries. A New World Order is the "power given over the fourth part of the earth" and it surfaces due to war (sword) and famine (hunger).

The Christian church has distorted many of Jeshua's teachings, as he most certainly did not teach that the only way to heaven was through him. In fact, he said, "the kingdom of God lies within,"[10] within meaning inside of oneself. You are a part of God, and your relationship with yourself is more important than your relationship to Jesus or God, because in the end this stimulates all the other relationships of your life, including that with God. Remember, men wrote what became the Christian Bible, not God. It is impossible for a person to die for the sins of humanity. Each and every person is responsible for creating his or her own reality. This also defers to the belief that there even is such a thing as sin, when really sin is an illusion. Every soul is a creator son (son of God) endowed with consciousness and infinite love, and is, was, and always will be perfect. Going to church doesn't mean you will go to heaven. Heaven is a future template that society can mold and anchor down to the Earth at will. It is not an afterlife. The main reason for the power of the Church is the political ambitions of the clergy. In 553 C.E. the Second Council of Constantinople issued a decree stating that all references to reincarnation in the Christian canon be expunged. Isn't it obvious? This was an important step for the royal aristocracy in securing total control. To rule out of fear is the name of the game. Preachers could now scare people into thinking they would go to either heaven or hell when they died. This would subvert the masses into clinging to a religious doctrine.

---

[9] This is the basis for the title of Milton Cooper's book, *Behold a Pale Horse*, and it comes from the Bible, chapter 6 verse 8.

[10] This is taken from *A Course In Miracles* (unknown author/date).

When Jeshua preached his true spiritual teachings, the authorities of the Holy Roman Empire became frustrated with this man teaching people how to empower themselves and question authority; they so brought him to the cross. The part of Jeshua forgiving his assailants because they knew not what they did is real, as he taught everyone how to forgive and embrace unconditional love and compassion. Unconditional love to me means you love everyone no matter what, even if they do not believe what you believe. When Jeshua was brought to the cross he left his body immediately. He did not suffer for three days. He also had no need to resurrect his body because he could project himself into human form holographically once he merged back with his higher self at 8th density. He appeared to his disciples and Mary Magdalene many times, telling them to carry on with his teachings. His body disappeared from the tomb because grave robbers stole it.[11]

Jesus posed a threat to the Roman elite during his time because the people saw him as a spiritual leader. A political satire was bestowed upon Jesus when a purple cloak was draped around his shoulders and a crown of thorns placed on his head because of the esoteric significance. The purple cloak was worn during initiation into the Adonis mysteries of pre-medieval Europe, while the crown of thorns was an augury of initiation into the Eleusis mysteries. Although Jesus was not a hierophant of any mystery school, he was the prime antagonist of the Sadducees, the begetters of initiatic knowledge in the stead of the ruling elite. If Jesus' reign marked the end of the mystery schools it most certainly marked the beginning of secret societies.

During zero point, the Anunnaki attempted to institute a new calendar based in the Holy Roman Empire in order to set up a new stage of control over Earth, however, Earth was to be free according to the Galactic Federation. For this reason, Christ incarnated as Jeshua and pioneered the Eucharist to activate the plant realm. This stirred up the telluric realm, which in turn stirred up the blood of the humans. Jeshua transubstantiated the plant realm into blood and erected a sacrament operating through time in order to increase the resonance of Gaia in the plant realm. The plant realm is the green expression of the second-dimensional elementals. Humans transduce elementals into electromagnetic communication systems (kundalini energy) and plants

---

[11] Sal Rachele, "The Founders on Earth History Part 9," http://www.salrachele.com/webchannelings/foundersonearthhistorypart10.htm.

transduce the elementals into a breathing system composed of oxygen and carbon dioxide. The Annunaki tried to take over the planet at zero point, but when Jeshua elevated the planet realm into blood, they knew that this would evolve the people right out of their control range as they would begin to feel Gaia in their blood. To compensate for this, the Annunaki devised a program from zero point to 325 C.E., and they slowly took over humanity through the Roman Emperor Constantine by establishing the Christian Church to dominate the diverse religious movements of Rome, Greece, the Levant, and Egypt. In 325 C.E. at the Council of Nicaea, the Roman Catholic Church was set up as the official dispenser of the Eucharist. The Annunaki-controlled Caesars knew what Jeshua was doing when he transmuted wine into blood and so they immediately tried to shut this power down by taking control over it—hence, the Roman Catholic Eucharist millions of so-called Christian's celebrate every Sunday at church.

When Jeshua transmuted the wine into his blood during the "Last Supper," seventy-two disciples watched as Christ transfigured into a lightbody. As Jeshua became a nine-dimensional human, each of the disciples awoke within all nine dimensions and were able to see the blue-white light of their kas (Egyptian for 'spirit'). As the disciples staggered and shook from the kundalini rising up their spines, a burst of power spread out to all the ancient power points where churches would later be constructed. This event became known as the Pentecost. Of course, the Romans and the Annunaki did not like this, so the Eucharist and the Pentecost were stolen and placed in a story where Jeshua became a pagan sun god and Mary Magdalene was turned into a prostitute. The bloodline of Jeshua as well as the real Eucharist had to be covered up. After the Popes murdered the Cathars, all priests were made to be celibate so people would eventually believe that Christ was celibate. Mosaic Law was the Nibiru version of the Eucharist.[12]

Lord Sananda (as he is called in the higher dimensions) has fragmented his soul several more times, there currently being eight fragments on the Earth now. There are fragments in the higher densities that guide the fragments in the lower densities. A high density soul will often fragment itself twelve times to perform work in the lower, physical worlds, although this is not a rule. The "Second Coming of Christ" is the return of the Christ Consciousness, the perfect balance

---

[12] Barbara Hand Clow, *The Pleiadian Agenda* (Rochester, VT: Bear & Company, 1995), 120-126.

between male/female, light/dark, and physical/spiritual. Christ actually means "anointed one"; those who are a "Christ" are anointed with enlightenment and divine status. Jeshua could very well have been the spiritual master the Jews were waiting for. Although Moses is the prophet who bequeathed the Talmud to orthodox Jews today, the esoteric Jewish religion began with the Order of Melchizedek, of which Sananda was a high-ranking member. The Essene Brotherhood evolved within Judaism, and gave it many of its phonetic practices. In effect, the Essene, orthodox Jewish, Melchizedek, and Christian lineages are all part of one pedigree that began with the ancient mystery schools.

Jeshua was the World Teacher throughout the Piscean Age (the last 2,000 years), in carnation and in the spirit realm (after he was crucified). During his incarnation he was overshadowed by Lord Maitreya, another ascended master, and now, it is Maitreya who is training the next world teacher, who is Dr. Joshua David Stone. In the mid-1990's during his incarnation on Earth, Dr. Stone became the first ascended master teacher ever to admit a U.F.O.-related entity, Ashtar, to the ranks of the ascended masters by incorporating the teachings of the medium Tuella (Ashtar's channel) into his own teachings. Dr. Stone told audiences that "Master Ashtar" is the commander of a space fleet of thousands of flying saucers watching over the Earth and that Vrillon is the communications director. According to Stone, these flying saucers are based on several oblong artificial asteroids approximately 100 miles in diameter which function as mother ships for the spaceship fleet, which has a total population in the millions. The saucers in Master Ashtar's fleet are manned by Venusians (extraterrestrials from Venus who live in the fourth dimension) and aliens from the Galactic Federation. Also according to Stone, "Master Jesus," under his galactic name of Sananda, works with Commander Ashtar and is the Commander-in-Chief of the Ashtar Galactic Command. Another name for Ashtar's fleet is "The Airborne Division of the Great White Brotherhood."

Dr. Stone also formulated a chart he called the "Cosmic Map" in which he detailed the structure of the ascended master hierarchy within the Milky Way Galaxy. He stated that there is a powerful cosmic being functioning at the core of the Milky Way Galaxy named Averran who governs the galaxy and is the personification of the Galactic Logos. In 2004, Dr. Stone was told by the Spiritual Hierarchy and ascended masters that he had completed his spiritual mission on Earth and was

A New Order of the Ages

free to go back to the spirit world to continue his work on the inner plane in the Synthesis Ashram and the Office of the Christ, run by the Planetary Logos. This position now held by Stone's spirit was formerly held by Djwhal Khul. Stone was also voted by the Hierarchy to become the next World Teacher for the Aquarian cycle, following in the footsteps of Jeshua. He is working with Lord Maitreya, the current president of the inner plane spiritual government of Earth. On Earth, Dr. Stone founded I AM University, a spiritual academy based on the lost teachings of the Essenes and order of Melchizedek. Gloria Excelsias was appointed by Stone to be the next director of I AM University since she is an ascended master channel.

Three In One

Christianity, Judaism, and Islam all share common roots. Moses, Solomon, and David were of royal Egyptian families while Abraham was from Babylon. By zero point, the law was the Mosaic code and it was descended from the Sumerians and through the Babylonians and Israelites. The Hebrew, Arabic, and English languages are all neo-Indo-European. Language and numbers were the vestiges of the Annunaki system, and the Caesars planned to use them to take over the Earth through the Temple of Jupiter. Just as planned by the Galactic Federation however, the Eucharist instituted by Jeshua was absorbed right into the Roman Empire. Every time a Catholic mass was performed, the two-dimensional telluric realm was pampered with cosmic energy, and even though the Catholic Church insists the second coming of Christ is just around the corner, they are really activating the Christ Consciousness grid with that inception. Power and greed is truly a double-edged sword. In the Age of Aquarius, Mosaic law will be replaced with the Christ Consciousness.

In all likelihood, Sananda was the savior the Jewish people were waiting for. Jeshua was a member of the Essene brotherhood and the Great White brotherhood, vowing to end the corruption that had strangled central Europe in the beginnings of the new Era. He was born from Jewish parents, however the term 'Jew' is a misnomer. In the King James Bible the Gentiles were any non-Israelite people, the inhabitants of the nation-state of Israel being labeled as Jews. Being anti-Semitic does not mean you hate Jews. There were many Semitic peoples in ancient Anatolia and parts of Northern Europe who migrated southeast into Mesopotamia and Southeast Asia; their ancestors were small proto-Indo-European tribes who evolved naturally in warm weather areas. When Jeshua incarnated he was already a member of the Essenes because he had been initiated in a past life and had incarnated into the body many know as Jesus to complete his work in establishing a Jewish religion centered on wisdom, love, and compassion. It was not the Jews who persecuted Jesus, it was the Roman Empire. When studying the information, it becomes clear how the Judeo-Christian movement was pioneered by the reptilian bloodlines through the Babylonians, Egyptians, and Roman Catholic Church. Inasmuch, I do not believe Islam falls into the same category. It is a separate religion based upon the conversations between the Prophet Muhammad and the archangel Gabriel and the subsequent debate over the successor caliphate. It borrows history from the Torah of Judaism and New Testament of Christianity, but was not inspired by them. Islam is a similar monotheistic religion to Zoroastrianism, Christianity, and Judaism in that there is worship of an almighty, omnipotent creator that is split between good and evil parts, but it more of an offshoot religion than the primary establishment. Nevertheless, it is used for political motivation as Islam is a target for terrorism. It still serves a purpose in the reptilian agenda.

In its genesis, Islam focuses on the Prophet. In 570 C.E. a child named Mohammed was born in Mecca, Saudi Arabia. By the age of twenty-five he was one of the wealthiest and most renown citizens of the city with a beautiful and rich wife. At that time the religious center of Mecca was a large black granite cube called the "Kaaba." It was purported to have been built by Abraham at the behest of God.[13] Later, you will understand further the significance of this stone. Outside of the Kaaba, there was little piety as Mohammed witnessed that people were only interested in making money, gambling, horse racing, and getting drunk on wine. They adhered to hedonistic pleasures while caring little about spirit. One day Mohammed was sitting on a hill outside the city contemplating how he could unite the people of Arabia and become a revered leader like Jesus Christ had been when the angel Gabriel appeared to him and offered up a golden tablet for him to read. Mohammad confessed he knew not how to read, but upon further prodding he found that he suddenly could. A

---

[13] Abraham is seen as the official Patriarch of the three major worldly monotheistic religions. He also shows up in accounts from Babylon and the Nibiruan Royal Family.

series of like encounters with this angel eventually led to Mohammed adapting the Qur'an. He went back to Mecca and began to preach. His creed was facile:

> My teachings are simple.
> Allah is the One God
> Mohammed is his prophet
> Give up idolatry
> Do not steal
> Do not lie
> Do not slander
> And never become intoxicated
> If you follow my teachings, then you follow Islam.

Whatever intentions Mohammed had of educating his people, he did not wish to perpetuate a dogmatic monotheistic religion like the early Christian church. The Christian Church can be viewed as the royal institute for dogmatic monotheism representing all three religions. The Pope has officially accepted Judaism and Islam as valid expressions of religion.

Giving up idolatry means not worshipping anything. The Creator is the source of everything. The name Allah implies practically nothing, it just means "the one God." When prompted to demonstrate a miracle like Jesus Mohammed refused, stating that the world in which Allah created was good enough and the people need only relish in it. This storyline does take a similar twist, however, to the time of Jesus, and as such Mohammed's preaching instigated a plot to assassinate him. Like with Jesus, Mohammed was becoming too famous. He escaped to Medina and eventually returned to Mecca in 629 C.E., and in the four years before his death had established control over all of Arabia. His disciple Abu Bakr became his successor, the new Muslim religion taking in elements of Zoroastrianism, Buddhism, and Hinduism. Islam is the world's third and final major monotheistic religion that spread out of Arabia after the death of Mohammed.

Just like the "heretical" movements of the Judeo-Christian religion like the Gnostics, Templars, Cathars, and Kabbalah worshippers elaborated on the mystical elements of life behind the face of orthodox religion, Sufism represented a contrary thought to Sunni and Shi'a Islam. Esoteric

Islam was that of a gentle, more feminine feeling. What constituted one's self in Sufism was a combination of fears, attachments, dislikes, likes, habits, and compulsions. A whole separate entity was made up of these component parts, operating independently from what we conceive to be our individual self. Our physical vehicle is just a conduit for this entity to manifest itself through. The Sufi way involved breaking down this false self so the real self, the soul pure of all toxins, could become manifest instead. Universal love and compassion embodied this self. Mohammed's brother-in-law was named Ali and was to him as John the Baptist was to Jesus. At Cairo, Ali and Mohammed's daughter, Fatima, inaugurated a school for esoteric philosophy called the "House of Wisdom" where seven initiatory levels were taught. One of its initiates was the "Old Man of the Mountains," Hassan-I Sabbah.

In Islamic lore, the Old Man of the Mountains controlled the whole world without ever leaving his hideaway through his agents, this idea being likened unto the film by Fritz Lang in which a demented Dr. Mabuse hypnotizes the world from his cell in a lunatic asylum. It is like the way the people of the world today are hypnotized. The global elite have the media and newspapers do it for them. You think this is fantasy? In 1953, renown journalist John Swinton had this to say when he gave a toast at the New York Press Club:

> There is no such thing at this date of the world's history, in America, as an independent press. You know it and I know it. There is not one of you who dares to write your honest opinions and if you did, you know beforehand that it would never appear in print. I am paid weekly for keeping my honest opinion out of the paper I am connected with. Others of you are paid similar salaries for similar things, and any of you would be so foolish as to write honest opinions would be out on the streets looking for another job. If I allowed my honest opinions to appear in one issue of my paper, before twenty-four hours my occupation would be gone. The business of journalists is to destroy the truth, to lie outright, to pervert, to vilify, to fawn at the feet of mammon, and to sell his country and his race for his daily bread. You know it and I know it, and what folly is this toasting and independent press? We are the tools of rich men behind the scenes. We are jumping jacks, they pull the strings and we dance. Our talents, our possibilities

and our lives are all the property of other men. We are intellectual prostitutes.

As well as newspapers, television networks apply this same ideology.

Today in America, most people hold religion at the zenith as the platform for all historical knowledge about God and spirituality. Unfortunately, most of the factual knowledge has been hidden by secret priesthoods. Erudition concerning the Essenes, the Kabbalah, reincarnation, and the Tree of Life was withdrawn so powerful reptilian bloodlines could control the masses. Several modern researchers, following the traces of the Essenes and the Kabbalah, agree that the Bible is a coded message. Michael Drosnin, in his acclaimed book *The Bible Code*, wrote that Israeli mathematician Dr. Eliyahu Rips believed he had found a hidden crossword-like code within the Bible, which accurately foretold of both Kennedy assassinations, World War II, the moon landing, the bombings of Hiroshima and the Oklahoma City federal building, as well as the election of Bill Clinton. Resent researchers have also found references to Barack Obama. Harold Gans, a senior code breaker for the U.S. National Security Agency, was aghast when he verified this same code using his own computer program. I am sure most people have also heard at some point in their lives about Nostradamus, perhaps the most august and celebrated prophet of the last few millennia. He too prophesied about these happenstances.

As usual, one can trace all the symbols back to ancient Mesopotamia. The connection between Hebrew traditions and Egyptian mysticism may be even stronger than previously believed, as many authors, including Jewish scholars, now believe the Kabbalah was an oral tradition concerning ancient Egyptian mysteries handed down from Moses through the leadership level of the Israelites. Some traditions say Abraham possessed a tablet of symbols representing all of the knowledge handed down from the time of Noah (or Utnapishtim if you study the Babylonian accounts). This knowledge was known to the Sumerians as the "Tablet of Destinies" and it was this knowledge, known to the early Jews as the Book of Raziel, which King Solomon supposedly garnered during his reign.[14] The philosophical cipher of this tablet became known as "Ha Qabala" (light and knowledge) and it was purported that he who

---

[14] The "Tablet of Destinies" is proclaimed in the *Enuma Elish* as the fate of the Earth granted to Marduk when he slew Tiamat.

possessed Qabala also possessed Ram, the highest expression of cosmic wisdom. The Tablet of Destinies is said to be the same as the Tablets of Testimony in the Bible and the Emerald Tablets of Hermes/Thoth. To the Greeks and Romans (such as Virgil, Homer, Plato, Pythagoras, etc.) the tablet was a source of cosmic understanding.

Religion and Astrology

Religion is really a form of astrology, a brew of science, art, and religion, along with a hint of mathematics, metaphor, and mythology. Ancient stargazers knew they were consociated with the stars and planets. To the ancient astrologer the planets, stars, and constellations were symbols for gods and heroes alike, the fundamental archetypes for the creed, "As above, so below." Within the carefully calculated movements of the heavenly bodies a meaning was transcribed, and however menial it seems to modern people today, it was of great import to those who fancied the connotation in times past. Today, religion is a way for people to jettison their spiritual burdens, but in ancient cultures, religion was closely related to astrology, and especially the precession of the equinoxes.

Due to the fact that the Earth is tilted on its axis at 23.5 degrees, it maintains a slow wobble as it spins on its axis. This concept is called "axial precession." If a line were drawn connecting both of Earth's poles extending out upward ending into an arrow tip, that tip would trace an ellipse in the sky due to the wobble of the Earth as it spins on its axis. The time it takes the ellipse to be drawn out once was referred to in ancient times as the "Great Year." The equinox occurs twice a year when the Earth's axis does not tilt toward or away from the axis of the Sun. The precession of the equinoxes was labeled so due to the westward movement of the equinoxes along the ecliptic path relative to the fixed stars. This transpired opposite to the motion of the Sun across the ecliptic (the apparent path the Sun takes across the sky throughout one Great Year). From the perspective of someone in the Northern Hemisphere, the solstices (winter and summer) occur when the tilt of the Earth is farthest away from (winter) and closest to (summer) the Sun. The ring of twelve constellations that align to the Sun's ecliptic path—or in other words the constellation the Sun rises up by every age—was well known to the ancients, so much so that they were personified. They were known as: (1) Aries-the ram, (2) Taurus-the bull, (3) Gemini-the twins, (4) Cancer-the crab, (5) Leo-the lion, (6) Virgo-the virgin, (7) Libra-the scales, (8) Scorpio-the scorpion, (9) Sagittarius-the centaur, (10) Capricorn-the goat, (11) Aquarius-the water bearer, and (12) Pisces-the fish. Together these twelve constellations make up the Zodiac, which is depicted as a circle intersected by two lines at 90 degrees. These two intersecting lines represent both the equinoxes. Each section is divided into three parts, in total there being twelve sections for each of the constellations.

To understand how this fits into religion one must look back and see how history repeats itself. Horus was the sun god of ancient Egypt and his mythology declared him to be born from a virgin on December 25th, his birth being accompanied by a star in the east. At birth he was adorned by three kings, and when he was old enough he traveled about with 12 disciples performing miracles. He was known as the "good shepherd" and the "lamb of god," and after he was crucified he resurrected himself after three days. Attis, a demigod from Greece around 1,200 B.C.E., was also born from a virgin on December 25th. He was crucified and after three days was resurrected. Krishna, the savior of India from around 900 B.C.E., was born from a virgin as well. His birth was accompanied by a star in the east and he performed miracles. He too was resurrected after death. The god Dionysus from Greece was known as the "king of kings" and the "alpha and omega" and he too was born of a virgin on December 25th. From around 1,200 B.C.E. the deity Mithra from Persia also shared many of these same characteristics. He was born from a virgin on December 25th, had 12 disciples, performed miracles, and was resurrected after three days of death. It is interesting that the sacred day for worship of Mithra was Sunday. Obviously, these stories bear a striking resemblance to the one most heard of in America, the story of Jesus Christ. The myth of Jesus shares all the aforementioned characteristics. What is more, there are numerous myths of other gods and saviors from the far past which share these same general characteristics. I have outlined a table of the most prominent below:

Name	Region/Tribe	Time period
Krishna	Vrindavan, North India	3000 BCE
Buddha	Lumbini, Nepal	500 BCE
Shalivahana	Southern India	100 CE
Zulis	Egypt	1700 BCE
Odin	Scandinavia	1000 BCE
Crite	Chaldaea	1200 BCE
Zoroaster	Iran	1500 BCE
Baal	Phoenicia	1100 BCE
Indra	India	1300 BCE
Bali	Indonesia	1500-500 BCE
Prometheus	Greece	800 BCE
Wittoba	India	2000 BCE
Thammuz	Mesopotamia	1500 BCE
Atys	Greece	1200 BCE
Xamolxis	Greece	500 BCE
Zoar	Rome	400 BCE
Adad	Babylon/Akkad	1100 BCE
Deva Tat	Thailand	500 BCE
Alcides	Greece	1200 BCE
Mikado	Japan	700 CE
Beddru	Japan	300 BCE
Hesus	Gaul	50 CE
Thor	Europe	800 CE
Cadmus	Phoenicia	2000 BCE
Feta	Greece	800 BCE
Ischy	Formosa	1500 BCE
Fohi	China	3000 BCE
Adonis	Greece	600 BCE
Ixion	Italy	600 BCE

Risen savors like Jesus

So why these characteristics? Why do all of these stories share the same attributes? It is simple. It is all astrological. From the summer solstice to the winter solstice the days get shorter and the Sun appears lower and lower in the sky until December 22nd when it is at its lowest point. For three days the Sun does not move and then on December 25th it moves one degree upward. At this time, Sirius (the brightest star in the night sky) aligns perfectly with the three stars in Orion's belt and the Sun, appearing in the vicinity of the Crux constellation. Just as the constellations of the Zodiac were personified, so the stars were as well. The three stars on Orion's belt represent the three kings or "wisemen" who follow the star in the east (Sirius) to meet the risen savior (the Sun) on December 25th when the Sun begins its ascent back up in the sky. The Crux constellation represents the cross Jesus died on and the constellation of Virgo relates to Bethlehem. Bethlehem translates to "house of bread" and the Virgo

A New Order of the Ages

was usually depicted has carrying a sheaf of wheat (or bread). It is said that Jesus was resurrected on Easter because it is during this time that the dark side of Earth is officially overshadowed by the light, creating longer days. The 12 disciples of Jesus represent the 12 constellation of the Zodiac. Just as Jesus traveled about with 12 disciples, the Sun travels about along the 12 main constellations seen in the night sky. The number twelve is replete throughout the Bible as it was a sacred number to the ancients. There are 12 tribes of Israel, 12 brothers of Joseph, 12 judges of Israel, 12 great patriarchs, 12 prophets, 12 kings of Israel, 12 Princes of Israel, and so on. That is why the Greek/Roman pantheon consisted of 12 deities. The cross superimposed on a small circle you often see on church steeples is not Christian at all. It is a pagan representation of the cross of the Zodiac.

Among numerous mistranslations in the Bible one is most notable. The "end of the world" is a total misconception. World should be exchanged for "Age," as the Bible symbolically relates the period and transition of three ages while foreshadowing a fourth. When Moses descends Mount Sinai he is antagonized by the fact that the people are worshiping a golden bull. This was blasphemous because Moses officially instigated the Age of Aries (the ram). That is why Jews today still blow the ram's horn. Jesus ushered in the Age of Pisces (the fish) and foreshadowed the Age of Aquarius (the water bearer). When his disciples asked him what the next pass (or Age) would be Jesus proclaimed, "Behold, when ye are entered into the city, there shall a man meet you bearing a pitcher of water." This is obviously a reference to Aquarius the water-bearer.

The story of Moses is lifted directly from ancient accounts. Sargon, the king of Akkad, was also placed in a reed basket and set adrift in a river to avoid infanticide. He was rescued and raised by a royal family. Moses was not Hebrew, he was Egyptian and he did receive what could be likened to the Ten Commandments on Mount Sinai, which is not what it seems. The Ten Commandments were lifted from book 125 in the Egyptian *Book of the Dead*. In the Bible, the passages in Exodus 20 and Deuteronomy 5 actually contain fifteen commandments, although Exodus 20 reveals only 10. In the *Book of the Dead*, the deceased appears before 42 judges:

> Homage to you, Great God, the Lord of the double Ma'at (Truth)! I have come to you, my Lord,

I have brought myself here to behold your beauties. I know you, and I know your name, and I know the names of the two and forty gods, who live with you in the Hall of the Two Truths, who imprison the sinners, and feed upon their blood, on the day when the lives of men are judged in the presence of Osiris. In truth, you are "The Twin Sisters with Two Eyes," and "The Daughters of the Two Truths." In truth, I now come to you, and I have brought Maat to you, and I have destroyed wickedness for you.

I have committed no evil upon men.
I have not oppressed the members of my family.
I have not wrought evil in the place of right and truth.
I have had no knowledge of useless men.
I have brought about no evil.
I did not rise in the morning and expect more than was due to me.
I have not brought my name forward to be praised.
I have not oppressed servants.
I have not scorned any god.
I have not defrauded the poor of their property.
I have not done what the gods abominate.
I have not cause harm to be done to a servant by his master.
I have not caused pain.
I have caused no man to hunger.
I have made no one weep.
I have not killed.
I have not given the order to kill.
I have not inflicted pain on anyone.
I have not stolen the drink left for the gods in the temples.
I have not stolen the cakes left for the gods in the temples.
I have not stolen the cakes left for the dead in the temples.
I have not fornicated.
I have not polluted myself.
I have not diminished the bushel when I've sold it.
I have not added to or stolen land.
I have not encroached on the land of others.
I have not added weights to the scales to cheat buyers.
I have not misread the scales to cheat buyers.
I have not stolen milk from the mouths of children.
I have not driven cattle from their pastures.

I have not captured the birds of the preserves of the gods.
I have not caught fish with bait made of like fish.
I have not held back the water when it should flow.
I have not diverted the running water in a canal.
I have not put out a fire when it should burn.
I have not violated the times when meat should be offered to the gods.
I have not driven off the cattle from the property of the gods.
I have not stopped a god in his procession through the temple. (*The Coming into Day: Egyptian Book of the Dead*, chapter 125: the Judgment of the Dead)

The only commandment altered in the Jewish Talmud was the first one: "I am the Lord your God and you shall have no other gods before me."

When one studies how history repeats itself it becomes clear how those in power stay in power. They just perpetuate an already existing story and tweak it a little to make it their own. It should be no mystery that the Egyptian religion acts as a precursor to the Judeo-Christian religion. Baptism, afterlife, final judgment, virgin birth, crucifixion, death and resurrection, ark of the covenant, circumcision, saviors, communion, deluge, Easter, Christmas, and Passover are just a few of the many similarities. Osiris the sun god was the premier deity to the Egyptians, and this is nothing different then mainstream Christianity today. Instead of Osiris Christians worship Jesus the pagan sun god. Jesus is the son of God because in the past 'sun' and 'son' were used interchangeably. Thomas Paine, one of the founding fathers of the United States, once said, "The Christian religion is a parody of the worship of the sun, in which they put a man called Christ in the place of the sun, and pay him the adoration originally paid to the sun." The fact of the matter is that Christianity is a Roman story developed for political reasons.

In 325 C.E. the Roman emperor Constantine convened the Council of Nicaea where the politically motivated Christian doctrines were established. Texts left out of the officially sanctioned versions (canons) of the Bible are known as the "Apocrypha." This esoteric literature casts a bright light on the true meanings of events and teachings. For the past 1,600 years the Vatican has maintained a tight political hold on Europe and the rest of the world. The Dark Ages, the Inquisition, and the Crusades were all byproducts of greedy men in positions of power. Jesus,

Paul, Solomon, Moses, John the Baptist, Mary, Joseph, and Pontius Pilate were all real people. They were simply placed into a convenient story that has been told since the dawn of our planet. The Bible is not the real story of these people. It is an astro-theological literary hybrid. For the unwist, religion is the ascent of morality. For the wise, religion is slavery.

The supposition of a "virgin birth" and "immaculate conception" not only implies the divinity of a savior-like figure, it also hints at the true nature of pre-history. According to esoteric author Michael Tsarion, a virgin birth related in antiquity to production of hybrid offspring from a human female crossing with an alien being. The woman was a virgin not only because this is in reference with the constellation of Virgo, but because it indicates a bloodline link to the alien gods who were often called the "Serpent Masters." The "immaculate conception" implies progeny created genetically, not sexually, and this could relate to the creation of the human race in test tubes. Queen Elizabeth I was known as the "Virgin Queen" because she was a Virgo baby as well as the prime carrier of the reptilian genetic stream. The name Elizabeth means "beloved of the Gods," and the Queen of England is beloved by the Serpent Masters because she carries their bloodline. In Hollywood today we have the practice of cutting the red tape and walking down the red carpet because both are symbolic of the perpetuity of the ancient bloodlines that control the world.

On a less pernicious note, astrology relates to cycles. In reality, everything is a cycle. When you get out of bed in the morning your brain releases serotonin, a chemical that wakes you up to the three-dimensional world. When you fall asleep at night melatonin is secreted, producing the opposite effect. Balance is always the key for survival and perpetual suspension. The Harmonic Formula (13th dimensional formula for compassion) is the atonement for the current precession of the equinoxes. In *A Course in Miracles*, the atonement is described as the purpose to any miracle, which is an action. The movement of the heavenly bodies is a miracle because it represents balanced action. The atonement is the reason and the end result of the miracle taking place, and in the Aquarian Age it will be forgiveness and ascension. This contemporary precessional cycle was set up by Prime Creator in order to facilitate our ascension.

The Sphinx was built in 22,819 B.C.E. and it symbolizes the "Lion King," the king of the beasts in the lower universes. It is located at the exact center of the land masses on Earth and represents the "Cycle To End All Cycles" (for the Earth). In the early 20th century the precessional cycle (the Great Year) was calculated to be 25,800 years. In the later part of the century it was calculated to be 25,920 years. The actual duration is 24,832 years with an acceleration factor of 6.18 percent. The acceleration factor must be accounted for because time is speeding up. I acknowledged before that time changes when your perception of it changes. This is happening now. The construction of the Sphinx initiated this current cycle and the speeding up of time. When calculated with the accommodation of the acceleration factor, this cycle ends on March 21, 2013, and that is when Earth will ascend into 5th density. The date of December 21, 2012 is the most anticipated date, although the real date is in March of the following year. December 21st is an important date though because it activates the opening of the dimensional doorways all around the planet. People will literally walk into the 5th dimension beginning on that date and even before. On March 21st the cycle will have ended at 26,366.618 years (24,832 × .0618 + 24,832). Notice how 618 appears synchronously on the end of 26,366.[15]

The number 24,832 is also recursive, recursion being the numerical expression of wisdom (Sophia): 2×2=4, 2×4=8, and 4×8=32. When dealing with harmonics one is in effect working with correlation. The language of computers (artificial intelligence) is the polarity based binary system of 1's and 0's and should not be confused with the language of life, which is the inter-relational energy exchange of light. The cycles of stars and star systems reside within the cycles of galaxies, in turn residing within the cycles of universes. The microscopic life (individual human consciousness) in these cycles maintain cycles of its own existing within the larger framework of the largest possible cycle, the cycle of life. This is the "alpha and omega" ancient ideologies talk about. Every cycle in creation has an alpha (beginning) and omega (end). The Sphinx was built in 22,819 B.C.E. and consider now that 81,918 meters per second is the gravitational acceleration of the speed of light at 60 degrees latitude. 819 correlates to both numbers, linking the two, for the erection of the Sphinx was the initiation of the 24,832 year cycle for this current pass.

---

[15] George Kavassilas, "Harmonic Equation of Ascension," http://www.georgekavassilas.org/theharmonicequationofascension.pdf.

The midpoint for this cycle was 10,403 B.C.E. which marked the construction of the great pyramids. The numbers 8, 1, 9, 1, and 8 take on a higher significance when one interprets what each number insinuates. The 8 is the infinite wisdom of Prime Creator represented as the infinity symbol turned on its axis. The image of the Vesica Pisces is also seen in the 8 with the top portion cut off. The Vesica Pisces represents the Age of Pisces, the last age of the cycle, as well as the womb of the Earth mother. The Male aspect of the Universal Consciousness expresses the matter grid per cycle. The Female aspect of the Universal Consciousness expresses the anti-matter grid per cycle. Together, the Father Sun and Mother Earth are the Twin Flame. The 1's represent the two pillars of polarity, light and dark. The 9 is situated between the two 1's because it denotes the ending of the cycle; 9 is the last number of the numerical code starting at 0. The Holy triangle of Light is the source of the Holy Trinity contended in numerous religious institutions. The Father, Son, and Holy Ghost of the trinity morphs as Prime Creator, Creator Son, and Eternal Spirit of the Holy Triangle of Light. The all-seeing eye adorns the centerfold of the pyramid:[16]

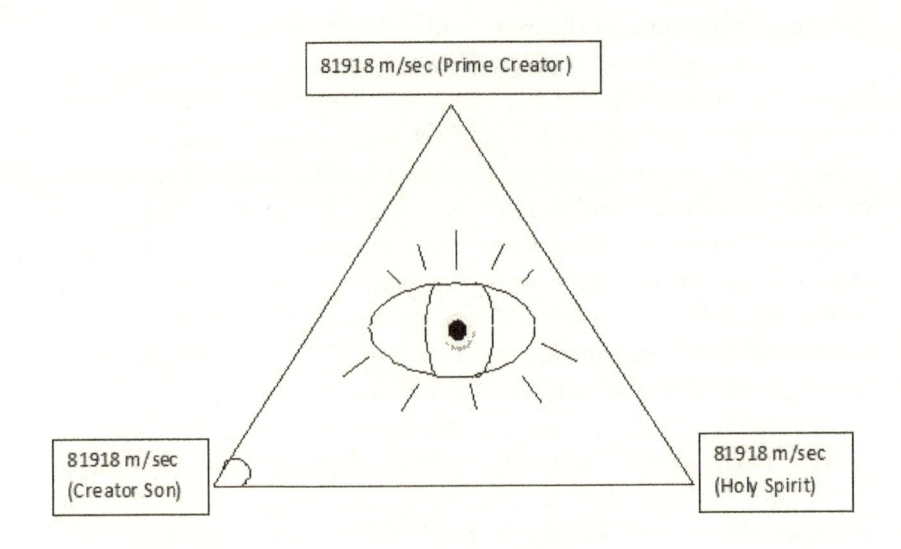

The Holy Triangle of Light

---

[16] The Holy Triangle of Light is associated with the Arcturians. See *Teachings from the Sacred Triangle* by David Miller.

This holographic reality is made of five general frequencies known as the five Platonic solids. They are the icosahedron, tetrahedron, dodecahedron, octahedron, and hexahedron, polyhedrons which exist in three dimensions (height, width, length) as geometric objects composed of flat sides. In the *Timaeus*, Plato, an initiate of the mystery schools and the Great Pyramid, discourses about how each solid is related to one of the five elements. The hexahedron represents the earth and the mineral masses, the octahedron represents air and the gasses, the tetrahedron represents fire and energy, and the icosahedron represents water and liquids. The final Platonic solid corresponds to the ether, or the spirit. The spirit is the intention that organizes the other four Platonic solids (the four elements) according to what it wishes to manifest. In many forms of classical artwork the four earthly elements are symbolized by four Cherubim, the angels of the pagan world, who are often depicted as animals with wings. The four cherubim, working form the four corners of the cosmos, hold the material world in place. The sun god is the fifth element who dissolves matter by spiritualizing it. It is all related to six-dimensional sacred geometry and the fifth-dimensional light body. A spiritual transformation is now purging Earth of all negativity. Earth will ascend to the 5th dimension, however this comes to pass, via the Planetary Logos (headed by an ascended master), who speaks on behalf of the Spiritual Hierarchy. On March 21st, 2013 at the spring equinox the Platonic solid governed by the intent of the eternal spirit will be morphed into a higher vibrational state and the planetary Merkabah vehicle will be activated. The following diagram illustrates this point:

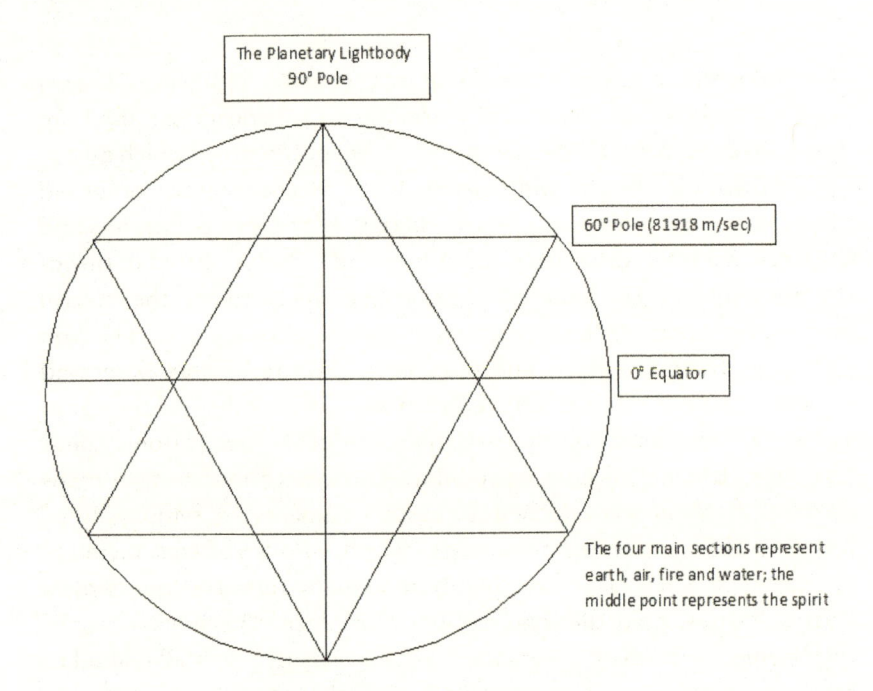

```
                The Planetary Lightbody
                      90° Pole


                                      60° Pole (81918 m/sec)


                                      0° Equator


                                   The four main sections represent
                                   earth, air, fire and water; the
                                   middle point represents the spirit
```

The Planetary Merkabah Vehicle

When ascension occurs one exits the earth plane and linear time at 90 degrees. One will ride the elevator, so to speak, up the ascending dimensions on the vertical gravitational plane, which holds together the vibrational frequencies that keep our bodies intact (the 1st through 9th dimension on the Pleiadian dimensional scale). When linear time is exited, one's consciousness is transported to the only moment in time which is the present moment; all things become possible. Time is not linear. It is like a loop that goes full circle and comes back to where it started. It is not time that moves, it is energy, and when energy moves or changes form it creates the illusion of time. Ascension is living fully in the present moment with no misconceptions about time. Past and future are only projections of the eternal now. Your consciousness is the embodiment of the eternal now as your subconscious and superconscious minds hold the knowledge and wisdom of the entire universe, as well as unconditional love and compassion. The following diagram illustrates this point; the x-y plane is the circle (2D representation of our space-time

A New Order of the Ages

continuum) and the z plane is the arrow travelling up from the middle (the elevator which carries one's consciousness to the "eternal now"):

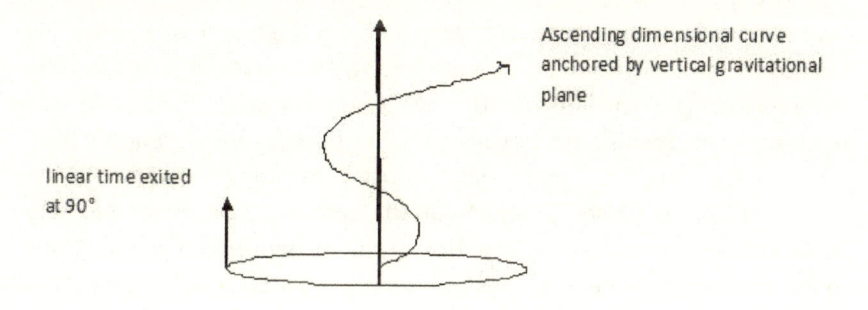

Ascending dimensional curve anchored by vertical gravitational plane

linear time exited at 90°

Linear time exited at 90 degrees

The Gregorian calendar, instituted by Pope Gregory XIII by a decree signed on February 24, 1582, reformed the Julian calendar to match the Mayan calendar on two dates: October 28, 2011 and December 21, 2012 at 11:11 a.m.[17] A German mathematician name Christopher Clavius was hired and he assembled a team to match these dates, along with the spring and winter equinoxes. This was desired by the Pope and the powers-to-be because 11 (11:11) is the number of mastery in occult lore and 22 (11 + 11) is the number of ascension. October 28, 2011 is a date predicted by the Mayans to have a great significance on the space-time continuum of the planet. On this day, time is supposed to speed up to such an extent that people will start to shift in and out of the fifth dimension, since in this dimension there is no time or space. The calendar we use today is altered to match 2012, although those in positions of power would never admit that.

These two dates—October 28, 2011 and December 21, 2012—also correlate with the process of D.N.A. transmutation, since that is what this process is about. There are 64 possible codes of amino acids in our D.N.A. from 20 amino acids and four atoms: carbon, hydrogen, oxygen, and nitrogen. We should have all 64 codes activated, but we only have 20. After 2012 the other 44 codes will be activated.

---

[17] These two dates are important because they signify large changes in planetary vibrational density.

Gods of Heaven and Earth

The post-diluvian Earth is under the jurisdiction of demonic extraterrestrials, especially the Annunaki and Draconians, and the subjugation of the population is advancing its course. Sir John Dee was court astrologer and ambassador to Queen Elizabeth Tudor and was embroiled in opening up portals to other dimensions during his life's work. In fact, many pre-Industrial scientists, cosmologists, and chemists were master occultists. Throughout the centuries, the Black Nobility (Black Venetians) under the direction of the 4th density reptilian factions have employed alchemists, necromancers, diviners, and clairvoyants to predict the future and communicate with these higher-dimensional beings. Famous personages like Robert Boyle, Count Saint Germain, Cornelius Drebbel, Casinova, Nostradamus, Machiavelli, and Cornelius Agrippa have been used in the past by these evil powers as conduits for placation. Many celebrities even today live double lives. They participate in black magick rituals and call upon evil spirits for guidance and protection.

In the past, the gods of heaven were also the gods of Earth. Upon inspection of documents and tablets from antiquity it becomes abundantly clear that everything beautiful and worth worshiping was brought forth from the "gods." Who were these gods and why did they have human characteristics? In the Bible, much of the Old Testament works to describe the origins of the Hebrews, saying they descended from the Sumerian city of Ur around 2,000 B.C.E. This group of people was ruled by a personality/god named Jehovah. He is the supreme god of the Jewish canon and his name derives from the Hebrew word "Yahweh" meaning "is, was, and always will be." The early Biblical narrative tells of Jehovah convincing the early Hebrews to leave Ur and travel to Haran, a caravan center in northeastern Mesopotamia. The clan's patriarch, Abraham, was then told by Jehovah to migrate towards Egypt. When they settled in Goshen they lived peacefully under the pharaoh, but a change in reign led to the Hebrews being forced into slavery and servitude. After 400 years of toil a man named Moses led the slaves on an exodus out of Egypt and through many bloody battles to the land of Caanan, the "promised land" granted to them by their god Jehovah. Thus, according to the Bible, the Jewish religion was born. That is why Jehovah (Yahweh) is the god of the Jewish cannon.

A New Order of the Ages

It is also evident that Moses was chosen by Jehovah to lead the conquest of the new monotheistic religion escaping Egypt and the pharaohs' grasp. Egyptian history according to the High Priest Manetho (c. 300 B.C.E.) unveils much about Moses and his childhood. Manetho states in his writings:

> Moses, a son of the tribe of Levi [one of the Hebrew tribes], educated in Egypt and initiated at Heliopolis, became a High Priest of the Brotherhood under the reign of Pharaoh Amenhotep. He was elected by the Hebrews as their chief and he adapted to the ideas of his people the science and philosophy which he had obtained in the Egyptian mysteries; proofs of this are to be found in the symbols, in the Initiations, and in his precepts and commandments . . . The dogma of an "only God" which he taught was the Egyptian Brotherhood interpretation and teaching of the Pharaoh who established the first monotheistic religion known to man.

This "brotherhood" was none other than the Brotherhood of the Snake, and it was under the guidance of Jehovah that the Hebrews wished to instill their new religion throughout the world. Early teachings of Judaism were deeply mystical, employing many symbols from the Brotherhood. Most of these axioms have been deleted from the official Hebrew scriptures, but many are still utilized today in the Kabbalah, which is guarded over by a secret sect of Jewish rabbis. The six-pointed Star of David has been a symbol of the Brotherhood of the Snake for thousands of years and it appears on modern Israel's national logo.

Who was Jehovah really? According to Alex Collier, Jehovah was an extraterrestrial who used technology to promote himself as god, and it was the fear issued to the minds of the people which served as their capitulation. A major controlling factor was the water supply. When the extraterrestrials controlled the water supply they controlled the people, because water was necessary for life. The languages and social structures were also introduced by the extraterrestrials as well as the letters and their numerical values. Just as one religion stems from a previous one, language follows suite. All the modern languages spoken today can be traced back to ancient Mesopotamia and the early Indo-European languages.

Jehovah was only one of the extraterrestrials fighting for power over Earth, his competitors being Marduk and his offspring. Each had their own groups of humans who worshiped them, but it was only after much bigotry that they decided upon a truce. In the Biblical account the Nephilim were the giants, the progeny of the gods, but they were also known as the Magi. During this interbreeding process there were predominantly 13 families from Orion, Sirius B, and Nibiru who established bloodlines. When the progenitors of the bloodline families left Earth they abandoned the old technology referenced in the Veda's from ancient India. This was the technology Saddam Hussein found and partially activated in Iraq. He was attempting to open up a stargate (a dimensional portal) in Iraq in hopes of bringing in the Annunaki. The Magi were left with certain types of technology proving useful in mind manipulation and space travel. Other technology was left buried and is still being discovered by archaeologists all over the world. Of course you are never told this.

As the Magi were left in charge of Earth, they interbred themselves among their own families and also other families who weren't part of the original bloodlines but exhibited many of the same characteristics (greed, superiority complex, occult philosoph, etc.). The Priesthoods were erected as an inner circle of initiates who were bequeathed the knowledge handed down by the ruling bloodlines and their extraterrestrial counterparts. These priesthoods are discussed at length in ancient Sumerian and Egyptian lore, and every major religion has one. Each religion has its canon (scriptures) and its origin (priesthood). Just as the Magi were left in charge of Earth, the Greys under the control of the Draconians were left in charge of the space around Earth. They were sent here to manipulate the social structures of the planet so when the Draconians graced the Earth with their presence once more there would be two categories of humans on Earth: royalty and worker. Over the past 200 years the focus for this goal has been the United States because it is the freest country in the world.

In fact, the whole hierarchy of the manipulation of planet Earth can be mapped out. It has even been reported that the reptilians living underground are responsible for 32,000 missing children in the United States in the last 25 years. That is a staggering number. They usually fast for several weeks at a time, but when it is feeding time they go into a frenzy. The royal members of their kind get first meat, and the victim is always brought into a state of terror because the adrenaline is a "high" for the reptilians. That is why it is mainly children who are eaten. They are pure of toxins that exist in most adults and they frighten easily. The violence in movies, television, and video games is desensitizing to the youth of the planet, which is why not only is there so much physical violence in our society, but also non-physical violence (angry thoughts and emotions).

Above all, the virus of life is religion—organized religion. The major monotheistic religions of the world have kept ancient knowledge for themselves, feeding the public lies and testimony. They do not want an informed population because that is too self-empowering. The way the ancient peoples worshiped the extraterrestrials with advanced technology is no different than the way people today worship Jesus or Muhammad. History repeats itself. People today give away their power just as the ancient people did. Before Judaism and Christianity the ancient Greeks and Romans worshiped the extraterrestrials and wrote about them often. Is it any wonder why the Greek gods were anthropomorphized? It is because they weren't really gods. They were extraterrestrials who were advanced and powerful but who had human characteristics.

The Greeks inserted anthropomorphic gods into nearly all of their stories. The gods intermingle in human affairs in Homer's *Illiad* and *Odyssey*. Hesiod was a Greek shepherd who composed the *Theogony*, a literary work describing the birth of the universe and the gods, from whence all human life then came. The Greeks are not specific concerning where mankind came from, but they do say that certain heroes and famous figures were the offspring of a male god and female mortal, or vice versa. According to Hesiod, first there was Chaos, the great void. From Chaos spewed Gaia (Earth) and Uranus (the heavens). The two were lovers and they produced the twelve Titans, six males and six females. Cronus and his sister Rhea procreated and brought forth three sons and three daughters: Zeus, Hades, and Poseidon; Hestia, Demeter, and Hera. Just as Cronus had overthrown his father Uranus, Zeus did likewise and Cronus was disposed by castration. Many battles between the gods ensued after this period, the main altercation taking place between Zeus and Typhon, a serpent deity. Zeus won and he was proclaimed king of the gods, although he had to share rulership with his brothers. Zeus was given the skies, Hades the lower world (known in popular culture as Hell) and Poseidon was given the seas. The six children of Cronus and Rhea came to make up the upper half of the pantheon of twelve, the lower half composing the offspring of Zeus.

When the Romans adopted the Greek pantheon they altered the names and many came to represent celestial bodies. The original Greek pantheon of twelve consisted of the Titans: Male—Oceanus, Hyperion, Coeus, Cronus, Crius, and Lapetus; Female—Mnemosyne, Tethys, Theia, Phoebe, Rhea, and Themis. When the Titans battled Zeus and his brothers and sisters, it was the Olympians who wrestled away command and ultimately the pantheon. The adaptation of the Greek pantheon of twelve were the Olympians: Male—Zeus, Poseidon, Ares, Apollo, Hephaestus, and Hermes; Female—Hera, Athena, Demeter, Artemis, and Aphrodite. The twelfth member of the pantheon came to be Dionysus, who was a male, making seven males in all. Although he was not a female, Dionysus was always described as being very effeminate and womanly. He was the god of wine and fertility, and was also in charge of carnivals, ceremonies, and ritual worship. When the Romans adopted the pantheon of twelve they changed the names which appeared as such: Zeus → Jupiter, Poseidon → Neptune, Ares → Mars, Apollo → Apollo (same), Hephaestus → Vulcan, Hermes → Mercury, Hera → Juno, Athena → Minerva, Demeter → Ceres, Artemis → Diana, Aphrodite → Venus, Dionysus → Bacchus.

In the Greek tradition, Zeus was placed on the island of Crete by his mother because it was prophesied that he would kill his father Cronus and take over the throne. This led to Cronus eating all his children save Zeus, who was able to flee to Crete and hide in a cave. After abducting the beautiful daughter of the Phoenician king of Tyre, Zeus had to flee Crete and that is when he came to the Greek mainland. It is naturally agreed upon by most scholars that the Minoan culture on Crete was the precursor to the Greek civilization. The Greeks themselves never claimed their Olympian gods came from heaven. Zeus came to the Greek mainland by swimming from Crete, Aphrodite came via the sea from the Near East (Cyprus), Poseidon came from Asia Minor on horse, and Athena came from the lands known today as Israel, Iraq, and Iran. There is very little doubt in most scholars' minds that the Greek religion came from Asia Minor and the Mediterranean Islands. The relationship with the number twelve and the pantheon in deed came from Asia Minor and the surrounding lands.

A New Order of the Ages

It is the same with the cultures from the Far East. The Vedas are a composition of hymns and sacrificial formulas, as well as general maxims attributed to the gods. Hinduism was the ancient religion of India and considered the Vedas to be its canon. They were written in an ancient Indo-European language, the predecessor of Sanskrit, Greek, Latin, and other European languages. When the Vedas were translated many similarities were found between them, the Greek tradition and other religious customs. Just like the Greek gods, the gods from the Vedas were all part of one large family. They married one another, fought one another, interbred with mortals, and interfered in human affairs. The head of the Devas was Kash-Yapa, him and his consort Prit-Hivi producing ten children. This family made up the pantheon of twelve deities, each member given a sign of the Zodiac and a celestial body. When Indra took over as supreme deity of the pantheon he was known by the symbols of lightning and thunder, just like Zeus. He also had to share dominion of Earth with his two brothers, Vivashvat and Agni. These three can be likened unto Zeus, Poseidon, and Hades. Agni was responsible for bringing fire down from heaven so mankind could use it. In the Greek tradition it was Prometheus who stole fire from heaven.

One region of Asia Minor was known as Anatolia, and it is here where the Hittite civilization was birthed. The supreme deity of the Hittites was Teshub, and he was associated with thunder and lightning, also like Zeus. He was known as "the Bull," bull worship being prominent in ancient Hittite culture, as it was in Greece. On Crete, the Minoan king Minos had a wife named Pasiphae who mated with a bull producing a half-man, half-bull child. This child was called the Minotaur as bull worship is often depicted in Minoan artwork. Most of this type of artwork is accompanied by a cross symbol. This cross could be a depiction of the cross of the Zodiac and the bull worship could be a reference of the constellation of Taurus, the heavenly bull. When Teshub was rendered in drawing he was usually seen sitting on a bull. His nemesis, Yanka, was a dragon he had to battle to achieve full supremacy over Earth. This translates to Zeus fighting Typhon. Yanka literally translates to "serpent." Predating Hesiod's tale of theology, the Hittite version was known as the *Kingship in Heaven*. In this epic, Alalu is king of the gods who has his position taken over by Anu. Anu, in turn, was defeated in battle by Kumarbi. There is little hesitation on the part of scholars in accepting the *Kingship in Heaven* as the forerunner to the *Theogony*, as it was composed over a thousand years previous.

When the Hittite stories were translated, scholars were astonished to find that Sumerian pictographic signs, syllables, and whole words were contained within the works. It became obvious that not only did the Hittites study the Sumerian language, they also borrowed from the Sumerian pantheon of gods. Anu, Antu, Enlil, Ninlil, Ea, and Ishkur are names seen in both pantheons. When the Hittite people had migrated to Babylon circa 1,500 B.C.E., the Sumerians had long been departed, so how did their language, religion, and literature come in the hands of the Hittites? For this answer we must look to another group of people encompassing the area between Sumer/Akkad and Anatolia. In light of the facts that the Hurrians absorbed Sumerian religion and myth and that they comingled with the Sumerians in the third millennium B.C.E., no connection is left unscathed. The Hittite "gods of old" were the gods from the Hurrian culture, which were the gods from Sumer.

The Egyptians followed suit as well, borrowing from earlier religions, ideas, and pantheons. All Egyptian celestial affairs were governed by the divine number twelve. The heavens were divided into three parts, each containing twelve celestial bodies. The afterworld was divided into twelve parts. Twelve hour intervals composed day and night. The Egyptian pantheon included twelve deities, the head of which was Ra-Amen. Ra brought forth Geb (Earth) and Nut (sky). His depiction was a winged globe, a symbol recurrently seen on ancient tablets from Mesopotamia. Hitherto, we have a story line: the Romans adopted their pantheon from the Greeks, who adopted theirs from the Hittites. The Hittites were influenced by the Hurrians, who no doubt took their culture from Sumer. Akkad and Babylon were establishments which branched from the cities of Sumer, and they in turn influenced the ancient people living in India who composed the Vedas. In this argument, the point of origin is of course Sumer, the land of the original gods who "from heaven to earth came" before 4,000 B.C.E. Sumer, the place all organized human life appeared suddenly. Cro-Magnon man was abruptly transformed into homo-sapien. How did this happen so quickly and urgently? It is because everything on Earth was bequeathed from the gods.

It is bright as day that Anu, Jehovah, Marduk, Enlil, and the other extraterrestrials that came to earth were the "gods" referenced in the Bible, the Eastern scriptures, the Greek and Roman cultures, and ancient

Mesopotamia. Of all the thousands of tables found and deciphered a story was depicted, however fragmented. In this narrative, a race of reptilian extraterrestrial beings came to earth and created a worker class to mine gold for them. The workers called their gods the "Nephilim" or when translated, "those who from heaven to earth came." The gods who came down gave themselves a numerical rank based on a sexagesimal numerical system. The highest number was 60 and was assigned to Anu, king of the gods. The pantheon of the gods consisted of 12 deities. The six male gods in the pantheon were given the multiples of ten and the six female gods were given numbers ending in a five. The table appears below:

Male		Female	
60	Anu	55	Antu
50	Enlil	45	Ninlil
40	Ea/Enki	35	Ninki
30	Nanna/Sin	25	Ningal
20	Utu/Shamash	15	Inanna/Ishtar
10	Ishkur/Adad	5	Ninhursag

Male/Female gods of Sumer

It is of palpable observation that the gods from the Sumerian tablets were the very gods from Nibiru. Nibiru was often illustrated as a globe with wings, an image glimpsed in many traditions. The pantheon of 12 gods from Nibiru has directly influenced the most ancient theological cultures, and as you will see, this has led to the clout witnessed today.

Religious symbolism

Keeping in mind how history repeats itself, a panorama of pictures and symbols seem to echo throughout societies all around the world. Inherent in every picture is a thousand words, or maybe even more. When one is confined to a particular area it becomes difficult to see how an image can mean something totally opposite of what you think. One example is the iron cross, a cross with its arms splayed out in equal fashion on all sides. It was used as a military decoration issued by King Friedrich Wilhelm III of Prussia in Breslau on March 10, 1813 and was also given as a sign of bravery among soldiers and sometimes among civilians during the Napoleonic Wars, the Franco-German War, World War I and World War II. Its meaning is "as above, so below," a dictum adopted by the Teutonic Knights of Malta and the Knights Templar. Before, it was a universal symbol denoting the similarity between the microcosm and the macrocosm, the atom and the universe, which is really just an elementary particle in an even larger universe. Furthermore, it was used as an official emblem of the German Army from 1871 to 1915, and in 1956 symbolized the Bundeswehr, the new German armed forces. Black is the traditional color of the cross with red or white trim, although it takes on numerous forms.

It replaced the German swastika when that symbol was banned and has since evolved into a wider variety of shapes and decorations. The Iron Cross has become very iconic in recent decades. It has been worn by bikers, skinheads, and hot-rodders promoting non-conformity and a "tough guy" image due to its militaria connotations. Adolf Hitler used to wear the Iron Cross pinned to his uniform. American surfers endorsed the image in the 1960s, many plundering old war metals from their fathers and seeing the symbol as freedom from authority. The early Christian churches of the 20th century must have employed cynical overtones when adopting the Iron Cross as an official pennant. Kingdom Church places the symbol on the front cover of many of their magazines, and I don't know how many countless churches erect the symbol on top of their steeples. For those of you fundamentalists you can buy online "hardcore Christian" memorabilia. For only a limited time you can buy a Christian Iron Cross shirt that says, "Hardcore Christian: I am a prisoner of Jesus Christ." How ironic. The prisoners of war who saw this symbol on German military officers during World War Two are now prisoners of the church's anointed savior and of the church itself.

The swastika is another major symbol that has cropped up almost in every culture. It represents a fire wheel, but in metaphysics we call it a "chakra." Both the Earth and human body contain chakras, which are like spinning vortexes of energy denoting varying aspects of consciousness. The swastika can be depicted in many forms. It also represents the Sun because it is like fire that spins around in a circle. When the sun's radiation field strikes Earth, it merges with the planet's electromagnetic field and the effect looks sort of like a swastika. Of course, this can only be viewed from space, but the ancients knew this because they were in contact with aliens. No matter how it is depicted, the swastika generally stands for the same thing:

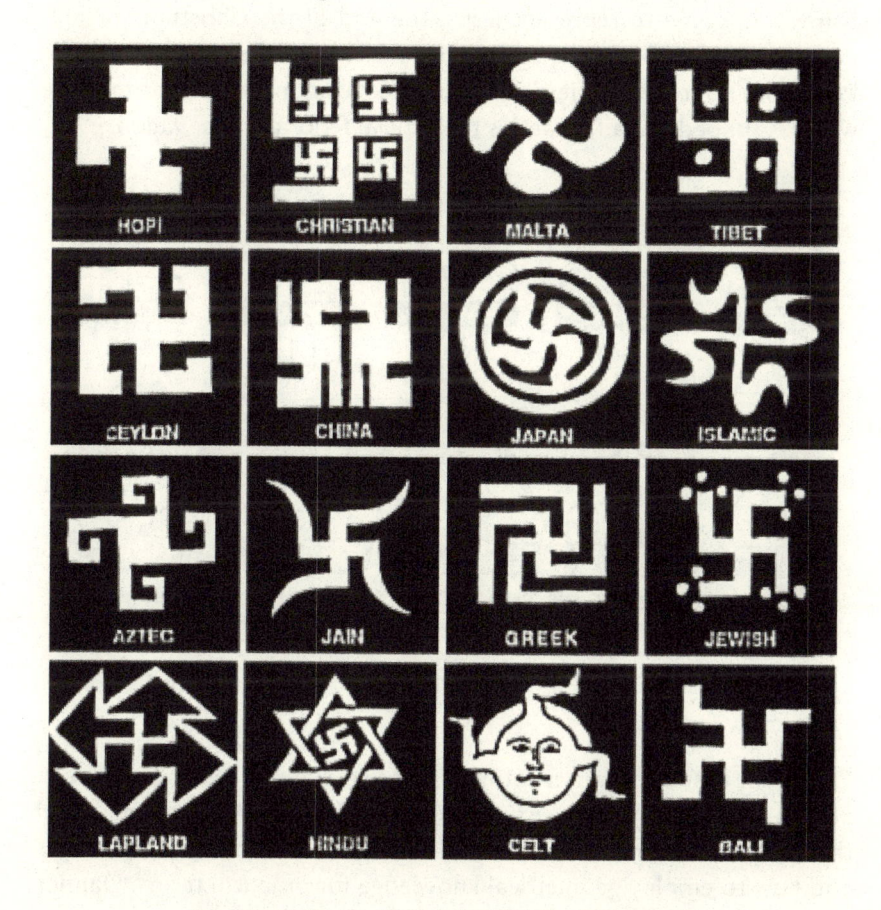

The Swastika and its cultural interpretations

The Hindu version is very interesting.

Another symbol of the Christian church and Jesus is the fish. Many people put the Jesus fish on the back of their cars with little idea of what it really means. The fish does not represent Jesus, it represents the constellation of Pisces. In 2005 an ancient church was discovered buried under prison ground in Israel. A large mosaic tiled the floor and depicted was two fish, facing opposite directions and stacked on top of each other. This two fish picture is a classic representation of the age of Pisces. In the Bible, Jesus comes across two fishermen and says,

"Come and I will make you fishers of men," and later feeds an entire crowd of people with a few loaves of bread and two fish. Eventually the fish would come to represent Jesus, the god of the Christian religion. Predating Jesus, however, Dagon was the Piscean fish god. The Catholic Pope does not represent Jesus, he represents Dagon. In fact, the mitre he wears is shaped like a fish and is the official fedora of the Dagon.

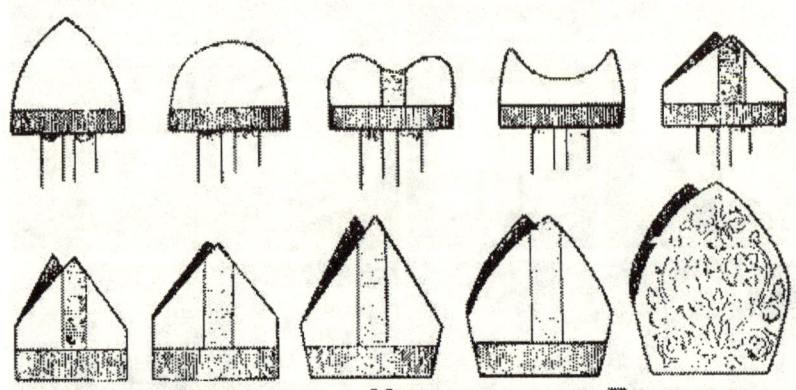

DEVELOPEMENT OF THE MITRE FROM THE ELEVENTH CENTURY TO THE PRESENT TIME

The mitre

One of the first historians in Babylon was Berosus and he wrote about an animal called Oannes whose body was that of a fish. He taught mankind the sciences and arts of every kind, how to build temples, compile laws and how to employ geometrical knowledge for practical terms. Oannes later became Dagon, the fish god. The hat the Pope wears is a direct offshoot of the symbol often attributed to Dagon. The Pope does not represent Christianity, he represents the Piscean Age supposedly initiated in 1 C.E. This too, is untrue. The Piscean age actually started a century before the generally accepted dawn of the new era.

Just as Dagon is the god of the Piscean age, so is Saturn the god of earlier ages. The cult of Saturn was originally a Semitic group who worshiped the god Saturn, referring to the planet Saturn (Saturn is also a pagan Egyptian god). Renderings of the god Saturn usually depict him bearing a sickle. Along with the hammer held by Thor, the sickle and hammer combined form the memento of communism. In its primitive form the swastika also resembles the hammer of Thor as each side bears the resemblance of a stick hammer. Also, the sickle of Saturn relates to the sickle used by Zeus to castrate his father Cronus. Together, the sickle and hammer represent both usurpation of the throne (sickle) and the power of authority (hammer). Black was the color attributed to Saturn, which is why black robes are seen everywhere today. When you graduate from school you wear a black robe, the same black robes worn by judges. The mortarboards perched on top of graduates' heads represent the square mortarboards used by Freemason's for their plaster. It was how temples were built. A school, just like a courtroom, is nothing more than a temple. It is a temple where the god Saturn is worshiped, but in conventional society these details are covert, not overt. Alumnus is a Masonic word, and that is why when you graduate from high school or college you become an alumni, an initiate in the great order of the god Saturn.[18]

The control of education in the United States lies in the hands of the Freemasons who employ their symbols everywhere. When you pay 'tuition' to gain entry into a 'university,' you are disregarding your "intuition" to receive indoctrination concerning a condensed form of "universal" laws. When you receive a 'master's' degree you are in effect gaining a Masonic distinction in a particular "degree." There are varying levels of initiation of Freemasonry, so you might hear that someone is a 33rd degree mason. This is the highest level. Many illuminati are at this level. Degrees are purely Sabaean in nature. In ancient times, a person was given a degree when they effectively demonstrated that they, like the Sun, had ascended to an exalted place. Once you had mastered the stars, hence "mas-Star," you had acquired the next level of degree. The true meaning of 'graduation' is "gradual indoctrination."

Judges and Roman Catholic priests wear black robes because they are above the law. They are the god Saturn imposing the law. Instead of a sickle, though, they carry a hammer, the hammer of Thor. Judges use the hammer, or gavel, to declare the Law of the Land. The law of the land is civil law and is governed over by the demi-gods. That is why when ships are approaching land they must dock in the harbor and sign a certificate of manifest, declaring all goods brought forth onto the land. When your mother births you she must sign a birth certificate. Just like

---

[18] Jordan Maxwell, "Hidden Roots of Religion," http://www.jordanmaxwell.com/articles/religion/index.html.

a certificate of manifest, your mother must declare all goods (you) she is delivering to the "land." That is also why when a ship is in harbor it is "birthed" in port. It is 'birthing' goods to be brought onto the land, which are then under the rule of the demi-gods. When your mother's water broke before she had you, a parallel is drawn between her "water" and the "harbor" ships dock into. Maritime Admiralty Law is the law of water and the banks. You are in fact the property of the New York Stock Exchange. There is a code of numbers on your social security card which corresponds to a single dollar bill with the exact same code on it. Currently, there are nearly seven billion dollar bills bearing everyone's birth certificate numbers. Just as the goods brought forth from ships are property of the "law of the land," when you are brought forth into this world you are the property of the New York Stock Exchange. That is why everything costs money. You are property and therefore you must pay to live on the planet you are born on. People go to work every day because they must pay off the debt owed the Federal Reserve Bank when they loan the United States government money. The government gives the Federal Reserve everyone's birth certificate number as property in collateral for the loaned money.

 The Ten Commandments were said to have been engraved on stone tablets because of the expression "breaking the law." When you break the law you are metaphorically breaking the stone tablets carried by Moses. The reason judges sit on a three tier high platform is because it is a representation of the first three degrees of Freemasonry (Blue degrees of initiation). This same tritier platform is encountered in the room inhabited by Congress. In Latin, 'bench' means "bank" and the judge rules from the bench because he is ruling from the bank. No matter what decision he makes he will still get paid. Altars in many Protestant and Catholic churches are also three tiers high. Just as congregations at church stand up to recognize the entry of the priest, all must rise in courtrooms when the judge walks in. The same types of pews are seen in both churches and courtrooms and this has been so for centuries. When you rise to pay homage to either the priest or the judge you are in fact acting out the rising of the Sun every morning.

 The game of tennis is a good analogy for the way courtrooms operate. When you play a game of tennis with someone you hit a ball back and forth from the back court to the front court. When lawyers defend their clients they bounce back and forth their statements between the defendant court and the prosecution court. The judge takes a "recess" because his is in "court" playing a game. When a witness is asked to place his/her hand on the Old/New 'Testament' they are swearing that they will give an accurate and verifiable "testimony." When they come up to give their statements they must ascend a platform in order to reach the witness stand. Judges sit on a platform a level higher because they are the authority. The audience sits on the first level. In church, you must usually ascend two levels before you reach the place where the pastor gives the sermon. He speaks from the third level because in Egypt it was always done that way.

Also in ancient Egypt, the lawgiver was the sheriff and was always male. In today's society the sheriff is usually male and he represents the "riff" between "she" and he, the division between male and female. Males are usually dominant and expansive, while females are compassionate and passive. The law is very dominating. If you break the law you go to jail, and the judge (who is usually male) has the largest vote. It is instilled into our minds that if you do wrong you will be punished. The police do not help you when you get in trouble, they handcuff you. These are all patriarchal characteristics of a society. The Merkabah is a three dimensional star tetrahedron and represents the union between male a female. The badge worn by the Egyptian sheriffs was a six pointed star, a two dimensional representation of the three dimensional star tetrahedron. This is another symbol for the god Saturn. Sheriffs in the Wild West also wore the six pointed star, as do many still today. Ever wonder where the number 666 comes from? It is not a sign of the devil; it has to do with Saturn. Saturn is the 6th planet from the Sun, Saturday (or "Saturn" day) is the 6th day of the week, and Saturn's symbol was the six pointed star—hence, '666.' Also, the 6th chakra of the human energy system is the 3rd eye chakra. 6, 3 times wields 666.[19]

Just as angels were always depicted with rings or haloes around their head, Saturn is the only planet in our solar system with rings around it. When you get married today you get married before the god Saturn and a ring is exchanged. When Catholic monks shaved their head during the Middle Ages they did so in a circular fashion. Another name for Saturn is

---

[19] In the Bible, "666" is the number of the Beast, the Antichrist. It represents the future rule of the pagan God Saturn, or Satan. Saturn and Satan are two names for Lucifer. In the higher degrees of Freemasonry, Jahbulon is the real god. At the 33rd degree, Jahbulon is revealed as Lucifer.

El. That is why 'el' appears as either a prefix or suffix to names of gods, people, places, and labels in the Bible: elect, elder, elevated, elohim, temple, circle, gospel, apostle, angel, disciple, Michael, Uriel, Raphael, Gabriel, Emmanuel, Bethel, and many others. When witches cast a spell on you they are said to "hex" you. Hex denotes '6'. When they do this they usually chant a particular passage or phrase three times, hence '666.' The word Israel is another representation of past themes. The Elites are the international bankers who run the world today. Elite comes from Isra-ELITE. Isis was the Egyptian moon goddess. Ra was the sun god of Egypt. Saturn was the god of the Elohim. Isis (Is), Ra, and Elohim (El) = IsRaEl.

As far as Islam, Mecca, the holiest site in Islam, houses a large black cube called the Kabba that is worshiped every day. The same cube is found in Vatican Square. Black, of course, is the color of Saturn. Yahweh was known to the ancient Jews and Muslims as the Tetragramaton, meaning "four-letter God." When Yahweh was written down in ancient scripture it was usually chalked as YHWH. The Kabbalah from Jewish mysticism comes from 'KabbaAllah' meaning "Cube God." This is also where the Muslim god Allah comes from. When the ancient Semites worshiped their god they gathered around a large black cube and walked in circles around it in ceremonial fashion. It is from this origin where the Masonic "circling the square" expression comes from. The 'G' in the freemason emblem denotes "geometry" or "god," these two correlating because the universe was thought to be based on geometric forms. Also, God was called by the freemasons the "Grand Architect." That is why a compass and a T-square adorn the Masonic emblem. Just as people used to encircle their cube god Kabba, Masons today use a compass and T-square to encircle their god of sacred geometry. Statues of gigantic black squares can be found in Santa Ana, New York, Denmark, Australia, and many other places.

In Islamic myth, Muhammad ascended to heaven on the famous rock escorted by the angel Gabriel. The Dome of the Rock is an Islamic shrine erected on Temple Mount in Jerusalem in 600 C.E. It was won back by the Israelites on June 7, 667; (666). The Dome's outer walls measure 60 feet wide and 36 feet high. $60 = 6 \times 10$ and $36 = 6 \times 6$; (666). The Templum Domini, a shrine constructed by the Knights Templar adjacent to the Dome of the Rock, was claimed to be the site of the ancient Temple of Solomon. To understand the Temple of Solomon one

A New Order of the Ages

must go back to Babylon. The conspiracy of religion today hearkens back to the worship of the god Saturn and the number 666. Rome was not called so when it was first instituted. It was called Saturnia or "the city of Saturn." In many cultures Saturn was associated with Lucifer and evil.

With the fall of the divine feminine, the advent of phallic worship has also dominated society. The phallus, of course, represents a patriarchal society. The Lia Fail Stone in England is a holy shrine depicting a large phallus. The Worldwide Church of God in Pasadena California has phallic-shaped bushes all along the perimeter. Countless other churches employ this symbol in architecture and design. Sculptures unearthed of the god Shiva show him often with an erect phallus. There is also a phallic sculpture in the Dead Sea Scrolls in Israel. Most church steeples are stone representations of phallic worship done in the days predating Christianity and Judaism. The more we change the more we stay the same. The United States today is no different than Nazi Germany in the 1940's. The group procedure of Christian kids and adults gathering around a pole with a United States flag perched on top is very symbolic, like the way men and women did in the Nazi religion, but they were not the first. Children gathering around a pole was a pagan ritual practiced in ancient Greece and Rome called the "Maypole Dance." It was done before the advent of spring, the pole representing the earth's axis, the phallus, and male fertility. Min was a Greek god exhibiting fertility, and sculptures of unearthed reveal him with an erect phallus. Min was also an Egyptian god, renderings of him showing likewise. The Bethel Stone referenced in the Old Testament, the one Jacob used as a pillow, was not really pillow-shaped. It was in fact a stone representing a phallus in which the pagans of the ancient world poured oil over, signifying the anointing of the Christos. The Christos was not Jesus—it was a sexual ceremony practiced when choosing "sons of God." The stone was called a Lingam. An online encyclopedia has this to say about it:

> In the temples there were smaller, human-sized linga, or priapic statues of the gods, intended to deflower brides before their wedding night. This operation was what biblical terminology called "opening the matrix." Firstborn children were regarded as fathered by the god upon mortal virgins, because of the defloration custom—which was prevalent not only in southeastern Asia but also throughout the Middle East and

in Rome. Such divinely begotten "sons of God" were often chosen for lives of religious devotion. The phallus or lingam was usually painted red and anointed with holy oil, to which the Greeks gave the name *chrism*. Thus the divinely begotten one was given the name of Christos, meaning "anointed." Of course, oil was necessary to the insertion of a stone phallus into a virgin. Later, the oil itself became a symbol. Kings' heads were anointed with oil, being likened to the "head" of the god-penis. (Encyclopedia Britannica online, 2005)

How interesting.
Most people today are in no way cognizant of the fact that they covertly worship the god Saturn, a pagan star god whose symbol was the six-pointed star. The Star of David is not Jewish at all. Saturn was known in Talmudic Hebrew as a representation of the Shabbat, or what was frequently called the "Sabbath." So remember the Sabbath and keep it holy? No, remember your patronage to the god Saturn. Shabbat references to the seventh day of the week in the Jewish calendar. In St. Peter's Basilica in Rome sits a statue of Jupiter that has been modified and re-titled as a statue of St. Peter. Many thousands of Catholics who kiss the feet of the statue have no idea that it is in fact Jupiter. Everything unfolds from a single source. We are all Greeks and Romans worshiping the same gods. Circe was a Greek goddess who maintained herself by hypnotizing men and seducing them, thereby taking their minds away and turning them into animals. Worship of Circe traveled to Scotland where Circe became "Kirk." The Scottish word 'Kirk' then became "Church" in England. Churches are money-making enterprises, and that is why they are divided into "denominations," just like money.

The Ten Commandments, large stone tablets believed to be truly iconic in the Judeo-Christian sense, are replete throughout medieval pictography. The laws themselves reverberate a spiritual significance, however they have been used by the Church as its own. Most fundamentalists think they were two large stone tablets carried in each hand by Moses as he descended Mount Sinai. Renderings of what most scholars would call the tablets, in their most simplistic form, take the shape of two elliptical-topped tablets standing adjacent to each other, or in other words, two phallic-shaped stones. The phallus appears again, but this time with a twin. The twin phalluses represent the real Babel Stone used to anoint the Christos. Two is of classic Masonic numerical symbology—two fish, two towers, two fishermen, two royal lines of D.N.A. (reptilian and human). When people flash the number two with their fingers a 'V' is displayed. When Mason pledges flash the 'V' they are not saying, "peace, man." The 'V' represents two things—the chalice or the female womb and the Roman numeral five. The five represents the fifth element. The fifth element, spirit, is close guarded by the Illuminati who wish to keep the masses ignorant.

Spirit is said to be "all encompassing," "all-seeing," and "all-knowing." The true meaning of the pyramid with the all-seeing eye on the back of the one dollar is very elusive. Whether the eye represents the third eye of the Chitauri, the right eye of Amen-Ra, or the hidden knowledge kept by Lucifer and his secret societies, parallels can no doubt be drawn between the two. While there are subtle nuances behind the eye, the meaning of the pyramid is concrete. It is in effect a ruling hierarchy, each higher level embodying more knowledge and greater authority. Those at the bottom serve the very foundation of the enterprise. They compose the worker class, the drones. While not entirely programmed with complex algorithms, the simple algorithms that run our everyday lives attest to the structure of our society. The people at the top run everything. They have all the money, prestige, and power. The vanity of their presence traces an outline of stereotypical fascism penetrating into the very core of the Matrix. The might is the right to rule, the position of demi-god. The Global Elite serve their hidden masters, the prison warders, the very constructs of the eye itself. The reason the eye sits above the pyramid in a non-connecting fashion is because it represents the hidden authority which stands above the people. The Global Elite are the visible authority, while the real prison warders are never seen on television or in public political rallies. They are rarely even talked about. To them, the people must never know who truly rules them. If they did, much chaos would ensue, and the goal is always to maintain order out of chaos, not vice versa.

The Latin phrase surrounding the pyramid on the back of the one dollar bill reads, "Annuit Coeptis, Novus Ordo Seclorum," or in other words, "Our enterprise is crowned with success, a new order of the ages." The title of this book is derived from this phrase. There are thirteen letters in the first title referencing the thirteen bloodline families (or Magi), this number appearing in other sectors as well as can be seen in the thirteen arrows and thirteen leaves on the olive branch clutched in the claws of the eagle. Originally, ancient cultures employed the use of the phoenix, which later adapted to the image of the eagle. The phoenix embodies rebirth and the secret of reincarnation kept by the Illuminati. There are also thirteen stars in the star tetrahedron above the eagle's head which represents a Merkabah vehicle, as well as thirteen stripes in the American flag. Moving back to the pyramid you can see that a star tetrahedron can also be traced with lines connecting the 'O,' 'A,' and 'S' in the phrasing as one triangle and lines connecting the top of the pyramid with the letters 'N' and 'M' forming the reverse triangle. Two miniscule snake heads adorn the top two corners on the back of the bill and on the front a tiny owl is perched on the top left corner of the '1.' The owl represents wisdom, Lucifer, and also Queen Semiramis from Babylon.

Two other important symbols are the acorn and the equilateral triangle inscribed within a circle with a point in the middle. The acorn represents the pineal gland of the human brain, which is the physical annexation point to the protoplasmic spirit (light) body.[20] In ancient cultures, the walking stick or ruling staff of a chief was often adorned with an acorn at the top because it represented spiritual wisdom. The other symbol, the equilateral triangle inscribed within a circle, denotes Satan's ruling hierarchy and is referenced by Madame Helena Blavatsky in many of her alchemical and occult writings.

---

[20] According to Dr. Bill Deagle, the pineal gland in the human brain is not only the center for third eye vision but also the connecting point for the spiritual body.

A New Order of the Ages

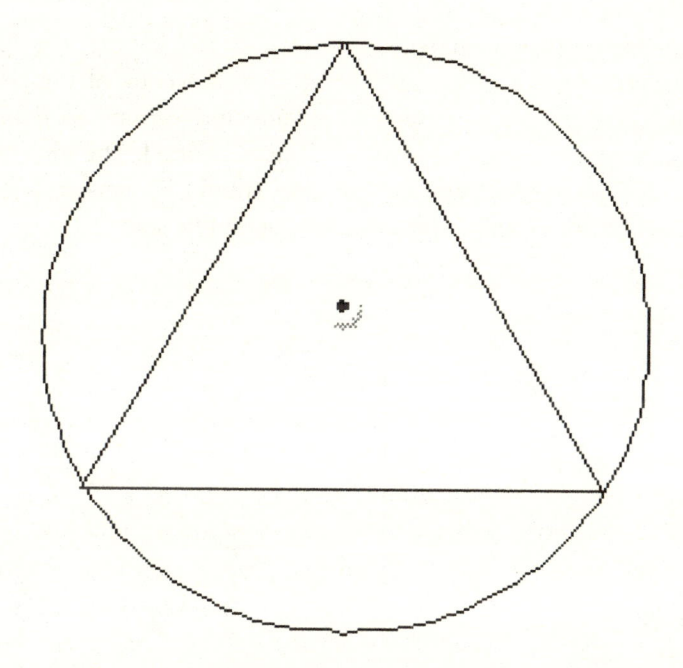

The hierarchy of Satan

The circle represents the ignorant and controlled masses while the triangle denotes the ruling hierarchy of Satan (Lucifer/Jahbulon/Saturn) positioned in a pyramidal ruling system. The black dot exemplifies Satan himself as the sole ruler over Hell on Earth.

    The wizard lurks behind the electronic curtain, his wand conjuring up a gossamer reality for the everyman, merely electrical signals fired into his forebrain. Clusters of photons and electrons enter his eyes and pass through neural pathways where they discombobulate and assimilate a structured reality. For everyman, everyday reality is not the truth, it is wholly a mental construct offered on a silver platter by his superiors. Why does everyman accept this diabolical gift? Because his eyes are entranced by the colorful reflections off the silver platter, an illusion not fully escaped from. The vibrational prison which entraps everyman grows stronger everyday as the belief that this is the only reality solidifies into dense thoughtforms. Now, everyman has reached a fork in the road. Three paths lay ahead of his gaze. The culmination of events has led to a varied ulterior. Currently, the flow of life produced by all the inhabitants of Earth is projecting three distinct possibilities for the future. In the 1960's an emblem was forged for this import. The "peace sign" adopted by the Hippie culture is a carbon copy of the symbol from this epoch, where new ways of thinking and learning set the stage for a mass demonstration of liberty and justice for all. The three paths aforementioned are laid out as such and should be viewed from the perspective of one traveling south down the middle line:

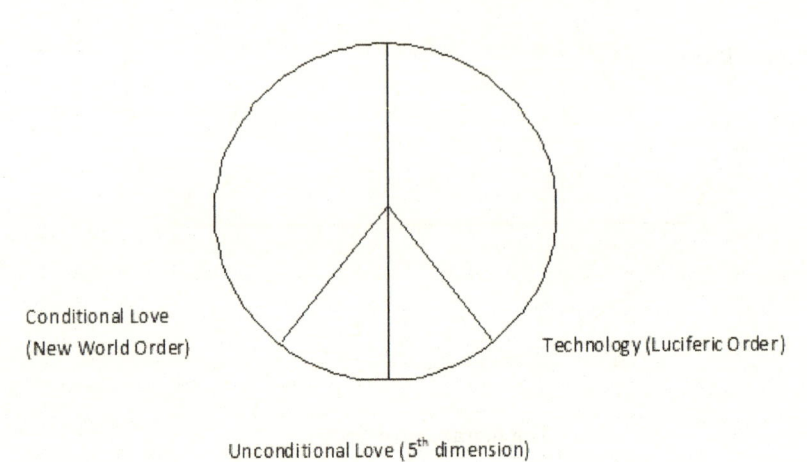

Conditional Love (New World Order) — Technology (Luciferic Order)

Unconditional Love (5th dimension)

The Peace Sign as a future signpost

The ruling elite wish for the New World Order headed by Lucifer. David Spangler, Director of Planetary Initiative at the United Nations once said, "No one will enter the New World Order unless he or she will make a pledge to worship Lucifer. No one will enter the New Age unless he will take a Luciferian initiation."

That Old Time Religion

Religion and history are astro-theological. According to Zecharia Sitchin, a scholar capable of translating ancient proto-Indo-European languages, the "men of renown" referenced in the Christian canon is a mistranslation. It should say, "men of the sky vehicles." That makes a lot more sense. In fact, the English word hero comes from the Egyptian word 'heru' whose precise meaning is, "a human being who was neither a god nor a daemon." A daemon was a spirit who influenced events on the physical plane and communicated with human beings. It wasn't until later that daemon became 'demon' and took on malevolent connotations. The Greek poet Homer wrote about heroes such as Hercules who were exalted above mortal men. Another poet, Pindar, used the word hero to denote a race 'between gods and men.' Many first century writers studied at the University of Alexandria and learned the true history of the human race on Earth. According to several novellas and other written documents, the word angel originally meant "messenger" but later became associated with nonhuman entities interbreeding with humans. Angels, daemons, heroes, and the men of renown are nothing more than references to the extraterrestrial presence on the Earth. The "divine right to rule," the bestowment of the gods' blessing on a king or a pharaoh, originated in Sumer, the first major human civilization on this planet. That old time religion was not the ones known today. It was the worship of the demi-gods, the bloodlines, the heroes, the hybrid children of the angels or the gods. The theme of royal families claiming the right to rule because of their bloodline is seen all around the world and continues even today. The Egyptian Pharaohs were a monumental testament to this divine right as they would don python-like hats and elongated lizard chins to signify their divine powers.

Today, the Magi and their extraterrestrial parents hide behind the Jewish conspiracy, although it is only a façade. The great personages of so-called "Jewish" history like Abraham, Jaacob, David, and Solomon were not Hebrews at all nor did they live in a holy land called Israel. They were in fact pharaohs of the Egyptian royal line. The pharaohs of the Hyksos, or the "Shepherd Kings," ruled in Egypt. In lists of kings dug up in Sumer, two names appear as "Shepherd Kings" as one can take into account how similar the Egyptian and Sumerian religions are. Shamash was the Mesopotamian sun god while Ra was his Sumerian counterpart, both gods depicted as a winged sun-disk. Historical scholar Ralph Ellis writes in one of his studies:

> The historical record of Sumer runs substantially parallel to that of Egypt, dating back to some 3,000 B.C., with king lists much the same as to be found in Egypt. Historically, it would appear that at some point in history, elements of the Sumerian culture sailed across to

Egypt and that the first dynasty kings of Egypt, therefore, had much in common with the Sumerian peoples.

According to Ellis, the Hyksos were Egyptians who followed the religion of the sheep when the astrological age of Aries commenced. The reigning pharaoh at the time, still practicing bull worship, was in opposition to this new epoch initiated by the priests at the mystery school at Heliopolis. The Shepherd Kings worshiped the sheep instead of the bull.

Abraham was the son of an Egyptian pharaoh and became the first Hyksos king whose real name was Sheshi, although his throne name was Mayebra. Place the M on the end and you have a perfect phonetic match for Abram: Ma-aye-bra → aye-bram → Abram, or what later came to be Abraham. In Christianity Isaac was Abraham's son, but in real life his name was Anather and he was a Hyksos pharaoh. Isaac's son was Jacob, the pharaoh whose throne name was Jacobaam. The Israelite (Hebrew) exodus out of Egypt occurred at the time of the reign of Jacobaam and was when the Hyksos line departed the region. The royal line of Hyksos returned from exile in Canaan to Egypt with Joseph. No, not the Biblical Joseph; this Joseph became chief minister of the pharaoh and married the daughter of a priest at the mystery school at Heliopolis. This daughter was from the Egyptian royal bloodline. I must insert an important note here: it is always the D.N.A. of the mother that determines the purity of the child in regards to bloodline D.N.A. Joseph was the first born of his father Jacob's wife Rachel. Rachel was of pure D.N.A., thus Joseph was the heir to the throne of Egypt. Joseph's wife was also from the Egyptian royal bloodline. Tuthmoses (Moses) was from a family of priest-kings, his brother being the pharaoh Amenhotep IV. Amenhotep IV usurped the right to rule from his brother when Tuthmoses expressed altercation with the ruling Hyksos line and hence the early Illuminati bloodlines.

Amenhotep married Nefertiti from the line of Joseph because he knew they were from the same bloodline. During his reign, Amenhotep sought to move the capital of Egypt to Amarna and with it a new monotheistic religion. In the religious conflict that ensued Tuthmoses and his followers were exiled to a remote part of Egypt (called Canaan) and placed in stone quarries. The Exodus of the Hebrews from Egypt has traditionally been placed in the reign of Ramasees II, but this cannot have been because if you look you will not find any traces of the Hebrews during the reign of Ramasees II. You will also not find the Temple of Solomon or Jericho in

A New Order of the Ages

any of the archaeological places they are pertained to be. Contemporary evidence has revealed that Moses was born in about 1,540 B.C.E. and was brought up an Egyptian prince during the reign of Neferhotep I. He was also initiated into the mystery school at Heliopolis. Biblical mythology tells us that Moses' brother was Aaron, but we can see now that it was really Amenhotep IV. As an anti-Amenhotep priesthood grew, Tutankhamen (King Tut), Amenhotep's son, was made the new king. He was eight years old at the time.

As he was an initiate in Heliopolis, Tuthmoses was well studied in the Cabala, which taught that the Golden Proportion, *pi*, and the Fibonacci sequence are universal constants explicating the patterns of astronomy, music, and physics. The Hebrews have not left us a large composite of heritage save the Torah, the five books of Moses. The great book of the Cabala is in fact the Zohar, a commentary on the first five books of the Old Testament. The Cabala instructed that as the physical world is simply materialized thought, so words and letters are the means by with this process unfolds. It has been argued that Akhenaten was the source for the monotheistic religion posited by Moses, but paradoxically this cannot be so since Moses, or Tuthmoses, came before Akhenaten. Akhenaten's father was Amenhotep III, who had numerous sons. Among them where Tuthmoses, Akhenaten, and Amenhotep IV. Tuthmoses was the first-born son of the Pharaoh, but he opposed the despotic rule of his family. He led the enslaved Hebrews out of Egypt during the Exodus, but the question is, who were the Hebrews?

In 2,000 B.C.E., Ibiru was a clan of royal descendents from Ebla (an ancient city in Syria), and they were the wealthiest miners and traders of precious metals. By 1850 B.C.E., the Ibiru became known as the Hibiru and it is this word that is the root of 'Hebrew.' The Hibiru had acquired historic knowledge and inventions which made them powerful businessmen. They had also established themselves as influential Egyptian priests and provincial rulers. In Egypt, the Hibiru were granted the settlement of Zion, a major trade center on the Red Sea, and they built a famous channel linking the Red Sea with the Nile River from Zion westward to Cairo.[21] As they reigned Egypt, the Hibiru intermixed with the royal line of the Egyptian pharaohs; Tuthmoses was half royal-Egyptian and half royal-Hyksos. When his younger brother,

---

[21] This is where we get the Jewish political movement of Zionism today. It comes from the Hibiru settlement of Zion bestowed by the Egyptian royal line.

Akhenaten, became ruler, Tuthmoses did not agree with the heretical religious changes instituted henceforth. He left Egypt with a group of Hibiru and founded Jerusalem, which later became a major trade city. Akhenaten later exiled other Hibirus from Egypt who traveled back to Ireland, the original home of the Hibiru (before they set up a colony at Ebla). The Hibiru who traveled back to Ireland eventually merged with other powerful bloodlines of Europe and they became the Phoenicians. The Phoenicians set up the founding colonies of many of the great empires of the ancient and modern world like Greece, Rome, and Persia. They later captured Jerusalem, becoming kings and calling themselves "Israelites" after the new home they crowned Israel. There they merged with the Khazarian bloodline and became what we call today "Jewish."

King Solomon and King David, his father, were also Egyptian pharaohs. David was Psusennes II and Solomon was Sheshonq I. The Eastern Delta lands sheltered the court Tanis of Psusennes I, who was the last pharaoh of the twenty-first dynasty. The true location of the Temple of Solomon (an Egyptian temple, not a Jewish one) was indeed this court palace. The Hebrew name for King David was Duad, djuat being the name for an Egyptian star. This is where we get the Star of David, but it is an Egyptian symbol and not a Jewish one. The Egyptian Pharaoh Psusennes II of the Hyksos bloodlines had an army ready to overthrow the Israelite tribes under King Saul and he had passed this dynasty on to his son, Sheshonq I, who was formerly known as King Solomon.[22] The reason why King Solomon was always portrayed with powers is because he was of the priest-king line, the bloodline of the gods. He recorded his secret knowledge in a book that was later laid in the foundation of the second temple in Jerusalem. Jewish folklore relates that Solomon's reign was filled with gold and silver, but this exaggeration hardly baffles scholars as up until this time the Hebrews had no tradition of building elaborate temples. For this reason, Solomon employed an architect named Hiram Abiff to construct this edifice. In the middle of the temple sat the Holy of Holies containing the Ark of the Covenant and the tablets of Moses. In some ways it was characteristic of the rich temples erected in Babylon, as you can hopefully see by now that the mystery schools of Sumer, Babylon, and Egypt have laid the foundation for the secret societies today that covertly rule the world.

---

[22] Icke, David, *Tales from the Time Loop* (Wildwood, MO: Bridge of Love, 2003), 239.

A New Order of the Ages

The stories depicted in the Judeo-Christian tradition were written by these bloodlines I just discussed. Real characters were inserted into an allegorical story based on the Zodiac, and these doctrines were bound together by the Emperor Constantine during the Council of Nicaea. At the behest of his Draconian rulers, Constantine declared this the new religion. King Solomon, King David, Moses, Ramsees, Jesus, Mary Magdelene, Paul, Abraham, Jacob, Noah, and all the other characters found in the Bible were real historical personages placed in a story based on a monotheistic doctrine demanding worship of a god name Jehovah (YHWH). Jesus was made the pagan sun god of this religion and his twelve disciples represented the twelve signs of the Zodiac. Christmas was celebrated during the winter solstice and Easter was celebrated during the spring equinox, but to the blind followers of Christianity, these dates represented the birth/resurrection of Jesus. The doctrines of the Bible were written by these bloodlines (Hyksos, Phoenician, Roman) so they could control the masses via religion. Islam was set up later to oppose Judaism in the Middle East while Christianity spread rapidly to the West.

Zionism is not about fulfilling Biblical prophecy. The sacred Jewish place, Zion, is claimed to be Jerusalem, the place of Mount Sinai, but this is just a fable. Zionism is really about the global dictatorship of the Egyptian-Sumerian royal bloodlines through Israel. The *Protocols of the Learned Elders of Zion* was written by the same bloodlines in order to have a worldwide doctrine with which to rule the world. The official scapegoat for this world takeover became the Jews, although this lineage is highly controversial. Israel is not the home of the Jews, it is the home of the bloodlines that control the world today. In the last century, most of the presidents of the United States have been genetic members of these bloodlines. Today, President Obama is controlled by the Trilateral Commission, a secret society linked to the Council on Foreign Relations (New York) and the Royal Institute of International Affairs (Great Britain).

The state of Israel today was the place of Mount Sinai and it is controlled by the Rothschild bloodline, which can be traced back to Egypt and the Hyksos kings. In antiquity, their name was "Red Shield" because of their decorum, the Knights Templar bearing similar attire. The Star of David can be seen on the flag of Israel because the Hyksos pharaohs wore a talisman called a "star shield" around their necks for protection. It was in the likeness of a two-dimensional star tetrahedron. The reason the Pope holds a shepherd's crook is because it is a symbol of the Egyptian Shepherd Kings. The title given to the Pope should also be put in its proper place in Egypt under the reign of Apopis II. From Babylon to Rome did the Illuminati (Magi) transplant their operation.

The trinity of Christianity, the Father, Son, and Holy Ghost, is a makeover of the stories from the Babylon church. The Babylonian trinity was Nimrod (the fish), Tammuz (the savior of humanity), and Queen Semiramis (the dove), which is derived from the 'ka,' Egyptian for "soul." In Egypt, Nimrod is Osiris, Tammuz is Horus, and Queen Semiramis is Isis. Both the Egyptians and Babylonians used the story of the immaculate conception to bequeath the stories of Isis and Semiramis, respectively. Isis was the virgin mother of Horus, the sun god, and Semiramis was the virgin of the god Tammuz. The halos used in pictures of Jesus, Mary, John, the disciples, and angels are representations used by the ancients of portraying their sun gods. Many, back when the vibrations of Earth were higher, could see the auras emanating from people, as some who were enlightened had a glowing light projecting from their crown chakras. Auras and halos can be seen in many pictures from long ago. It is a well established fact that Jesus had an aura (halo) as well as Saint Paul and John the Baptist. Even the Buddha is sometimes depicted with a halo around his head.

Ishtar, the Babylonian goddess, is the origin of the Christian celebration of Easter. Ishtar had a son Tammuz who was dubbed "the only begotten son of the Moon goddess and Sun God," Semiramis and Nimrod. Queen Semiramis is said to have descended from the moon in a giant egg, later to be called the "Ishtar egg." The Easter eggs and the Easter bunny come from the Ishtar eggs and the fact that Tammuz was fond of rabbits. Celebrated Illuminati personages go to church, but unlike other people they understand that they are really participating in an ancient pre-Christian and pre-Jewish ritual aimed at commemorating their bloodline. Just like Freemasons worship the Grand Architect, the Egyptian pharaohs were called the "greatest of architects," their Illuminati progeny creating the present-day justice and education systems. The hammers banged in the courtroom by judges are representations of the hammer of Thor and the hammer depicted on the seal of the Freemasons. In fact, the very craft of freemasonry is to rebuild the temple of Solomon, the El-Aqsa Mosque on Temple Mount

A New Order of the Ages

being the temple of Sheshonq I. The secret knowledge from Egypt and Babylon was carried to Rome by one of the first major secret societies called the Comacine Masters. The Dionysian Artificers is the mystery school offshoot of this sacred knowledge. The symbols employed by modern Freemasonry have direct ties to this school in Rome. The British monarchs ruling throughout medieval Europe and even today practiced the Coronation, the crowning ceremonies of the Egyptian pharaohs.

As in Egypt, the right to rule from serpent gods is seen in most ancient tablets and stories.[23] The royal families were created from the gods, whose signs echo throughout all ancient cultures. The Buddhist text in India deals with a list of kings who descended from the Nagas (serpent kings). Hindu legend maintains the Nagas could shapeshift into human and reptilian form interchangeably. The early Chinese emperors were known as the "Lung" or the "Dragons," and many were depicted by artists as having reptilian-like features. The Chinese emperor Huang Ti was said to have been born with a "dragon-like countenance" and conceived by a ray of golden light that entered his mother's womb from Alpha Draconis, the star of the Egyptian god Set. Genetic descent from the reptilian gods has also been witnessed in Central America. The Peruvian Incas were known by the symbol of the snake. The first Mycenaean king of Athens, Greece was drawn as a human with a serpent tail. King Kadmus of Greece was also said to have shapeshifted into a reptile upon his moment of death.

The Illuminati blood drinking rituals where sacrifices transpire are no different from the ceremonies and rituals performed in Sumer and Babylon. The reptilian gods drank human blood and fed off human energy, the story of Dracula perpetuating from these notions. *Dracula* was written by Bram Stoker in 1897, and he claimed his story was inspired from a man called "Vlad the Impaler," the fifteenth century king of Wallachia (a country in what is now Romania). He brutally slaughtered tens of thousands of people and impaled them on stakes, and was also known for eating corpses. Vlad Dracul was his father and an initiate of the Order of the Dragon in the late fifteenth century, an order of the Holy Roman Empire. The most famous vampire legends transpire from this region, which was once known as Transylvania. Like the Chitauri

---

[23] The Annunaki (Sumer), the Children of the Serpent (Africa), the Royal Court of the Dragon (Egypt), and the Nagas (China/India) are only a few examples of this type of serpent worship.

of ancient lore, Dracula has fangs, horns, pale skin, and masquerades around at night. He sleeps during the day in a coffin, this most likely representing the advent of death upon the densification of the material world after the fall from grace. Moreover, the stake in the heart, or the special wood that was used to kill the Chitauri, was also known as "holy wood." Later this became Hollywood.

Heresy, the child of orthodoxy

The wizard who lurks behind the electronic curtain dazzles movie theater audiences world-wide with his wand. He has us all hypnotized by the "magic of Hollywood." In the movie *Fantasia*, Mickey Mouse is a sorcerer who can command ordinary objects to dance with his wand. In *Aladdin*, the Sultan of the kingdom is hypnotized by the Royal Vizier with a stick shaped like a python. In *Breeders*, another classic movie, a doctor and a detective are greatly addled when a string of women are found brutally raped and covered in a strange organic material. After slipping into a coma, the women wake up one by one and hypnotically journey down into the sewers where the doctor and detective find a nest hosting the birthing of other-worldly offspring. This last one is a reference not only to the hypnotism of Hollywood but also the interbreeding done between aliens and Earth human females. All across the globe, audiences are dazzled by the "magic" of Hollywood when they are really being hypnotized and implanted with subliminal programming.

There is a lighter side to the story. To fully comprehend it one must be taken to a new perspective, the perspective of those benevolent higher intelligences who watch over planet Earth. They have no permission, nor do they ever interfere with the free will of humans. They do though, on occasion, send a gift. A gift is not interference because it must be accepted as such. Those who watched World War II from space came to a mindset of great concern after the atomic bombs were dropped on Hiroshima and Nagasaki. The Galactic Council (referred to often as the Galactic Federation of Light) sent out a call to all souls not associated with Earth to journey to the planet and incarnate in order to help out in any way possible. The watchers over Earth were perturbed concerning the idea of atomic warfare (imploding atoms) because this is the only way that the soul matrix can be damaged. The souls who came to help were given a karma shield, which lent them great freedom for their work on Earth.

Karma is like sticky paper. It holds lower vibrational energetic residues, keeping one in the incarnational cycle. The first wave of souls who heard the call and began incarnating in the 1950's had an immensely difficult time adapting to the dense vibrations of Earth. Many attempted suicide. The second wave of souls was not as traumatized, many retaining connections to the outside world (the universe) through channeling abilities. The third wave of souls coming to help Earth encompasses many children being born now and in the last decade. They have 3,4, and 5 strands of D.N.A. and are quick learners. They are typically more evolved than others on the planet from older generations, which is causing disharmony among social groups. Myriad discrepancies have arisen because of the extreme vibrational differences among these varying groups of incumbents.

Many of the third wave souls are diagnosed with Attention Deficit Hyperactivity Disorder because they get bored easily and wander around. They can multitask and are very efficient workers, the medical industry destroying their abilities with drugs such as Ritalin and Adderall, psycho-stimulants composed of numerous types of amphetamines. The children diagnosed with A.D.D. and A.D.H.D. never get "better" because amphetamines raise a person's blood pressure and force the body to work harder. Those diagnosed with an attention deficit disorder really do take on the effects of the supposed disease because of the stimulant drugs, not because of the physician's medical expertise. Adderall and Concerta have replaced Ritalin in most areas of the United States, both drugs carrying a high abuse potential and both being used as "study drugs" at universities. William Frankenberger, a psychology professor at the University of Wisconsin at Eau Claire, conducted a study at the university in 2004 and reported that 14% of the campus had used some form of an A.D.H.D. drug, including Adderall. In more recent studies done across the country, colleges known to be highly competitive had up to 25% of students misusing A.D.H.D. medication. One must also take into account the rate at which people (especially younger people) lie about their drug use.

There is, at this time, the necessary critical mass of new souls for the Earth to make the transition to the 5th dimensional paradigm, however, most people on the planet are still at a low level of consciousness and are holding this process back.[24] More people need to wake up and realize that they have been conned. You are not a victim, you are a god with amnesia. When you incarnate the blinds come down and you forget. It is all part of the learning and evolution process. Your soul is experiencing all of your past and future lives simultaneously, this being the realm of your higher self. Your conscious mind proper (your waking consciousness) can only focus on one life at a time and move along a linear progression until your soul becomes evolved enough to move out of the cycle of reincarnation.

Even Carl Jung admitted that there was a human collective unconscious. He believed that disease occurred when communication between your minds (superconscious, conscious, and subconscious, all of which make up the collective unconscious) shuts off or battens down. The key to this connection is the heart (the physical heart as well as the heart chakra); the physical heart and brain maintain a continuous two-way dialogue. The heart sends far more information to the brain than the brain sends to the heart, as signals sent to the brain influence perception, emotional processing and higher cognitive functions. The heart also generates the strongest rhythmic electromagnetic field in the body. This can be measured in the brain waves of the people around us. According to the HEARTMATH Institute:

> The heart's field is a carrier of emotional information and a mediator of bio-electromagnetic communication, within and outside the body. Research shows our heart's field changes distinctly as we experience different emotions. It is registered in people's brains around us and apparently is capable of affecting cells, water and D.N.A. studied in vitro.

Fear is the negative energy (just as love is the positive) which creates a distinct bio-electric signal and disseminates it to organisms within a community or world. The cells in our body communicate through biophotons, tiny particles of light that act as a single unit of an electromagnetic field; this communication system also exists between organisms and is known as "morphic resonance." When fear dominates the collective conscious or unconscious, that emotion is emitted to every

---

[24] Dolores Cannon, "Convoluted Universe," http://www.youtube.com/watch?v=ihH0L_bffAA (May 3, 2010).

A New Order of the Ages

individual. The only opposing force to this and way to counterbalance is love. Just as there are positive (+) and negative (-) charges in matter (atoms), so too are there positive and negative charges among organisms. Love is the only counterbalancing force.

Your soul contains your collective unconscious (superconscious, conscious, and subconscious minds) and has been measured to weigh anywhere between 14-22 grams. It holds together your physical, emotional, mental, and spiritual bodies, which are just varying frequencies of light. Your physical body is the lowest frequency and your spiritual body is the highest frequency. People are really just holograms, like the universe. When a cephalogram is used, the memories from one conscious mind are beamed into another body that is soul-less. When this is accomplished, you have a walking, talking, breathing cloned personality.[25] Many famous personages are really just clones. As part o the "Plan 2000" the Global Elite are trying to reduce the world's population down to 500 million. When this is brought to fruition the populace will be much easier to control, since it is hard to keep tabs on nearly 7 billion people. Imagine the fright the New World Order specialists would face if 7 billion people decided to stand together. The case of Billy Meir from Sweden is a well-documented event of benevolent alien interaction with people from Earth. The Pleiadians contacted Billy and visited his house on numerous occasions, teaching him metaphysical concepts and helping him to build a meditation catalyst pyramidal machine capable of taking one's consciousness into higher dimensions. They took him, Billy, to the future (remember there are many possible futures) and he took pictures of World War III. In one of these pictures California is underwater and New York City is totally annihilated.[26]

This is not meant to scare you, merely to inform you. The "other side" is not heaven or hell. It is the 4th dimension where there are three dimensions of time and one dimension of space. To move is to move forward or backward in time, not to move to any special x-y-z location. When a soul incarnates into a physical body on Earth it gathers itself at

---

[25] George Green, interview with Project Camelot, http://www.youtube.com/watch?v=sSYXrWIA618.

[26] There are many debunkers on the case of Billy Meier and the Pleiadians. Some say the pictures he took were faked and that he is really working for a secret organization, but that is up for debate. The reason the Pleiadians broke off contact with Billy was because some people in the organization founded by Billy and the aliens grew parsimonious.

the middle point between this reality (three dimensions of space and one dimension of time) and the "other side" (one dimension of space and three dimensions of time). It then attaches itself to the central nervous system of the body it wishes to inhabit, once permission is granted from the higher self and angelic hierarchy. Can you see now why knowledge is power? If everyone knew this there would be no control or suppression. Once you take away knowledge, there are only three currencies left: gold, oil and drugs. Money is not a currency because it is backed by absolutely nothing. Money is only worth its weight in whatever economy distributes it. The bloodline families control all the real currencies, of course, like technology and knowledge. The result? Here are some facts:

- Half of the United States population is over 50 years old
- The average weight of a woman in the United States is 163 pounds
- Fat retains toxins and poisons effectively and that is why everyone is sick all the time
- The population of Earth increases by 250,000 people a day
- Oil is not replenishable like the governments say
- Inflation increases by 20% a year on average
- When you use a cell phone you are microwaving your brain, which is why people get brain cancer
- The current unemployment rate in the United States is 25%
- 1/3 of the United States adult population works for the government at any level
- One branch of the Bank of America only has $2,500 in cash on an average day, the rest is numbers on a computer screen
- 33% of the world's population lives on $1 a day
- According to the Constitution, wages are not taxable, although the average American loses ¼ of his/her paycheck every year
- Sugar is carcinogenic and highly addicting although it is in much of the food we eat
- Hundreds of animal and insect species die every day due to the destruction of nature
- No country wants the American dollar anymore because it is worthless

- Walmart has the largest computer database of goods sold, and now new televisions are linked to computers that record what everyone watches
- There are two mafias, one controls Las Vegas and another controls Reno
- Nevada has no taxes and that is why people live there, however gambling takes much of the people's money
- Concentration camps are being built all around the United States and nobody is asking questions

I say that heresy is the child of orthodoxy because the global elite create the orthodox paradigm by establishing organized religion and an economy that runs on money and oil. They did not create this paradigm for themselves, they created it for the people. Those who backlash against orthodox belief are branded as heretics. Why? Not because they are wrong, obviously, but because they are seeing the maneuverings behind the curtain. Few people who label others as "heretics" know what they are doing or saying. Orthodox does not mean "right," it means "most." That is why the Spartans thought democracy was the worst form of government. The people can be led to believe anything.

It is time now for the ground grew to receive the new indoctrination, the new paradigm. Take your eyes away from the television and listen to a message from the sponsor of truth. We are all one race. We are all one consciousness. On March 21, 2013 the planetary lightbody will activate and Earth herself will ascend into the 5th dimension. Get ready, because the Earth and everyone on it are turning into stars. The evil Nordics and Reptilians are trying to prevent this. They control the secret world government. In the movie *Star Wars*, there is a group known as the Empire. Few people know that this is a real group. The real Empire spans from 1st density through 4th density and is in control of planet Earth. The Alpha Draconians have created a fake lightbody hologram and will try to teach a false version of ascension. Those who fall into this trap will be taken away in 2012 on reptilian and Nordic spacecraft and will be used as slaves or as food. The Dark Ages were when all the ancient mystery schools were wiped out and organized religion took over. Let us try to avoid a repeat, shall we? We can all start by ceasing to watch television. The change from analog to digital television looks like this:

Analog (few channels, muddy picture) → digital (many channels, clear picture)

Or in other words:

Mind programming → super advanced mind programming

Get the picture?

Secret Societies: The Roots of Control

The control and suppression seen today can be traced back to esoteric secret mystical orders. Esoteric religion is the history of magick and the very roots of the operation of secret societies around the world today. Esoteric can be likened to the occult, which simply means that it is beyond the perception of most the population. As the mystical experiences of life were codified into religious canons based on idolatry and false worship, a seal was tightened on the freedom of mind of the average individual. Conformity was preached and heretics were either beheaded or burned at the stake. It became obvious after the Feudal ages that there was a power behind the king, and this power has kept many secrets. Although most secret societies which have ever operated during the post-diluvian times are not demonic, do not worship Lucifer, and are not a part of reptilian bloodlines and the New World Order, they all share a common trait in that something is kept secret amongst the group. In this section, I will discourse not on orthodox religions but the secret mystical orders that lay behind not only religions but also politics. Secrets are kept so power can be bestowed upon only the chosen few, but today that power is disintegrating as real knowledge is being leaked out from the dark corners.

Our discussion of secret societies begins with esoteric religion and philosophy. After Sumer and Babylon (the Brotherhood of the Snake/Babylonian Brotherhood), Zoroastrianism was the first monotheistic religion, the predecessor to the Judeo-Christian and Islamic traditions, the "religions of the book," so to speak. Contemporaneous to the height of the Egyptian empire, Zoroastrianism borrowed such concepts as

A New Order of the Ages

belief in one God, heaven and hell, the resurrection of the dead, the final judgment, and the victory of good over evil in the end times. Zarathustra, who lived possibly as early as 1,000 B.C.E., declared Ahura Mazda the one true God and that all the other Egyptian, Persian, and Greek gods were just servants of the real God. Most Zoroastrians today are known as Parsees or Persians (especially in India). Mithra was the Persian god of contracts and was associated with the Sun, like many of the other gods. From the second century to the fifth century C.E. Mithraism was the popular religion in Rome and was held as a religion for men only, its precursor Zoroastrianism identifying with men and women equally. As Mithras was a savior god, the elements of Jesus and Christianity bear a striking resemblance to Mithraism, a practice much more common in the Holy Roman Empire than was Christianity during the early centuries of the New Era.[27] There were seven levels of initiation with the initiated and the practitioners of the ritual meeting in secret to perform such duties.

This hearkens back to Egypt and initiation in the Great Pyramid. It has been reported that these secret rituals involved the initiated making his way through a dark passage until he came across a light, a metaphor for death and resurrection. The most important goal of initiation is self-realization, and Mithraism fits this perfectly. Among other titles, Mithraism was in fact a religio-magickal cult in that it kept secret spiritual and magical knowledge and revealed it only to initiates, more and more knowledge being admitted the higher they climbed the ladder. Other mystery religions before and after Christ were based on the gods Dionysus, Isis, Osiris, Cybele, Attis, Demeter, Persephone, and Orpheus. The movement commemorating the god Orpheus taught that there is a spark of God the eternal creator in each and every person.

The rituals in the highest degrees of modern Freemasonry today draw precise parallels to these ancient rites of passage to higher levels in the Kabbalah. Texe Marrs, renown Christian occult researcher, details quite vividly in his books the extent to which Masonic hand signs and handshakes resemble ancient Babylonian and Egyptian rites of passage. In *Codex Magica*, one can find more than enough pictures and magazine/

---

[27] Christianity did not become the dominant religion in Europe until the rise of Byzantium and the Emperors Constantine and Theodosius I after the split of the Holy Roman Empire. The New Era began in 1 C.E., although the calendar for which started in 45 B.C.E. as the Julian calendar adopted by Julius Caesar.

book scans portraying these hand signs and what they really mean. It is quite evident from Marrs' research that religious, political, and military leaders as well as famous musicians and actors employ these symbols on a regular basis, most likely demonstrating their allegiance to secret societies and the false god Lucifer. In *Mysterious Monuments*, Marrs describes how monuments erected today embody the concepts preached in the mystery schools. It is not only Hollywood and hand signs but also satanic monuments that act as subliminal messages to our collective unconscious. In fact, our subconscious mind is very powerful and perceives everything. Peggy Kane is a U.F.O. researcher who is an expert in Electronic Voice Phenomena (E.V.P.) and Reverse Speaking (R.S.). According to the R.S. theory, when humans speak their vocal chords simultaneously emit a backwards speech that sheds light on the true nature of the inner thoughts and emotions of the person speaking. This backwards tonal frequency is emitted from the subconscious at the same time the conscious mind speaks in forward language.[28]

Pythagoras, the mathematician living during the fifth century B.C.E, was also a religious/spiritual philosopher. In 530 B.C.E. Pythagoras set up a school in the Greek city of Croton where he taught the relationship of numbers to the universe.[29] He explained to his students that the universe is in constant vibration, a state which produces the "music of the spheres," or in other words, the sounds the planetary bodies make when they rotate on their axes (seventh-dimensional harmonics). He taught in reincarnation and the connection between the microcosm and the macrocosm. He also taught in the purity of body-mind-spirit. Members of his school were obliged to follow the ascetic way of life, meditating every day and abstaining from sex and eating meat. As Pythagoras and his followers construed the rational element in life, they subsequently identified that a vast irrational element existed as well. Life can only be explained in rational terms up to a certain point. At this point the imagination must be invoked. Contemporary to Pythagoras were the philosophers Heraclitus from Greece and Lao-Tzu from China,

---

[28] Reverse Speaking is relevant here because it adds to the growing belief that words, pictures, and symbols have a heavy impact on our subconscious mind whether we perceive them consciously or not. The leaders of our world employ this subliminal technique on a daily basis, unbeknownst to most people.

[29] Numbers exist in a symbiotic relationship with universal resonance—the two are almost inseparable.

A New Order of the Ages

both attempting to explain the irrational element of life. According to Heraclitus, one cannot step into the same stream twice because it is constantly changing. This recurrent evolution marks the path to full comprehension. Everything is constantly evolving to a higher state of consciousness. Today, these teachings would either be deemed occult, which means "hidden," or esoteric, which means "recondite."

Other figures in different parts of the world were coming to similar conclusions. In Nepal, Prince Siddhartha was born into a royal family, never tasting the experience of rags, poverty, or illness until he one day came across four sights—an ascetic, a sick person, an old man and a corpse. Realizing that people suffered no matter where they were in the caste system, Siddhartha sat under a Bohdi tree one day and vowed to remain unmoved until he understood the meaning of life. After three days he understood. He apprehended that life is suffering and that this suffering stems from attachment for material things. Freedom from this desire can be attained by following the Eightfold Path. Siddhartha became the Buddha and released this knowledge to his people. The Eightfold Path is the path to enlightenment and involves right belief, conviction, teaching, action, living, intention, thinking, and contemplation. The followers of Buddha devised their own methods for initiation and understood the mystical, or irrational, element to life.

Plato, one of the most influential Greek philosophers, was another prominent figure in the epoch following Pythagoras, Siddhartha, and Lao-Tzu, his teachings derived from Pythagoras. Neo-Platonism is the movement started by Plato in the fourth century B.C.E. that receded with the later Greek philosophers of the sixth century C.E. Many of Christianity's founding fathers were well studied in Neo-Platonist thought, as few at the time were not. There is no one set of Neo-Platonist ideas, so it is useful to apprehend the knowledge taught by its advocates. Plotinus taught virtue and chastity and was utterly opposed to magic. His student Porphyry sought practical ways for the soul to move to higher levels of consciousness and was much more in favor of white magic. His pupil in turn, Iamblichus, stressed the practice of mystical philosophy, employing numerous types of magical rituals and ceremonies aimed at invoking kindly spirits. The impact that Neo-Platonism (especially the kind taught by Iamblichus) had on esoteric religion and secret societies cannot be underestimated. Iamblichus taught the hierarchy of spiritual beings, which did very well in explaining the relationship of the one true god to the lesser deities. The dichotomy of monotheism and polytheism was thus explained away. There is only one infinite creator and every other soul is a lesser deity. Those souls who are more evolved can appear as gods when they really aren't.

It is also important to note here how Hermetic philosophers and alchemists, constituents of the earlier esoteric traditions, used to call down daemons in rituals and offer sacrifices to them. They rarely attempted to call down demons, the modern translation of daemon. This was known to be very dangerous and is known today as "selling your soul to the devil." The ceremonies of the Hermetic Order took on the aspects of Neo-Platonist thought that there is one true god and every other soul is a lesser deity. Those souls who were spiritually evolved were evoked and made an offer. People today who worship the Devil or Satan are offering sacrifices to a dark spirit in exchange of money, sex, and power. The more people in on the ritual and the sacrifice the more powerful it becomes. That is why in secret Illuminati rituals today a victim is always sacrificed amidst a crowd of silent but eager spectators. The evil spirits (most likely reptilian entities) feed off of the fear and negative energy and they grant the worshipers some sort of knowledge or power.[30] Esoteric Christianity employs these concepts today, however, the teachings have been distorted for centuries. The Vatican and other related organizations have practiced devil worship, blood sacrifice, pedophilia, and black magick for centuries, and they maintain a veil of secrecy over esoteric philosophy. When mystical Christianity split from Rome it moved to Constantinople, which was a better fit due to its nature of being a melting pot for cultures and ideologies. Saint Maximus (580-662) came from this area and taught that the ultimate aim of the worshiper was to become God. This position united the Neo-Platonist desire for ecstatic communion with purity, and the early mystical Christian belief that full initiation made the devotee a Christos. Such beliefs lay at the core of esoteric Christianity, a fact greatly misunderstood considering the Church's monopoly on salvation.

The Egyptian pantheon and its connection to other pantheons has already been touched upon, but it is of greater interest to me now to speak of the origins of alchemy, which may very well lay in ancient Egypt. The English word alchemy derives from the Arabic word 'al kimiya,' itself coming from the Greek 'chemeia' and the Egyptian 'khem.' The

---

[30] Peggy Kane, "U.F.O. Hypothesis," http://www.youtube.com/watch?v=fNDwiifO-eU (2006).

earliest Egyptian alchemists were also chemists and they knew how to combine different types of powders and chemicals together; they also had the ability to refine gold, one of the most precious metals. Gold was reserved for royalty and the priests who guarded this secret were early metal-workers and chemists (the Hibiru are a good example of this). It should be no surprise to the reader by now how gold was important in the workings of the early human civilizations on Earth. Thus, the linkage was bonded between magick, scientific knowledge, and religion. Today, the three are enemies of each other, but back then they were all different expressions of the same thing. Just as the Egyptians influenced the early Christians, they also stamped a heavy impact on the Greeks.

A man who sought the unification of magic and science was Hermes Trismegitus. It is impossible to say who Hermes Trismegistus actually was in real life, however we know what his name means—"thrice greatest." If Hermes Trismegistus was indeed three people who placed their teachings together then that would make sense, but it does not matter much as the teachings have been passed on for centuries. Hermes is most notably identified with Mercury, the Roman messenger god, and Thoth, the Egyptian god of writing. When you add the fact that Mercury is a planet and a liquid metal used in alchemy you see a partially completed picture. Writing, alchemy, and the gods (which were sometimes depicted as the planets in the solar system) were indispensable to secret orders. Writing was important because it was the way in which records of rituals were kept as well as knowledge written down in books. Being able to read and write in the days of the Greeks and Romans was no small feat, so to be in a secret society back then it would most certainly help one to be able to perform these tasks.

Thoth was not only the god of writing and record keeping but also the god who instituted the calendar and the methods by which the movements of the planets around the Sun could be measured. These methodologies are extremely important today. Everyone is bound to the calendar, night and day, and the cycles of months and years. Everyone's personal schedule revolves around these compartmentalized procedures. The Hermetic texts have inspired the sixteenth century alchemists and Hermetic philosophers who were of great significance to the perpetuation of esoteric teachings. Modern day science can lay claim to beginnings in the Hermetic Order. Hermes' famous dictum was, "As above, so below," which has come to mean the unity of all.

The bridge between the microcosm and the macrocosm can be summed up nicely in the *Emerald Tablet*, the refined wisdom of the much longer *Corpus Hermeticum*:

> It is true, without falsehood, and most real: that which is above is like that which is below, to perpetrate the miracles of one thing. And as all things have been derived from one, by the thought of one, so all things are born from this thing. Here is the father of every perfection in the world. His strength and power are absolute when changed into earth; thou wilt separate the earth from fire, the subtle from the gross, gently and with care . . . By this means thou wilt have the glory of the world. And because of this, all obscurity will fell from thee. Within this is the power, most powerful of all powers. For it will overcome all subtle things, and penetrate every solid thing. Thus the world was created. (*Corpus Hermeticum*, The Emerald Tablet)

This passage means that everything stems from one source. All knowledge is connected to one fact, and that fact is that everything on the inside is the same as everything on the outside in likeness. God is infinite and we are all part of that unified field of consciousness. This is also the basis of Ayurvedic medicine in India. There is one thing in which everything else can be known by, and that is consciousness.[31]

When speaking of knowledge and consciousness, a reference must also be made to the Gnostics. Gnosticism deals with the Greek word gnosis which means "knowledge." The Gnostics took it upon themselves to look for the divine spark within them, thereby opening the allowance for the divine spark without to be apprehended. This all relates to 'as above so below.' Gnosticism is most known as a combination of Zoroastrianism, Greek/Roman philosophy, Egyptian theosophy, and esoteric Judaism/Christianity. Gnosticism, in an attempt to reconcile the differences between light and dark, good and evil, proclaimed that there was a god of good and a god of evil. As a part of a dualistic approach the Gnostics sought to answer the question, "why would God, in all of its benevolence, allow for so much evil?" The Gnostics had an answer. Above all is the good God, the perpetuator of all benevolence. Below is the actual creator God, the creator of the physical realm. This concept underlies the belief that the spirit is inherently good, but it is trapped in

---

[31] Deepak Chopra is a heavy advocate of Ayurvedic medicine. See *Quantum Healing*.

a body which is inherently evil. The god who created the physical world was known as the Demiurge, and it was this god who was worshiped for material gain. In order to purify the spirit, one must attain a perfect lifestyle and abstain from sex, drugs, perverse pleasures, and ego. In contrast to popular Gnostic belief, the Christian church has taught that man and God were divided by sin and that the only path towards absolution was faith in Jesus Christ.[32]

So who did the Church want Jesus to be? The Infancy Gospels of Thomas and James are two of the books left out of the Bible, mainly due to their explicit nature concerning the childhood of Jesus. The interest in how Jesus was born and raised takes on a slight tweaking in these two accounts, the *Infancy Gospel of James* relating the story of Mary (mother of Jesus), and the *Infancy Gospel of Thomas* recounting Jesus as a young child. In the latter account Jesus is portrayed as a brilliant but short-tempered young child who makes clever prophecy about his own life. Many scholars would agree that Jesus was psychic, but few would take the *Infancy Gospel of Thomas* as actual accounts from the time when Jesus was but a child. One of the tales is written as such:

> The son of Annas the scholar, standing there with Jesus, took a willow branch and drained the water Jesus had collected. Jesus, however, saw what had happened and became angry, saying to him, "Damn you, you irreverent fool! What harm did the pond of water do to you? From this moment you, too, will dry up like a tree, and you'll never produce leaves or root or bear fruit." (*The Nag Hammadi Library*, The Gospel of Thomas, 15)

This was left out of the Christian canon because the way the *Infancy Gospel of Thomas* portrays Jesus as a child does no justice to the Church's renderings of him as a savior god.

The *Infancy Gospel of James*, adding to that, paints a different birth scene than that which is portrayed in the New Testament. In this account, Jesus is born in a cave near Bethlehem instead of a manger in a stable, and it is a Hebrew midwife who accompanies the birthing and not three kings or wise men. Both would have derailed Christian myths had the Church allowed them in. The *Infancy Gospel of Thomas* is thought by some scholars to be the lost source document "Q," the lost sayings of Jesus

---

[32] This notion has come to be an aberration of real spirituality.

Christ. While convening on the books they wished to place in the New Testament, the Church Fathers forcefully left out the lost source of Q, and it is probably because of sayings like this one:

> Jesus said to them, "When you make the two one, and when you make the inside like the outside and the outside like the inside, and the above like the below, and when you make the male and the female one and the same . . . then you will enter the kingdom." (*The Nag Hammadi Library*, Gospel of Thomas, 22)

Sounds like the *Emerald Tablet* doesn't it? For those who did not accept the official Christian version of the New Testament, an answer was made ready. The heretics were condemned to the stake. The real sayings of Jesus were hidden and the final Christian authority fell into the hands of the Vatican.[33]

The Persian teacher Mani (216-76 B.C.E.) was the founder of Manichaeism, another opponent of the Christian church. Manichaeism acted as an alternate religion, drawing in elements of Christianity, Buddhism, Gnosticism, and Zoroastrianism. Much like its predecessors, Manichaeism believed in a god of light and dark, the god of light being the creator of the soul and the god of dark being the creator of the material body and world. It also claims that the serpent in the Garden of Eden was in fact trying to help Adam and Eve by bestowing knowledge onto them. Manichaeism also lays claim to teaching others that god and man are not separated by anything. Man is two parts—one part soul and one part body—so he therefore embodies both aspects of God (light and dark). The Manichaeans also believed in reincarnation, and that in order to transcend the cycle one must practice a purely ascetic lifestyle. One particular reason why Manichaeism lasted longer than most Gnostic movements is because it did well to set up a church hierarchy with bishops and apostles. There is still a small Gnostic religion in modern-day Iran and Iraq called the Mandaeans. They claim spiritual descent from John the Baptist and employ aspects of both Gnosticism and Manichaeism.

Cabalism is another esoteric religion practiced by non-fundamentalist Jews and Christians. Varying spellings of the word render different

---

[33] Today, the Black Pope dominates the Judeo-Christian movement and he sees to it that these ancient texts are kept hidden in the Vatican's secret vault.

A New Order of the Ages

belief systems to different scholars. Most see 'Kabbalah' as the original Jewish teachings, 'Cabala' as the more renaissance Christian version and 'Qabala' as the modern occultist version. Above all, knowledge of the spirit world was the determining factor in the secrecy of these alternate sects. It was this knowledge which made the initiates powerful. It is interesting to note that Cabalist writings usually take the form of parables, stories with a message or meaning between the lines. This can be seen quite evidently with Jesus. My favorite is the parable of the seed: a seed planted among a grove of horny vines will get choked, a seed planted in a dry desert will become dehydrated, but a seed planted in fertile soil will bear fresh fruit. Jesus was using the seed as a metaphor for the spoken word and how it could or could not produce wisdom within the body. In the right context the word of the Kingdom of God will multiply one hundred-fold. It is simple wisdom teachings like these that often distract the reader from the real intention of organized religion. One must practice discernment at all times, and only when love in the heart chakra is activated will one see the truth.

Originating over 2,000 years ago, Cabalism sought to find the hidden meaning behind religious scripture. The outer shell must be shed away and the soul living inside brought to the light. During the time of Jesus, there were the Jewish Cabalists—the Pharisees and the Sadducees. The Pharisees followed the oral tradition in their teachings while the Sadducees were more conservative and did not believe in angels, demons, or resurrection. The Sadducees were the more aristocratic families, although both traditions formed a network of educated Jews. Jesus himself was part of the Essene order, the Essenes at the time joining many Gnostic groups. The more politically motivated zealots were nationalistic patriots. They took a more literal approach of the Torah (the Pentateuch). All of the aforementioned sects did indeed follow the Torah, although each group had its own methods of interpretation. In their search for spiritual enlightenment, the Cabalists were much more radical, borrowing ideas from Jewish Gnosticism and Neo-Platonism. The Jewish rabbis later developed as interpreters of Torah Law and became judges and teachers, holding more authority than the priests, who conducted ritualistic ceremonies. The rabbis were deeply respected in their literal interpretation of the law, while the Cabalists took a more allegorical approach. They adopted the Tree of Life, the primary connection between God and Creation. The Tree of

Life displays 10 sephiroth, 10 rays emanating from God, which were as such: Kether (Crown), Chokmah (Wisdom), Binah (Understanding), Chesed (Mercy), Geburah (Power), Tiphareth (Beauty/Harmony), Netzach (Victory), Hod (Splendor), Yesod (Foundation), and Malkuth (Kingdom). The theoretical and practical ideals are embedded within the complex Cabala.

Sufism is mystical Islam, and much akin to esoteric Judaism and its affect on Orthodox Judaism, Sufism has made orthodox Muslims uneasy. The beginnings of Islam are full of complexities, but in a way very similar to the methodology employed by the esoteric and orthodox Jews. Sufi writings have been highly influential on both Christian and Jewish mystics alike, and the depth at which Sufi's extract wisdom is much like the way the Cabalists read "between the lines." Many current New Age beliefs stem from Sufism. Shortly after the death of Muhammad, a bold line drew itself in the sand between the Sunnis and the Shi'ites, the Shi'ites taking on a more radical approach before splitting off into further groupings. The name 'Sufi' derives from the Arabic word for "wool-clad," referring to the rough wool robes worn by the Christian and Muslim mystics. All the religious movements, conservative and esoteric, stem from a single movement. In the beginning it was the Brotherhood of the Snake (taught to Adapa and Lilith), which taught all the mystical concepts and personal union with spirit. Next it was the Babylonian Brotherhood, which was the first feature secret society headed by the Draconian bloodlines. Today, the Babylonian Brotherhood is called the Illuminati, although many occult scholars will defer to the Committee of 300 and the Druidic Council.

Mystical Sufism is no different than the arcane movements before it. Allegorical is the Sufi's interpretation of the Koran, a book undoubtedly written in similar fashion to the Bible. Sufis sought personal knowledge of the divine, and like many esoteric religions before them, they were persecuted by the Church. In the twelfth and thirteenth centuries, after much belittlement, Sufism became well accepted. However so, the orthodox Muslims today, especially the Shi'ites, hold an antagonistic stance against Sufism which they deem heresy. Even today in Pakistan, members of the Ahmadi sect of Sufism can be arrested for saying anything that is against the beliefs of the orthodox Muslims. The Sufis have always maintained close ties with spiritualists and mystics from other religious orders, and as such have been influenced by esoteric Christianity,

A New Order of the Ages

Neo-Platonism, and the Advaita Vedantism sect of Hinduism. As most esoteric traditions, the Sufis saw God in all things, past or present.

The radical Shi'ite branch of Islam contained within it a schism between a group called the "Seveners" and a group called the "Twelvers." These two cults thought that the seventh and the twelfth imams, respectively, were the later-to-return saviors. Just like in the "Book of Revelation" in the New Testament, the return of the Mahdi, the savior, was predicted in the Koran to restore the purity of Islam. The Persian Hasan-i-Sabbath was a Twelver who converted to Ismailism (the Seveners). When he was young he studied alongside the future prime minister of Persia, Nizam ul-Mulk, who was later assassinated by Hasan. In 1090 he took over a Sunni fortress in the mountains of northern Persia called Alamut, and there instituted his operations center. Hasan's followers were in total dedication to their master, killing and dying very bravely under his orders. There is a story told of how once when Hasan wanted to prove to several visitors to his palace how powerful he was, he signaled to one of his followers on a high peak who subsequently cast himself down to his death. It is quite reasonable to assume the ecstasy Hasan's followers felt when, upon initiation, they were drugged and taken to a beautiful garden owned by Hasan where they delighted with palaces, musicians, singers, dancers, honey, and wine. A direct parallel bridges the way so-called "terrorists" today employ the use of suicide bombers and the way Hasan got his initiates to obediently follow him. He simply promised a luxurious life in heaven upon their death. The drug with which Hasan introduced his followers to blissful happiness was cannabis. The reason this drug was so powerful was because when it was smoked, tetra-hydro-cannabinoids entered the brain where they posed as dopamine. The newly released and imitated dopamine entered the neural synapses where they attached to the dopamine receptors. Since dopamine is the chemical that makes you happy and feel good, the cannabis brought the inhalers to a state of biological paradise. Since cannabis is also known to bring one to a higher state of consciousness, Hasan's followers entered into a state of mental bliss as well.[34]

While helping to promote political schisms in Persia, Hasan destroyed many of his rivals in due process. After a very short while he was powerful and feared by both Christians and Muslims. At the end

---

[34] The Christian Crusaders who encountered Hasan's followers called them the "Assassins." Since they smoked hashish, they were also known as "Hashshashins."

of a 35-year reign Hasan died at the ripe old age of 90, his successors instigating many of the same techniques employed by him, such as promising a heavenly paradise to assassins who took out religious and political leaders. One other technique proved successful by Hasan on many a fortnight was the planting of "sleepers" in the courts of rulers who would not reveal themselves until years or even decades after the planting. The sleepers would kill the unsuspecting ruler after seeing a hand signal or some other sort of sign. This relates to the way the C.I.A. today plants Manchurian candidates in other countries and even within the United States itself. These assassins are hypnotically programmed to kill and then to not remember, so when they are interrogated later they will have nothing to confess. The fourth Grand Master of the order instantiated by Hasan, also named Hasan or Hasan II, was so powerful during his reign that he claimed himself to be the next Imam, known to Muslims at the time as the "mouthpiece of God." In the early stages the Assassins acted like ordinary and even kosher Muslims, but under the kingships of Hasan II and his son Muhammad II they disregarded the laws of Islam entirely. They drank wine, ate pork, and procreated incessantly. All the while, the Syrian branch of the Assassins became an independent body with continuing contact with the Syrian Crusaders. This branch of the Assassins had the most connection with the Knights Templar and paid them 2,000 pieces of gold a year to avoid military conflict.

    In the thirteenth century C.E. the Mongols defeated the Assassins, although they were not wholly wiped out. They had spread all over Europe including Russia and India and they still exist today as a small Ismaili sect called the Nizari. The Assassins were one of the original secret orders with levels of initiation, oaths of obedience, and secret signs, just like many of the secret orders today. The Assassins had a heavy influence on the Knights Templar who wore the same types of uniform; the white tunic, red sash and black boots of the Assassins complimented the Templar's white tunics displaying the red cross. The iron cross used as a medal of honor in Germany is most undoubtedly an evolution of the red cross of the Templars. The cross with its arms splayed out is first seen in drawings and renditions in the *Corpus Hermeticum*. The hierarchy of the Knights Templar also closely resembled that of the Assassins. The Assassins were organized under the Grand Masters into the missionaries, companions, and laymen. The Knights Templar, under the Grand Masters, had grand priors, priors, knights, esquires, and lay brothers.

The religious climate following the tenth century C.E. was unstable, mainly due to the fact that the Roman Catholic Church had to deal with the most heretic orders since the founding of Christianity by the Church Fathers. These heresies could have easily become the dominant form of Christianity, one such movement known as Arianism, which stated that Jesus could not have been a god because there was only one eternal God the Father. Arianism exists today under the guise of the Unitarian movement and the Jehovah's Witnesses. Dynamic Monarchianism was another heresy which held the belief that Jesus was an ordinary man with divine power in him. This belief still clutches to the fringes of Christian movements today. Pelagianism, a British heresy, was founded in the fourth century C.E. by either a Scottish or Irish monk and stated that the way to salvation was through personal achievement and not through Jesus Christ alone. The Waldenses were founded in 1176 and were the first Protestants, rejecting the ideals of the Catholic Church. They have survived until the present day although they were burned at the stake by the Inquisition.

The Paulicians were a group which extracted itself from the Manichaeans and became established in Armenia in the mid-seventh century C.E. They too, were opposed to the Catholic Church and in turn influenced the Bogomils, who were founded by a tenth century Eastern Orthodox priest. Bogomil, as his name appeared, taught the Gnostic dualistic belief that the world was created by an evil God and Jesus had come to save man from the clutches of the Demiurge. They held the view that Satan was Jesus' older brother, just as Mormons today believe the Lucifer was Christ's brother. The Bogomils lasted until the fourteenth century when they were taken over by the Muslims, many Bogomils in effect converting to Islam. The Bogomil priests and monks were called "perfecti" because they practiced abstinence, ate no meat, and maintained a purity of spirit. This is a common theme among many esoteric groups, especially in the higher positions of authority. The evil material world was held in a low regard as spirit and union with God was held in the highest regard. What became the orthodox religious movements and canons sought to victimize people, thereby lending the hand of salvation so the people could in turn be saved. The interests of the Christian and Muslim clergy were purely political and anti-spiritual.

Among other accusations, the Bogomils were accused of sodomy. According to the Catholic Church, sodomy was the way Bogomils and Cathars had sex without bringing offspring into the world.[35]

In the thirteenth century C.E. the Beguines was a largely female movement in Europe which most likely took its name from the Cathar Albigensians. Their independence, adherence to the virtues of chastity, and reverence for the poor led to them causing a great irritation to the Church, and what was once a thorn in the side became potentially lethal. They took on highly mystical beliefs and wrote that God was in everything and everything emanated from God. Amid arid accusations by the Inquisition the Beguines believed they were above the law, whether that law be moral, religious, or state. This infuriated the Church, which fought to become the law. The Beguines believed they were absent of sin because sin, according to their definition, was the "will to offend God." Since they had no such will they adhered to the mindset that they were God's will. As always, the Church met the Beguines' demands for separation from the might of the clergy with torture, persecution, and death. It is no different than today.

The Bogomil-influenced Cathars were another esoteric group functioning at the time. A fully fledged alternative to orthodox Christianity, albeit similar in structure, the Cathars had a church hierarchy composed of bishops and other spiritual leaders who quickly condemned the riches of the Catholic Church. 'Cathar' is Latin for "pure one," a theme recurrent throughout many esoteric groups. At the behest of renown scholars, most Cathars are known as Albigensians, labeled so because of the town Albi, a major Cathar center in southern France in the Languedoc region. The Cathars first appeared, however, in Cologne, Germany, mention of them appearing in 1143. By the 1160's the Cathars had vagabonded their way to parts of southern France and northern Italy. They had an impetuous lifestyle; they abstained from eating meat and participating in sexual acts and also vehemently believed in equality of the sexes. They believed that one could be saved from the cycle of reincarnation by living a perfect ascetic life, their branding of 'heretics' coming from a most ambitious King Henry II of England. In 1166 thirty German Cathar missionaries were recalled to England where they were flogged, stripped of their clothing, and subsequently left out in the brutal winter to die of exposure. However deceitful to the spiritual nature

---

[35] David Barrett, *A Brief History of Secret Societies* (Philadelphia: Running Press, 2007).

of man, the kings of Medieval Europe had more on their minds than befriending political and religious rivals. In 1184 Pope Lucius III began the Inquisition and stated that all deemed heretics were to be banned from the Church unless he or she could prove otherwise. It is amusing that after excommunication from the Church, the heretics were handed over to the secular authorities. It seems the Church had instituted itself not only as a religious authority but also a secular state authority by this time, and this was only the beginning of the atrocities to be committed by the Papacy. In 1199 Pope Innocent III declared all heretics to be branded as such and put forth that heresy was "high treason against God," convicted heretics owing all their possessions to the Inquisition and the civil authorities. So it was said. The Pope giveth and the Pope taketh away.

In 1208 Pope Innocent III sought full retribution for the damage done to his empire by the Cathars and sent a papal legate named Peter of Castelnau to negotiate a treaty with Raymond VI, ruler over most of the Cathar lands. Peter was discharged by the blade of one of Raymond's knights and the pope had had enough. Originally, the Crusades had aimed at killing Muslims and non-Christians, but a new creed issued by Innocent III pulled out all the stops. According to the pope, it was "God's will" that orthodox Christians should kill heterodox Christians. Under the leadership of Simon de Montfort, over 30,000 crusaders from northern France besought, beseeched, and utterly annihilated the Cathar towns in the Languedoc with the promise that their rage would bring them as much plundering and booty as their hearts desired. Although both Cathars and Catholics alike lived side by side in the town of Beziers, over 15,000 men, women, and children were slaughtered due to the wish of the papal legate whose words were, "kill them all, God will know his own." The Cathar towns of Carcassonne, Minerve, and Lavaur fell and Raymond VII surrendered in 1229, pledging allegiance to the new king of France Louis IX. After twenty years of the Albigensian Crusade most of the Cathar wealth had fallen into the hands of the Church and the king.

During the end of the jihad many Cathars had withdrawn to Montsegur, a sturdy fortress that had withstood the penetration of de Montfort thus far circa 1209 CE. In 1243 a band of crusaders decided to lay siege to the fortress, an attack which lasted twelve months because of local villagers smuggling in food to the hostage Cathars. The night before the Cathar surrender in 1244, a particular witness claimed to have seen four Cathars descending the walls of Montsegur on ropes and then vanishing into the wilderness with the Cathar treasure, most believing it was the Holy Grail. With the fall of the stronghold Queribus in 1255, the Cathars had all but vanished, a few escaping to northern Italy and even fewer retreating into the Balkans where they conformed back into the Bogomil movement. There was a Cathar revival in the village of Montaillou in the early 14th century, however menial. The Inquisition orchestrated by Jacques Fournier and later the Avignon Pope Benedict XII from 1318-1325 did well to quell whatever Cathar revivalism resurfacing during that time. This period of French history is shameful, and it seems that if Catharism had not perished the cultural and spiritual influence of the Languedoc could have altered the course of European history. The notions of chivalry, questing knights, and the Holy Grail most likely came from this epoch.

As well as being known for the resurgence of Gnostic beliefs in the late Middle Ages, the hundred year epoch of the Cathar reign was most notably responsible for the development of the Inquisition. During the Albigensian Crusade a Catholic preacher of orthodox faith named Dominic traveled about with the Bishop of Osma and debated the two belief systems—Catharism and Catholicism. In 1216 Pope Honorius III was so impressed with the preacher's work he sanctioned the Order of Friars Preachers, more commonly known as the Dominicans. This order was bestowed the task of converting Cathars and other heretics. Twelve years after the death of Dominic, Pope Gregory IX placed the Dominicans in charge of the Inquisition, no doubt to the belittlement of Dominic's memory as a gentle but wise teacher.

Much information about the Knights Templar is speculation, but it is often conjectured that the Cathars had a major influence on this order. The founder of the Knights Templar is said to have been Hugues de Payen, a knight from Champagne who, along with eight other knights, instituted this order in 1119 towards the end of Hasan's rule over the Assassins. Their initial aim, however suspicious and arduous, was to protect pilgrims travelling to Jerusalem, a city captured by Turkish Muslims in 1076 and established as a Christian kingdom in 1099. At the Council of Troyes in 1129, their statutes were officially drawn up by Bernard of Clairvaux and their order was labeled the "Order of the Poor Knights of Christ and the Temple of Solomon." Saint Bernard advocated the systematic training of the imagination by proposing that imagining the birth, life, and death of Jesus Christ would invoke his spirit to descend upon you. The right brain, the forerunner of all imaginative thought, was well respected by Bernard as it held the key to the Holy Spirit of God. The Knights Templar respected his teachings and incorporated them into their secret rituals. They were given room and board in the royal palace of Baudouin I, the king of Jerusalem at the time, the palace according to lore presiding over the ruins of the original Solomon's Temple. Prerequisites for gaining admission into the order were strict. One had to be from a knightly family, born from wedlock, unmarried, and an adult free from all obligations and debt. One also could not have been from any other order and had to swear to vows of poverty, chastity, and obedience. The Templars were primarily a military order and they were well respected, as they did an unusually exemplary job keeping the path to Jerusalem safe. They were honored as well as feared, and in 1139 Pope Innocent II gave them independence from all authority save that of the pope himself. It seems the Church clergy had bigger plans to eventually use the Templars for other purposes, but were they to become too powerful in the meantime?

In 1161 Pope Alexander III granted the Templars exemption from all tithes while being able to receive tithes, and they were also given their own chaplains and burial grounds. They were granted land from kings and nobles and in time, came to own not only land and fortresses but also ports and fleets.[36] Although now encompassing a much wider range of influence, they remained a protection team for the Pilgrims, who could now employ the Templars as a banking cartel. Due to the fact that many nobles had joined the order, first going through an intense initiation where demons were confronted, they came to own much property and subsequently invented letters of credit so money could be transferred without the risk of it being abducted. The very first checks were given to the Pilgrims as promissory notes when they did not want to haul large amounts of gold. This gold was given to the Templars who promised to hold it until a promissory note was returned, the gold in the amount of the note then being returned. The Templar temple in Paris assumed the form of the center of French finances. The Templars posed as early European bankers, loaning money to kings, nobles, and merchants,

---

[36] This is when the Templars became very rich and powerful and came to indebt kings. It is also during this time that the order expanded so greatly that the original ambitions were lost.

which eventually gave rise to the merchant class. They were also placed in charge of state coffers. Additionally, the patrons of the first trade guilds independent of the Church and nobility were connected to the Templars and other such secret orders. The Compagnons du Devoir, as these guilds were called, were responsible for building projects spanning over many acres of land as well as maintaining ethical and decent business codes and regulations in the Holy land and across other countries in Europe ruled over by the aristocracy.

Although the Templars maintained many of their bases in the Holy Land, their official stronghold was in Europe. As you will see later on, Europe has been totally conquered by the Snake of Zion, the bloodlines instilled by the Alpha Draconians (the Knights Templar were only one order commandeered by these bloodlines, they just happen to be the most famous). Endowed between the first and second Crusades, the Knights Templar had set up their headquarters in what is believed to have been the stables attached to the Temple of Solomon (which was an Egyptian temple). They wore sheepskin breeches beneath their outer clothing and were forbidden to cut their beards as an image of chastity. In 1252 King Henry III of England demanded that the liberties of the Templars be constrained, as they were no longer doing the duties they originally sought out to do. They had become much too rich and powerful by this time, infuriating the crowned heads of Europe.

One of the reasons the Templars were so powerful was because so many kings were indebted to them. One of the kings heavily in debt to the Templars was King Philippe le Bel of France who was owed a favor from Pope Clement V as Philippe had helped him secure the papacy. Most undoubtedly the Pope had political motivations of his own, but under the orders of King Philippe, Pope Clement had coordinated large raids in 1307, forcing the arrest of numerous Templar groups. The date this occurred was Friday the 13th of October, this infamous date resonating throughout the rest of history as an ominous day. On this day the kings of the world moved to eradicate the esoteric influences from such groups as the Knights Templar and other secret spiritual orders who taught virtue and self realization and condemnation of the ruling elite. It is a most curious thing that the Templars had learned of this plan beforehand, finding the time to clear their treasure at the Paris preceptor before Philippe could lay his hands on it. When the Paris temple was excavated, a secret chamber containing a skull and two thighbones was discovered. This, of course, is the skull and crossbones that you will find in any Freemasonic temple today. As always, the captured Templars were charged with heresy and tortured.

Even though the Templars were all but expunged from France and middle Europe, they reconvened in Spain and Portugal where they instituted two new orders; the Order of Montesa and the Order of Christ were brought forth, the latter becoming a revealing maritime body in which Christopher Columbus sailed under. The flag of the Order of Christ was the Templar Red Cross. When they were captured and interrogated, the Templars were accused of allying with the Saracens, the aggressors of many Christian nations and indeed the Holy Land during the 12th century C.E. The debauchery of letting the Holy Land fall in the hands of the Muslims was a heavy charge, among other charges of homosexual acts, blaspheming against Christ, and most shockingly, worshipping a severed head calling itself "Baphomet." This head, incredulous and insidious as it sounds, was reported by several Templars under torture as being able to communicate with whomever it wished. It was the conduit of a particular demon the Templars had invited in, although further details remain obscure. The head was used in many Templar ceremonies and was claimed to be able to bestow a certain amount of power on those who participated in the rituals. It was confessed to have been goat-headed with a long beard, sparkling eyes, and four feet.

Thirty-six Templars died under torture, another incentive for others to confess, however it must be assumed, and rightly so, that most told the torturers what they wanted to hear in the hope that they would be set free. Most of the charges made against the Templars by Guillaume de Nogaret, one of Philippe of France's chief ministers, had been later leveled by Nogaret including sodomy and spitting on the cross. I do believe some of the accusations were valid, but others seemed not only ridiculous but purported, as any charge would be against those standing accusations of magic and heresy. Recurring themes conjured up by the popes, in a league of their own no doubt, led to the dissimilation of not only the Cathars but the Templars as well. Pope Lucius III instigated the Inquisition in 1188, Pope Gregory IX placed control of this movement under the Dominicans in 1233, and Pope Innocent IV authorized methods of torture to obtain confessions in 1252. The hypocritical Catholic church is now officially a tyrant. Hugh Schonfield, a scholar of the Dead Sea Scrolls, did well to explain the Jewish roots of the New

Testament and the ATBASH cipher, a code in which the first letter of an alphabet is substituted for the last, the second for the second last and so on. In the word 'Baphomet,' Schonfield found the word 'wisdom.'

The Knights Templar were known by other names, their order sanctioned into component parts before the official release of the Templars from mainstream written history. Since, their operation has moved underground and it takes on many forms today. In 1885 the French village of Rennes-le Chateau received a new parish priest named Berenger Sauniere, who found an encoded message which he brought to his superior, the Bishop of Carcassonne. Sauniere was then sent to Paris where he made many influential friends and somehow accumulated a mass wealth. When Sauniere was on his deathbed he conferred a secret to the presiding priest, who later appeared from the room in a shaken stupor. The priest suffered a terrible depression for the next several months. Was this the secret the Templars had been protecting for so long? Marie Denarnaud was Sauniere's close friend who shared his life and secrets and had amassed a fortune in similar fashion to the way Sauniere did. When she was asked to account for her revenue she chose poverty instead. How conspicuous. She also promised the purchaser of her villa, Monsieur Noel Corbu, to give him a secret before she died that would make him rich and powerful. In 1953 Marie suffered a sudden stroke and was unable to give the secret away, much to the chagrin of Corbu. What was this secret and why was it so powerful?

When the Knights Templar were formed they only had nine members and for nine years did not accept anyone else, but these facts have been later debated. If they were indeed a police force then wouldn't they have needed more members? And why were they so secret? New evidence has linked the Knights Templar not only with the Cathars but also with the Rosicrucians, a secret order supposedly formed around the time when the Temple Mount was sacked in 70 C.E. by Roman legions under Titus. Among the Dead Sea Scrolls unearthed there was one known as the "copper scroll" which made reference to a treasure and sacred vessel of an indeterminate kind. This was most likely the secret kept by the Templars that made them so powerful. There is also evidence that several of the Templars were linked to the papacy. In 1285 Roussillon Templars traveled to Bezu to guard a treasure of some sort. Of all the Templars they were the ones left unmolested by King Philippe in 1307, their leader at the time being Seigneur de Goth who later became Pope

Clement V. The mother of Bertrand de Blanchefort, Grand Master in 1153, was Ida de Blanchefort, of the same family that kept a secret until the 18th century, a secret revealed when Abbe Antoine Bigou (priest of Rennes-le Chateau) composed the parchments found by Sauniere.

Confirmations of a third order behind the Templars and Cistercians became obvious to many scholars in search of the secret which made kings fall from their thrones more swiftly than any external foe. The secret order behind the Knights Templar was called the Priory of Sion and it was directed by a series of Grand Masters, many being famous personages in Western history. The Knights Templar were the military and administrative arm of the secret order that remained unscathed after the dissolution of the Templars in 1307. When Jerusalem fell in 1099, Godfroi de Bouillon was elected king of the region, but he declined and instead took the title "defender of the Holy Sepulchre." The conclave who offered Godfroi the throne was of Calabrian origin, as were the Monks of Orval. After the fall of Jerusalem an abbey was erected at the command of Godfroi on Mount Sion, subsequently housing an order of the same name. By 1114 the Knights Templar are fully active, the first Grand Master recorded as Hugues de Payen. The Order of Sion remained in the Holy Land in the abbey outside Jerusalem. Until 1188 the Order of Sion and the Order of the Temple had shared the same Grand Master. Hugues de Payen and Bertrand de Blanchefort presided over both institutions simultaneously. In 1188 the Order of Sion changed its name to the Priory of Sion and adopted a nickname. Besides that of "Ormus" the Priory of Sion adopted the subtitle "Order of the Rose-Croix" or in modern terminology, "Order of the Rosicrucians." The Priory of Sion was so powerful during its time that it could compel a king to do its bidding. The Knights Templar were active long before 1118, but during that time when King Baudouin was on his deathbed he was coerced into granting the Templars official status, thus giving them a constitution.

There must have been some driving force behind the coercion powers of the Templars, and I assume it had something to do with the secret they held. Before the secret is revealed several prominent pieces of the puzzle must be gathered. I will now relate to you an excerpt from the book *Holy Blood, Holy Grail* by Michael Baigent, Richard Leigh, and Henry Lincoln. The facts surrounding such matters have been scrutinized and they appear below as such:

viii. In the late 11th century a group of monks from Calabria appear in Ardennes where they are given land at Orval by Godfroi de Bouillon's aunt and foster mother.
ix. A member of this group may have been Godfroi's personal tutor and may have co-instigated the First Crusade.
x. Some time before 1108 the monks at Orval decamp and go to Jerusalem.
xi. In 1099 Jerusalem falls and Godfroi is offered the throne by an anonymous person of Calabrian origin.
xii. An abbey is built at Godfroi's behest on Mount Sion.
xiii. By 1114 the Knights Templar are already active as an armed entourage for the Order of Sion. Their constitution is not negotiated until 1117 and they are made public in 1118.
xiv. In 1115 Saint Bernard, a member of the Cistercian Order, emerges as a spokesman of Christendom. All the while the formerly destitute Cistercians become one of the most influential and wealthy institutions in Europe.
xv. In 1131 Saint Bernard receives the abbey of Orval, vacated some years before by the monks from Calabria. Orval then becomes a Cistercian house.
xvi. Count Champagne donates the land for Saint Bernard's abbey at Clairvaux, establishes a court at Troyes, and in 1114 contemplates joining the Knights Templar.
xvii. Andre de Montbard, Saint Bernard's uncle and member of the Order of Sion, joins Hugues de Payen in founding the Knights Templar. Shortly thereafter Audre's two brothers join Saint Bernard at Clairvaux.
xviii. Saint Bernard becomes a public relations exponent for the Templars.
xix. Between 1115 and 1140 both the Cistercians and the Templars begin to prosper, acquiring vast sums of money and tracts of land.
xx. The Order of Sion, which had created the Knights Templar, separated from its offshoot in 1188. This ceremony was known as the 'cutting of the elm' and took place at Gisors.
xxi. In 1188 the Order of Sion selects its own Grand Master named Jean de Gisors. Its name then changed to the Priory of Sion.

xxii. The red/rose cross could have been adapted from Ormus, an Egyptian sage who in 46 CE started a religious sect which combined the teachings of Christianity and the Mystery Schools.

xxiii. According to the Prieure documents, the Priory of Sion was not an extension of the Order of the Temple. The separation of the two occurred after the cutting of the elm. Some rapport continued to exist, though. (*Holy Blood, Holy Grail*, 106-109)

The connection between the power of the Templars and the Church becomes obvious. A tower constructed by Berenger Sauniere was dedicated to the Magdalene. The church at Rennes-le Chateau was also dedicated to the Magdalene. Considering the mother goddess of Christianity was in fact the Magdalene, and assertion can be made that the secret kept by the Templars and discovered by Sauniere was the bloodline of Jesus and Mary Magdalene, also referred to as the "Holy Grail."[37] The grail was not a chalice, it was the womb of Mary Magdelene which held the bloodline of Jesus. In ancient cultures, 'holy grail' was blood that spewed from the birth canal during menstruation; the Catholic Church stole this ritual so they could erect a patriarchal society. Men cannot give birth, so any act of drawing blood symbolized a womb. The blood of Jesus offered in communion ceremonies in modern Christian church services does not symbolize the blood of Christ, it represents menstruation blood. This secret was in demand of being guarded by the Templars, and that is why they were instituted as a separate authority. All the Popes bowed to the graces of the Templars until they became too powerful, and power was the Church's motto. If the people knew about the Holy Grail they wouldn't revere Jesus as a god, and the Church would lose most of its power. This secrete made those who knew it powerful because it allowed them entry into many prominent political and religious circles, and they would no doubt hold on to it for fear of persecution.

Most assured in my mind is the way the Church victimized the Templars by putting them at the head of the sword. The new might of Europe could not have been the Templars, and according to the Church

---

[37] The Holy Grail is purposely depicted falsely in popular culture and in Christianity so Jesus can be viewed as a god worth worshipping. If knowledge of his bloodline was released, he would seem like a mortal and nobody would want to worship him.

the heretics had to be feared. Most the charges leveled against them were inaccurate to say the least, and it is interesting to note that in 1129 the Crusaders, the Templars, and the Assassins had formulated a plan together to seize Damascus from the Muslims so it could be given to the Christians. Enemies or allies? No, fodder. The Church was quick to side by the Templars when they first began, but when the power started to fade from the clutches of the clergy there was only one thing to do—brand the accusers as heretics and look the other way. The Church and the Popes were quick to disown the Templar powers; even so, they have always been connected. There is no such thing as an enemy, only a victor, and every time the Vatican saw itself as sliding from this position, it took hold of the straw willy nilly and did what it does best. Point the finger the other direction.

The Religions of the Book, the canons of ancient history, and the Egyptian and Greek influences on the Holy Land helped stir the melting pot of religious ideals. The links between religion, philosophy, mysticism, and magic have been dug up and rediscovered, the real truth lurking in the shadows. It is as Napoleon Bonaparte said. History is always written by the victor, and we must put our minds together now and assume the Church is behind all the debauchery and treachery since the reign of Marduk officially began. The political has nothing to do with the moral, remember? It is obvious that not only did many of the surviving Cathars migrate to the ranks and files of the Knights Templar, but many esoteric orders long predating either group did likewise when assimilating into bigger and better movements. The Templars, independent of the Church hierarchies, carried the knowledge that the divine lies within, and the primary rift between the Orthodox Church and the esoteric religions was indeed this knowledge. For some it was freedom, for others, the opportune moment to seize power. Everything evolves from a single source, and later, you will see how far one can truly wonder off into the darkness.

Jan van Helsing, in his revealing book *Secret Societies and Their Power in the 20th Century*, opines that the Templars were originally a benevolent order that wished to serve the teachings of Jesus Christ. They resented Judaism and exalted Christianity as they thought their savior Jesus referred to the Jewish god Satan. Even today, Yahweh is considered Satan. As the Templar order grew it eventually became corrupted, and when Jerusalem was sacked by the Muslims the Vatican ordered the Templars be disbanded. Afterwards, many Templars fled to Portugal, England, and Scotland where some joined Masonic lodges while others became incorporated into a group known as the "Knights of the Order of St. John." In subsequent years the Knights of the Order of St. John lived in the Mediterranean where it became known as the "Knights of Rhodes" and later the "Knights of Malta." After their defeat to Napoleon in 1789, their headquarters was transferred to Rome and it is today known as the Sovereign and Military Order of Malta of which the Pope is the head. Members of this order include/included William Casey (Chief of the C.I.A., 1981-1987), Alexander Haig (former U.S. Secretary of State), James Buckley (Radio Free Europe), John McCone (C.I.A. chief under Kennedy) and Alexandre de Marenches (former head of French Secret Service).

Manly P. Hall was a high-level Freemason until he discovered the true purpose of the secret society he was involved in and left. In his book, *The Secret Teachings of All Ages*, Hall discourses on the ancient mystery schools and how they were taken over by greed and avarice.[38] One of the most efficacious priesthoods was known as the Druids, and before the order was corrupted it resembled the Bacchic and Eleusinian Mysteries of Greece and Rome. When Marduk took over in 2,200 B.C.E. he commandeered some of the more prominent mystery schools by helping the 13 primary bloodline families infiltrated the highest echelons of these orders/priesthoods which included the Druids, Knights Templar, and the Freemasons. Orthodox religion was established to control the masses and esoteric spirituality was kept as a secret to be passed only to the initiated few. In *The Secret Teachings of All Ages*, Hall writes:

> The Druids were initiates of a secret school that existed in their midst. This school, which closely resembled the Bacchic and Eleusinian Mysteries of Greece or the Egyptian rites of Isis and Osiris, is justly designated the *Druidic Mysteries*. There has been much speculation concerning the secret wisdom that the Druids claimed to possess. Their secret teachings were never written, but were communicated orally to specially prepared candidates. Robert Brown, 32°, is of

---

[38] Hall recounts in his recollection of secret proceedings how the Freemasons today employ many of the same symbols and rituals used by the Knights Templar and the Rosicrucians. This should show one that all of these orders are connected at the top by the Brotherhood of the Snake/Babylonian Brotherhood, colloquially known today as the "Illuminati."

the opinion that the British priests secured their information from Tyrian and Phoenician navigators who, thousands of years before the Christian Era, established colonies in Britain and Gaul while searching for tin. Thomas Maurice, in his *Indian Antiquities*, discourses at length on Phoenician, Carthaginian, and Greek expeditions to the British Isles for the purpose of procuring tin. Others are of the opinion that the Mysteries as celebrated by the Druids were of Oriental origin, possibly Buddhistic.

The Druids were a powerful order and clearly they borrowed from numerous traditions. The Arch-Druid was the spiritual head of the organization and he wore a crown of sun rays (a tiara) and carried a sickle (the sickle of Saturn). The Druids were sun worshipers, just like any Christian today (because Jesus is the pagan sun god), and they also worshipped Mercury under the similitude of a stone cube (just like the black stone of Mecca worshipped by the followers of Islam).

The Mysteries existed to teach deeper, esoteric doctrine (the dimensions and energy) to the chosen initiates while the simpler, exoteric doctrine (simple and entrapping creation myths) was taught to the people. Over time, most of the mysteries (especially the Druidic Order) became corrupted and infiltrated by the Reptile-Aryan bloodlines. Today, the Druidic Council oversees all the mystery schools of today and consists of thirteen chairs, one chair for each of the thirteen primary bloodline families. The Arch-Druid is Baron Guy de Rothschild and he is the C.E.O. of Earth, which is a giant corporation run by the Illuminati.

Other secret societies worth mentioning here (which are connected to the Illuminati) are the Hermetic Order of the Golden Dawn, the Jesuits, and Opus Dei. Around the turn of the 20th century, the Hermetic Order of the Golden Dawn was England's leading occult society and it was founded by three Freemasons: Dr. William Robert Woodman, Dr. William Wynn Westcott, and Samuel Liddell Mathers. The full gamut of Masonic and neo-Rosicrucian mysticism was coalesced into this order as it was organized into three degrees of membership (like many of the contemporary and pre-existing societies during and before it). Its tenets of spell casting, tarot cards, yoga, astrology, and channeling were inspired by the Cabala, Hermeticism, alchemy, and the Enochian magic of John Dee, and it most likely influenced the Thule Society, the German occult group in Munich which Hitler transformed into the

A New Order of the Ages

National Socialist German Workers Party (Nazi Party). Aleister Crowley, the "Beast" and the "wickedest man in the world," got his start in the Order of the Golden Dawn. Crowly would later leave and develop his own society of magick.

The Jesuits are another occult group from Europe. These are Roman Catholic priests who belong to the Society of Jesus, the real name for the Jesuit Order which was founded by the Spanish soldier and cleric Ignatius of Loyola in 1540. Loyola wrote his *Spiritual Exercises* while recovering from wounds he received at the Battle of Panteluna, and this dialogue later became the foundation for the Society of Jesus. The Jesuits have accrued a malevolent and satanic occult connotation over the past century, and they are most assuredly connected with the New World Order, but Ignatius most likely did not have these intentions in mind when he founded the order as his followers were rigorously disciplined, ascetic, profoundly educated, skilled in dialectics, and foot soldiers for the Pope. Loyola's band of followers undertook missionary work and opened schools throughout the world, all the while igniting the Counter-Reformation and pressing for reform within the Roman Church. The Society of Jesus spawned many enemies, and as a result the organization was suppressed between 1773 and 1814 by order of the Pope. Today, it is the largest religious order in the Roman Catholic Church with over twenty thousand priests serving in more than one hundred countries. At face value, the Jesuits appear to be deeply religious ascetics on mission to make the world more peaceful, but their pledge to the New World Order is argued by many scholars to be undeniable.

Opus Dei (translated to "the Work of God") is another faction of the Roman Catholic Church.[39] It was founded by Josemaria Escrivá in Spain in 1928, and in his own words, the group's mission is to:

> Foster the search for holiness and the carrying out of the Apostolate by Christians who live in the world, whatever their state in life or position in society. The Work of God was born to help those Christians . . . to understand that their life, just as it is, can be an opportunity for meeting Christ: that it is a way of holiness and apostolate.

---

[39] In Dan Brown's book *The DaVinci Code*, Opus Dei is not given a good reputation and in fact is seen to be the secret service of the Vatican.

How appropriate. Unfortunately, just like the Society of Jesuits, former members have accused Opus Dei as being a cult, a secret society, and a conspiracy. It has been referred to as a "brainwashing cult" because of its high-pressure recruiting tactics (especially on college campuses), corporal mortification techniques (like the cilice seen in *The DaVinci Code*) and an extraordinary degree of censory (some members say they were encouraged to break off ties with their families). All members are urged to make substantial financial contributions to the movement as Numeraries donate their entire salaries. Opus Dei is a secret society because it does not reveal the names of its members and it is a conspiracy because it is involved in right-wing politics. The Vatican and its extending arms (the Jesuits, the Knights of Malta, Opus Dei, and the Priory of Sion) work for a New World Order along with the Scottish and York Rites of Freemasonry complete with the worship of Lucifer and total facilitation by reptilian and Grey aliens.

Most people will reference the Illuminati when talking about the takeover by secret societies, and they are correct to a certain extent, but that is only the façade. The real commandeers are reptilian hybrids perpetuating secret knowledge and technology. In Germany in the 14th century, the highest initiates of the Brotherhood of the Snake appeared for the first time under the Latin name of "Illuminati." The mystical order of the Rosicrucians was one of the main branches of the Illuminati in Germany at this time and it was introduced by Charlemagne in the early part of the 9th century. The Illuminati and the Rosicrucians were the driving force behind the religious zeal following the epoch of the Crusades. Harboring close ties to these organizations were the Knights of Malta, Martin Luther, Lorenzo de Medici, and Sir Francis Bacon. Today in the United States, it is not only the Illuminati composed of Rosicrucians and Freemasons that run the country but also the Elders of Zion, the religious and political leaders of the Hebrews and Khazars.

An Epic in Three Parts

The "Children of the Serpent" are the Magi, and upon their inheritance of the Earth, set up a series of mystery schools predicated upon genetics and more specifically eugenics in order to suppress technology and knowledge from the general population.[40] The knowledge and wisdom taught in each school varied, but more or less they were designed to teach the initiates about two things: death and the real history of the Earth. Many famous personages were initiates, few disclosing all the secrets. In the original mystery schools creation was acted out in three parts. The first part was dramatized as Saturn's oppression of Mother Earth. The ancients knew Saturn was a planet, but they also deified it as they did with other planets in the solar system like Venus. The god Saturn was depicted as an aggressor.[41] Just as science uses biorhythms to address the Earth's relationship to our physical bodies—like how the processes of day and night are built biochemically into our brains—as well as the Sun and the Moon, the ancients used the planets in the place of key characters in history. The Age of Saturn preceded the Age of the Sun, the birth of the Sun precipitating the protection of Earth. A play with special effects coupled with elements of a séance is what initiates would find themselves in, the original schools evincing drama and real-life effects like was never before seen until Greek theater. The candidate was taken to the spirit world by priests in an altered state of consciousness, usually brought on by psychoactive drugs or other dissociative techniques.[42]

The third act consisted of a snake slithering down into the Garden of Eden in the Age of the Earth, when she is fully separated from the Sun. The snake coils around Adam, but Adam in this sense is not really a person, per se. He is more like a vegetable. The mystery schools taught that as vegetable life evolved before animal life, so humans were in a more vegetable state before they evolved more complicated and more physical bodies. The image of the snake coiled around Adam, or in most cases now a tree or a pole of some sort, is very illustrating of the formation of the brain and spinal cord needed for intelligent animal life. The Garden of Eden here symbolizes the E. Den set up by the Nibiruans and Adam represents the first of the Lulus. The snake of course represents Marduk. The fall from grace as acted out in the mystery schools is not only characteristic of the transition to animal life

---

[40] These mystery schools evolved into the secret societies that control the world today.

[41] The ceremonies for graduation and law enforcement resemble ancient rites attributed to the god Saturn because he was the "Lord of the Rings" and hence a baron of structure and order. Today, governments oppress the people and that is why they are associated in the United States with an aggressor pagan god.

[42] Mark Booth, *The Secret History of the World* (New York: The Overlook Press, 2008).

but also of the way the Lulus were taken out of the E. Den compound and positioned to live on their own. Sex, hunger, and desire conjugated with dissatisfaction, sorrow, frustration, and fear brought on a whole new state of consciousness.

As this state of perception enveloped the animals upon their evolvement and later the human evolvement we can see that Satan, the Dark Lord, is the very agent of materialism and was identified with Saturn in Greek and Roman mythology. In the Roman tradition Venus is associated with Lucifer, but as a necessary evil so humanity could evolve past a vegetable state. In an early German adaptation of the transgressions of Venus/Lucifer, the poet Wolfram von Eschenbach composed this in his play *Parzifal*:

> See! Lucifer, there he is!
> If there are still master-priests
> Then you know well that I am saying the truth.
> Saint Michael saw God's anger . . .
> He took Lucifer's crown from his head
> In such a way that the stone jumped out of it
> Which on earth became Parsifal's stone. (*Parzifal*, 47)

Make any connections to the stone of Babel? Well, perhaps, but what is more interesting is the way the battle between Michael and Lucifer was delineated in the initiations into the ancient mystery schools. In the beginning was the void, but it wasn't nothing. It was infinite possibilities. Even the ancients knew this. They understood that matter came from mind, and the longer it manifested the denser (or more real) it became. In the first act the Earth goddess is mauled by Saturn. In the second act the Sun god appears and saves Earth by defeating Saturn in a great war in the heavens. Here, Lucifer is affiliated with Saturn and Michael is affiliated with the Sun god. The battle between Michael and his legions and Lucifer and his legions in the higher dimensions has also reverberated in other cultures around the world. In India Krishna faces the snake-demon Kaliya in a skirmish, in Greece Apollo clashes with the Python, and in Mesopotamia Perseus combats the dragon that threatened Andromeda.

The third act witnessed during the initiation ceremonies in the early mystery schools was the fall from grace, or in other words the transference into lower human consciousness. As warring factions competed for territory, food, and mating rites, the human condition formed as a mind rejoicing in forcing another to submit to one's authority. The euphoria of being dominant over another human being sunk the vibrations of the planet into the lowest levels glimpsed yet so far. After this occurrence the age of demi-gods and heroes commenced. Full-scale conflicts resulted between humans and armies of other creatures like centaurs, humans with wings, and other deformations and products of genetic experiments. The demi-gods like Hercules were more highly evolved souls and were sent down in order to aide humanity. Even figures like Enoch did not experience death. Enoch ascended in his body, which is why it says in the book of Enoch that he rode a "fiery chariot into heaven."

The story of Jason's quest for the Golden Fleece as well as the labors of Hercules personify the movement of the Sun through the signs of the Zodiac, but these narratives also represent something else. Initiates have stated the Fleece also represents the purging of the animal spirit of negative thoughts and emotions. This catharsis rendered the Fleece, and the spirit, an object of radiant gold brilliance. A snake protects the Fleece and Jason must wrest it away. It should be no question to the reader now why a snake is in this place. Here the snake protects the wisdom, just as in the Garden of Eden the snake confers the wisdom to Eve. In any case, the snake can be likened to Lucifer and wisdom. The iconic owl sees in the dark and he too is the bearer of wisdom.

The Bible does well to paint a picture of at least one important parable to the ancient mystery schools, and that is the element of language. In the Old Testament Job is a good, hardworking man who comes across a series of troubling events. He loses all his money, his offspring perishes, and he contracts a plague of boils. All the while the wicked were prospering. It was during this time that language was becoming more complicated as humans thought in words instead of pictures. The story of Job is the first that poses the question, "is life unfair or is it just a dream?" Even though language allows us today to break down experience into bits and pieces we can operate and maneuver, it bars us from developing our telepathic nature. The wicked in Job's time prospered because they thought of ways to deceive and keep secrets, such feats not being possible in the time before the Garden of Eden. Before there was no deceit, but now the malevolent were getting away with murder. What saved Job was his ability to transgress his negative experiences and see life from a different perspective. Just as he had prospered earlier in his life, now he was troubled. He was able to distinguish good from bad and therefore became enlightened. He saw the bad not as terrible, but as a necessary tool for learning. In the ancient mystery schools it was taught that music, mathematics, and language were catechized in this age, the age of the heroes. Heroes like Gilgamesh, Hercules, Orpheus, and Jason seek the more meaningful things in life while at the same time discovering how the darkness can be a tool for integration.

The transition from etheric matter to solid matter was embodied in the Sphinx. The four elements coming together to form physical matter accompanied the four cardinal constellations of the Zodiac, the four corners of the cosmos (Leo, Taurus, Scorpio, and Aquarius). In the Greek tradition the Sphinx asks Oedipus, king of Thebes, a riddle: "What walks on four legs, then two legs, then three legs?" The answer was the progression of man from birth: first you crawl on four limbs, then in adolescence you walk on two legs, and finally in old age you require a walking stick to aide you. Before, in the golden age, the gods walked the Earth alongside humans and peace reigned. In the age of the demi-gods, heroes ventured on quests and discovered wisdom. In the age of the Sphinx, man was learning about the travesties and the setbacks of life in the lower vibrations. Even though Oedipus had learned of the prophecy revealing that he would kill his father and marry his mother, his actions unconsciously led him to his fate. It seems the laws of nature had become fixed and mechanical. Humans were trapped in the lower pleasures of life while bouncing back and forth in the wheel of reincarnation. The Sphinx marks the end of the age of metamorphosis, the fixing of the biological forms we know of today.

Perhaps the most important teaching of the ancient mystery schools concerned the way the spirit worlds are experienced after death. According to these ancient teachings, in sleep the animal spirit leaves the vegetable and mineral parts of the body behind; in common terms we can call the animal spirit the astral body and the mineral part the physical body. Upon death, the vegetable part leaves with the animal spirit. The vegetable part was seen as the memories stored from each lifetime, and upon death this disintegration of the vegetable part caused the spirit to review the life just completed. After this the spirit moves on to a place in the spirit world where demons attempt to corrupt the soul with all amounts of evil impulses. In the Christian tradition this place is called "Purgatory." In the esoteric tradition the initiate was compelled to form the right attitude towards death and see the demons as not evil but actually as angels coming to set him/her free. In Egyptian art the spirit was depicted leaving the body as a bird with a human head. In all the ancient religions the being who guides this spirit into the underworld (or the 4th dimension as it is called now) is the god Mercury.

As orthodox doctrine instills a simplified theory of manifestation (God → Adam → Eve → Lucifer), the esoteric dogma explains a much different version of events. First there was the golden age. The Sun and the Earth were one body of light, and after a period of time the Sun separated from the Earth, causing it to materialize into a dense form and cool down. When Lucifer the lightbringer, externalized in many forms, deceived the human inhabitants of the Garden of Eden the vibrations of the Earth sunk even lower and men descended into wickedness and tyranny. The god of the Sun (Jesus, Osiris, Mithra) returns and infuses his holy spirit into the Earth so that the whole universe would one day dematerialize and become spirit once more. This cosmic vision of splendor and the return of the Sun god helped shape the churches of the Middle Ages and the art of the Renaissance, however, the vision and the glory have succumbed to the greed of exoteric Christianity and the Vatican.

The Eleusinian Mysteries

In Athens, Greece around the fourth and fifth centuries B.C.E., individuals were seeking a free form of thought and a free form of will, a movement pushing its way to Sparta and other Greek colonies. We have been blessed with the works of Plato, Aristotle, Pindar, Sophocles, Euripides, and other playwrights, poets and authors who hail from these epochs. Cicero said that the mystery schools in Greece accorded a great gift to the rest of the world. Pindar himself stated, "Happy is he who has seen the Mysteries before being buried beneath the ground, because he knows what happens as life ends." Sophocles said, "Thrice happy are those who have seen the Mysteries before they die; they will have life after death; everyone else will only experience suffering." Even Plutarch orated that 'those who die experience for the first time what those who have been initiated have already experienced.' Some say that Socrates was an initiate but there is not much evidence to back this up. The religious officials coveting Athens at the time exhausted much effort in seeing Socrates sentenced to death for corrupting the youth and blaspheming against the gods, creating new ones. The most known of the Greek mystery schools was born in Eleusis, a populace a few miles outside of Athens. The purification process of plants coming back to life and warmth restoring itself over Earth in the spring was celebrated in the Lesser Mysteries, which contained dramatized interactions between the gods of the pagan world, a ceremony where singing, dancing, and a person bearing a torch while wearing a crown of thorns were carried out. Ioachos, the god who was the son of Zeus and Demeter, was sacrificed and after three days was resurrected. That sounds familiar doesn't it? What also rings a bell is the overtly sexual themes displayed in the ceremonies where the goddess Venus was parodied rising out of the sea. Later Persephone marries Hades and in another drama the god Athenagoras is seen as having a horn on her forehead over her third eye.

Such ceremonies, being concerned with not only worship of the female goddess but also life after death, oftentimes epitomized the milk from the breast. Accounts of the pouring of milk from a golden vessel shaped like a breast have surfaced, and this couples with the 'Milky' in Milky Way Galaxy. The Greater Mysteries were celebrated during the autumn equinox. A candidate for initiation would fast for nine days, the hunger eliciting a visionary state and a propensity for hallucinations. When a potion called "kykeon" was drunk, the roasted barley, water, and poley oil became a narcotic and propelled the initiated into an altered state of consciousness where he could experience expanded awareness and perception. Wild fears were brought to the surface of people where they seethed and culminated into independent thoughtforms. The thoughtforms then attracted spirits and other discarnate entities. In his *Description of Greece*, Pausanius chronicles a demon named Euronomos. The entity possessed blue/black skin and devoured the flesh of rotting corpses. Through much speculation and doubt, a reference to incarnated demons must mean a possession, and there have been well-documented cases of exorcisms throughout this era and up through the Renaissance. Initiations and ceremonies have also been maintained to perform séances where spirits were invoked and asked for a certain type of power. What can be viewed as a typical case of an ancient person personifying the gods can also be glimpsed in the way the Egyptians and Sumerians intended for the gods to occupy the large statues they manufactured. The gods would have the statues as their physical bodies and whichever person possessed the statue would have reverence from it.

What is today called "out-of-body experiences" is glimpsed in a quote from the orator Aristides who proclaimed: "I thought I felt the god draw near and I touched him; I was somewhere between waking and sleeping. My spirit was so light – in a way someone who hasn't been initiated wouldn't understand." The god he is referring to is Dionysus, who also goes by the names of Bacchus and Iachos. In this state of being when a candidate was living in his astral body he was a 'spirit among spirits' and a 'god among gods' and when he was re-entered into the everyday material world he retained many of his psychic powers of perception from his out-of-body experience. On one level the ceremonies and initiations were aimed at maximizing agricultural results, but another element was hidden underneath. The harvesting of souls and soul energy has been studied for thousands of years, as well as the relationship between matter and spirit. In New Age terminology today we know that the Merkabah is the interface between the material world and the spirit world, but back then it is more mystical. That was during the times of Merlin the Magician and King Arthur.

One prophetic element did exist in the teachings handed down through the initiations, and this can been witnessed in the final initiation at Eleusis which involved a candidate being shown a plucked green wheat ear. This wheat was the star Spica, the divine seed held in the left hand of the virgin goddess of the constellation Virgo. Isis was this Egyptian goddess who held in her palm the "seed time," the current of time-space continuums which flowed together into a beautiful tapestry. This grain was purported to be made in the bread ate in the Last Supper and it symbolized the vegetable body in Jesus and also the vegetable dimension. This dimension was the altered state of consciousness taught by esoteric Christianity to be the place where you would meet Jesus. Socrates sometimes spoke of his daemon, his guardian angel who guided him through the course of life. Socrates was very much guided by his subconscious and he demonstrated it in his speeches and writings where he attempted to reconcile the instinctive wisdom of the lower animal self and the esoteric wisdom of the higher self. When he was accused of corrupting the youth of Athens and worshiping pagan gods he stood up for his cause and stated that the god he worshiped was inside himself. This might seem alien to many people, but these influences of the spirit world can be noted by many historians. One pupil of the Russian esoteric philosopher P.D. Ouspensky announced that a major influence on great writers, scientists, and artists of the twentieth century like T.S. Eliot, Frank Lloyd Wright, Kazimir Malevich, Georgia O'Keefe, Thomas Edison, and Albert Einstein was spirit guides.[43]

The aspiration of Greek drama was always to invoke within the audience member a catharsis, a purging of emotions. The emotions were always seen as the gift from the creator, the feelings that made you feel alive. New ways of feeling, thinking, perceiving, and understanding were portrayed in the plays of Aeschylus, Socrates, and Euripides. In some ways these plays were representative of initiation and what was experienced during these secret ceremonies. The animal body, during the fall in vibration, took on the form of a rough carapace, a hardened shell which protected the spirit from the harshness of the environment. Deep down inside of us a longing to be set free is realized in these plays, which articulated ways humans seek to live in the moment. When Socrates said, "An unconsidered life is not worth living," he was no doubt referring to the esoteric thinkers who repeatedly sought to understand the greater meaning behind life and the ideals of transformation. It has often been reckoned that such ancient people had no faculty for abstract thought and that people like Socrates and Plato were way ahead of their time, but I think that people have always had a deeper connection to the home from whence they came buried deep in their subconscious, and sometimes this inner knowing is forgotten and stashed away.

When Socrates died, his pupil Plato took over as the leading figure in Greek philosophy. Born in 428 B.C.E., Plato founded one of the first institutions teaching how to read called the "Academy," which was located in the garden of the tomb in Academus in Athens. The mind before matter way of thinking is reflected nicely in the *Dialogues*, writings that aim at posing philosophical questions through intricate dialogues. The idealistic mindset offered by Plato naturally assures that matter precipitates out of mind and that mind can influence the material world in any way, shape or form. In his *Allegory of the Cave*, Plato hints at sacred geometry. The prisoners of the cave can only see the shadows which they

---

[43] Spirit guides are included in most New Age writings and videos as evidence of the world beyond the physical.

interpret as the only reality. When one person escapes the cave he sees the objects which form the shadows and even the Sun itself. He realizes that there are perfect forms (sixth-dimensional geometry patterns) which act as blueprints for everything in the material universe.

The ancient initiatic teachings involving the sun god were revealed to the Caesars of Rome when they insisted on gaining entry in the mystery schools. Due to the fact that the Druids prophesied the sun god would return to eradicate the evil on the planet, Julius Caesar eradicated the cult. Emperor Augustus condemned astrology because he feared what the astrologers could see in the sky that allowed them to make predictions of futuristic events. *The Golden Age* of Apuleius is one of the great initiatic works of the Roma era. The story of Cupid and Psyche resonates well with the life of the spirit, an esoteric understanding crowning the warnings about curiosity. Cupid falls in love with Psyche, but their love-making must take place in total darkness. Amongst warnings that Cupid is a giant serpent and not a boy-god, Pysche shines a lamp on him but burns him in the process. Psyche is banished from Cupid forever and learns a harsh lesson. The true initiates of Rome eventually disappeared into shadowy schools in Rome that were totally independent from the original Mystery cults. The apex of intellectual and spiritual revelation became the movement of Stoicism, the outward expression of the initiatic esoteric impulses. When Cicero was beguiled by the machinations of Rome's political empire he gracefully bared his neck to the centurion's sword. It was he who said to "live joyfully and die hopefully."

The Early Church and Rival Movements

The early Church father Clement of Alexandria most likely knew those who were in close contact with the Apostles of Jesus, but it was his ambition to distance the real teachings of Jesus Christ from official Christian doctrine. Many early Christians, however, had already apprehended the fact that Christianity was a literary hybrid of what had been taught in the mystery schools of Egypt, Greece, and Rome. Clement and his pupil Origen educated more advanced students in the *disciplina arcane*, magical practices which would today be considered arcane. In the second century C.E., Neo-Platonism took full form and structure, Plato's ideas of mind before matter merging into a living philosophy that erudite men like Clement adored and adapted. All magic is henceforth a power of mind over matter, practitioners of this skill adept in the arts of mind manipulation. Plutarch, most notably an advocate of the Neo-Platonist movement, in his *On the Delay in Divine Justice*, wrote extensively on what different spirits look like on their journey into the spirit realms. Some are enveloped in a flame like aperture, others dappled with blanched spots like adders. Porphyry, apt pupil to Plotinus, often reported seeing his master in ecstatic raptures, unified with the "One." Men like Iamblichus and Jamblichus who followed these acts emphasized that godly, magical practices were a "total union with God." This state of ecstasy, however mystical, was promulgated throughout the centuries with a flavor of Hermeticism and the Cabala.

As an initiate of the Persian Mystery schools, St. Augustine was a follower of Manichaeism, and as an imperial intellectual, sought to render a comprehensive account of Church doctrine in terms of Platonism and even Gnosticism. According to Augustine, the light of the soul was superior in contrast to the light of the intellect, the smart man in effect no wiser than the spiritual adept. In the end, the intellect must bow to the spirit, but conventional Church history has undermined the intense, spiritual experiences of Augustine and other mystery school initiates. In these experiences, the conjunction with Jesus Christ is often independent of the religious encounter with the divine. The Roman Emperor Constantine, upon entering battle, claimed to receive a dream in which Jesus told him to place the cross on his battle flag with the words, "In this sign thou shalt conquer." When the rebels were defeated Constantine proclaimed Christianity the official religion of the Empire. Was this vision like the one Paul had on his way to Damascus? It is fitting to note how both Paul and Constantine adopted a Christian logo after their encounters with Jesus, as I am sure politics weighed heavily in the equation.

In promotion of the new Christian doctrine, Constantine offered freedom to any slave who converted and twenty pieces of gold to any who were free. You have to spend money to make money, right? Even so, as the Christians exalted meekness and humility, the face of the Roman Empire was turned on its nose. It was originally known for conquest and expansion, but deeply vexed by the prophecy in the Sibylline Oracles—which expounded that Rome would once again fall

A New Order of the Ages

into abominable depths—Constantine hoped with vigor that this new religion would slow the decline. In this advent he also transported the Palladium, the statue that had been carried from Troy to Rome in its inception, to the city that would soon become Constantinople. Under the aegis of Constantine and his reptilian (Annunaki) superiors, the Council of Nicaea was congregated in 325 C.E. and it stationed the gospels that were to be interpreted as valid and those that would not. Pagan practices were also forbidden by imperial edicts. As a result however, this rigid dogma imposed by Constantine was lessened by his nephew Julian when he came to the throne in 361 C.E. As a student of Iamblichus, Julian gave permission for pagan temples to resume worship, instituted equal rights for all subjects independent of their religious beliefs, and above all revered the being he called the "Seven-rayed god." The seven emanations from the Cosmic Mind were a topic of great study in the schools of Iamblichus, Julian's god undoubtedly mirroring this concept. The gods that Julian had encountered during initiation were denied by the strict dogma that had been imposed on the Roman people during the reign of Constantine, which is why the new emperor led a military campaign into Persia in order to absorb the knowledge of the Manichaean Mystery School positioned in Persia. Before he could carry out his mission, though, Julian was assassinated by a devout follower of Constantine.

The Emperor Theodosius came to power and the knowledge of true initiatic spirituality was vehiculated underground. Much like when President Kennedy was disposed of after he compromised the stranglehold of the international bankers, so too was Julian gotten rid of when he undermined the power of religious and political authority. In the wake of their deaths (both Kennedy and Julian), evil men were placed on the pedestal by the real powers hiding behind the curtain. In his conquest of the spiritual truth, Theodosius confiscated all property supposedly owned by "heretics," rededicated statues of Isis (Egyptian) to Mary (Christian), and converted the Roman Pantheon into a temple of monotheism. Was this the same Theodosius who apportioned the statue of Saturn and made it into the statue of Saint Peter in Saint Peter's basilica? What is most revealing is the way the new emperor closed down the mystery schools in the wake of besieging the Serapeum in Alexandria, one of the great wonders of the ancient world which housed a grand library of the planet's most extravagant collection of books. Most fortunately, many books were smuggled out before the library was razed to the ground, but where did they go? I would not be the least bit surprised if they ended right back in the hands of tyranny and suppression.

If that wasn't enough, Theodosius organized the murder, nay, extermination, of Hypatia, daughter of a prominent philosopher and mathematician. She lectured at the Neo-Platonic school of philosophy in Alexandria, a preserver of sizeable intellectual knowledge of the mystery schools. She argued amidst large crowds that Christianity had evolved out of the teachings of the more ancient mystery traditions. Well-versed in the wisdom of Plotinus and Iamblichus, she posed a major threat to the new Roman dogma. One day in 414 C.E., a group of black-robed monks besieged Hypatia, forcing her off her chariot and dragging her naked to a nearby church. There they tore her apart and scraped the flesh from her bones with oyster shells, later burning the remains. Just as the priests of Amun had tried to erase Akhenaton from history, the Church endeavored to do the same with Hypatia.

The Romans, stamping out doctrinal differences across the state, were in fact more concerned about Attila the Hun and the barbarian hoards from the East than any internal foe. China composed a rapidly growing empire and blackmailed the Goths, Visigoths, and Vandals to invade the eastern parts of Europe. In the fifth century C.E. the Mongolian tribes were united under Attila the Hun and invaded the plains of Central Asia to northern Gaul and into Italy where they razed Constantinople. When Attila's forces conquered the Roman city of Corinth he found a prostitute on every street corner. Attila was known as a barbarian, albeit a moderate one, and so he gave the prostitutes the option of exile or marrying one of his men. Attila forbade his people to live in Roman territory or buy Roman goods, all the while destroying Roman buildings through raids and stealing thousands of pounds of gold. In 452 C.E. the Roman Emperor sent the Bishop of Rome, Leo, to meet Attila when he had Rome in his death grip. Leo, the future pope, struck a deal with Attila that the Mongolian invader would receive the daughter of the Roman Emperor as his wife and thousands more pounds of gold. Why was Attila so successful when others were not? The primary aide to Attila and his forces was a practice known as shamanism. In fact, the guides of Attila during battle were confessed by Attila himself to be shaman priests of the spirit world. The spirits of the dead guided

Attila and his people to victories in battle, and in some accounts they bequeathed to them supernatural powers.

Shamanism is another interesting practice the Church has tried to attenuate. The word comes from the Tungus-Mongol noun meaning "one who knows." Shamans in Attila's life were probably spirit shamans, but this most likely also evoked warriors to practice the shamanic ways of inducing oneself into trance states by hyperventilation, frenzied self-mutilation, sensory deprivation, dehydration, and sleep deprivation. Psychoactive plants were also ingested like ayahuasca, peyote cactus, the ergot fungus, and cannabis. In these trance states the Shamans could astral travel to the spirit worlds in their etheric bodies. There is an enzyme secreted in the pineal gland called dimethyltryptamine that points modern science to the dream world. In roughly two percent of humans it is in great enough quantity to deliver spontaneous and voluntary trance-like states where hallucination occurs, but science mostly attributes the chemical to dreams. In ancient practices, shamans would experience extreme trance states where they would be taken in their astral body to a higher realm of consciousness. These sometimes involved puking, blacking out, chanting, speaking in tongues, convulsing, and conversing with spirits. A disembodied spirit could be either benevolent or malevolent. In all the accounts from antiquity the results of these journeys into altered states of consciousness recurrently produced supernatural powers like the ability to heal, gather secret information about enemies, channeling mind to mind impressions with animals, and the gift of prophecy.[44]

This all fits in perfectly with the narratives from initiations in the mystery schools, all of which required candidates to travel out of body and experience demons on the astral plane. Modern esoteric teachers have unraveled the teachings and drawings of the old Hunnic and Mongol hordes that practiced shamanism and concluded that the ancient tribes were very interested in reaching higher states of consciousness where they could communicate with spirits and angels. They did this to gain knowledge and certain healing powers. In conventional history, animism and totemism give rise to the complex cosmologies of the great ancient civilizations. In secret history lore, the primordial vision and questing of mankind was complicated and epic. This then descended

---

[44] In *Awakening to the Spirit World: The Shamanic Path of Direct Revelation,* Sandra Ingerman and Hank Wesselman posit that the Shamanic path to illumination is the most universal and does not adhere to any specific religion.

into animism, totemism, and shamanism. Attila and his forces practiced shamanism because it gave them strategic information, but modern shamans practice because it allows them to traverse freely through the spirit realms when the material realm offers so many restrictions. In 453 C.E. Attila was found dead, right when he was preparing to celebrate marriage to a beautiful young woman. It appeared that he had suffered a massive nosebleed. Probably poison. He had been arranging the end of the Roman Empire, or so he hoped.

In the days when the Roman Empire really did decline it was the result of too massive an empire to defend. Constant invasions from the Germans, Visigoths, and other tribes ensured a constant need for soldiers to protect the cities. Political avarice also added to the downfall. The oracles fell silent and Pan saw his demise. Harsh economic and political realties swam through amidst the advent of technological improvement. Incredible engineering projects of the time like aqueducts, drainage systems, and roads thousands of miles long propelled the people into a new way of thinking. Even so, the delicate growth of human consciousness was distracted. God and the gods become nothing but abstract ideas as poets like Lucretius theorized that everything was made up of tiny atoms and God was not real. He wrote that every action in the universe was random and unpredictable. At this critical juncture in human history it is revealed to us the shift from the age of the mystery schools to the age of the secret societies. The soul was on a roller coaster ride. Is *Alice in Wonderland* a good allegory for this idea? I think so. A mechanical grinding of the wheels of economic and political development quieted the spirit inside the average human, and all the while Church fathers were scheming ways of forcing the people into submission from a demanding, monotheistic god.

Regardless, the capacity for abstract thought has been developing since the days of Pythagoras, Confucius, and Socrates. Siddhartha spread Buddhism from India to China. Zen became a philosophy of intuitive enlightenment as a fusion of Buddhism and Taoism (Daoism) over a period of two hundred years in China. It was one of a new view of abstract thought which purported that the vegetable consciousness is centered in the solar plexus chakra and it is that which connects us to the rest of life in the universe. To quote Saint Augustine, the "light beyond the light of the intellect" was this form of consciousness. It offered universal compassion and love, and when operating from this mode one could see everything as himself or herself. Acting on his predecessors, the Byzantine Emperor Justinian closed down the remaining schools of Greek philosophy and banished this form of consciousness. The works of Aristotle, Socrates, and Plato were smuggled out by terrified professors who feared for their lives. Many eventually settled in Persia where King Khusraw spoke of founding an academy like the Greek one. The epoch of the sixth century saw a magical influence of abracadabra and Arabian magic, which stemmed from the alchemical material of Aristotle. Caches of self-generating gold, flying machines, and tomes of magical knowledge arise from this period when the intellectual ferment which observed the components of Neoplatonism, Gnosticism, and Hermeticism tore through the front.

Crazy in Love

Amid all the muck of the Annunaki/bloodline/Roman oppression after the death of Jeshua, the Renaissance and the age of love/enlightenment was a great sidetrack. Giordano Bruno wrote about multiple dimensions and extraterrestrials civilizations in 1600 C.E. and so the Pope burned him at the stake, but the Roman Catholic elite would not have the last laugh during this era. Many great Renaissance artists and musicians successfully captured the power of sacred geometry, extraterrestrial influence, and alchemical codes. Alchemy presents a multidimensional awareness, and artists like DaVinci and Michelangelo captured this essence beautifully. People were also remembering how to love again. The odes of Pindar, Sappho, and Horace paint a picture of love on the canvas of life, expressions of romantic love that dance in the moonlight. In conventional history people have been falling in love since the dawn of time, but was this always so?

In the secret history, overtly sexual themes have perpetuated the dwindling ecstatic delight of romantic love. The religious understanding of "love your neighbor as you would yourself" is seen to have sprung out of the Hebrew prophets' conceptualization of grace. Grace can be remembered as Jesus dying on the cross, but what about amorous love expressed between a man and a woman? For centuries since the dawn of abstract and abstruse thought, sexual energies had been channeled into the development of the mind and human intellect, and by the time of Thomas Aquinas and Roger Bacon this transformation was reaching completion. People were discovering new alchemical sciences and a new way of understanding the universe. Aquinas' *Summa Theologica* is over two million words testifying to the diligence and capacity for continuous intellectual focus. As an impulse radiating out from Arabia, people were indulging in a new delight for the material world, a pleasure garden of light, sound and space. A new and extravagant sexual sheen was drawn like a curtain and the evolution of human consciousness was about to take a unique twist.

In the twelve century C.E., the Languedoc and Provence were the most civilized regions in Europe. The Arabic-Andalusian poetic forms were adopted by the Troubadors, poets who composed tender, yearning love songs; the first of these poets was Guillaume, Count of Poitiers and Duke of Aquitane. Quite a title; his courtly visions of love were a direct counter to the bloody fighting of the Crusades. With the coming of Troubadors like Bernart de Ventadorn and Pierre Vidal, the poetry took on a colloquial scent with metaphors and similes comparing love to everyday objects. Against the traditional view, Troubador poetry also made men the subject of women, marriage being an agent for a new form of love which spontaneously flowed between individuals of varying social and economic status. These revolutionary poets affirmed that this new state of ecstasy can be reached by propelling oneself through a series of trials like solving riddles, escaping a dense labyrinth, and slaying wild beasts. Finally, In the presence of his beloved, the lover is overcome with eternal bliss and in the ensuing consummation achieves an amended state of consciousness which confers supernatural powers like the power to heal. It must be noted here that these documented experiences of being in love were identified with the process of initiation. Troubador literature is stock full of symbolism emblematizing initiation, the most popular sigil being the rose.[45] As an obvious allusion to the chakras, the rose was most likely derived from Sufism where it was the motif of the entrance to the spirit worlds. Also, alchemical techniques were employed for sexual ecstasy. As Guillaume of Poitiers wrote: "I want to retain my lady in order to refresh my heart so well that I cannot age. He will live a hundred years who succeeds in possessing the joy

---

[45] Shakespeare was most likely influenced by the Troubadors. Some accounts say Shakespeare never existed and it was really Count Saint Germain who wrote all his plays. The rose is a powerful Rosicrucian symbol and it appears in many of these writings.

of his love." This sexual impetus was the cause of the Renaissance. Secret societies and heretical groups were catechizing such techniques of mystical ecstasy, but would the hard-fought intellectual faculty of human thought be overcome by this?

Once again we must differ to the energy of the imagination which flourished during the Renaissance.[46] The literature from this epoch was illumined by the stars and the planets as it was said that through love and emotion our spirit is reunited with the rays of the stars. Upon imagining with full intent and conviction the spirits of the planets and the star gods, these powers were believed to flow through one. As the Middle Ages integrated the age of alchemical magic, the Renaissance was the age of spiritual magic. With paints and colors artists could render these newfound feelings on parchment and canvas. Botticelli's painting of the *Primavera* illustrates the process of the creation of matter in terms of the continuous emanations of creative energies from the cosmic mind. The artist's preference for minor tones and lighter colors suggest the etheric nature of beings who are not fully materialized. As our minds are protrusions of the Universal Consciousness, everything that is experienced, felt, and thought in history is held in the memory of the cosmic mind, that which we know today as the Akashic records. Painters like Leonardo DaVinci stressed notions like these in subtle overtures as towering geniuses were becoming known for the clarity of their visions and not intellectual data in their head. One need only gaze at Raphael's *Madonna and Child* or DaVinci's *Mona Lisa* to sense a divinely guided paintbrush and a spiritual understanding.[47]

One of Leonardo's influences was an architect named Leon Battista Alberti, designer of the Rucellai Palace in Florence, one of the first classical edifices in Renaissance Italy. He was also the grand architect of the façade of Santa Maria Novella, also in Florence. His vision on love was grandiose; his book *Hypnerotomachia Poliphiliis* translates as "the lover of many things in his struggle for love in a dream." In the story, a hero awakes one day to go on an adventure but suddenly falls into a dream. He follows his love through a strange wilderness of monsters and a labyrinth of half stone/half organic buildings. Alberti proposed that

---

[46] The Renaissance was a shift in human consciousness to a more artistic and compassionate form. It started in Florence and spread to the rest of Europe between the 14th and 17th centuries C.E.

[47] Leonardo da Vinci and Raphael were both initiates of secret societies.

the architecture of the Renaissance, which he helped spur, contained the logic of a dream, a surreal adventure where past, present, and future collided with the living organism that is the universe. In this new state of mind nothing is forbidden and recondite thought is encouraged. At the end of the story the hero is united with his beloved in the Temple of Venus. The beloved stirs a cistern with a flaming torch which causes the hero to fall into a trance, and as nymphs dance around the altar, doves are sacrificed and a basin of whale sperm, musk, camphor oil, and almond oil is set alight. The beloved rubs the ground at the base of the altar and the whole building collapses as a tree emerges from the top of the altar. When the hero and the beloved eat from the fruit of the tree they are transported to a higher state of consciousness. A direct parallel can be drawn here between this fruit and the fruit from the Garden of Eden. In this case, though, the eating of the fruit is recommended for the attainment of knowing. In this series of mystic rites the channeling of sexual energy is procreated and the two lovers are at one with the cosmos. An illustration from the *Hypnerotomachia Poliphiliis* reveals a tree transforming into a human, most undoubtedly delineating the shift from vegetable life to animal life.

Born at the end of the fifteenth century, the poet François Rabelais traversed the streets of Chinon fifty years after the death of Joan of Arc. The spirit of the Troubadors coursed through his veins as he composed *Gargantua and Pantagruel*, a novel which tells of giants maintaining large appetites for the material world. According to Rabelais, the Church's censure of spiritual heights proved to be unhealthy as the love of laughter and lovemaking adorned his prose. To Rabelais, love of the existence was the healthiest form of consciousness. At the end of his novel the protagonists arrive at a mysterious island denoting the Matrix. They are led into an underground chamber where a fountain is overflowing with wine, which in consonance with Rabelais, represented the character of humanity. Wine was the spirit of truth and philosophy as it was associated with the secretion of chemicals in the brain that spur a mystical state of ecstasy. This ecstasy was amrita, the nectar of immortality the ancient cultures claimed to be the nectar of the gods. Amrita was also associated with the feeling of being in love. Love, to the men and women of the Renaissance, was the ultimate expression of life. Love could crown or it could cripple. It was well documented but incomprehensible at the same time. In the words of the Roman poet

A New Order of the Ages

Horace, love conquers all. This concept is properly distinguished in his odes:

> Tell me, Lydia, in the name of all that's holy, why are you set on wrecking Sybaris with loving? Why does he loathe the sunlit field? Dirt and sweat never bothered him before.
>
> Why won't he join his fellow soldiers at cavalry practice, or curb his Gallic stallion with a jagged bit in its mouth?
> Why is he scared of a splash in yellow Tiber? Why does he avoid the rubbing oil as if it were the blood of a viper? Why doesn't he show off now all the bruises on his arms?
> And to think he once threw for the record with discus and javelin!
>
> Why does he lie low, like the son of seaborn Thetis before the fall of Troy with all its bitter tears, afraid that
> Trojan troops and death would come of wearing the clothes of a man?
> (Horace, *Odes and Epodes*, 1.8)

Beautiful.

Prosecute the Witch: Descent Into Tyranny

The esoteric suppositions which continued to cultivate from the Late Middle Ages through the Renaissance to the Age of Reason were for the most part individual yearnings for the spirit, in other cases aggregations perpetuating their knowledge through secret rituals and ceremonies. There were many obstacles to this shifting, howsoever. From 1347 to 1350 the Black Death decimated a third of the population of the entire European continent while Cathars and Templars were tortured, hunted down, and burned. The Inquisition was having its way as the Hundred Years War, precipitating 1337 to 1453 C.E., upheld the degradation in France and especially the Languedoc. An individual of an independent mind sought refuge during this period when the Church attempted a coup d'état on spiritual and temporal order.

In the Late Middle Ages Europe was a madding pot of religious turmoil as ordinary country people struggled to survive amidst the witch hunt. Estimates of the number of 'witches' burned throughout Europe during these epochs vary from 50,000 to over a million.[48] In the minds of the clergy, the "will to offend God" became the central offense, and as society grew more and more sophisticated, the morality emphasized by the Church shifted from the Seven Deadly Sins to the Ten Commandments. The Seven Deadly Sins accentuated the chastity, decency, and conduct of an individual and a community, whereas the Ten Commandments set the standard that only one god could be worshiped, and that of course was the wrathful and jealous god of the Church (Jehovah/Jahbulon/ Lucifer). More specifically, the Dominicans were the members of this institution who influenced the Church fathers. In 1486, *Malleus Maleficarum*, the "Hammer of the Witches," was composed by Dominicans who wished to propose a do-it-yourself Inquisitor's manual for hunting down and prosecuting witches and others accused of heresy.

More than three-quarters of those dispatched for witchcraft were women. The females of society were seen to hold a powerful sway over men, those of lower stature and even those of higher stature. The Church mistrusted women because not only did they hold the mysterious key to childbirth, but they could also sexually entice men. Even when their sexual allure was lost they still possessed "women's intuition." The authors of the *Malleus Maleficarum* were misogynistic as they feared women, and during this time set up Christianity as the dominant religion. Most medieval men and women did not understand much theology, but they most undoubtedly were all Christian because that was simply the primary religion. Even though many small villages in Europe harbored minute traces of the old pagan beliefs which loitered for centuries, there was most definitely a stratum of folk-belief and superstition still lingering. The Devil depicted in the Bible is wholly a construct of the medieval Church. Pan, the male personification of nature, and Bacchus, the hermaphrodite Greek god of wine, were admixed to form the modern representation of Satan or the Devil. Both Pan and Bacchus embodied the concept of the natural generative force, although their projection was sewn into the image of a red man with a black pointy beard, a trident, and horns. Satan was the new weapon for combating the dissidents and nonconformists that arose as the demonizing of superstitious peasants became commonplace.

---

[48] David Barrett, A Brief History of Secret Societies (Philadelphia: Running Press, 2007), 62.

Viewed as an immediate threat to stability, deviant beliefs were not a luxury anyone could possess. It made little difference whether the clerics who prosecuted the heretics were Roman Catholics, Lutherans, Calvanists, Dominicans, Jesuits, or Purity Presbyterians. The tribulations continued betwixt the development of political, religious, intellectual, and social thought. Difference was not accepted by those in charge. The connections between religion and astrology, the secrets of the heavens, posed an uneasy relationship with the Church because of the potential for knowledge and understanding coded within the codes of the stars and constellations. In the Middle Ages, many astrologers bedecked the ranks of priests and monks, and were repeatedly sought out by the popes for astronomical interpretations. The Borgia pope, Alexander VI, hung a zodiac on the ceiling of his apartment in the Vatican. Remember when the esoteric religions were beseeched by the Roman and early medieval nobleman? It wasn't because they disagreed with these movements, it was because they agreed with them and therefore saw them as hazards to their empire. The same applies with astrology. The popes and kings did not banish astrology and astronomy because they regarded these concepts as fiction, they did it because they vehemently believed them and saw anyone who used this knowledge as a threat to their political and religious stability.

Alchemy has always been an amalgam of science and spirituality. It was the "royal art" that so-called fraudulent magicians practiced in ancient Egypt, Greece, Rome, and Italy during the Renaissance. These practitioners were chemists, physicists, astronomers, mathematicians, botanists, and biologists. They discovered that one could focus a beam of sunlight through a polished lens of glass to produce one of the first lasers and that what was seen through this lens could be magnified. Physiologists also fell into this category. They studied the component parts of the human body and how they could be healed. Roger Bacon, who was altercated earlier in the dissertation, along with Albertus Magnus (1193-1280), were both monks and scientists. Being a monk or scientist back then did not mean one was confined to a particular field of study as oftentimes people sought to expand their horizons. Bacon invented eye-glasses and the modern scientific method of observation. Albertus was a Dominican, and although he spent a lifetime studying Aristotle he eventually merged as a bishop who walked on the dark side more times than not. Both Albertus and Bacon were imputed with possessing a speaking brazen head. They both most likely heard the stories of the Templars and Baphomet and probably used similar methods of opening up portals to the spirit world.

Even though it proved useful, alchemy was regarded by the Church fathers with cynicism because it involved non-Christian ideals. The Arab mathematician Jabir Ibn Hayyan, who lived during the eighth century C.E., was one of the most influential early alchemists whose texts were so obscure that the word 'gibberish' originates with his works. This, however, could have been used to hide the deeper meaning of his teachings. Alchemy was never solely applied to turning base metals into gold, it was in fact a language for deeper psychological, philosophical, and spiritual truths. The twentieth century occultist Israel Regardie once wrote: "The entire object of all magical and alchemical processes is the purification of the natural man, and by working upon his nature to extract the pure gold of spiritual attainment. This is initiation." I will allude back to the *Metamorphoses* by Ovid and say that esoteric thinkers were primarily concerned with transformation, not only the transformation of objects or epochs but the transformation of people from infancy to enlightenment.

With the advent of the Middle Ages passing over to the Renaissance a desire for learning multiplied through the fray. Cosimo de' Medici was a Florentine who contracted a monk by the name of Marsilio Ficino to ferret out intellectual and spiritual manuscripts, one of these being the *Corpus Hermeticum* which was later translated into Latin and published in 1471. While Neo-Platonist and Gnostic in nature, it also appended elements of Greek and Egyptian, studies which related the cosmic bodies to the sub-atomic bodies. The Hermetic philosophers of the next two centuries advanced the knowledge and wisdom that was really known thousands of years ago. Most people today think the knowledge, technology, and data studied now is something new, but it isn't. Man has been thinking like this since his inception. During this epoch scholars around Europe were studying texts such as the Cabala and *Corpus Hermeticum* and applying these ideas to God and Creation. Just as today, the smartest and most well known litterateurs of the ancient world studied and learned the texts of many different religions and belief systems, not just one or two. When Henry Cornelius Agrippa von Nettesheim (1486-1535) told authorities that a witch should be spared the fire, he was ridiculed immensely, the basis of which resulted from his applications of Christianity, Cabalism, and Neo-Platonism. His composed works such as *The Nobility of the Female Sex* and *The Superiority of Women* brought him to a level of much contempt to the eyes of the Church fathers, who did not understand the significance of the Divine Feminine. In his *Occult Philosophy*, Agrippa professed that magic is a philosophical science combining physics, mathematics, astrology, and theology. Of course, the Church condemned him, not because he was wrong but because he was right.

Around the time of Agrippa was a physician and surgeon named Theophrastus Bombastus von Hohenheim. He reformed medicine and argued that the truly effective physician is one who understands the influences of the soul, not just the body. He was one to purport that the physical body, being a three-dimensional projection of the spirit body, broke down in function and became diseased when communication with spirit shut off or dwindled. He demonstrated an immense wealth of knowledge concerning psychosomatic illnesses and alchemical studies and also discovered chemical and mineral cures for illnesses. John Dee was another pioneer, a true Renaissance man who was a doctor, astronomer, cartographer, mathematician, philosopher, theologian, and advisor to Elizabeth I. Ironically, Dee's success as a mathematician led to his felicitous aptitude for summoning angels and other daemons. Following in the steps of Agrippa, Dee was also a Christian Cabalist who saw numbers as the basis for all creation. Just as the Cabalists had pilfered the ideas and theories of Pythagoras, so too did the Hermetic Philosophers. In 1583 an angel warned Dee of his impending demise and he fled to Prague. It seemed he too was to become a victim of the Matrix.

Giordano Bruno (1548-1600) began his career as a Dominican monk, although he had to abscond when it was discovered that he was holding certain 'suspect' works by Erasmus in his monastery's privy. These were most likely works which disputed the authoritative claims made by the Church. While spending time as a Lutheran and Calvinist he quickly became antagonistic to all forms of orthodox Christianity. In opposition to the Church, he was a free thinker who took Copernicus' heliocentric theory and expanded it to include other star systems as well. By applying this theory he was able to surmise that all the stars were in fact suns like our own with planets revolving around them. The common, accepted view at this time was that the Earth was the center of the solar system and was circled by the Moon, Sun, and other planets, as well as the other stars in the night sky. God was perceived to be beyond the circle of the stars, but to Bruno this was ludicrous. He saw that God permeated all aspects of creation. God was not "out there" but in fact "in here." Bruno taught that man could become God not by any saving act of grace or death, but by his own extended efforts in any incarnation. This thought was even at more variance than the orthodox belief. Lo and behold, Bruno was accused of heresy and imprisoned in Venice. Later, in 1593, he was taken to Rome. After seven years of imprisonment and interrogation by the Inquisition he was burned at the stake in 1600.

The Dark Ages, Middle Ages, and the Renaissance, although stock full of new and inspired ways of thinking, bore witness to the ego of man and especially the Church. The Roman Catholic Church's view on astrology varied from pope to pope, but it was always alchemy and real spiritual knowledge that was held in deep suspicion. Oftentimes considered black magick, the summoning and raising of spirits, angels, and demons was held in utter disdain by those who did not understand. Those who showed an interest in the esoteric field of thought were suspected and accused of dealing with the Devil, as most the wars fought in the sixteenth and seventeenth centuries C.E. were over religion. The barbarity of burning supposed witches and heretics continued right up through the Renaissance, the last person to be burnt at the stake in recorded history being as late as 1781. The Spanish Inquisition took on all the attributes from its predecessors, perpetuating the search for heretics until 1834. In Britain, the anti-witchcraft law was not repealed until 1951.

Even today, religious fundamentalists are quick to dismiss someone or something as blasphemous when it is not in accord to what they believe. They are simply scared of the wrath of their God and do not much care for the free will and free thinking of others. They are quick to conform, and see everything else as a threat, not as a beautiful diverse element of life. The more we change, the more we stay the same. People even today are ridiculed incessantly by those with rigid belief systems who are afraid because their masks are falling down. Just like the Church and the Inquisition, they are insulting spiritual people who have love in their hearts and are willing and able to teach others the truth. How much longer are we going to allow this? The real light of knowledge is not ego, envy, greed, or power. It is not dogma, a wrathful god, or the deceitful Church. It is love and creativity. The Roman Catholic Church has always been a conduit for the Annunaki. Today, Satanism, witchcraft, and black magick are practiced not only in the White House and British Royal Family, but by many famous personages like athletes, actors, and musicians. It was branded centuries ago as heresy, but obviously because it has significant merit.

The Book of Knowledge: Keys of Enoch

The Book of Enoch, one of many discluded in the official Christian canon, relates the story of Enoch, great grandfather of Noah, and his interaction with a race of ascended beings called "the Watchers." In the text the leaders of this group of beings are many. They aid mankind and are referenced as such:

> And Azâzêl taught men to make swords, and knives, and shields, and breastplates, and made known to them the metals of the earth and the art of working them, and bracelets, and ornaments, and the use of antimony, and the beautifying of the eyelids, and all kinds of costly stones, and all colouring tinctures. And there arose much godlessness, and they committed fornication, and they were led astray, and became corrupt in all their ways. Semjâzâ taught enchantments, and root-cuttings, Armârôs the resolving of enchantments, Barâqîjâl, taught astrology, Kôkabêl the constellations, Ezêqêêl the knowledge of the clouds, Araqiêl the signs of the earth, Shamsiêl the signs of the sun, and Sariêl the course of the moon. (Dead Sea scrolls, Book of Enoch)

Compared with the original source of 1 Enoch 1:9, which may be in Deuteronomy 33:2, the parables of the Watchers are seen to assist mankind on its evolutionary progression to higher consciousness. It is proclaimed, "The Lord came from Sinai and dawned from Seir upon us; he shone forth from Mount Paran; he came from the ten thousands of holy ones, with flaming fire at his right hand." As with the story of Moses, we can see similarities between the mountains ascribed in both texts as well as wording used to describe the gods. A burning bush is a flaming fire that must assume the form of powerful radiation and energy emanations from metallic and/or etheric spacecraft. Accounts from eyewitnesses attest to the fact that both Moses and Enoch, as well as others described in these types of encounters like Ezekiel and Elijah, appear to light up in a "chariot of fire" and ascend to heaven. Heaven, of course, was the sky and above to the ancients, not the dimensional frequency which metaphysicians attribute it to today.

The Arcturians, the Watchers in some accounts, are known to be the keepers of the Arcturian Stargate[49] and are mentioned in the book *The Book of Knowledge: Keys of Enoch* by J.J. Hurtak. They are acquainted as "shepherds watching the faithful on the other side of the river of crystal," or in other words, the Milky Way Galaxy. Arcturus is considered to be the midway programming center for the physical brotherhoods of the universe; the Arcturians are the shepherds who corral souls between incarnations on Earth and other planets in this sector of the galaxy, and they are also the governing body for this universe, Arcturus being the home of the most ascended of beings. The Eye of Horus was a motif used in ancient Egypt as a portal into the higher heavens, or higher dimensional frequencies inhabited by the consciousness. The Eye in the Triangle is the Eye of Horus as well as the denotation for the Arcturian Stargate. The Holy Triangle of Light is this triangle and the eye is not the all-seeing eye but in fact the fifth eye chakra, an extension of the third eye chakra. In his book, Dr. Hurtak writes that until the Eye of Horus arrives, the consciousness of man is forever trapped in the karmic cycles of life. The Adam Kadmon, or the primeval man, was the original blueprint for the seeds of human life on Earth instigated by the Arcturians and Lyrans (note here I mean the original seeds of all life on Earth, not the genetic tampering performed by the Nibiruans). The Illuminati operating today has used the symbol of the all-seeing eye for many centuries, but the concept is not originally theirs. They have borrowed it because of the power it holds. The Arcturians are the real guardians of the Eye in the Triangle, the Arcturian Stargate and the Holy Triangle of Light.

Hurtak's work posits the spiritual and scientific issues of the future as well as the methodology in which we humans exist in this three dimensional reality. Prime Creator's manifestation can only be fully realized when we discover the higher thoughtforms and mathematical rhythms of light vibrations that connect us to the macrocosm of the

---

[49] It is reported through channeling that many souls on Earth passed through the Arcutrian Stargate when they incarnated on Earth. The Arcturian Stargate can also be likened to the Holy Triangle of Light. Arcturian Channel, http://ourreturnhome.com/.

collective unconscious, the divine blueprints for all biological and mineral manifest forms. *The Book of Knowledge: Keys of Enoch* does quite well in demonstrating the relationship between D.N.A. coding and the transmissions and emanations of all higher manifest thoughtforms, since everything in creation originates as a thought in the Universal Consciousness. The Arcturians profess that the human unconscious will soon merge with the Universal Unconscious. Above all, this work describes the Divine Genetic Code within the human body that will prepare mankind for new vistas of life within the spectrum of higher evolution of the species, the transformation of light succeeding aspects of identical central genetic light information. What Jesus Christ referred to as the "house of many mansions" is a revelation of the greater meaning of life in which we are all participating. Shakespeare once said that life is but a play, and Beethoven, upon his passing away from the material realm, said, "applaud friends, the comedy is over." Life is a dream, and we are dreaming. We are free-willed multidimensional beings who create reality with thoughts and emotions in every moment. The Keys of Enoch are an archetype for different levels of spiritual consciousness, and through intensive study, an understanding of the methods in which there are varying levels of coding in the biological framework of physical existence can and will be apprehended.

Visions of the future reveal a new science. Medical astronomy will be applied towards adjusting pressure fluctuations that underlie mechanisms administering new axiatonal lines which according to Hurtak are stimulated by noise temperature calibrations (seventh-dimensional sound pulsations). The following is an excerpt from *The Book of Knowledge: Keys of Enoch*; here overself is a synonym for oversoul:

1. There is at work within all biological systems a path of interchangeability to standardize unique vibratory levels. Our galactic body of creation controls its renewing functions through meridian *axiatonal lines* which are the equivalent of acupuncture lines that can connect with resonating star systems.
2. These *axiatonal lines* are not limited to a physical body or a biological creation, but are open-ended and can connect the body vehicle with axiatonal lines that emanate from the various star populations and exist as chemical code mechanisms.

3. When Man can discover the connection between his life space and the axiatonal grids controlling the body through endless cell division, Man will have a new superscience known as *medical astronomy*.
4. For the human body is a microcosmos or small space-time field within a larger field. If we can maintain this view, we can recognize that acupuncture is one of the first empirical demonstrations of biological scaling within the universe.
5. If we are to approach acupuncture from the standpoint of biophysics and also under stand the higher force fields which go through the human system as a small openended universe, then we can understand how this thinking organism known as the human being can be attached to other thinking organisms within the local universe.
6. In essence, Man is a floating biological sub-system existing between Magnetic fields. The Magnetic fields shape the embryological lines of growth and correspond to magnetic grids delineated within the body.
7. These embryological lines are controlled by biochemical clocks which, in turn, are controlled by the magnetic resonance factors in the immediate universe.
8. Answers to problems of growth, connected with the biochemical clocks in the human body, will come from experiments conducted outside the earth's gravitational and electromagnetic field.
9. The human evolution is a "preconditioned experiment" within a world of happen stance relativity. Without higher evolutionary programming or direct programming by an Overself intelligence, the human biological system must go back into the overall flux of Magnetic fields when the system is discorporated.
10. When Man is directly programmed by an Overself, he is no longer kept in biochemical slavery within a three-dimensional consciousness by the "apparent realities" of the earth.
11. In this case, the body is a grid of magnetic domains which moves between the primary blueprint of the Overself and the pattern angles of the human organs (i.e., the axial relationship).
12. The lines which tie together these magnetic domains are the axiatonal lines.

13. The axiatonal lines can exist independent of the Overself but still require the governing functions of the Higher Evolution.
14. The governing functions are required because the axiatonal grid structures pass through several evolutionary orders, all sharing and working in the same local life space on different dimensions of activity.
15. Therefore, the axiatonal grids tend to enter and interface with the biological activity taking place on higher and lower vibratory frequencies within the space being used by various biologies. Yet, these grids are not governed by the laws and mechanisms controlling physical evolution, for they operate by means of their own accretion of energy for maintenance.
16. However, on this planet it is important to know that acupuncture lines *qua* acupuncture lines can be acquired with "progressive" and "regressive" axiatonal lines. This is due to the residual effects of the human rebellion.
17. Therefore, acupuncture, as used during the last 12,000 years of evolutionary existence, was cut off from the "progressive" higher start programming channels when the root races revolted against the programming of the Father. This caused the twelve biophysical meridians to be truncated from direct connection with the Overself.
18. Furthermore, the biological interconnection with the higher astronomy was lost at that time which requires the intervention of the Office of the Christ to restructure the axiatonal lines.
19. Until this time, the body has been left to work on molecular biological levels with only limited magnetic resonance patterns to continue the functions of the amino acids, the basic building blocks of life.
20. Thus, non-Adamic characteristics appeared in the human race because the molecular biological levels were cut off from the data transmission system sustaining the mechanisms of both higher medical astronomy, as well as bioelectrical activities of the Higher Evolution.
21. In other words, Man was cut off from the higher star points that are necessary to maintain a perfected form of the Adam Kadmon.
22. In order to reconnect the biological interconnection with the higher energy planes serving higher evolutionary programming,

the acupuncture lines of the old program have to be attached to "new" axiatonal lines (at their intersections) if the cellular grids are to be in harmony with all physical manifestations permitted by the governing hierarchy.
23. This is the bringing together of molecular biology with medical astronomy within programs of creation.
24. Man, at this time, is being advanced to a new biological program of creation.
25. This advancement requires his acupuncture lines be extended to axiatonal lines that will be connected directly with the Overself, for if Man is to go on into further soul progression, he must connect his axiatonal lines to his Overself which is also making an ascension into the next quantum level of the Adam Kadmon, just as the Adam Kadmon body is making an ascension into a completely new program in our Son universe . . . .
29. The axial lines are part of a fifth-dimensional circulatory system combining color and sound, which are used to draw from the Overself body the basic energy used for the renewing functions of the human evolutionary body . . . .
32. Hence, the axiatonal lines can be used for the complete regeneration of an organ and even to resurrect the dead, when activated by the proper energies.
33. The key is to be used at the time when the human evolutionary molecular grids are in direct alignment with the higher evolutionary resonance grids, permitting ultrasonic pulsations to allow for direct changes within vascular bodies. (*The Book of Knowledge: Keys of Enoch*, key 3.1.7)

Through intellectual and para-scientific fervor, Hurtak details an astonishingly accurate depiction of what appears in the flesh to be a metaphysical correlation to the modus operandi proposed by Hermes Trismegistus. The full potential with lies in our cellular and D.N.A. structure can only be fully realized when a projection of light and information, coming from the recorder cell, manifests the perfect blueprint of our physical structure, referred to in Hurtak's book as the "Adam Kadmon." Is Adam Kadmon synonymous with Lulu? I don't think so. I believe the Adam Kadmon was the original human blueprint and the Lulu design was bestowed by the Nibiruans.

Hurtak's vision for the future subsumes a macroscopic understanding of the way the Earth and the universe provide a direct connection to the body's magnetic grid, merely a fluctuation of electromagnetic impulses influenced by the magnetic resonance variances in the cosmic mind. The axiatonal lines in effect provided a chemical and electrical code resonance for the manipulation of all biological forms throughout the universe. The body is nothing more than an electro-chemical computer and it is programmed for upgrades called the "evolution of consciousness." Hurtak also does quite well in stating that the two-stranded D.N.A. structure trapped in three dimensions of consciousness is an experiment of higher density beings. For long we have not been masters of our bodies because we have not been masters of our minds. Total adroitness over the body is a result of a clear mind.

More specifically, magnetism and the attractions of the fifth dimension are a result of a clear mind. Only a frequency of pure light and love will activate mental clarity, and two races that can provide assistance in this endeavor are the Arcturians and Pleiadians. As stated by the Arcturians, much of the cause of manifestation in this and other realities is the unconscious and subconscious minds of the human, as well as the universal and galactic unconscious. The Arcturian subconscious is also providing a sturdy connection between your subconscious and the Andromeda Galaxy. The star Arcturus, home to many ascended beings, is also the residence of the Great White Brotherhood. The Andromeda galaxy provides a tenacious connection to the Milky Way Galaxy. As the Andromedan Council provides guidance to the Great White Brotherhood, the development of the consciousness and spiritual awareness of the Earth inhabitants will be intensified, as will the light and love. In this, the linkage between the third dimension and the fifth dimension will be strengthened, a corridor of light serving the bond between your individual subconscious and the Arcturian mothership. From the Arcturian mothership, the corridor is solidified and travels directly to the Arcturian stargate. The linkage from your aura and etheric energy is then encoded into the stargate.

Because of karma, the crystalline block substances around the mental bodies of the inhabitants of Earth must be removed, and this can be accomplished by special tonal sounds which are assimilated in the mind and unconscious of not only the Earth humans but also the Earth herself. The Arcturians provide a wealth of feminine energy, the type of energy which has been abused on the planet. The Andromedans have also shown the way for living a pure thought consciousness existence, as Prime Creator has no manifest physical mind or body. Purity of thoughtforms is essential when clearing blocking energies and emotions and when opening up the third eye, the psychic doorway of the third dimension. When the Arcturians take you in your etheric body to the crystal temple in Shamballa you can better conceive of this type of being, a consciousness substantiated in accordance with the crystal light body. In pure thought you can manifest healings in your etheric body, which then incarnate into the physical body. When you are at this level of thought you are closest to the Godhead energy, the source of everything.

The etheric body of humans correlates with the etheric body of the Earth, which has meridians that are either grids or matrices, there being a vibratory grid and a light and consciousness grid. The axiatonal lines, or acupuncture lines of the human body, are extrapolated up and out to the consciousness grid, one of which is the Christ grid. The Christ grid, or Christ consciousness, was not only demonstrated by Jesus in his incarnation on Earth but also by many ascended masters who have traveled here in the past. The axiatonal lines connect our bodies to the Earth grid and to the intergalactic grids. Both the ley lines and meridians of the Earth are related to the planetary vibratory grid.[50] Just as each chakra in the human energetic matrix composes varying levels of awareness and consciousness, the axiatonal lines connect to different Earth grids depending on a person's evolution and which chakras he or she mostly focuses on. The Earth also has a memory matrix where the imprints of experiences are recorded, these experiences not being judged as good or bad but simply as occurrences which fluctuate the state of vibrational being of the planet. When Marduk took over in 2,200 B.C.E., humanity was separated from the Earth grids with the exception of the Native Americans and Aborigines. Many from these groups today are stepping forward and voicing concern about the destructive tendencies of our young race. As we have not been true to ourselves, we have not been true to the planet. As the separation between humanity and the Earth grids transpired, the Earth was disconnected from the galactic grid. The chakra energies of the Earth receive on a gigantic scale energy from not only our sun but also the central sun of the Galaxy, Alcyon.

---

[50] These are used in some forms of anti-gravity planetary travel.

The Cosmic Party

"Before the Sun throws out light, where is the light? Photons come out of nowhere, they cannot be stored, they can barely be pinned down in time, and they have no home in space whatsoever. That is, light occupies no volume and has no mass. The similarity between a thought and a photon is very deep. Both are born in the region beyond space and time where nature controls all processes in that void which is full of creative intelligence."

-Deepak Chopra

Earth has roamed the "Galactic Night" since 8,800 B.C.E. Now it is time for the light of awareness to bathe the planet in wisdom once more.[51] This party, which begins on the winter solstice in 2012, will activate our own cellular memory banks. Coded holograms in our bodies (galactic morphogenetic fields) have been hidden from us because light precipitation from higher dimensions has been stymied by an electromagnetic reticulum which has been cast over our planet. We are like fish caught in a net. When the current 26,000 year cycle comes to conclusion and the rays of the photon belt pelt our dimension, we will be like liberated fish swimming out of the Age of Pisces and into galactic synchronization with the other stars in the Alcyone spiral. Our sun is the eighth star of the spiral, and as such the Pleiadians and Arcturians are here to assist humanity on entering another dimensional frequency. Maya is the third star of the spiral and will move into the Photon band at the same time as our sun, this reunion echoed in Pleiadian culture as the "return of the twin." The Pleiadians carry a female vibration while the Sirians carry a male vibration, and it is the merger of both the masculine and feminine which will save Earth from annihilation. Since there has been an abundance of male energy over the recent centuries, a female touch must free the beast within, inside all of us.

This reticulum of which I speak is an electromagnetic net which has been thrown over Earth by the Annunaki, their group of conspirators known colloquially as the "World Management Team." They have effectively manifested an immense power grid from the Vatican in Rome

---

[51] The Pleiadians refer to the "Galactic Night" as the time period when Earth is not aligned with the Galactic Photon Band.

and clairvoyants can see dark, negative energies surrounding the area. As the Annunaki and their collaborators (several subtypes of Zeta Reticulum Greys and Orion and Sirius reptilian species) have deposited their memory codes in the vortexes on Earth (which connect the telluric fields with all nine dimensions), they have made it possible to play in this dimension. They cannot, however, erase these codes because such an act would cause the Earth vortexes to go out of form, and if such primordial memory was blocked in linear space and time the Annunaki would not be able to play here anymore for they would lose their own memory banks. Our species is dying, and obviously if we die the Prison Warder (Draconian) Consciousness cannot control us anymore. If Earth is too weakened by manipulation of her energy fields, her species will be erased from memory in time, and the Annunaki can never again access these vortexes.

The reticulum exists in the fourth dimension, so that's why from the perspective of the third dimension it seems like there is no "net." The reptilians have used their puppets in the religious and political realms to layer lies upon lies on the public so this entrapment would become more dense and encapsulate the third dimension. Reverse Speaking analyst Peggy Kane has hosted television shows in which she has invited guests and discussed the 'net' that has been cast around Earth. She has discoursed that after speaking to souls who are trapped in the fourth dimension (since the net only reaches 4th density), there is no escape to 5th density for a misguided soul who passes away in 3rd density carrying dense emotions and thoughtforms. Many souls are trapped in the fourth dimension on Earth and they are hunted by the reptilians, who are themselves 4th density souls. The human souls are taken to Mars where the reptilians own a colony and to Orion in several locations including Alpha Draconis.

The Age of Aquarius is crucial to the dissolution of the net. When Earth is deep in the Photon Band, laser beams will no longer split into two parts in solar light and create dense realities for exploring feelings. The holographic images which are created by laser beams will not exist for us to worship and use as sixth-dimensional archetypes; instead, their multifaceted lenses will open to the fifth dimension and those who are in the third dimension will be able to look out into the cosmos through those lenses. It will be like looking through a kaleidoscope. Souls who are anchored in light and love will ascend to the fifth dimension. The higher dimensions are like mirrors for viewing oneself, as the third dimension provides only a limited perception. The Pleiadians and Arcturians are here now, mirroring back the vibrations we send their way, and unless a transmutation of the heart ensues, that which is mirrored back to us might not be pleasant. It truly is a superlative drama. While two people are having sexual intercourse in the third dimension, beings in the fourth dimension can trigger emotional energies, beings in the fifth dimension can become excited by the kundalini fire and have cosmic orgasms, beings in the sixth dimension can expand and amplify the fields of these pulsations throughout the galaxy, beings in the seventh dimension can carry the feelings via galactic information highways, entities in the eighth dimension can organize new morphogenetic fields from sexual seismic waves and ninth-dimensional entities can birth new biological forms in the galactic center black hole![52]

A photon is a quantum (smallest particle) of electromagnetic energy with zero mass, so it has no electrical charge and exists indefinitely. As a positronium is composed of both an electron and a positron and as the positron is the electron's antiparticle opposite, the two eventually collide and form two quanta of light (photons). The collision merges inherent duality into light, and as the electron is a basic unit of activation (life) it triggers the transmutation of the positron (karma). In this way, as the photonic light increases in the solar system, the karma on Earth will transmute into information (since light is information). As the karma is released, the antiparticles and electrons collide forming quanta of light. As the photonic light increases in the Earth realm, the collective subconscious and unconscious will be activated and you will receive more information about yourself. The miasms in your body (karma) must be released because they hold the memory of genetic or past-life disease patterns, present-life diseases patterns and memory of disease that was pushed down into the subconscious by the introduction of antibiotics, chemicals, or radiation. Since March 14 of 1994, these miasms have been intensely activated by the Photon Band. As long as the miasms are cleared, elements of your physical body will fly off in 2012 during the culmination period and reunite with the antiparticles melding into light. Once fully emerged in the Photon Band, your lightbody will be your embodiment of consciousness on the Earth in the 5th dimension.

---

[52] Barbara Hand Clow, *The Pleiadian Agenda* (Rochester, VT: Bear & Company, 1995), 57-59.

Because the brain is holographic, your higher self knows how to help eradicate hold behaviors which limit the body. Sometimes, these rigid patterns of past conditioning are miasms that need to be released before light activation. Zero Point was when the World Management Team casted the electromagnetic net over our dimension and occurred roughly around the time Christ was born. From the Age of Cancer in 8,800 B.C.E. through the Age of Pisces, Earth has roamed the Galactic Night. Our sun re-entered entered the Photon Band in 1998 C.E., but the inhabitants of Earth won't really feel the effects until 2012. The Galactic Night commences when the solar system is not in the Photon Band, but when it is the Pleiadians call it the "Cosmic Party." It is time now for the party and all evil traditions and orthodox religions must fade away.

II

COLUMBUS AND THE NEW WORLD

In America today, we technically live in the "New World," but what is that? Colombus is a patriot of the history books and labeled as the official "discoverer" of the New World, but looking back at the more unorthodox history I present in the preceding chapters, how could the land masses of North and South America be such a secret? The extraterrestrials visiting the Earth most undoubtedly knew about them, and knowing full well the real hidden hand behind the secret societies of past and present, Columbus and his cohorts should have also known about them.[1] From its earliest beginnings, America has been the bassinet for secret societies and conspiracies. Even Columbus claimed to received a divine vision in which he was asked to found a new land that would be the new heaven (the new Jerusalem) promised by St. John in the "Book of Revelation." This vision did not end there as even Francis Bacon predicted that America would be the "New Atlantis."

Whatever his intentions, Columbus was not an ignoramus. His father-in-law was closely annexed with the Knights of Christ in Portugal and it is reported that the young Columbus spent many nights studying his father's charts and papers. The Knights of Christ are the descendents of the Knights Templar in Portugal, and it is no mystery the ships Columbus used to 'discover' the New World bore the Templar cross on their sails. It is also no secret Columbus was well connected to the Merovingian bankers like the Medicis of Italy. In his *Occult Conspiracy*, researcher Michael Howard writes:

> Columbus was associated with a political group that supported the ideas of Dante, one of the alleged Grand Masters of the Order of the Rosy Cross, who is known to have used codes and ciphers in his writings,

---

[1] They also knew the Earth wasn't flat, as the Babylonians even knew that. It is evident in the stone tablets and terracotta reliefs from that time period.

a practice associated with membership of a secret society. Columbus' voyages of discovery were sponsored by Leonardo da Vinci and Lorenzo de Medici, both initiates of secret societies, who found the explorer wealthy patrons among European Royalty and aristocracy.

It is surmised Columbus was in a Masonic secret society based on his ciphers and the hand signs he used. In this picture, his left hand is in the shape of an 'M' (the left hand also signifies the left-handed path of the dark arts and Satanism—see books by Texe Marrs).

Colombus giving a Masonic hand sign

The Papal House of Anjou financed Columbus, as well as the King and Queen of Spain, both European royalty. It is even said that Columbus married a woman tied to the Knights Templar and that they (the Templars) visited America long before the fifteenth century.

When Columbus and his crew first landed in North America they were greeted by the Arawak Native Americans with kindness and offerings, but that was not to last long. Upon this viewing, Columbus wrote in his journal:

> They brought us parrots and balls of cotton and spears and many other things . . . they willingly traded everything they owned . . . They do not bear arms, and do not know them, for I showed them a sword; they took it by the edge and cut themselves out of ignorance. They have no iron. Their spears are made of cane . . . They would make fine servants . . . With fifty men we could subjugate them all and make them do whatever we want. (Howard Zinn, *A People's History of the United States*)

The subjugation of the native tribes of North America commenced and Columbus was forever known as an imperialist and a gold digger, much less a hero. The Native American tribes he exploited had a spiritual connection to the Earth and held a vast history with their land and its resources, unlike the greedy European white men.

After the destruction of Lemuria and Atlantis, the toxic radiation from the nuclear wars caused mutations to humans, regressing them and reducing their intelligence.[2] The survivors of not only nuclear catastrophes but also the affliction caused by polar shifts, ice ages, and wars of reinforcement in space were forced to live in small, primitive groupings. Many went underground. The native human tribes living on the North and South American continents during the days of the Greeks, Romans, and the early European church were very spiritual. They communicated with the spirit of the Earth and the Sun. They had ideologies, but not dogma. Dogma spelled backwards is 'am God.' How interesting.

In the United States today, many indigenous peoples and tribes refer to themselves as "American Indian," and in Canada, "First Nation People." If they do not do this they just refer to their tribal name like Cherokee or Inca. Just like the diversity of extraterrestrials visiting the Earth, there were many divergent Indian cultures meshed together in these lands. From California to Maine, the Yukon to Argentina, these peoples wore different types of clothing, talked different languages, lived in different types of housing depending on the climate, and worshiped different gods depending on their respective philosophies.

---

[2] "Pleiadaian Message From the Galactic Federation," http://www.youtube.com/watch?v=I99vAwVDW7E&feature=related (2007).

They did all share commonalities, like worshiping nature and the Sun, developing tribal dances and chants to influence the weather, self made clothing, and one other thing . . . . ancestry. Some claim to be from the stars, others from the Earth herself. Still others claim to be from the ocean. They are all right. Most Americans today have no idea about the genesis of their family lineage let alone where the human race came from. Also, not many Americans today are spiritual and respect nature. We did well to wipe out those values so utterly idealized by the Native Americans, whether they be from North, South, or Central America. Before Columbus there were over 800 million natives and Indians living on these lands. Today, there are less than five million combined.

Some Native American tribes adduce they came here from Asia using ancient boats in prehistoric times, circa 20,000 B.C.E. It is well known today that Christopher Columbus was not the first to discover America as he was beaten by at least several centuries by ancient Anatolians and tribes from Mesopotamia who migrated from Sumer, Babylon, Italy, Spain, and Africa. That, and considering a native race of humans most likely evolved naturally in this area of the world and that extraterrestrial visitors knew about these continents all along, I propose that Christopher Columbus already knew about America before he traveled over from peoples who knew about America for thousands of years. It is also well known that the Vikings, coming from the North, pioneered the Western lands no later than 1000 C.E. There are archaeological remains of their settlements along the coasts of the Americas, both Norse sagas and Indian oral history chronicling these encounters. The Vikings the Native Americans most notably encountered were the Beothuk and the Micmac. Of course, these weren't the only ones.

The Bering bridge was a 1,000 mile long land bridge joining present-day Alaska and eastern Siberia at various times during the Peistocene ice ages. Archaeologists and anthropologists have discovered that ancient eastern Asian peoples migrated into North America through Alaska. This was accorded to have occurred 12,000 years ago in which early Paleo-Indians spread throughout the American lands. They primarily practiced aquaculture and agriculture, two activities typifying the early humans. They were also hunters and gatherers, hunting animals, and gathering fruits and vegetables. The early human Lyran colonies are a testament to this as they too were agricultural in nature. In some places these newly created tribes erected monumental architecture, edifices, pyramids, and cities. In some cases, they created empires. Extraterrestrials revisiting the planet after the nuclear warfare helped these people with astrological, technical, and spiritual knowledge. Some say the Mayans ascended to a higher dimension on the Earth. Other civilizations seem to also have all but disappeared with no trace. Where did they go? The indigenous Americans still in operation today are largely seen in Bolivia, Peru, Paraguay, Mexico, Guatemala, Colombia, and Ecuador. Although many have retained the ancient dialects such as Quechua, Guarani, Nahuatl, and some Mayan languages, many live in isolation from Western society and are accounted as un-contacted peoples. It has been speculated that these early migrants traveled into the Beringia land bridge between eastern Siberia and present day Alaska somewhere around 40,000 to 17,000 years ago when sea levels where relatively low.[3]

Myriad plant species were domesticated and bred among the American indigenous peoples, who cultivated through artificial selection exotic strains of plant and animal. In southern Mexico maize was grown from wild teosinte grasses in the local valleys. Early agriculture was a predominant attribute of the South American highlands to these migrates from the European continent around these time periods. Pottery became very common in the Archaic period of North American cultures. Vegetation was often burned in mimic of the natural occurrence of wild fires. The Mississippi River valley saw the prominent managing of nut groves and fruit trees in orchards. Numerous crops domesticated by the indigenous Americans are now produced globally in massive quantities for the profit of the large food distribution corporations. Large clothing companies like Tommy Hilfiger harvest income from the abuse of young children in many sweatshops in countries still harboring indigenous Americans, like in Bolivia, Peru, and Latin America.

The Pre-Columbian era incorporates the period of America before the appearance of sententious European influence on the American continents and after the original settlement during the Paleolithic period. Christopher Columbus' voyages between 1492 and 1504 significantly influenced the native tribes until their conquering and subsequent retreat into the western mountains. A more complete list of the native tribes ambushed by the Europeans reads like this:

---

[3] According to the New World Migration Model, the magnetic poles of the Earth were shifted over 10,000 years ago, so these peoples would have been migrating in warm weather.

Olmec, Toltec, Teotihuacano, Zapotec, Mixtec, Aztec, Maya, Andes, Inca, Moche, Chibcha, and Canaris. The wonders of the ancient world were discovered by Columbus, the Vikings, and other voyagers seeking adventure, land, slaves, and profit. The Aztecs had engineered a very impressive city, Tenochtitlan, in the antediluvian site of Mexico City, and it possessed a population of over 400,000 as well as secret astronomical and mathematical knowledge. Besides the Arawak tribe, the first indigenous group most likely encountered by Columbus was the Tainos of Hispaniola, a prominent culture of the Greater Antilles and the Bahamas. After 25 years, 75% of the Tainos had perished because they had no medical help for European diseases like measles and smallpox. Labor was forced on the unwilling natives, who often obliged due to the incessant threats that their limbs be cut off.

After some time of inoculation, a creed was established in which the Laws of Burgos prospered in 1512, however, its foundation also saw the conversion to Catholicism. In a distant colony, the Spanish crown was prepared to enforce political laws after religious laws came into being. The overwhelming agent in the decline of Native American populations was, inarguably, epidemic diseases, over 85% of the deaths attributed to diseases from Europe. In 1518 half of the native populace in Hispaniola was eradicated by smallpox; a few years later the smallpox trail relocated to the Inca population. In all, typhus, influenza, diphtheria, and measles ravaged the native denizens of Mexico and the United States. With the arrival of Panfilo de Narvaez in 1520, an epidemic of smallpox killed 150,000 citizens of Tenochtitlan alone, including the emperor. In 1521 Hernan Cortes was accredited with the overthrow of the Tenochtitlan Empire. During the first 100 years of European contact these repeated outbreaks of diseases decimated almost two-thirds of the Aboriginal population of eastern North America. Further exploration by Europeans of the Caribbean led to the uncovering of the Arawak peoples of the Lesser Antilles, which eventually became extinct by the latter half of the 17th century. Through the breeding of horses, the Europeans, especially the Spaniards, benefited greatly in expanding their empires. The term 'Indian' actually originates with Christopher Columbus, due to the fact that he had 'mistakenly' landed in the East Indies while searching for Asia. Once erected, the term 'Indian' was appraised into law, religion, and politics.

Columbus, himself an initiate, was married to a daughter of a former Grand Master of the Knights of Christ, a Portuguese offshoot of the

A New Order of the Ages

Templars which surfaced after the Templar order was forced to dissipate. The red cross patte was drawn on the sails on Columbus' ships which bore a resemblance to secret orders and secret societies, however the Knights of Christ, the new adjunct, did not stand for the same spiritual symbiotic as the Knights Templar. A feeling of being "one-upped" by the Templars led the Vatican to adopt a glamorous mystique for the Knights of Malta, another derivative of the Knights Templar. For the most part, the Knights of Malta, and later the Teutonic Knights, were conduits for the Roman elite to advance their agenda of spiritual secrecy and economic wealth. We are told in school that in "1492 Columbus sailed the ocean blue," a poetic overture for this time period when the battle lines for control of the world were being formulated, a war fought not only in the material realm but the spiritual realm as well. In 1492 Columbus had reached the mouth of the Orinoco, one of the longest rivers in South America, where he believed he had found the Gihon, the fringe of Eden. A new Golden Age was proposed to commence and Columbus wished to expose this prophecy. Although a new age was not brought to light, gold was indeed unearthed. Queen Isabella and her husband King Ferdinand, recently having re-conquered Granada in order to bring Spain back under the hold of the Church, expressed an interest in Columbus finding barrels of gold so the "new Jerusalem" could be built. This could very well relate to El Dorado. This legendary city of gold was lusted after by the European aristocracy, although the history books keep it in a haze of doubt.

European awareness of the Western Hemisphere most certainly did not start with Columbus as I stated before. Among the others, he was also preceded by the Norse, led by Leif Ericson. Ericson had erected a temporary settlement at L'Anse aux Meadows and established a healthy relationship with the natives, but it was Columbus who was credited with initiating widespread contact between Europeans and indigenous Americans. His voyage in 1492 precipitated a relief for the imperialists in Europe seeking wealth from the control of trade routes and colonies in China and India. Silk, spices, opiates, and gold were the primary motivating factors for ascendency of the land route to Asia from Western Europe. Under the hegemony of the Mongol Empire this became very possible, although the fall of Constantinople to the Ottoman Turks in 1453 did make this passage treacherous. Columbus and his brothers, together with others serving a cartel of navigators, wished to discover new resources, and with the hazardousness of the Silk Road turned their heads westward. What was west? If the world was flat then nothing was west, but did the Europeans really believe that? This could not have been because the maritime navigation techniques at the time relied on the observation of the stars and the curvature of the Earth as a sphere. Methods for calculating the diameter of the Earth using an astrolabe was well known to even the Greeks and Romans, an approach continued right up through the Middle Ages and the Renaissance. Plato knew the Earth was a sphere because of the circular shadow it casted on the Moon when it stood between the Sun and its orbiting satellite. This knowledge must have been known to a great majority of nobility, and most certainly anyone attempting to travel via the oceans.

Why would this be put in the history books? We have already seen how much more the initiates and instigators of secret orders and societies knew then we ever gave them credit for, but why profess ignorance? It was most likely to keep the people at bay. Christopher Columbus was supposedly connected with the Order of Saint John, or more commonly called the Knights of Malta. When the order of the Knights Templar decomposed in 1312, most of their property was granted to the Hospitallers, an order more 'hospitable' to the papacy. Their holdings and wealth were divided into eight "tongues" in the Crown of Aragon, Auvergne, Castile, England, France, Germany, Italy, and Provence. Each place was presided over by a Prior, and at Rhodes and later Malta the residing knights were headed by a Bailli. The papacy organized the Hospitallers, or the Knights of Rhodes, into a military force to oppose the Barbary pirates and other buccaneers in conflict. After withstanding invasions in the 15th century by the Sultan of Egypt and the Ottoman Mehmed II, the Knights of Rhodes built a stronghold on the Halicarnassus peninsula (now Bodrum). In 1522 a fleet of ships under the directive of Suleiman the Magnificent laid siege for six months, at the end of which the Knights of Rhodes withdrew to Sicily. In 1530 the Knights were given Malta, Gozo and the North African port of Tripoli by King Charles V of Spain in exchange for an annual fee.

The Hospitallers beseeched the Muslims and the Barbary pirates though they only had a few ships, and gained the wariness of the Ottomans, who were disgruntled when the order of the Hospitallers resettled. In 1565 Suleiman ordered a force to besiege the 1,000 or so soldiers and expunge them from Malta. Philip II of Spain contemplated giving aide to the Knights at the expense of his own forces and potentially the hand off of Sicily and Naples to the Ottomans. His delay, an irritation that almost proved fatal, subsided into a stronger effort by the Hospitallers to repair the breaches and hold the defense. As this was coming to pass, many Ottomans were falling ill as well as losing morale, and with the death of their commander and corsair Dragut, a serious blow was dealt to the Ottoman siege. Upon hearing of the arrival of Sicilian reinforcements, the Ottomans made a last ditch effort to overrun the fortress but were eventually denied. They subsequently departed from Malta. In 1607 the Grand Master of the Hospitallers was acceded the status of Reichsfurst, or in other words, "Prince of the Holy Roman Empire" even though the order's territory was south of the Roman Empire. In 1630 the Grand Master was given ecclesiastic equality with cardinals, a quality position indeed.

Facilitating the crusades in the Holy Land was now no longer an option, so the Knights Hospitallers became a police force in the Mediterranean. They opposed the Ottoman-endorsed Barbary Corsairs operating from North Africa and all other forms of piracy as well. In the advent of the Christian victory in 1571 over the Ottoman fleet in the Battle of Lepanto, the Knights were accorded the mission of protecting Christian merchant shipping to and from the Levant as well as freeing any Christian slave hitherto working for the Barbary Corsairs. A reduced income, however, plagued the struggling Order. Although they protected the naval city states of Venice, Genoa, and Pisa, they were economically hindered by the barren island in which they abided. They started raiding Muslim ships, thereby gaining local women, gold, exotic food, and treasure. The changing belief structures of the Knights Hospitallers, coupled with the corollaries of the Reformation and Counter-Reformation as well as the dwindling stability of the Roman Catholic Church, saw a decline in the religious attitudes of many of the Christian inhabitants of Europe. The decision of many Knights to serve in foreign navies, paired with the overall moral decline of the Hospitallers, was best witnessed in many joining the French navy and becoming "mercenary sea-dogs," an act negating the Knights' primary reason for existence. They faced the potential of meeting another Catholic force, and as Paris signed numerous trade agreements with the Ottomans, the moral ambivalence of the Knights increased even more. Scholar Paul Lacroix states:

Collin Robert Bowling

> Inflated with wealth, laden with privileges which gave them almost sovereign powers . . . the order at las became so demoralized by luxury and idleness that it forgot the aim for which it was founded, and gave itself up for the love of gain and thirst for pleasure. Its covetousness and pride soon became boundless. The Knights pretended that they were above the reach of crowned heads: they seized and pillaged without concern of the property of both infidels and Christians.

A cycle of increased raids and reduced grants from the nation-states of Christendom commenced and the island of operations of the Hospitallers was made dependent on conquest. Christopher Columbus was most likely a member of the Knights Hospitallers, who were also the Knights of Malta. They behaved like the Knights Templar in that they were a military force set up to protect Christian pilgrims and nation-states of Christendom. While the Templars were disconnected from religion, the Hospitallers vehemently favored Christianity over Catholicism, and constantly sought to commandeer ships entering their harbor carrying Turkish goods. Even though their funding was rapidly decreased by the thrones of Europe who did not see a need for them anymore after the withdrawal and assimilation of the Ottoman Empire into the French and British navies, they remained rich off of confiscated goods from ships, piracy and selling crew members into slavery.

When the Roman Catholic Church regained power after the Thirty Years War and the official abolishment of all heterodox religion, they turned their attention to the New World, the North and South American continents. After spirituality was decimated, along with the rights of the peasant workers who laid the very foundation for the kings and queens of Europe to dominate the economic and political landscape, the aristocracy of Europe (bloodlines) had no need for the Cathars, Knights Templar, Knights Hospitallers, or the Knights of Malta. They controlled many of the trade routes to Asia and India and were learning much about astrology, mathematics, and science. They needed explorers, though, people to step up to the plate and be the official pioneers of the history books. With Europe all but in the hands of a very few rich and knowledgeable people, more and more heads were being turned toward North and South America.[4]

---

[4] Author Jan van Helsing has stated in his books that the order of Freemasonry was documented to have carried secret meetings in 2,000 B.C.E. Considering that modern Freemasonry has

We know why Columbus, Leif Ericson, the Vikings, and the early Proto-Indo-European came to the New World. They were filling in new areas of the world map. But why did others come over, and why so suddenly? Historical evidence bequeaths to us the possibilities of migrants moving to the new world in search of economic, religious, and political freedoms, as well as refuge from persecution.[5] Others most likely traveled to the North American continents simply for a fresh start. Up until about 1820 many European countries were averse to meeting the costs of maintaining convicts in prisons, so they often gave the prisoners the option of going to the New World instead. Some Europeans, the profiteering gluttonous type, wished greatly to discover El Dorado, the lost city of gold. Most of these attempts were meet with desolation. If El Dorado was found, its caretakers probably kept it a secret.

The Pilgrims enter the New World

The forefathers to the Pilgrims, a Puritan bunch intent on freedom from King James of Great Britain, were quite fed up with the Church of England. It was a mandatory at that time that all peasants, regardless of religious affiliation, should attend the Church of England every week. This church was very centralized, although it was only a shell. The rituals and ceremonies executed and undertaken at this Church were solely dependent on the current ruler of England at the time. If he was a Protestant, his reign would see the practice of Protestant ritualism in the same church that would see the practice of Catholicism under a different ruler of Catholic faith. The Church of England was a State Church. The religion of this region was strictly dictated by the government. Why do you think the forefathers of the United States wanted a separation of Church and State? Under King James, any person (man, woman, or child) could be detained against his or her will, tortured, and thrown in prison simply because they did not adhere to the State religion. It wasn't even a religion. The reigning ruler of whatever epoch always appointed the archbishop of his choice to be the mediator between the people

---

stemmed from the secret orders mentioned in this paragraph, it could fit that modern Freemasonry, the secret organization that founded the United States of America, is nothing more than the most ancient post-diluvian secret societies ruled by Draconian bloodlines.

[5] This is a concept of Civil Law, which is different in every country.

and the ruler, who was always the demigod between you and Saturn. Or Satan.

One group of people wanted to stay in the Church of England and purify its forums. This group was called the "Puritans." Another group surmised the Church would never change because it was simply a conduit for the elect and whatever he wanted to pass off as spirituality. This group was called the "Separatists." Today we refer to the Separatists as the "Pilgrims." They utterly opposed the ritual and symbolism of the Anglican Church, as well as the complexity and intricacy of the religious communion in the Church of England. In their interpretation of the New Testament, the first Christian church was simple in adornment and practice but complex in spiritual knowing. Richard Clyfton mentored this small community of people in a form of democratic self-government. The will of the majority always ruled, and everyone was held in equal regard. The democratic system of government did not begin with the Pilgrims, it began in Athens, Greece, but the Pilgrims were a good example of the self-governing methodology mandated by the forefathers who supposedly won independence from England during the Revolutionary War.

In 1606 the Separatists in Scrooby, a northeastern county of Nottingham, made a hasty decision to leave England in search of religious and spiritual freedom, seeing the situation in England had become so intolerable they could no longer bear it. The Puritans, their opposition, thought they could reform the Church. Their methods were baleful to say the least. They despised those who opposed them, they dressed in black, prosecuted witches, and were generally much more violent. At this time there was a group of Separatists camped in Amsterdam, a place of more religious freedom. The Separatists in Scrooby were Amsterdam-bound when their plan was foiled by the English authorities who found out. The absconders were forced into bondage once more. In 1608 the congregation in Scrooby instigated another attempt to leave England once and for all. During this attempt they were deeply troubled again by the authorities who arrived just in time. Many had already boarded a ship departing for Holland, however the woman and children were still on the shore. When the English authorities came they arrested the remaining Separatists, but it was not long until they were reunited with their families in Amsterdam. In the early 17th century Holland was overpopulated in relation to the economic situation of the day, much like today in the United States. The only occupations

A New Order of the Ages

available to English immigrants were low-paying jobs in the textile and clothing industries. The vigor of their labors was brought to naught as the economy continued to slide. Some went back to England to endure the hardships offered there, but many stayed and eventually succumbed to the budgetary upheavals.

The religion of the Pilgrims was birthed out of the Puritan movement in England. They desired to advance the gospels of the Christian doctrine in remote parts of the world. They perpetuated a New Testament type of worship and were thoroughly opposed to the Catholic Church and its Old Testament paramount of a spiteful god named YHWH. In 1608 the Leiden Separatists provoked King James into giving them a Royal Charter so they could establish a colony in the New World. King James declined, but also stated that he would not attempt to thwart the congregation from leaving. The Leiden Separatists finally succeeded in receiving a patent from the London Virginia Company, an organization bent on budding financial gain from investing in new settlements in America. Two ships, one called the "Mayflower" along with a smaller ship called the "Speedwall," were purchased for the journey to America. After several difficulties, the Mayflower made its departure from Plymouth, England in 1620 without the Speedwall. It carried 102 passengers, of this number there only being 41 Leidens. The remainder of the passengers were strangers who wished to travel to America to find economic freedom.

The Mayflower arrived at Cape Cod, Massachusetts and a group of Pilgrims, led by William Bradford, signed the Mayflower Compact. This agreement stated that they, the Pilgrims, would govern themselves and would not take orders from other people. After a long and cruel winter, a Native American named Samoset entered the Plymouth settlement and greeted the bewildered Pilgrims with a warm, "Welcome, Englishmen." A peace treaty was signed between the Native Americans and the Pilgrims that saw a lifespan of more than fifty years. The Native Americans taught the Pilgrims how to plant, grow and harvest wheat, barley, corn, and peas. The first Thanksgiving occurred when the first harvest came to fruition later in the fall. As the Plymouth colony thrived, more and more settlers came from England and Europe, and eventually many colonies had sprung up on the Eastern North American coast.

The New World was a safe place where individuality and indigenous culture could prosper side by side. The insidious wickedness of the European tyrannical rule did little to suppress the newly found freedoms enjoyed by the Separatists and any other traveler coming to the North American continents either before or shortly after Columbus' voyage. Once the Vatican, the Knights of Malta, and the prominent secret societies had a stranglehold over Europe and parts of Africa, their attention was duly directed in the westward direction. In concurrence with Columbus was a plan to reach the East by going West, a contrivance labeled by Columbus the "Enterprise of the Indies." His marriage into Portuguese nobility allowed him access to charts, sailor testimony, and other maritime sources of information regarding travel across the Atlantic Ocean. Also, he learned much from those who dispersed stories about the Vikings and lands west of Iceland while he was in ports in England, Iceland, and Ireland. It is indeed so that the notion of sailing west to reach the east did not originate with Columbus as he drew on countless knowledge from Greek and Roman times which theorized that there was only one body of water on the surface of the Earth and that it connected Europe and Asia. Columbus later revealed that he also swallowed much information from early geographic works which include papers by Ptolemy, Pierre D'Ailly, and Marco Polo.

Patronage for Columbus' plan to reach the East by sailing west was granted in Portugal, due mainly to the Portuguese crown deeply applauding the idea of exploring new lands and acquiring new sea routes to the Indian Ocean and Asia. This would have optimized the trade route possibilities. In 1484 the king of Portugal enlisted his Council of Geographical Affairs to endow Columbus' plan with agreement and financing, although they rejected on the grounds that the trip was too expensive and provided little mathematical certainty. Disappointed but still encouraged, Columbus presented his case to the Spanish monarchs, King Ferdinand V and Queen Isabella I. Since Spain lagged far behind Portugal in exploration of the Atlantic and the fact that the two had been engrossed in open hostilities over Portugal's claims to certain lands in Africa and several Atlantic islands, Columbus' plan was rejected but openly debated and considered for several more months. In 1491 Columbus projected his final appeal to the Spanish monarchs and again he was rejected, but not because the plan was dubious. It was because Columbus demanded so much in reward for himself. The egos of the Spanish monarchs could not have possibly fit on the same elevator as the one Columbus was attempting to hijack, but after Ferdinand's treasurer interjected on Columbus' behalf he was granted that which he necessitated on the grounds that there was much more to gain than at first was perceived. When Columbus accidentally (or intentionally) landed in South America he instigated a new epoch.

The second Monday in October every year is celebrated across America as Columbus Day. In 1492 a hero was born, but be careful with this connotation. He was a hero for the European monarchs and merchants, not for the indigenous peoples and cultures he so utterly expunged with slavery, warfare, and inhumane acts. In various testimonies and even in Columbus' own letters, we are witness to the hostile and deceitful behavior exhibited by Columbus and those who accompanied him. In a letter to his friend and confidant Luis de Santangel, Columbus wrote, "And when I arrived I found very many islands filled with people innumerable, and of them all I have taken possession for their Highness." Even if Ferdinand and Isabella of Spain had ordered the proper treatment of the Native Americans encountered, Columbus would have met this request with disregard and triviality. He exploited the indigenous peoples and the resources of their lands openly and savagely. He began exporting slaves in large numbers in late 1494 and totally ignored the requests to cease this blasphemous activity when he saw how profitable it was. The Indians that were not exported were placed forcibly into slavery on the island, the children killed and the women made sexually available.

As well as positing corrupt tactics for political and economic control trough aggressiveness, violence, and warfare, Columbus controlled the native inhabitants of the Americas through religion. They were forced into the dogmatic belief and practice of Christianity, the religion of the European crown. Even though they had their own spiritual beliefs and practices that had incubated and cultivated quite nicely over the past thousands years, Columbus instilled a fear-based system rooted in grotesque punishment for those who did not adhere to either Christianity or slavery. Some Indians had their hands cut off and tied around their necks to serve as an example for others who dared deviate from the orders of the Europeans who considered themselves superior. In other cases, Indians were starved and tortured for weeks, and when they could no longer bear the agony they succumbed to the ruthlessness of the European travelers and especially Columbus, a tyrant unto himself.

According to Hopi legend, Younger Brother (those who traveled from the East) came to America and corrupted Elder Brother (the native tribes of the Americas). Younger brother brought ignorance, disease, weapons, and political and religious despotism. The Hopis were given a myth by the Great Mother (the spirit of the Earth) that America would come and go. America is now on its way out as it has totally annihilated not only the indigenous cultures but the resources, the sky, the land, human health, and human intellect, along with the spirit of everything above all. Supposedly, America is the "Land of the Free" and the "Home of the Brave." Is it?

No. America is the home of the Illuminati. It is one of their major centers of operation along with Great Britain and Italy. Columbus was a member of the reptilian hybrid secret society network in northern Italy and Genoa. At one time he was also employed by Rene d'Anjou of the House of Lorraine, one of the primary reptilian bloodlines. Immense financial support for Columbus came from Lorenzo de Medici, one of the most powerful Venetian families of the Black Nobility, and Leonardo da Vinci, a grand master of the Priory of Sion.[6] Other explorers like Giovanni Caboto took on similar assignments from the "Wise Men of the East," the expression Manly Hall uses to describe the leaders of the Venetian reptilian hybrid families, especially when Newfoundland and Nova Scotia were "officially" discovered. In his book, *America's Assignment with Destiny*, Hall writes:

> The explorers who opened the New World Order operated from a master plan and were agents of re-discovery rather than discoverers. Very little is known about the origin, lives, characters, and policies of these intrepid adventurers. Although they lived in a century amply provided with historians and biographers, these saw fit either to remain silent or to invent plausible accounts without substance.

As the reptilian hybrid families of Europe dominated the world, they held on to their systems of management (central banks, hierarchical political structures, war, etc.). The United States was not really founded on freedom, but fascism. The first settlement was at Jamestown, Virginia in the early seventeenth century, but it was not an independent colony

---

[6] King Ferdinand and Queen Isabella of Spain were the secondary financers of Columbus. Lorenzo de Medici was much more powerful and rich, and Leonardo da Vinci was a good friend of his.

A New Order of the Ages

as it was controlled by the Virginia Company, which was owned by the British Crown.

The Freemasons were at the forefront of the change from overt to covert control by the European aristocratic families, although I do believe many freemasons like George Washington and Benjamin Franklin actually had visions of a free and democratic republic for those who wished to be free from monarchy and the Black Nobility. Francis Bacon's *The New Atlantis*, published in 1607, is a parable of the way the dominant European families wanted to take over America, and if you read it, you will see how a group of supposedly independent colonies became an empire founded on satanic fascism. Just look at all the architecture and symbolism in Washington, D.C. People like Hall and David Icke argue that most of the signers of the Declaration of Independence were tied to the same bloodline and secret societies and so therefore were agents of the European Satanic cults (like the P2 lodge), but I believe they were actually double-agents. On one side, they wanted to please their masters and move up in initiation, but on the other, I think they actually believed the United States would one day become independent from Great Britain. Even so, the thirteen colonies have become one colony for their British masters.

The way powerful secret societies and governments fight for control is thinking it will be they who will one day rule the world. Although it appears many clandestine organizations work today to enslave the people, they all fight each other for ultimate power. If you want ultimate power besides technology and economics, think hybrid bloodlines. The first President of the United States, George Washington, the Grand Master of the Freemasonic lodge at Alexandria, was from an aristocratic bloodline. One of his ancestors was an English knight of the 12th century during the time of the Templars, and another was a relative of the Duke of Buckingham who had fought for King Charles I in the English Civil War. The Reptilian hybrid presidential dynasty has continued ever since up to families like the Bushes and Clintons. Benjamin Franklin was a grand master of other European Masonic lodges, and Thomas Jefferson erected the first central bank of the United States modeling that of England, but I am not in favor of blaming any one particular group of people. The United States never was free from England as it is a Crown colony tied to the European bloodlines, but we must not blame the founding fathers. Perhaps they wanted to be free as well?

III

Freedom From Oppression

It is obvious that many settlers coming from Europe to America wished for a greater freedom, as they did not enjoy the oppression offered to them by the kings, queens, and aristocracy of Europe. They hated despotism and wanted the option of open spiritual and religious practice of their own accord. The Age of Rosicrucianism and Freemasonry was inaugurated in Europe and propagated over many generations, and although these societies proposed a freedom of intellectual and spiritual thought, they were also the begetters of evil in the United States today along with the Roman Catholic Church and the Black Nobility. These secret societies, all taking bits and pieces from their precursors, struggled to maintain a stranglehold over esoteric knowledge of the divine. Even though alchemy was the core utility fastening the Rosicrucians and early Freemasons together, their outward expressions were quite varied. In the original Rosicrucian brotherhood there were only eight members, each of which combed the "House of the Holy Spirit," a meeting ground which existed on another thought dimensional plane of existence. By contrast, Freemasonry quickly spread after its inception and worked to foster a tolerant and prosperous society with a large degree of economic and social freedom offered to those who wished to pursue the inner universe as well as the outer one, must like the ancient mystical traditions.

Francis Bacon's *New Atlantis* was a vision of a perfect Rosicrucian state although it was never fully realized as the Industrial Revolution produced life-benefiting results which quelled the barking of the Church and religion, holding itself separate from materialism, a form of life that saw a shift in paradigm from idealism to science. It is often surmised that the early Freemasons were atheists, but this is an absolute misconception. They hated dogma, yes, but only in the way that demonstrated a vindictive heavenly father figure who punished those who sinned against him. The early Freemasons saw the age of materialism as a possible combatant to religion as it forced people to use their scientific brains more and develop logic and reason. Even so, the Freemasons continued to seek direct personal experience of the spirit worlds in a time of sporadic technological innovations, and constantly encouraged people to discard unthinking religion and false piety. Scottish and English Freemasons championed a constitutional monarchy working alongside a democratic parliament, but this was solely the vestige of their predecessors. Even though you will soon see that the secret societies which conspired to create the United States worked together for the most part, I will propose that the American colonies in the end wanted nothing to do with kings, queens, the Church and central banks.

The Freemasons immigrating to America played a crucial part in the American Revolution and the severance of the American colonies from the grasp of the English aristocracy, but today one must come to realize that America is not separate or independent.[1] In 1774 Benjamin Franklin met Thomas Paine in a Masonic Lodge in London and persuaded him to travel to America. He did well in arguing for the abolition of slavery and state funding for the education of the poor; he also coined the phrase, "The United States of America." Many of the founding fathers were Freemasons, but this means little except that they all carried a chip on their shoulders in regards to religion and political tyranny. The architecture of Freemasonry stems out of the occult, the magickal tradition of invoking disembodied spirits, an act travelling way back to ancient Egypt. A saying from Egypt goes something like this, "When the materials are all prepared and ready, the architect shall appear." In fact, none of the founding fathers were atheists like many scholars like to claim. They were very spiritual, it is just that they hated religion. George Washington had a horoscope expulsed for the founding of the Capitol building because he wanted to act in direct accordance with a Freemasonic tradition that charted the history of humankind according to the movements of the stars and planets. It all goes back to astrology. The night sky tells a grand story of birth, death, and creation.[2]

---

[1] The United States today is a British Crown colony controlled by the Rothschild Empire through the Bank of England.

[2] If not the most important, astrology is one of the most important factors in esoteric philosophy.

It is hard to ascertain where allegiances were laid when the United States was founded, but it is a fact that the founding fathers were most notably connected to the Bavarian Illuminati, the modern version of the Illuminati as opposed to the earlier organization. I discoursed earlier about the phrase "Annuit Coeptis, Novus Ordo Seclorum" and stated that it is the very mission statement of the globalists vying for control over the entire Earth today, but when the phrase was first adopted it meant something totally different. The endgame is however the same. The founding fathers were referencing the Roman poet Virgil when they venerated this phrase. In Virgil's *Eclogues*, he posits a new age when the people will be reunited with the gods, therefore creating a paradise where religion is obsolete. The phrase on the back of the dollar bill originally prophesied the end of the reign of the Catholic Church. The phrase did not appear on the dollar however until the aegis of President Roosevelt, himself a 33rd degree Freemason. When he tagged the phrasing on the dollar he made sure it was riddled with occult symbolism. His intentions remain obscure today, although a New World Order would today be a socialist dictatorship based on the worship of Lucifer.

The modern Illuminati was founded by the Rothschilds through Weishaupt, who was contacted in 1770 to found the Secret Order of the Bavarian Illuminati at Ingolstadt. The Bavarian Illuminati is not to be confused with the older Illuminati, the reptilian bloodline families. The original Illuminati infiltrated the Brotherhood of the Snake in Mesopotamia, and you can think of the Bavarian Illuminati as one extending arm of the inner circle of the most elite members. The Bavarian Illuminati attracted the brightest minds in finance, industry, and education, and Weishaupt used extortion to ensure control over the new initiates into the Order. Weishaupt's adepts knew how to advise those in government positions behind the scenes, and they were heavily influenced by their begetter's satanic manifestos. In politics today you literally have this exact same scenario.

Prior to the Bavarian Illuminati, however, appeared the Rosicrucians and the Freemasons. The birth of the Rosicrucians, a secret order paralleling the Age of Freemasonry, sprang out of nowhere and the first the world ever heard of them was with the publication of the *Fama Fraternitatis* in 1614, the *Confessio Fraternitatis* in 1615, and *Chymische Hockzeit* in 1616, although the order probably existed in some form or another beforehand. These fables tell of Christian Rosy Cross, a figure emulated by the Red Cross Knight in Edmund Spenser's *The Faerie Queene*. These three works became known as the Rosicrucian Manifestos, even though no author is attributed to either work. In one of these stories, the tomb of Christian Rosy Cross is discovered 120 years after his death. According to legend, he was born in Germany in 1378 and among his many travels founded the Brotherhood of the Rosy Cross, a group resolute on bringing good to the world through knowledge of spirituality, medicine, and a strict condemnation of the papacy. The charlatans who bring alchemy, astrology, and other occult arts to blemish are also condemned by the *Confessio*. The Rosicrucian Manifestos illustrate a complex fable where Christian Rosy Cross embarks on a journey of spirituality and self-discovery. John Bunyan's *Pilgrim's Progress* is probably an allegory of these earlier works.

The Rosicrucian Manifestos spoke of a secret brotherhood, operating under the auspices of the benefactor for the entire world.[3] Adepts were called forth, but nobody knew how or where to apply. Magical philosophers all over Europe ran around and petitioned to know how to apply, but the order was so secret that nobody knew. The symbol of the Rosicrucians became a rose superimposed on a cross, but this was nothing new to what Andreae and Martin Luther adopted for their family arms. The cross comes long before Christianity. It has long symbolized the mustering of heaven and earth, God and man, male and female. The rose was a symbol of both sensual and divine love as well as spiritual illumination. Before the Rosicrucians and Freemasons the rose emphasized secrecy, as a rose placed on a dining table meant that anything said under the influence of too much wine was kept "under the rose" so to speak and was not to be taken outside. Above all, the rose to the Rosicrucians derived from the Latin *ros* meaning 'dew.' This fits in nicely with the fact that the early Rosicrucian order was full of alchemists, for whom dew itself was a powerful symbol of regeneration. In alchemical symbolism dew is the universal alkahest, the most powerful solvent of gold. 'Dew' could also represent semen. Semen is another powerful generative and reproductive force.

Christian Rosy Cross is obviously an allegorical figure, and indeed there seemed to be no orderly Rosicrucian body at the time the Rosicrucian Manifestos were published, yet in the ensuing years there

---

[3] This is how secret societies operate today. They confess to be the saviors of the world when really they are the prison warders.

seemed to crop up many who joined themselves into the order without proper ritual. If the Rosicrucians did not exist before the 17th century in that particular form, they sure did during the 17th century out of sheer intrigue by those who deemed themselves worthy enough to fight for spiritual and economic reform during a time of heavy political and religious upheavals. By the 1640's, many Rosicrucian lodges had sprung up throughout Europe. Two men named Ashmole and Lilly incited a lodge in London in 1646, which is thought by some scholars to be the origin of the Freemasons, although we know now that the order of Freemasonry is far more ancient. In 1710 Sigmund Richter published the laws of the alchemical Brotherhood of the Golden and Rosy Cross which became the official proclamation of Rosicrucianism in Europe. Of course, the Church condemned those caught in Rosicrucian proceedings and dealings as blasphemers and correspondents of the devil, but to no avail. It seemed the people had grown tired of being scared of the devil and his followers, if there even were any. The Rosicrucian movement did not see any overt esoteric activity, but it did commence the emergence of the largest secret society in the world, Freemasonry, and two major revolutions—one in France and one in America.

Freemasonry appeared in North America around the mid eighteenth century, although it had occupied the Americas beforehand and Europe long before. Benjamin Franklin was a Grand Master in 1734 in the Province of Pennsylvania. In 1774 he became one of the Council of Three of the Rosicrucians operating in America at the time. George Washington was initiated as a Freemason in 1752 and was proposed to be the Grand Master of the central Grand Lodge of America, although this never occurred. As master of an individual lodge he did become the first president of the United States of America in 1789. Many Americans who played a prominent role in the American Revolution were Freemasons, such as Paul Revere, John Paul Jones, and Andrew Jackson. It has been largely speculated that Freemasons conspired and organized the American Revolution, but according to Masonic scholar John Hamill, this is a vast overstatement. Yes, there were many Freemasons who fought in the Revolution on the side of the colonists and America, but they did not coalesce together and instigate a war which took many lives on both sides. The colonists wanted to be free, and the British aristocracy wanted to control them. That is a simplified statement, but I believe it bellies a critical importance when attempting to understand why wars are fought.

Amid whatever bigotry prevailed among these secret orders, they were all influential in establishing the United States of America. After the Rosicrucians founded their first colony in 1694 in what is today Pennsylvania, the Freemasons established their first lodges around 1730 with the consent of the Mother Grand Lodge in England. One can see how Freemasons, the Rosicrucians, and the Bavarian Illuminati worked together in the lower echelons to found the United States in that most the signers of the Declaration of Independence were Freemasons and Rosicrucians and that the symbolism depicted on U.S. currency is old Illuminati regalia hearkening back to Egypt. Although these movements appear to be separate, they are well connected. After the American Revolution, the American Masonic lodges segregated from the English Mother Grand Lodge and created the American Grand Lodge which consisted of the York Rite with ten degrees and the Scottish Rite with thirty-three degrees.[4] Members higher than these degrees were initiated into the Bavarian Illuminati, which itself is controlled by the older Illuminati. To the Rothschilds, the establishment of a central bank was crucial in taking over the colonies, and even though Thomas Jefferson and Benjamin Franklin were inimical to this, Alexander Hamilton was persuaded by Rothschild agents in 1790 after Franklin's death to erect the First National Bank of the United States. The First National Bank was fashioned by the Bank of England and controlled by the Rothschilds. This power struggle over the nation's currency has maintained ever since.[5]

The argument for Masonic, Rosicrucian, and other esoteric influences in the birth of the United States rests bluntly on the Great Seal of the country; in 1782 the design was approved. The thirteen stars, the thirteen-berried olive branch, the thirteen arrows, and the thirteen stripes on the flag represent the thirteen original colonies. 'E Pluribus Unum' means "out of many, one," denoting the thirteen states merging into one country. Esoterically, thirteen represents the original thirteen reptilian bloodlines composing the old Illuminati. According to many Rosicrucians today, the New Order of the Ages stapled on the back of the one dollar bill is a reference to Francis Bacon's fictional *New Atlantis*,

---

[4] This the same pyramidal structure of modern Freemasonry today.

[5] Today it is the Federal Reserve that enslaves the American people through debt.

which proposed a utopian society that many claim was the ultimate goal of the founding fathers. The Declaration of Independence asseverates:

> We hold these truths to be self-evident, that all men are created equal, that they are endowed by their Creator with certain unalienable rights, that among these are life, liberty and the pursuit of happiness.

Was this really the goal of the founding fathers, or was it merely a ruse to fool the ignorant masses? You be the judge. Imagine of the United States government had this as its motto? Things today would be much different.

The same year the American Declaration of Independence was written and transmuted Adam Weishaupt founded in Bavaria the Order of Perfectibilists, also known as the Covenant of the Golden Dawn. Weishaupt was born in Bavaria, Germany and studied Satanism as a young adult. He was heavily influenced by Mayer Amschel Rothschild, who instructed Weishaupt to create these secret orders which would eventually infiltrate the United States. It is often conjectured by conspiracy theorists today that Adam was paid by the English aristocracy to found an order that would eventually take over not only the newly erected United States but also the world, and I believe they are right. In 1780, Baron France Carnegie was ordered to merge the Order of the Illuminati with Freemasonry, and this allowed the Illuminati to expand rapidly via the usage of Masonic Lodges, which seemed innocent to the general public. When Great Britain lost its domain over the American colonies it had a backup plan to reassert itself into the affairs of the New World. The Order of Perfectibilists, or more commonly referred to as the Bavarian Illuminati, was strictly casted on the order of the Jesuits, a group operating under the vestiges of the Catholic Church.

When the Bavarian Order was sanctioned in the latter half of the eighteenth century it represented more of a Rosicrucian ideal. Individual freedom and spiritual wisdom atop a utopian state were the monarchy is no longer in session represents what those who called themselves "illuminated" originally stood for. Abating the clergy and private ownership were also the overall goals of this group. Membership to the Illuminati was by invitation only, as was the case with many secret societies from the past. Extensions of the Illuminati proliferated throughout Europe, but after ten years the authorities had all but expunged the Illuminati as well as Freemasonry in many parts of Europe including Bavaria, and Weishaupt, once a university professor, was sacked and put under . . . or so many think. Since then the Illuminati has operated from underground, the bowls of the Earth forging secret chambers where rituals and ceremonies transpired. In 1783, Congress ratified a contract which stated that all bills of credit emitted, money borrowed and debts contracted by or under the authority of Congress shall be deemed a charge against the U.S. by the debtor, and that was King George of England. Many historians today know that Great Britain financed both sides of the Revolutionary War, but few are filling to talk about it. Today, Great Britain has a major hold over the United States. The Internal Revenue Service (I.R.S.) collects taxes from the American people for the English aristocracy. The C.I.A., F.C.C. (Federal Communications Commission), F.B.I., and N.A.S.A. are all organizations run by the United Nations and secret societies. The U.S. government only holds shares of stock in these groups, and that is why no government today has any power over the global elite, the Illuminati. The Illuminati remains corrupt, most powerful, and secretive.

When Weishaupt passed away in 1830, Guiseppe Mazzini assumed leadership of the Bavarian Illuminati and he collaborated with the Satanist Albert Pike, who was the Sovereign Grand Commander of the Ancient and Accepted Scottish Rite of Freemasonry and later the founder of the Ku Klux Klan. Mazzini had named Pike the leader of the operations of the Bavarian Illuminati in the United States. In a letter dated August 15, 1871, Pike outlined to Mazzini how to conquer the world with three world wars, which would accumulate into the New World Order. He emphasized how the first world war should be staged to bring Czarist Russia under the control of the Bavarian Illuminati. The second world war would then be started by manipulating the differences between the German nationalists and the Zionists which would result in the establishment of a State of Israel in Palestine. The third world war would then be the ice cap in that it would pit the Zionists against the Arabs and the result would annihilate Christianity and atheism.[6]

So where does a conspiracy theory begin and where does it end? In the 1960's British Prime Minister Harold Wilson had no rebuttal against the "Gnomes of Zurich," the international bankers and financers who

---

[6] The first two world wars went exactly to plan. Today, we are right in the middle of the third world war proposed by Pike.

really ran things. These men were shadowy figures who operated behind many pawns. Napoleon Bonaparte once said that we are all either kings or pawns of men. The Gnomes of Zurch are the kings and their minions are the pawns. Harold Wilson had no defense against these men who he called "shades" because he could not even pinpoint their actual identities. The "shades" were the beginning of the formation of the Bilderberg group, and they helped finance the Bolshevik Revolution and the Third Reich. As World Wars I and II ravaged Europe, the Gnomes of Zurich (Bilberbergs/Illuminati) were better able to create the European Union and annihilate free trade agreements. In 1973 Great Britain joined the Common Market leaving behind the European Free Trade Association, the rival trading block. In this shift, trade agreements with Austria and New Zealand, among other nations, was severely crippled. So why would Britain do this if it was already powerful politically and economically?

It was in fact the international bankers who wanted a single currency for all of Europe. When this comes to pass a central bank can be established that will control the flow of all the currency and commerce in Europe. Where would this bank be? Most likely in Jerusalem, the very site chosen by the global elite centuries ago. Back then, Jerusalem was the very center of the largest land mass on the planet. It sat right in the middle of two lines criss-crossing each other, one line coming southwest from the northern tip of Russia and the other traveling southeast from the Northern tip of Spain. It was the center of all business and trade. If you wanted to bring in goods you had to go through Jerusalem. That is why the New World Order primarily concerns Israel today. Israel has the most advanced atomic and nuclear weapons as well as the most advanced space program. Who do you supposed the United States gives Israel billions upon billions of dollars every year? Because it is the land of God's chosen people, the Jews and the Torah? No, because it is the chosen land of the global fascists who have been operating from behind secret societies for the past two thousand years. Remember? They created God. It all started with the control and distribution of money in Europe by the interbreeding aristocracy conspiracy researchers know today as the Black Nobility. The most important of these families were:

—The House of Guelph (Britain)
—The House of Wettin (Belgium)

—The House of Bernadotte (Sweden)
—The House of Liechtenstein (Liechtenstein)
—The House of Oldenburg (Denmark)
—The House of Hohenzollern (Germany)
—The House of Hanover (Germany)
—The House of Bourbon (France)
—The House of Orange (Netherlands)
—The House of Grimaldi (Monaco)
—The House of Wittelsbach (Germany)
—The House of Braganza (Portugal)
—The House of Nassau (Luxembourg)
—The House of Habsburg (Austria)
—The House of Savoy (Italy)
—The House of Karadjordjevic (Yugoslavia)
—The House of Wurttemberg (Germany)
—The House of Zogu (Albania)

This isn't a list of the original Illuminati, but these families were inexorably intertwined with the families of the Illuminati; in fact, many of the aforementioned families are offshoot bloodlines of the original 13 bloodlines.

To understand the Illuminati though, you really should understand Freemasonry, since it is perhaps the oldest secret society after the Brotherhood of the Snake. Ancient orders of Freemasonry were purported to have handled not only the Ark of the Covenant and the Spear of Longinus, but also secret anti-gravity technology. As with the Illuminati, there is the modern organization of Freemasonry as well as the ancient organization of Freemasonry, which could have influenced the Knights Templar.

One man, Baron Karl Gotthelf von Hund, perpetuated the idea that the Knights Templar society was the precursor to the modern Freemasons when he claimed to have been initiated into an Order of the Temple in 1742. No such order was perceived to have existed, but Hund was persistent. He claimed to have been ordered by unknown superiors to found a new rite of degrees known as the "Strict Observance." After this commandment the unknown superiors were never heard from again. Interestingly enough, the central figure of the Rite was Jacques de Molay, the leader of the Templars who was executed in 1314. It is supposed that he was succeeded as Grand Master by Pierre d'Aumont, the Templar Prior of Auvergne who subsequently hauled the Order to Scotland. He was then succeeded by an unbroken line of Grand Masters who kept their identity a secret. Were they the unknown superiors?

In 1776 Hund passed away with his newly created Rite, but his principles were undertaken by the Lodge of the Rite at Lyons and by the Provincial Grand Prior of Auvergne. These traits were then adapted into a Rite which today is still maintained by the Grand Priory of Helvetia. It is perhaps not so strange that the terminology and rituals instigated by the Knights Templar were picked up and reused by subsequent Rites and Orders passing into the seventeenth and eighteenth centuries under the guise of Freemasonry and Rosicrucianism. In *A Pocket History of Freemasonry*, it states:

> The Great Priory of England is in communion with the Grand Priory of the Rectified Scottish Rite, more often referred to as the Knights Beneficent of the Holy City. This is, in effect, the old Rite of Strict Observance of Baron von Hund. It is regarded as an exalted pinnacle of Freemasonry and its Swiss members have the privilege of attending meetings of the 33° of the Scottish Rite.

Great Britain still holds much power as the governing body of today's Masonic Knights Templar (The United Religious, Military and Masonic Orders of the Temple and of St. John of Jerusalem, Palestine, Rhodes and Malta in England, and Wales and Provinces Overseas). Under the control of the Masonic Knights Templar is the English Great Priory of the Holy Order of Knights Beneficent of the Holy City. In 1770 a man named Johann August von Starck organized the Clerical Chapter of Knights Templar. He claims:

> The original Knights Templar were divided into two classes, military and sacerdotal; that the Clerical branch possessed the inner knowledge of the Order; that it had been perpetuated in secret; that Starck was its present ambassador; that it was superior to the Secular Branch; and that if recognized by Baron von Hund, the treasures of its knowledge should be opened to him and his Rite.

It can be debated that the descendents of the Essenes, the Clerical Chapter, seems to bear a strong similarity to the Priory of Sion, and when the Templars were dissipated the Knight John Eures emancipated its secret documents and treasures and kept them hidden until his contact with Starck. According to one other author, James Burnes, the Priory of Sion did in fact evolve to neo-orders of Masonic Rites. In his 1837 publication of *A Sketch of the History of the Knights Templar* he writes:

> We are told by a learned French writer, that having deserted the Temple, they [the Templars] had arranged themselves under the banners of Robert Bruce, by whom they were formed into a new Order, the observances of which were based on those of the Templars, and became, according to him, the source of Scottish Free Masonry.

No doubt is there a connection between Freemasonry and the French and Scottish Jacobites of the early eighteenth century, and since it is well speculated that many of the disbanded Templars sailed to Scotland in 1307, they most likely in turn formed a new Rite under a new auspice.

When the Templars were officially dismantled, surviving members joined other orders such as the Knights of Christ, the Teutonic Knights, and the Hospitallers. The Hospitallers (also known as the Knights of Saint John) were not initially a military order but became more militant as the Templars rose to prominence. With the loss of the Holy Land, the Hospitallers had fallen back to Cyprus along with the Templars, and with the death of the Templar Order the Hospitallers increased their exorbitance. When they were besieged by the Turks, they (the Hospitallers) relocated to the island of Malta and became known as the Sovereign and Military Order of Malta (the Knights of Malta). Today, the Knights of Malta are headquartered in Rome under the direct supervision of the Pope and are recognized by more than forty countries as a sovereign nation. A British offshoot, the Knights of Saint John of Jerusalem, is a Protestant Order headquartered in London and headed by the king and queen. The Catholic and Protestant wings are the same cartel at the top. Americans in modern history connected to the Knights of Malta include William Casey and John McCone (both former C.I.A. directors), Lee Iacocca (former Chrysler chairman), William F. Buckley (columnist), Joseph P. Kennedy, William Wilson (U.S. ambassador to the Vatican), Clare Boothe Luce, and Alexander Haig (former U.S. secretary of state). Today, the Knights of Malta is one of the primary channels of communication between the Vatican and the C.I.A. The Rosicrucians are also an offshoot of the Knights Templar, the secret order which commenced numerous historical events and held a great deal of esoteric knowledge. The Templars were very influential, their backstop being the Priory of Sion. Past Priory leadership included Leonardo da Vinci, Robert Fludd, Sir Isaac Newton, Victor Hugo, and Jean Cocteau. The Priory of Sion, under different names at different times, was the secret society behind the Knights Templar and was the medium through which Templars escaped persecution to other orders.

The Priory of Sion was the nucleus of the atom which held together the societies of Freemasonry, the Illuminati, and the Round Tables. The avowed objective of the Priory was (and still is today) the restoration of the Merovingian dynasty and bloodline. The late Prince Bernhard was the leader of the Black families of Europe who claimed descent from the House of David through the Merovingian dynasty.

Even so, America remains a British Crown colony. The Queen of England is the head of the Royal Family and London is the capital of the British Empire, which is governed by the Prime Minister and the Cabinet. Just like the Vatican and Rome, however, there is a separate state within London called the City. The City is oftentimes referred to as the "richest square mile in the world" and it occupies about a square mile in the heart of London. It carries almost 5,000 inhabitants and a million jobs. The government of the City is the Crown, which itself is comprised of thirteen members led by the King of the City, the Lord Mayor. It is here were you will find the Bank of England controlled by the Rothschilds. Although the British Royal Family bows to the King of the Crown, there is cooperation between the two because the Windsor family is part of the Black Nobility, of which the Crown belongs. The British East India Company, which helped spur the advancement of the British Empire, founded the Committee of 300 at the behest of the Black Nobility. Today, the Committee of 300 is one of the most important secret societies working towards a one world government.

What we can see here is a hidden hand. Even though Rosicrucianism, Freemasonry, and the Black Nobility are at the front of control and suppression today in the United States, there is a real hidden hand behind the scenes. Negative extraterrestrials and the bloodlines they instilled are behind the real evil in this country. Most secret societies and orders had originally nothing to do with taking over the world, but once corrupted by these bloodline families, taking over the world became the modus operandi. The Duke of Brunswick, Grand Master of World Freemasonry, once said:

> I have been convinced that we, as an Order, have come under the power of some very evil occult order, profoundly versed in science, both occult and otherwise, though not infallible, their methods being black magic, that is to say, electro-magnetic power, hypnotism, and powerful suggestion. We are convinced that the Order is being controlled by some Sun Order [the Druids?], after the nature of the Illuminati, if not by that order itself.

Madame Helena Blavatsky, in *The Secret Doctrine*, wrote:

> While the real 'Brothers' died ignominious deaths, the spurious Order which tried to step into their shoes became exclusively a branch of the Jesuits (Illuminati) under the immediate tutelage of the latter. True-hearted Masons ought to reject with horror any connection, let alone descent from these . . . . There exists . . . another class of adepts belonging to a brotherhood also and mightier than any other they have to be ranked with the adepts of the Black Arts. These are our Roman Catholic 'Fathers' and clergy . . . A hundred times more learned in secret symbology and the old religion than our Orientalists will ever be . . . There are more profoundly learned kabalists in Rome and throughout Europe and America than is generally suspected . . . Thus are the 'Brotherhoods' of 'black' adepts more powerful and dangerous . . . than any host of Eastern occultists.

Both Blavatsky and the Duke of Brunswick reference the hidden hand that has covertly infiltrated the secret societies we associate with evil today. One must be wary who he or she labels as "evil" and "corrupt." The real evil in the world comes from evil extraterrestrials, and to say Freemasonry is bad or taking over the world is really an egregious statement although the notion is fundamentally valid. Remember, it is like Jordan Maxwell says . . . there is always more to the story than that which is revealed openly.

Matrix of Power

Power can do two things: control and subvert; these two actions are interchangeable and require victims. The display of power over the course of human history has taken on a pattern of such likeness: violent oppressive → mind oppressive → economic oppressive. Violence via the sword, arrow, and catapult was the archaic method of siege and conquer. Simply put, if you had a bigger army you could take over those smaller tribes with no arms and mostly women and children. When cities grew larger and kings were appointed in certain regions of the world, mind oppression emerged with the institution and the degradation of religious dogma. Monotheistic religions flourished while God was punitive and feared by all alike. Fear was the basal paradigm when peopled feared they would go to Hell if they sinned. Now, economic oppressions hold entire populations at bay financially and socially.

Money and economic political control (control over the world's resources) are in full effect today. In the book *Confessions of an Economic Hitman*, former "jackal" John Perkins testifies to his function within the United States "Corporate-ocrasy" to convince political and financial leaders in underdeveloped or third-world countries to accept development loans from institutions like the World Bank (owned by members of the Skull and Bones) and USAID. These loans were always too large to pay back, so the economic hitman would have leverage in persuading further entrapment by convincing third world countries to give up large amounts of resources at pennies on the dollar and forcing their governments to coalesce into extensions of the United States government. Fraudulent financial reports, rigged elections, payoffs, extortion, sex, and murder were the cards out on the table. Economic hitmen are in effect highly paid professionals who coerce and politically bully smaller governments and leaders of poor nations in giving up their power and resources. Often, the politician is paid off and no further penetration is needed. In more recent cases, plans B and C were taken into effect. These would involve assassinations and the military. According to Perkins:

> The first real economic hit man was back in the early 1950s, Kermit Roosevelt, Jr., the grandson of Teddy, who overthrew the government of Iran, a democratically elected government, Mossadegh's government who was Time's magazine person of the year; and he was so successful

at doing this without any bloodshed—well, there was a little bloodshed, but no military intervention, just spending millions of dollars and replaced Mossadegh with the Shah of Iran. At that point, we understood that this idea of economic hit man was an extremely good one. We didn't have to worry about the threat of war with Russia when we did it this way. The problem with that was that Roosevelt was a C.I.A. agent. He was a government employee. Had he been caught, we would have been in a lot of trouble. It would have been very embarrassing. So, at that point, the decision was made to use organizations like the C.I.A. and the N.S.A. to recruit potential economic hit men like me and then send us to work for private consulting companies, engineering firms, construction companies, so that if we were caught, there would be no connection with the government. (November 4, 2004 interview)

The Secret World Government uses powerful countries like the United States to eradicate small countries so when it was time for the United Nations to vote on a New World Order there will be few countries voting.

In America in the early nineteenth and twentieth centuries, private wealth consisted mostly of gold or silver, with gold being worth twenty dollars an ounce. This became a hassle to carry around, so gold and silver certificates were issued. The inscription "Pay to the bearer upon demand in gold or silver" bore on the papers. The true source of inflation occurred next when the bankers started to issue out more notes than they had gold for because the people rarely came back to withdraw their gold when they were using the notes all the time. Eventually, Federal Reserve notes came into effect and the gold standard was abolished, leading to worthless pieces of paper being traded on the notion that they are worth an inherent value corresponding to the economy and how many notes are in circulation. Today, when the Federal Reserve notes are printed they are loaned to the U.S. Treasury. A staggering eight and a half percent interest is compounded on the loaned notes, which cost only two cents to make. The interest is collected every year by the I.R.S. Repo Man. Interest in the value exceeding two hundred billion dollars every year is drained from the economy in the guise of income taxes.[7]

---

[7] According to the Constitution, federal income taxes are illegal and some Americans do not pay their income taxes because they have realized this. See *Zeitgeist* by Peter Joseph for more information.

When there is never enough money to pay back the principle plus the interest, inflation inevitably occurs, which is essentially a hidden tax on the people. The current debt the United States Government has trifled us with is ten trillion dollars and growing, which means that every man, woman, and child in the United States is in debt thirty-two thousand dollars. Overall, the debt total in the United States exceeds fifty-four trillion dollars when households, financial entities, and businesses are taken into consideration. The problem of money is even well documented in the Bible. According to the New Testament and the writings of the historian Josephus, the Pharisees were the ruling priest class in Jewish society during and after the time of Jesus. They developed a system of prayer worship in the temple where they would charge a half a shekel admission price, money-collectors being stationed outside the temples. They would not only make money this way but also by selling the cattle, sheep, and doves sacrificed during the rituals. Today, the bankers have much more clever ways of making money.

The Federal Reserve is a continuation of the Bank of England back in colonial times. Under the strict authority of the Church loaning money for profit was forbidden, but after the Protestant Reformation in the sixteenth century King Henry VIII of England subsided the lending laws and the power of money took on full swing. The power the bankers had back then and that they still hold now was the authority to take away property and assets from individuals who could not pay back loans. The bankers also realized they could make massive profits during war, and war we had. By the latter half of the seventeenth century the Bank of England was created and the British Crown posed as the largest debtor. The bankers, though, were clever. They created themselves, or rather put themselves up on a pedestal and declared themselves a private entity behind the government. The design of the scheme of the bankers was that the belief in a nonexistent enterprise was fostered by quick returns for the later investors who reaped the money from the earlier investors. The British government was forced to lay out the initial one million pounds while the bankers loaned out ten times that much to important rich people to buy shares in the owning of the bank. The bank agreed to loan the money back to the government of England plus the interest accumulated and paid for in the form of taxes by the people.

In the New World at this time, the economy was booming because the colonies were printing their own currency called "colonial scrip."

It was fiat money, but had a non debt-based value which accurately represented the value of goods and services without interest. In 1764 the Parliament of England passed the Currency Act prohibiting the colonies from creating and issuing their own currency. The 1766 Benjamin Franklin journeyed to London seeking the appeal of the law on account of the severe depression inflicted onto the colonies, but the action proved futile. The prime cause of the Revolutionary War and the strict observance of the Founding Fathers to have no national bank was this disagreement. In America, a battle raged for the first 120 years of its existence as the right to issue currency was ping-ponged back and forth between the government and the international bankers. The corporate-ocracy was also protected and secured during this period. In 1886, the United States Supreme Court ruled that corporations shall have the same rights as persons. Unfortunately, it was overlooked that the corporations were not subject to laws of morality burdened by the people. The bankers think they have created a self-perpetuating creature of deception, but they really have created a war on themselves. Pretty soon they are going to have mass riots on their hands, which is why they are working so hard on enacting Martial Law. The Happy Planet Index is a study that measures not only happiness but the cost of acquiring that happiness in terms of ecological impact and overall quality of life. The calculation looks like this:[8]

Life Satisfaction x Life Expectancy / Ecological Footprint = Happiness Index

The United States ranks 150th out of 178 nations, which is embarrassing considering we are the richest. The reason for our poor ranking is that our Ecological Footprint, or in other words our imperialism and our economic advancements on the world, is one of the biggest in the world. To achieve the happiness and life expectancy in Coast Rica the average America uses four and a half times more resources.

The happiness of each American would sure increase of debt was eliminated. One solution to the debt problem is to issue a coin worth whatever the debt costs and pay off the Federal Reserve. This could work because coins minted by the United States treasury are worth their face value as currency and there is a clause in the agreement that we,

---

[8] This equation was taken from *Spontaneous Evolution* by Bruce Lipton and Steve Bhaerman.

the people, can buy back the right to issue our own currency. President Kennedy passed an Executive Order in 1963 which called for the printing of $450 billion in U.S. backed debt-free currency. When he was executed for not only this but also threatening to disclose the alien presence his successor, Lyndon Johnson, suspended the order. The fact of the matter is that whenever an impediment arises, big name families quell the problem immediately through their wide influence. The Rockefeller family controls and finances the America Medical Association and the public educational system through textbook publishing. The Harriman family was directly responsible for the rise of the Rockefellers. Standard Oil of New York (SONY), now Exxon is a major economic influencer and player along with the Whitney Family, who own other large corporations. They do not serve the interests of the American people.

One further travesty administered by those in charge has been revoking of the use of hemp. The American colonies as well as the American Revolution would not have been possible without the cannabis/hemp plant that has been used throughout many areas of the world since the dawn of time. Paper made from hemp produced books, maps, and money. Hemp is so much stronger than paper made from trees and you can produce four times as much of it from hemp than you can from trees. Paper from made from hemp incurs 1/5 the pollution at 1/4 the cost, is 10 times stronger, and lasts 200 times longer. Case in point, hemp is the strongest natural fiber on the planet and is also the fastest growing plant. Also, the seeds from the hemp plant issue the highest source of complete vegetable protein and are the highest source of essential fatty acids. Fatty acids clean the cholesterol out of our arteries and are necessary for our survival. The oils in the supermarkets are as destructive as saturated fats and actually cause cholesterol buildup, leading to heart attacks, and cardiac arrests. Hemp could also replace petroleum oil mined in the ground as machine-grade lubricant. In America for the first 150 years, concentrated extracts of cannabis from the flowers were the second-most used medicines for over 100 separate medical illnesses. If Hemp were legal in America today there would be over 50,000 commercial uses for it. So why is it illegal? Because the main families in America (Harriman—Standard Oil, Rockefeller—American Medical Institute, Whitney—Eli Whitney-Cotton Gin, Rothschild—Federal Reserve, Dupont—chemicals in wood pulp processing and cotton pesticides, and Hearst—Newspapers and Media) do not care about us and want to profit immensely on selling us chemicals we do not need, pharmaceuticals that destroy our immune systems, petroleum oils that destroy the environment, and paper made from axed trees. Hundreds of billions of dollars are reaped in profit every year by the sale of petrochemicals, pharmaceuticals, machines, and other such products.[9]

The entire medical profession is founded on the false belief that genes control us and we are merely products of random chemical mixing and gene-mutating. The erroneous belief that our bodies are just biochemical electrical machines living in a machine-like universe has led to medical professionals being baffled by disease-curing miracles performed by the mind. Moreover, Luis Pasteur, shortly before he died, said that he was wrong about his germ theory. He stated that germs and viruses were the result of the disease and not the cause. The body overloads on toxic build-up and produces symptoms of stress, and coupled with a troubled mindset or bad karma, disease occurs. When the body is out of sync, it is out of balance with the flow of spirit. When toxins reach critical levels bacteria and other viruses swoop in and perform as scavengers. This leads to a super toxic waste by-product being left behind which the body has a difficult time getting rid of. On top of that, drugs introduced by the pharmaceutical companies are vastly over-priced and only work mask the symptoms, not cure them. These drugs are highly toxic, so they actually add to the increase in bacteria accumulation. Cures of cancer discovered have been voraciously suppressed by the pharmaceutical industry, although the media forces you to believe otherwise. It has been discovered that the cause of diseases are in fact parasites, worms in particular. These worms live in our bodies, and when their eggs are exposed to substances like Benzene and Propyl Alcohol they hatch quicker. Most foods ingested poison us and the air we breathe is no better. Nor is the water we drink, although water is the best alternative to any drink advertised on television. Fruits and vegetables are the best alternatives to any food advertised.

This economic struggle is really a result of money. The bank is duly called so because it represents a river bank. The river bank controls the flow of water, or current, and that is why banks today control the flow of 'current'-cy. Money by law is water under Maritime Admiralty Law

---

[9] William Randolph Hearst ran a smear campaign against hemp in the 1930's in order to protect his timber dynasty.

because it is liquid; it changes hands every day hundreds of times over. The ebb and flow of money is related to breathing and the tides. When the tide comes in it represents the loaning of money by the central bank to the government, when the tide pulls back it represents the flow of income tax paid by the people; Money going out and money coming in represents a breathing entity. Everything that lives breathes, and the way banks breath is by controlling the value and flow of currency. In the same sense, the bar exam attorneys are forced to take to become certified licensed lawyers represents a sand bar in an ocean. When you enter the gate to step up to the judge you are entering "deep water" and therefore you are dead because you technically drowned. Your lawyers must speak on your behalf because he passed the 'bar' and you 'drowned.' Your lawyer boarded the ship (represented by the gate) and he speaks to the captain who is the judge. The judge wears a black robe because he represents Saturn and he rules from the bench, which is the bank because the whole system is controlled by money.[10]

Judges, lawyers, and police officers are all part of the Law Society, whose laws do not affect you as a real person. They affect you as an artificial person, because that is what you are viewed as. In the Law Society, a special jargon is used which sounds like English but really is another language based on the corporation, which is classified as an artificial person. You are an artificial person in the Law Society because your body is a corporation. Under *Capitis Diminutio Maxima*, corporations are listed in all capital letters, and that is why your name is listed as such on nearly every document which applies to you. Your driver's license, birth certificate, social security card, and insurance cards all bear your name in capital letters because you stand for a corporation which makes money for the United States Corporation, your parent company.

Everything today is controlled by symbolism, which is etched into our subconscious minds through repetition and association. In the Hindu tradition the symbol for chakra and balance was the spinning wheel, but today it has taken on a darker connotation because it was used as the swastika by the Nazis during World War II. The Shell Gas station shell represents reincarnation and the body, which is the vessel for the soul. In Egypt, Horus was the sun god who was often depicted as a phoenix or an eagle. That is why we have left wing and right wing

---

[10] Jordan Maxwell, *Matrix of Power: How the World Has Been Controlled by Powerful People Without Your Knowing* (Daly City, CA: The Book Tree, 2003), 2003.

politics today, Republicans and Democrats. The phoenix also stands for reincarnation. In the popular science fiction movie *Star Wars*, the main protagonist is named Luke Skywalker. The Sun in ancient times was sometimes referred to as Luke, a being who walked across the sky (hence, sky-walker) in twelve steps (the 12 signs of the Zodiac). Over time, Horus became 'hours' (move the 'u' left) and we now have days composed of twelve hour intervals (12 hours of a.m. and 12 hours of p.m.). Darth Vader represented Set, the Egyptian god of Dark. Darth Vader commanded the "Empire," the same controlling force operating from behind the scenes today.

Since your body is collateral on the New York Stock Exchange, you are technically a corporation. That is why you are referred to as a "corpse" when you die. In this way, you have the power of free choice. Many people today do not realize the freedom they really do possess. You do not have to go to court, you can settle out of court. You do not have to go to school, you can be homeschooled. You do not have to go to church. You do not even have to pay a speeding ticket. When a police officer gives you a ticket it is called a "ticket of commerce." He signs it first and you sign it second, so technically you are the co-signer. You can choose to not pay and instead send it with the necessary paperwork to the Secretary of State, who then sends it to the Attorney General, who then sends it back to the cop. The cop then has to pay it, but if he does not want to he now has the right to arrest you and take you to jail. It is all written in the fine print on the ticket and in the law books, it is just that most people would never bother themselves which such trivialities.

Trojan Horse in American Education

When freeing oneself from oppression, the American education system would be a good place to start. The matrix of power weaves through the system of education as it is a bastion for a steady flow of information to be disseminated throughout the public arena. The powers-that-be have infiltrated the American education system in such a way that so-called "learning" today is nowhere near where it was a few centuries ago. Truth has been replaced with indoctrination and history has been replaced with a phony replica. The concepts of spirituality, extraterrestrials, reincarnation, free energy, hyper-dimensional physics, and ascension have been hijacked, and in the emptiness there has been placed a veil of amnesia. Today, education seems backwards, and it costs a lot of money. Most children in the United States today will not receive a full college education due to the fact that tuition costs have skyrocketed through the roof. Even so, this cult of learning we call "education" in the United States is nothing but a poor substitute for real knowledge and wisdom. The Magi have seen to that, as an informed and aware public is the last thing they want in their way to the socialist takeover of the entire planet.[11]

Founded in 1857, the National Education Association (N.E.A.) was created by individuals who had labored to promote the public school movement in the United States. The philosophical base of the N.E.A. was to place education in the hands of government so that it could be molded later to fit the needs of the international bankers. Public education in this country did not even exist until the 1840's, and the Constitution makes no mention of it. The notion of a state-owned and controlled education system was imported from Prussia, a country where an authoritarian monarchy used centralized schools and compulsory attendance for its own political and social purposes. Political and social control is the real endgame, and this tactic is not endemic to any one country or peoples. The reason the American government adopted the Prussian system instead of keeping its own government-free educational system is that the bankers who ran things in the West liked the idea of a system of indoctrination unlike any religious order. The subsequent decline in literary taste in this country most undoubtedly began with the growth and spread of public education with its watered-down literary standards.

The first fifty years of the existence of the United States was as close to a libertarian society as there ever was in this country. The education system was one of total freedom and diversity as there were no accrediting agencies, regulatory boards, state textbook selection committees, or teacher certification requirements. Basically, you could say that education primarily stayed in the family. Parents could send their children to any kind of school (church schools, academies for college preparation, seminaries, dames' schools, charity schools, common schools, etc.) and if they didn't want that they could just home school them, which was a common method. The common schools were the

---

[11] Every possible aspect of culture today in the United States is purposefully dumbed-down for this reason.

original public schools and they were founded in New England. They were first created in the early days of the Puritan commonwealth as a means of insuring the transference of the Calvinist Puritan religion. As the Reformation had replaced Papal authority with Biblical authority (really no difference), the Puritan leaders were impressed with the public schools erected by Luther and the German princes as a means of perpetuating religious doctrine and maintaining social order in the Protestant states. In addition to this, Harvard College was founded in 1636 with the aid of a government grant as an institution for higher learning (teaching future careers as magistrates and clergymen), and lower feeder schools were created in order to develop local talent.

When the common schools of New England came into being, Latin, Greek, and Hebrew were taught because these were the original languages of the Bible and theological literature, however, most of the schools were local (financed and controlled by local committees who set their own standards, chose their own teachers and selected their own textbooks). There was no central authority dictating how the schools were ran like there is today. There was a large enough schism between the civil authority and the clergy in that this system was much less of a theocracy than it had gained a reputation for being. Although this educational advancement was secure in its foundations and free of central influence, the common schools were religious instruments for teaching the catechism of the established orthodox Calvinist sect; all in all, there was a Biblical commonwealth. Inasmuch, this commonwealth did not last long. The growth of the colonies, the development of trade, the influx of other religious sects, the increased general prosperity, and the emergence of religious liberalism weakened the grasp of the Puritan orthodoxy. Enforcement of school laws and regulations grew lax, and private schools manifested as a means of teaching the more practical commercial subjects. By the close of the American Revolution, many towns had no common schools at all.

Over time, the private schools took over, but funding became a huge concern. The N.E.A. came into prominence as it promoted a nation-wide public education system that would be free for parents up through the level of high school. Funding for this system came from Great Britain, and today, the Rockefeller Foundation funds and selects the regional committees who themselves appoint teachers, textbooks, costs of going to college, and subjects in or out of the learning circle.[12] This sounded like a sound system, but unfortunately, the N.E.A. was controlled by the European aristocracy and the Black Nobility—it is quite evident today that the Rockefellers are a prime Reptilian/Aryan bloodline family. They openly promoted Marxism and Social Darwinism while attenuating reincarnation, alternate dimensions, extraterrestrials, and self-sufficiency. The American education system would become their playground, and they effectively subverted the system until its roots were shaken. The steady decline of proper education in the United States today as well as the failure of American children's A.C.T./S.A.T. scores matching those of children in China, Japan, and Russia is a direct result of what is referred to as "dumbed-down education." Moreover, the exponential rise of distractions (television, video games, etc.) has contributed immensely in this dumbing-down of the populace. Children are not the only one's affected. In many cases it is the failure of the parents in teaching their children proper morals, mathematical and reading skills, high standards, and self-sufficiency. People today totally rely on the system to keep them safe and aware, but in cold hard reality the system does the exact opposite. It serves as a prison warder.

The suppression of advanced technology also contributes to this dilemma of a virtually unaware public.

---

[12] The teaching of the theory of evolution has been one major debate in the American education system recently.

IV

THANK-YOU, MR. TESLA

Where is this advanced technology that is supposedly in the possession of our beloved leaders? I suggest that this technology is used behind the scenes, out of public view because it is used for negative purposes. The technology available to the general public, although advanced compared to a century ago, dwindles in comparison to that which is employed by secret brotherhoods. It is all relative, though, because spirituality transcends technology. To the ancients, a car would have been a miracle and an airplane would have been the vessel of the gods. Computers would be totally beyond their comprehension. So is technology magic? If so, Merlin the Magician must have been some sort of secret scientist working relentlessly behind the scenes in order to keep his audience captivated. Was Jesus a magician? One could say that technology is intellectual advancement and powers like the ones Jesus and Merlin demonstrated are spiritual advancements, but why stop there? I say that everything is a miracle and everything is magic. Is the Sun rising everyday not a miracle? Is my heart chakra not a conductor of magic? Why should men like Albert Einstein, Merlin, and Jesus be called either geniuses, wizards or saviors? If these abilities are innate in each of us then one could ask why more people do not put forth such a display of power. Well, I would argue that they do. Most people on the Earth now are in a complete fog as to who they once were and what they are doing now. We already are magicians, we have just forgotten, and the only power people flaunt today is social power. It's not what you know it's who you know, right?

Nevertheless, one cannot ignore how we have been lead to believe that we are not controlled and dominated by higher, incomprehensible technology. In recent history, Nikola Tesla was really the one who started the war over this suppression of new ways of living.[1] Tesla was most certainly a genius, and I would even go so far as to call him a magician. His contributions to the field of electromagnetism and engineering led to over 700 patents in his name for useful inventions seeking the relief of human effort in exchange for a luxury of living. As always, his efforts to help out his fellow man were thwarted by those with the kind of power mainly elicited today, and that is the power of money. When Tesla perfected his design for alternating current, a much more efficient schematic than direct current, he was accosted by his rival Thomas Edison. Even though Tesla expressed a great interest in exposing his A.C. design to Thomas, Edison held him in contempt and thought of his presence as a threat to his D.C.-based empire. Tesla offered to increase the efficiency of D.C. by 25 percent, and when Edison agreed to pay him $50,000 for accomplishing the feat, Tesla proved even more successful. However, his efforts were short-sighted as Edison refused to pay.

A group of investors subsequently contacted Tesla in interest of his design and thus, the Tesla Electric Company was founded. When the company became crippled with financial hardships, Tesla was ejected out of the company and the rights to his arc lamp were discontinued. Dispirited and depressed, Tesla planned on committing suicide at the age of thirty, but before that could happen, A.K. Brown of Western Union offered the genius a laboratory of his own and the restored plight to pursue alternating current. George Westinghouse, one of the members of a highly respected audience in hearing of Tesla's A.C. design, financed Tesla and together they produced Niagara Falls, the first application of the technology. In 1895 the Niagara A.C. power system transmitted streaming electricity to Buffalo, which was twenty-two miles away, and demonstrated an impossible feat compared to the workings and efficiency of D.C. Nonetheless, Tesla was quarreled with by the same powers people know and fear today.

His most well known invention, the Tesla Coil, was created in 1891 and soon became the prototype for radios, televisions, and wireless communication. The wireless transmission of energy was Tesla's ultimate passion, electrical resonance becoming the key to these feats of energy exchange. For instance, a vacuum tube held close to a Tesla Coil burst into illumination. It required no wires or filaments. Free

---

[1] This man has become obscured from the history books because the powers-that-be did not want his inventions going into the public arena where they could free people.

energy was established by determining the frequency of the needed electrical current. In this way, a series of lights were able to be turned on and off selectively from many yards away. So, energy could be sent through thin air, but Tesla thought of this method as cumbersome. It was much more efficient to send the energy through the Earth. This seems counter-productive, but it's actually genius. You see, the Earth itself could be turned into a colossal electric transmitter.[2]

In 1899, Tesla was offered a testing facility in Colorado Springs, a place where he erected a strange sort of laboratory topped with a 180-foot metal tower that was adopted as a magnifying transformer. As the magnifying transformer was tuned to match the resonance of the Earth, the citizens of Colorado Springs were literally walking on electrical current and lighting light bulbs from fire hydrants.[3] When Tesla was ready to turn his machine to full force, it pumped ten million volts of electricity into the Earth. The waves reached the other side of the Earth and returned with a weaker resonance, but the continuous pumping of volts forged a wave function of electricity which maintained a high degree of efficiency and power. The result busted his tower and the patience of his financers, but Tesla was not at all discouraged. He returned to New York in search of backing for the implementation of his resonant energy system to be applied to the whole Earth, in effect giving everyone free energy. Not only was Tesla proposing a free flow of energy, but also communication. Obviously, Tesla was way ahead of his time; he was already proposing the internet!

J.P. Morgan, the richest man in America at the time, was intrigued at the notion of a monopoly on world communications. He enabled Tesla to build a bigger and better laboratory on Long Island. After a series of accidents Morgan grew restless, and once Tesla expressed his real intention to bring free energy to the world and not necessarily new forms of communication, Morgan backed out completely. Obviously, Morgan was only in it for the money and power. Even though Tesla was better suited as a social conscience, the men in charge only wished to use his inventions to either build empires for themselves or go to

---

[2] The Earth is a conductor of electromagnetic energy. It is the second most efficient form of energy behind the Sun.

[3] The movie *The Prestige* (2006) details this time in history. In the film, Hugh Jackman is a magician seeking a real form of magic who stumbles upon Nikola Tesla in his laboratory and witnesses how the scientist is illuminating light bulbs from the ground.

war. Even Tesla once boasted that he could split the Earth in two with his resonance generator. When he could not find American financial backers, Tesla worked for the German Marine High Command building effective turbines in use of war. During World War I Tesla backed out of his post, in fear that he would be persecuted in the United States as a traitor. The death ray designed by Tesla was a particle accelerator, an excrescence of his magnifying transformer. When he aimed the devise at the Arctic Circle and fired, the beam traveled such a large distance that Tesla had no way of perceiving its effectiveness. Later, it was reported that a massive explosion had devastated the remote area of Tunguska in the Siberian wilderness. Five hundred thousand square acres of land were totally decimated. It is believe the explosion was audible from 620 miles away.

It is scientific fact today that for the hydrogen atom not to collapse in its primal (ground) state, it would have to be constantly sucking energy from the vacuum of space, or the ether. Everything you see around you emanates from an energy-rich background field that exists above time and space. To say everything happened all at once in a "big bang" is terribly off track. The energy that structures our bodies (because, as we have seen with Hurtak's work, our biological space-suites are connected to the cosmos through axiatonal lines) is surmised to have a potential energy equivalence of 10^{94} grams per cubic centimeter. In comparison, the human body emits energy at only one gram per cubic centimeter. In 1943, Tesla was scheduled to reveal this hidden potential to President Roosevelt, but he was unable to make it due to the fact that he had been poisoned the night before. The public was told that Tesla died by natural causes, but the official coroner's report clearly detailed that the scientist was poisoned by his dinner. Obviously, someone did not want Tesla convincing the president that he should let everyone in on the secret that they could obtain a form of free energy from any space they occupied.[4]

Just as Tesla was resisted by the international bankers who wanted to make massive profits on the burning of fossil fuels, he was also ridiculed and betrayed by Thomas Edison, most certainly not an American hero.[5] In fact, Edison was a fraud. Not only was he a liar, he was also a criminal.

---

[4] D. Trull, *Tesla: The Electric Magician* (ParaScope, Inc., 1996).

[5] It is amusing to note how cruel men like Columbus and Edison are deified when they were really autocrats.

The reason why so many stray dogs and cats went missing during this time period is because Edison captured them and used them in experiments where they were electrocuted by Tesla's alternating current. Edison did this in an attempt to match A.C. with electrocution in the minds of the people, a very devious propaganda scheme aimed at dismissing Tesla's brilliant designs. Edison and his entourage distributed pamphlets to people warning against 'deadly' A.C. current, and they omitted the fact that Tesla promised each American home would interface this current with a resistor so that the voltage would be reduced to a practical level. Not only was direct current far less efficient and powerful, it required one power house per every square mile compared to only one power house total per city for Tesla's design.

Tesla and Westinghouse won the electrical current battle in 1892, however, their success was short-lived as the Morgans pulled their funding from the institution. Tesla was talking wireless, meaning everyone could stick an antenna into the ground where they lived and receive the electromagnetic energy of the Earth. The way that this was possible is that wireless receivers can resonate with Tesla's transmitter frequencies, just like a piano string will vibrate when another instrument at a distance hits the same frequency as the piano string. By sending out electrical pulses which matched the frequency of the Earth's electromagnetic waves, everyone could receive this energy via a receiver which matched these pulses. This is the same way that multiple dimensions can exist in the same space. They operate on different frequencies. When you turn your radio dial you are tuning into radio stations broadcasting on different frequencies. You can get interference, like when you hear one station more clearly than another, which sounds like static. It is in this way that reptilians can manifest in this dimensional frequency by tuning their consciousnesses to it. Hilary Clinton in 3rd density is human, but in 4th density she is a reptilian demonic entity. Most people only see Hilary Clinton as a human because their consciousnesses are only tuned to 3rd density. People who are clairvoyantly gifted can see her for who she really is because they can tune their awareness to the 4th density and above.

What people today don't realize is that free energy was already patented over a hundred years ago. Tesla's patents referred to the Sun and other forms of radiant energy like cosmic rays, as well as the abundance of negative electricity in the ground. His first radiant energy receiver stored static electricity obtained from the air and converted it to a usable form.

Tesla's radiant energy receiver

The fact of the matter is that there are numerous methods for doing this; Tesla knew that and patented many devices. The problem is that the government took the patents and hoarded that technology for themselves—mainly because they were controlled by the Black Nobility.

No one can take away from the fact that the discoveries of Tesla would have changed life for the average person forever. At the age of sixty-five, Tesla managed to switch a gasoline engine with an 80 horsepower alternating current electric motor in a new Pierce-Arrow car. This design did not require batteries, as Tesla used a dozen vacuum tubes, wires, and resistors arranged in a particular way to accomplish the power supply. Tesla reached 80 miles per hour in this car. Later, he drove a car on free energy and wrote to his friend Robert Johnson, editor of Century magazine, that he had invented an electrical generator that didn't need an outside source of power. He also erected a moving device which operated on cosmic rays. This was the prototype for today's solar-powered cars. So why are solar-powered cars not even used today by the major motor companies? Think about it. When Tesla was assassinated, his scientific papers and patents were taken by government agents. The secrets were not to be divulged.

Even though he was a virtuoso and a humanitarian, Tesla was ridiculed, accosted, and shunned by the scientific community. To the people, Tesla was an unknown. The popular Max Fleischer Superman cartoons of the 1940's pitted the Man of Steel against the death rays and electromagnetic weapons of the mad scientist. Ironically, this scientist was called Tesla. The main reason for Tesla's misfortunes was that he was a terrible businessman. He always wanted his inventions to benefit the people, demote warfare, and be free! Greedy and arrogant men like J.P. Morgan could not understand this humanitarian effort as they only wanted to profit. One hundred years ago there could have been free energy and communications for all, as well as such a powerful weapon that the nations of the world would surely have signed peace treaties with each other for fear that their enemies would use the device. The great technology brilliantly created is always patented by those who only want to profit.

Tesla is not the only inventor who has been vehemently suppressed by the powers-that-be, he was just the most prolific. Other scientists, physicists and doctors have made remarkable discoveries and inventions over the past century which have been suppressed by the international bankers because they want to enslave you.[6] Any technology that sets people free is kept by the Secret World Government (Illuminati) so they can use it for their own selfish reasons. This is not making love, this is making war, and war is hell. World War Three will not be any one country against another; it is a war against the people of this planet. Healing technologies (like cures for cancer and other diseases) are suppressed so that the populace must endure sickness and cellular deterioration. This helps reduce the world's population and keeps people in a low vibratory state.

Thank-you Mr. Tesla. If only.

---

[6] Jonathan Eisen, *Suppressed Inventions & Other Discoveries* (New York: Perigee Trade, 2001).

V

MAKE LOVE, NOT WAR

The suppression of hemp, technology, and spirituality and the fostering of religious dogma and satanic politics has benefited only a few handful of people, all of whom see themselves as separate from everything and everyone else. Consolidation of wealth and the establishment of fraudulent enterprises have fine tuned the demonstration of power, all the while turning the people into a zombie nation. How to create zombies? Suppress information and introduce harmful chemicals and drugs. How to control zombies? Erect institutions founded on untruth with hierarchical systems of authority. The beasts of prey ill-restrained within man will abuse authority and power if only they can, thus giving those in low positions of authority the pleasure of thinking they are on top. Those above them have more power and think they are in fact at the top, and if not, at least have the intention of making quantum leaps to the highest positions of clout. After all the information and truth is sucked out of a particular energetic matrix of time and space, the only other thing to do to manifest a zombie nation is to create fear, and what better way to do this than to foster wars?

In a controversial 1966 study of war and peace called the "Report from Iron Mountain," it was contemplated whether or not secret societies foment wars by influencing both sides of the conflict. The study that led to this report began in 1961 with Kennedy administration officials such as McGeorge Bundy, Robert McNamara, and Dean Rusk. In 1963 a special study group was called to cogitate the hypothetical problems of peace just as government think tanks such as the Rand and Hudson Institutes studied war. The members of this group have never been publicly identified, but it was conjectured that this group consisted of highly regarded intellectuals of various fields, and their principle meetings took place at a large underground corporate nuclear hideout near Hudson, New York called Iron Mountain. According to a report presented by the "Iron Mountain Boys," as they called themselves, "war itself is the basic social system, within which other secondary modes of social organization conflict or conspire. It is the system which has governed most human societies of record, as it is today." The report's authors viewed war as necessary and desirable as a "principal organizing force" as well as an "essential economic stabilizer of modern societies." It was concluded that war was indispensable until a form of social control was ready to be put in its place and class relationships were ready to be maintained.[1]

As possible replacements for war, the Iron Mountain report presented these substitutes:

- A comprehensive social-welfare program
- A giant, open-ended space research program aimed at unreachable targets
- A permanent, ritualized, elaborate disarmament inspection system
- An omnipresent, virtually omnipotent international police force
- An established and recognized extraterrestrial menace
- Massive global environmental pollution
- Fictitious alternate enemies
- Programs generally derived from the Peace Corps model
- A modern, sophisticated form of slavery
- New religions or other mythologies
- Socially oriented blood games
- A comprehensive program of applied eugenics

Along these lines, the establishment by presidential order of a permanent and top-secret National Security Council was also recommended which would exist outside the purview of Congress, the media, and the public and which would also be provided with non-accountable funds. Hmm, sounds like the F.D.I.C. doesn't it? Remember, these agencies are only increasing their dominion and power. Universal healthcare, a top-secret space fleet, F.E.M.A., the P.A.T.R.I.O.T. act, the worldwide police force of the United Nations, Grey aliens, a total environmental collapse,

---

[1] In *Rule by Secrecy*, Jim Marrs details how the Report from Iron Mountain has led to continual warfare since the Kennedy assassination. This was all planned by secret societies going back to Rome and Egypt.

fictitious enemies like Osama bin Laden, Saddam Hussein and Timothy McVeigh, the Federal Reserve Bank, Scientology, the National Football League .... nearly all of these requirements have been meet. The only thing left to do is crash the economy, nuke a major city and impose the New World Order.

The main storyline used by the globalists to achieve conflict, fear, and ultimately dependence on a fraudulent system looks like this: create a problem or a conflict → nurture a reaction of hatred or fear toward a particular enemy → create a solution that further restricts freedoms, consolidates power, and advances a certain agenda. The megalomaniacal sadists that control the world and the influence of events wish to bring about a New World Order where everyone is chipped and logged into a database and further restricted by central banks, bodies of government, and an international police force. When wars are instigated, populations shift into mindless "group think" and are easily manageable.

You can bet the Rothschilds and Jesuits were behind every major war in the 20th century, as it was all planned out by Albert Pike and Weishaupt's successor. One must also look to the Round Table group, which oversees all the major political secret societies such as the Committee of 300, the R.I.I.A., the Trilateral Commission, the C.F.R., and the Club of Rome. The Round Table organization in England grew out of the life-long dream of gold and diamond magnate Cecil Rhodes, who wished for a one world government. In his first will, Rhodes stated that his aim for the future was the extension of British rule throughout the world with English as the world language and world domination by a secret society modeled after the Society of Jesus. The originator of such a secret society was Adam Weishaupt, and when he founded the Bavarian Illuminati, he used the model of the Jesuits and wrote his code for taking over the world in Masonic terms. In his third will, Rhodes left everything to Lord Rothschild (his financier in mining enterprises), and after his death, the Round Table network was established using Rhodes' money and Lord Alfred Milner was positioned at the helm.

Author William Bramley writes on the Round Table group:

> Rhodes was certainly on the right track. If he had reached his goal, many of the negative effects . . . by the network of the Brotherhood of the Snake might have been undone. By a world language the detrimental effects touched upon in the story of the Tower of Babel, having to

do with people talking in different tongues, might have been reversed. Fostering a feeling for world citizenship would help to overcome the forms of National Socialism that help to unleash wars. But something went wrong. He thought of realizing his objectives via a network of the corrupt Brotherhood of the Snake. So Rhodes set up institutions that ended up by falling into the hands of those who would use these intentions for the suppression of humanity.

Again the Brotherhood of the Snake crops up in our story. Never forget that all this evil has a common origin. For the First World War, it was the task of the Committee of 300 to set the stage. From the Round Table group emerged the Royal Institute for International Affairs, which received orders from the Committee of 300 to study possible ways of staging this war. A subsequent propaganda campaign was unleashed on the public to convince hardworking men and women that they had to send their sons to their deaths in a fomented world war. In America, President Theodore Roosevelt said during his election campaign in 1912, "Behind the visible government there is an invisible government upon the throne that owes the people no loyalty and recognizes no responsibility. To destroy this invisible government, to undo the ungodly union between corrupt business and corrupt politics is the task of a statesman." Nobody listened.[2]

Here is an outline of the major wars and conflicts and how they were fomented behind the scenes:

Nero and Rome

In 64 C.E. the emperor of Rome, Nero, set the city on fire one night while he was fiddling. Since the Christians were gaining too much favor and popularity, Nero had a scapegoat while he performed his shenanigans. After the problem was quelled, the citizens of Rome cheered as all the Christians were persecuted and killed.[3]

---

[2] Eisenhower and Kennedy warned the American public in similar fashion regarding the Secret World Government. It stopped with Kennedy as no subsequent president would risk assassination for exposing secrets.

[3] Alex Jones, *9-11: Descent Into Tyranny* (Oklahoma City: Hearthstone Publishing, 2002), 15.

The Revolutionary War

The only reason for this war was the fact that King George had banned the colonies from printing their own debt-free money. If he hadn't had done this, there would probably have been no war. King George wanted a war with the colonies because he thought his fancy generals and relentless redcoats would crush the American rebels. He was wrong, though, and the United States was born, a free country that should not have been. Even so, Sir Francis Bacon, serving as England's grand chancellor under King James I, was a Grand Commander of the Brotherhood Order called the Rosicrucians and very much involved in the underground operations of the traditions of the Knights Templar. Both he and Adam Weishaupt were the forerunners for English Freemasonry in America, along with most of the founding fathers. Even though they carried freedom on their shoulders and opposed central banks, most of them represented European secret societies in one form or another, although their true intentions can be debated. Mayer Amschel Rothschild also helped instigate this war.

The French Revolution

The French Revolution devastated France between 1787 and 1799 and was largely inspired by European secret societies. The German Illuminati and French Masonry sent revolutionary leaders to overthrow the monarchy of King Louis XVI. Wars, riots, and coups continued in France until Napoleon Bonaparte seized control in 1799. Although he fomented terror in Europe for years, he quelled the revolution and saw an end to both the monarchy and the monolithic church. In a sense, the projects of the Cabalists, Gnostics, and secret societies found fulfillment with a new way to rule the people.

The Napoleonic Wars

The Napoleonic Wars were a series of conflicts between Napoleon Bonaparte's army and changing sets of European allies including prominent British politicians. These altercations took place between

1803 and 1815 and were a continuation of sorts of the French Revolution. French power had conquered most of Europe, but went asunder after a disastrous invasion of Russia in 1812. These wars between European armies resulted in the dissolution of the Holy Roman Empire (not total dissolution but partial, as the Roman Catholic Church still influences world political events today) and the restoration of the Bourbon monarchy in France. With these conflicts, the seeds were sown for fascism in Germany and Italy. In 1815, as agents of the Rothschild family watched Napoleon fight to save his army from a British onslaught, the artificial news of Napoleon's victory over Lord Wellington was given to Nathan Rothschild so he could give it to London. When Nathan placed this rumor in the London Stock Exchange, stocks plunged by 98 percent and the Rothschilds were able to buy up the entire British economy. When the news of Napoleon's defeat reached London, stocks soared and the Rothschild family took dominion over England.

The American Civil War

The young United States during this time was fractured somewhat between the northern states and the southern states. The sovereignty of the state was put into question, as many southerners thought their statesman was not represented enough. Also, each state had to pay apportioned taxes to the federal government, and since the south was abundant with agriculture and slavery, many southerners thought they should pay less taxes because they contributed more. The northerners did not necessarily dislike the notion of owning slaves, they just saw an unfair advantage in the south using slaves from Africa to work in their fields for them. The Civil War did not result from the northerners wanting to abolish slavery and the southerners wanting to retain slavery, it occurred because the south was told by members of the British Royal Family that they would be aided by Britain if they seceded from the Union. Of course, the Royal Family drew back their promises, and a civil war ensued between the Union (northern states) and the Confederacy (southern states). After the war the Union was so economically crippled that it had to accept loans and retributions from British bankers.

Enter into the Brits once more, only this time they did it covertly. Great Britain helped finance both sides again with the help of the

Rothschild family, and the goal was to erect a central bank. The United States was reduced to an agrarian economy (north and south) that was easily infiltrated and manipulated by British powers. They did not have to fight the Americans; this time they got the Americans to fight themselves. This mission of erecting a central bank was not accomplished, and many more attempts were made shortly afterwards, but success finally ensued with the Federal Reserve. During the American Civil War the International Banking Syndicate, headed by the Rothschild family, funded the southern states to attack the U.S. federal government, effectively creating an enemy that would require massive war expenditures and debt. German chancellor Otto von Bismarck is quoted as saying:

> The division of the United States into federations of equal force was decided long before the Civil War by the high financial powers of Europe. These bankers were afraid that the United States, if they remained in one block and as one nation, would attain economic and financial independence, which would upset their financial dominion over the world. The voice of the Rothschilds prevailed . . . . Therefore they sent their emissaries into the field to exploit the question of slavery and to open an abyss between the two sections of the Union.

It has been well-known for years that Europe's aristocracies had never been happy about the success of the Yankee democracy. The American Civil War was like an extended Revolutionary War.

Ulysses S. Grant, the general of the Union, was recruited by the elite occult families because of his family ties. His father had worked with E. A. Collins, the Collins family of course being one of the 13 bloodline families. Grant went from private in the army to colonel to general in a snap and it was because of his friends in high places. After the war, Grant became president and his cabinet consisted of eight Freemasons including Alphonso Taft and Columbus Delano. You all know Taft and Delano as ensuing U.S. presidents. William Taft was the son of Alphonso Taft and Franklin Delano Roosevelt was the grandson of Columbus Delano. It is also intriguing that Abraham Lincoln's father, A. A. Springs, was part of the Rothschild dynasty, and his half brother (Abraham's) worked for the Merovingian family. The Merovingian family owned Jekyll Island, the place where the Federal Reserve was birthed.

The Maine and the Lusitania (World War I)

In 1898, William Mckinley and his navy blew up their own ship in Havana Harbor, the *Maine*, as a pretext for war against Spain. After this manufactured conflict, the United States was able to gather and control dozens of islands in the Pacific Ocean. In only a few decades time, the American population was averse to the prospect of war in Europe. As such, the British sailed one their largest naval auxiliary ships, the *Lusitania*, into waters they knew to be highly contested where it was sunk easily by German U-boats. Even though the Germans ran multiple full-page warnings in the New York times telling Americans not to travel on the ship, many went and perished. Later, the American population was ready for a war that was started when Archduke Franz Ferdinand (heir to the Austrian throne) was assassinated. The shooter who took credit was a member of a Serbian secret society who had connections to French and British intelligence agencies. So in effect, Americans were forced to fight in a war started by secret societies under the false pretenses that a U.S. naval ship had been blown up by an enemy.

The goals of World War I were massive profit for the international bankers and the establishment of a League of Nations. The latter was not done properly, so President Wilson's advisor, Edward House, aided Wilson in erecting the Institute of International Affairs, which has two branches. One branch sits in Great Britain as the Royal Institute for International Affairs and the other sits in the United States as the Council on Foreign Relations (just another way of Great Britain controlling the affairs of the U.S.). J. P. Morgan and John D. Rockefeller helped found the Council on Foreign Relations. The international bankers had a heavy hand in both world wars and today, they sit above all governments. Secret meetings each year are convened by the varying groups that make up the Round Table Group. The arms of the Round Table Group are the Club of Rome, the Bilderberg Group, the Trilateral Commission, the United Nations, and the Institute of International Affairs. The Bohemian Group and the Skull and Bones society are offshoot organizations. By 1930, promoters of world government was split into two factions. On one side stood the Fabian socialists (United States, Russia, and Great Britain), who thought that the inception of a world government could be brought about by a steady transformation of socialist systems through gradual incrementalization. On the other side stood the Bavarian fascists

(Germany, Italy, and Japan), who thought that world government could be brought about by a military takeover. One side wanted to use stealth (socialists) and one side wanted to use force (fascists). Today, both tactics are used to enslave massive populations of people.

Hitler's Reichstag (the Third Reich)

In 1875, Russian-born mystic Helena Petrovna Blavatsky founded the Theosophical Society in New York City. In 1878, Blavatsky and U.S. Army Colonel Henry Steel Olcott moved the society's headquarters to Madras, India, where it remains today. This kind of theosophy drew its thinking from the same early philosophers venerated by the secret societies of Freemasonry, the Illuminati, and the Round Tables. Blavatsky, in forming the German branch of the Theosophical Society in 1884, brought her belief in channeling, reincarnation, racial superiority, and extraterrestrial visitation to people who later formed the theological basis of the Nazis and the Thule Society in which Adolf Hitler was a member. Following World War I, the occult societies began to merge with political activism, particularly in Germany where Hitler was gaining power and prestige. Dietrich Eckart was the Master-Adept of the Thule Group who enlisted Hitler to fulfill ancient occult prophecy.

Hitler and his gang of criminals performed the usual business of creating catastrophe and blaming it on others. In 1933, Hitler's Stormtroopers razed the Reichstag government building to the ground. The people went into mass trepidation and Hitler told them he would protect them and instill a utopia where this would never happen again. He declared himself "Fuhrer," a position of power above the chancellery, which was the German republic in operation before the reign of the Third Reich. The people bought the lies that they would receive everything they needed from the state, and henceforth they were totally enslaved. Hitler used the Hegelian dialectic perfectly and it worked to make himself dictator. He attacked his own country, he blamed his enemies, and he told the German people that he would be their savior and protect them if they gave up their freedoms. Many Germans today are still embarrassed about Hitler and how he seduced the people with propaganda, false claims, and empty promises.

A New Order of the Ages

FDR and Pearl Harbor (World War II)

Even though the Japanese attack on Pearl Harbor sent waves of surprise and shock through the American people, the federal government and the military knew exactly what was going on. Not only had the Japanese broadcasted that they were building up for an assault in the Pacific, but twelve days prior to the attack, the government had in its possession a communiqué concocted by Admiral Yamamoto and the Japanese saying, "On the morning of December 7 we will attack the Pacific fleet at Pearl Harbor and deal a death blow." In fact, the United States Secretary of the War Department, Henry Stimsom, wrote in his diary on November 25, 1941, "President Roosevelt brought up the event that we are likely to be attacked perhaps as soon as next Monday, for the Japanese are notorious for making an attack without warning, and the question was how we should maneuver them into the position of firing the first shot." On November 30, 1941 the front page headline in *Honolulu Advertiser* read, "Japan May Strike over Weekend." Totally disregarding the warnings, the military went to the lowest level of readiness, the ships in the harbor were lined up in tight rows, and the aircraft were placed into circles, nose tip to nose tip. Before the attack, Roosevelt had done everything he could to anger the Japanese. He halted trade agreements, froze Japanese assets, and also aided Japanese enemies, an act which was forbidden by official world war protocols.[4]

Roosevelt's financial backers had been funding the Japanese war machine as well as Hitler's blitzkrieg, and even though Roosevelt had campaigned heavily on keeping America out of the war, his hands were tied due to the pressure he faced. The Anglo-American establishment in New York and London wanted a global crisis to usher in a global government and a United Nations. Is it any wonder then why six months before the attack on Pearl Harbor Roosevelt told the naval command at the site to dismantle the radar mount and remove the code-breaking machines? When the creation of a League of Nations had failed after World War I, World War II was fought on the grounds that it had to be bigger and cost more lives so that the people would be scared into accepting a world government. During World War II, the American company I.G. Farben produced 84 percent of Germany's explosives. Rockefeller-owned

---

[4] Hollywood movies like *Pearl Harbor* do well in convincing people that the catastrophe in Pearl Harbor on December 7, 1941was a total surprise even though it was well-known in advance.

Standard Oil Company had a patent on oil used by German planes, military trucks, and U-Boats. Union Banking Corporation, partially owned by Prescott Bush, was the official laundering bank of the Nazi party.

A the conclusion of the second world war, secret societies pushed for the creation of the United Nations with the excuse that further wars could be prevented. Obviously, that was not the reason as wars have continued in every decade ever since. The real reason of the United Nations was so a world government could be brought about gradually via national socialism through the implementation of population reduction and the instituting of three trans-national unions: The European Union (Council of Europe convened in 1949), the North American Union (Bilderberg group convened in 1954) and the Asian Union (dictatorships in China, Korea, Vietnam, and Japan). The African and South American Unions would be the next step in a pool of five unions which would unite in a world government, world religion, and world police force. John D. Rockefeller donated land in New York City to be the headquarters of the U.N.

What we have in America now is the Bilderberg Group (started by Prince Bernhard of the Netherlands) and the Trilateral Commission (created by Zbigniew Brzezinski and David Rockefeller) directing foreign political policy regarding the North American and European Unions. In his book *With No Apologies* (1964), Senator Barry Goldwater wrote that the Trilateral Commission is the 'vehicle for the multinational consolidation of commercial and banking interests by seizing control of the United States government.' After World War II, Eisenhower warned the American people about the takeover of the military-industrial complex, but that warning was not heeded. Today, every facet of life is controlled and monitored by the military-industrial complex, which runs the army, navy, military, and all advanced technology such as free energy and space travel. Today, the human herd is suppressed, monitored, and forced to bear the monetary yoke of financing major wars and bank bailouts, and all the while the corporate-mass-media worships *Dancing with the Stars* and LeBron James.

The Korean War/Cold War

The Korean peninsula had been ruled by Japan from 1910 until the end of World War II. Following the surrender of Japan, American administrators divided the peninsula on the 38th parallel, with American troops occupying the southern part and Soviet Union troops occupying the northern part. As tensions rose between the two sides, North Korea invaded South Korea on June 25, 1950. What started as a civil war soon became a proxy war as the United Nations (particularly the United States) came to the aid of South Korea while China came to the aide of North Korea, these two larger powers involved in the wider-spanning Cold War. The United States participated in both wars because it wanted to increase its sphere of influence in Europe, justify an arms race, scare the American people with the threat of Communism, establish N.A.T.O. and of course, so the international bankers could profit off of loaning money and war necessities. The U.N. organization, headed by John Foster Dulles (who had helped found the Council on Foreign Relations), created the Southeast Asia Treaty Organization which provided the legal rationale for war in Korea and also Vietnam.

When it was discovered in Korea that Russian commanders were running the conflict on both sides and that Communist Russia was financed and controlled by the inner circle of America's secret societies, it became apparent that this war was not fought to be won. Like Vietnam, this war was fought only to be sustained. Even C.F.R. member Dean Acheson admitted that the only reason he told the President to fight in Korea was to validate the North Atlantic Treaty Organization (N.A.T.O.). Again, it was all about consolidation of control. After World War I, when it was understood that the League of Nations was not powerful enough, the United Nations came to the fore. Today, the U.N. supervises the World Bank and the International Monetary Fund, as well as houses a number of social agencies such as the International Labor Organization (I.L.O.), Food and Agriculture Organization (F.A.O.), World Health Organization (W.H.O.), Scientific and Cultural Organization (U.N.E.S.C.O.), and the United Nations Children's Fund (U.N.I.C.E.F.).

The Cuban Missile Crisis and the Operation Northwoods Document

On October 22, 1962 President John F. Kennedy announced these words in a national broadcast: "Good evening, my fellow citizens. This government, as promised, has maintained the closest surveillance of the Soviet military buildup on the island of Cuba. Within the past week, unmistakable evidence has established the fact that a series of offensive missile sites is now in preparation on that imprisoned island. The purpose of these bases can be none other than to provide a nuclear strike capability against the Western Hemisphere." The notorious Operation Northwoods document published the plan of the federal government to use a pretext to invade Cuba. On A.B.C. news in 2001, a media report was issued with this headline: "Friendly Fire: U.S. Military Drafted Plans to Terrorize U.S. Cities to Provoke War with Cuba." Meanwhile, the Northwoods document stated that the federal government considered blowing up airliners full of Americans so that a wave of indignation would sweep through the population, turning anger and hatred toward Cuba. The architect of the plan was General L. L. Lemnitzer, Chairman and Joint Chief of Staff.

His plan was approved all the way up to the Secretary of Defense, but when President Kennedy saw it he was not impressed. Lemnitzer's plan called for the bombing of Washington D.C. or the disguising of U.S. Army soldiers as Cubans so they could attack Marines at Guantanamo Bay. Another suggestion proposed the blowing up of an American ship, just like what happened with the *Maine*. A nuclear war with Cuba and the Soviet Union was idealized by the federal government and the military. There was a problem, though, a real one. When President Kennedy distanced himself from the Operation Northwoods document, he signed Executive Order 11110 declaring an abolishment of the Federal Reserve System. He had also started pulling soldiers out of Vietnam and had signed an order abolishing the C.I.A. Kennedy chose to be a leader of the people instead of the secret government and to stand up for our Constitutional Republic. Kennedy's assassination should be no shock now.

War in Vietnam

Ever since World War II the United States wished for a greater sphere of influence in the Pacific and Southeast Asia. France, however, maintained control over French Indochina and so U.S. plans for the region were put on hold until the Japanese overran Indochina in 1945. Ho Chi Minh (leader of the Indochinese Communist Party) and General Vo Nguyen Giap (leader of the Vietnamese military) worked alongside the American Office of Strategic Services to oust the occupation forces. Once Japan surrendered, Ho intended to create an independent Vietnam which would give his American handlers entrée to the area of land, much to the chagrin of Charles de Gaulle and France. In October of 1945, de Gaulle ordered French troops into Saigon hoping to restore emperor Bao Dai to power, but he was defeated. At the Geneva conference in 1954, Ho's delegation was met in rivalry by the French-backed Bao Dai and the resulting conflict was reconciled by dividing Vietnam along the Seventeenth Parallel with Ho given the North and Ngo Dinh Diem (supported by Colonel Edward Lansdale, head of the U.S. Military Advisory and Assistance Group) was given the South, which contained most of Vietnam's resources and wealth. Lansdale's group was there to aid the 234,000-man Vietnamese National Army, created and financed by the United States. As tensions grew, aid to communist North Vietnam came from Russia and China, while South Vietnam remained heavily dependent on American support.

President Kennedy disagreed with the globalists' intent to invade North Korea and instead levied a new system of government in the United States that wasn't predicated on secrecy. Well, that was short-lived as Kennedy entered a coffin only a short while later, and his successor, Lyndon B. Johnson, saw no problem with war in Vietnam. In hopes of provoking a North Vietnamese attack, Johnson authorized the resumption of destroyer patrols in the Gulf of Tonkin, although this was a highly patrolled area. One day in the early 1960's a newspaper article read: "North Vietnamese P.T. Boats Attack U.S. Destroyer." This soon became known as the Gulf of Tonkin incident, and it did carry the United States into war with North Vietnam, but there was one problem. The episode did not even occur! It was a staged falsity, a contrived story by the New World Order Globalists and President Johnson to drag the United States into yet another war.

Were World War I, II, and the Cold War not enough? Apparently not. Years after the incident, Secretary of Defense Robert McNamara declared that the event was a huge mistake. Other insiders eventually came forward later and admitted the truth, that the event never happened and that its sole purpose was to carry us into another pointless war. The Rockefeller family funded the Soviet Union, which in turn funded and made war vehicles for North Vietnam. The war took the lives of 58,000 U.S. soldiers and 3,000,000 Vietnamese soldiers. These totals do not include civilian casualties, which were many and close between. Looking back, this war was never meant to be won, only sustained. The ludicrous rules of engagement proposed by the United States is revealed as follows:

1. North Vietnamese anti-aircraft missile systems could not be bombed until they are known to be fully operational.
2. No enemy could be pursued into any surrounding areas.
3. Critical strategic targets could only be engaged via high approval only.

Not only were these rules totally misaligned with an efficient victory strategy, but the North Vietnamese were made totally aware of these restrictions foisted onto U.S. soldiers. When Lyndon B. Johnson campaigned for office he expressed a great interest in pulling the troops out of the war. When he was elected, however, he perpetuated the war for many more years. When Obama was campaigning for office of president in 2008 he called for the retreat of the United States out of Iraq. When he took office, though, thousands of more soldiers were deployed into the Middle East, especially Iraq. Understand that all this evil comes from the same script.

The Persian Gulf War

President George H. W. Bush gathered a U.N.-authorized coalition force comprised of thirty-four nations to invade Iraq and Saddam Hussein.[5] The only reason Bush wanted to invade Iraq was because

---

5   Saddam Hussein did not make the Illuminati happy, and when he was executed by the United States, the Middle East was up for grabs. The Persian Gulf War was the precursor to the

A New Order of the Ages

he wanted the Kuwaiti oil supplies, which were a target for Iraqi troops. This war was fought for oil. Saddam Hussein was funded by the Bush administration through a Paris branch bank in Atlanta, Georgia. Hussein was also armed through Illuminati front organizations, and even though this was exposed in several magazines, the loans and armament continued and the American taxpayers were forced to bear the price for American troops storming Iraq when it was conditioned into their minds that Saddam had weapons of mass destruction. In 1990, Saddam's Iraq was a primary threat to the balance of power between Israel and its Arab neighbors, but Hussein was low on cash due to the Iran-Iraq War and couldn't pay back his loans. Under duress from the international bankers and from the Organization of Petroleum Producing Countries, Saddam saw Kuwait as a force of income. Although the Bush administration played indifferent to Saddam's financial woes, a military task force was organized by Father Bush and U.S. Ambassador April Glaspie to invade Kuwait because of course, the oil was so valued. Not only was 5 billion dollars passed to Saddam Hussein in the 1980's though the Atlanta, Georia branch of Banca Nazional del Lavoro (B.N.L.) so he could by weaponry to attack American servicemen, but the U.S. taxpayers picked up the tab!

This war dealt heavily with the C.I.A. and the Shah. In 1979, the Shah of Iran was chased away by the revolution, and since most employees at a U.S. embassy are members of the C.I.A., the Iranian rebels took the U.S. employees hostage. In turn, the C.I.A. retaliated by telling Saddam Hussein (the leader of Iraq at that time) that this was an opportune moment to invade Iran. The invasion was successful. At the same time, William Casey, the C.I.A. director, had established contact with Khomeini and Iran's leader decided to forge a guild with him. In October of 1980, George Bush and Richard Allen met with agents of the Iranian Hizbollah extremists in Paris and it was agreed that the U.S. would transport arms to Iran via Israel and that the Iranians would free the U.S. hostages the moment Ronald Reagan was declared president. This was the beginning of arms for drugs dealings between the United States and Iran and the official time for a third world war to commence according to the plans of Albert Pike.

War on Terror. Both either have worked or are currently working to build bases, secure oil pipelines, and control the ancient stargates that were left by the Annunaki.

In June of 1989, a delegation consisting of Alan Stoga (member of Kissinger Associates), members of the Bankers Trust, Mobil, Occidental Petroleum, and others agreed to an invitation to Baghdad given by Saddam Hussein. The Badush Dam project was discussed and it proposed that Iraq be made independent of food imports within five years. This was turned down by the delegation, which stated that Iraq had to pay its national debt and partially privatize the oil industry. Hussein declined and George Bush blocked all loans to Iraq from Western banks. Sheik Al-Sabah, Emir of Kuwait and friend of the British Royal Family then entered the scene. Kuwait had been channeling money into Iraq as bidden by London and Washington to keep the eight-year war afloat, a conflict that brought the arms dealers money and Israel political advantages. A quarrel between Kuwait and Iraq escalated thereafter, and even though the decision was made at a Bilderberger meeting on June 6, 1990 that the U.S. not interfere in the war between Kuwait and Iraq, President Bush sent U.S. troops into the Gulf on January 15, 1991. The aim of Bush and his cohorts was to start the third world war, a conflict that would end in the New World Order.

Assassination of President Abraham Lincoln

Lincoln made angry nearly everyone in the Illuminati power system because he refused to follow the orders of his financiers. He had expressed an interest to make the Greenback the official currency of the Union, although the international bankers wished for a new central bank in which they could control the newly-emerged United States. His assassin, John Wilkes Booth, was a Knights Templar Mason as well as a member of the Carbonari, a Masonic French Lodge. Booth did not act alone, though. The original plan was to kidnap Lincoln and hold him hostage in Richmond, Virginia, but that plot was implicated by unexpected changes in the president's traveling plans. Booth's confederate conspirators were supposed to kill Vice President Andrew Johnson and Secretary of State William Henry Seward while Booth dispatched Lincoln in his box at Ford's Theatre (effectively severing the head of the federal government and throwing the Union into such a void that the Confederacy could renew itself), but the plan was foiled because George Atzerodt (the man who was supposed to kill Johnson) got too drunk. Lewis Powell, the other assassin, did manage however to stab and seriously wound Seward. Both Powell and Atzerodt were hung, along with David Herold and Mary Surratt. Surratt had owned the boarding house where the conspirators meet and Herold was connected to several other conspirators, including Edman Spangler, a carpenter who held Booth's horse in the alley while he did the deed.[6]

Secretary of War Edwin Stanton and Andrew Johnson did not escape speculation for the murder, and many writers over the years have even pointed to the Jesuits. In 1924, the ex-Romanist Burke McCarthy wrote in *The Suppressed Truth About the Assassination of Abraham Lincoln*:

> The death of President Lincoln was the culmination of but one step in the attempt to carry out the Secret Treaty of Verona, of October, 1822 . . . . The particular business of the Congress of Verona, it developed, was the Ratification of Article Six of the Congress of Vienna, which was in short, a promise to prevent or destroy Popular Governments wherever found, and to re-establish monarchy where it had been set aside.

One should never count the Vatican out of any conspiracy. Lincoln was the first U.S. president to batter ties with the Vatican, and it wasn't until the aegis of Ronald Reagan that those ties were re-sowed.

Assassination of President John F. Kennedy

Not only was Kennedy killed for the words and deeds stated above, but also due to the fact that he had threatened to exposed all secret societies and the alien presence. Shortly after his inauguration, Kennedy launched a variety of sweeping initiatives to increase both the human and technological potential of the nation. Kennedy was quite the economic guru, and he incessantly pushed for tax breaks and a shift in the power of property from the power elite to the individual. The President also harbored acrimony towards the big business tycoons and attempted to force major U.S. steel companies to rescind price increases. In June of

---

[6] Arthur Goldwag, *Cults, Conspiracies, & Secret Societies* (New York: Vintage Books, 2009), 186-187.

1963, Kennedy went even further and authorized the issuance of over 4 billion dollars in "United States Notes" through the U.S. Treasury and not the Federal Reserve in an attempt to withdraw back to policies conditioned by the Constitution which clearly states that only Congress can coin and regulate money, not a private bank. In his attempt to even the economic playing field, Kennedy:

- Offered tax proposals to redirect the foreign investments of U.S. companies
- Made distinctions in tax reform between productive and non-productive investments
- Eliminated the tax privileges of U.S.-based global investment companies
- Cracked down on foreign tax havens
- Supported proposals to eliminate tax privileges for the wealthy
- Proposed increased taxes for large oil and mineral companies
- Revised the investment tax credit
- Made a proposal to expand the powers of the president to deal with recession

These are all good things, but you must remember who really calls the shots. To the globalists, international bankers, oil companies, and steel conglomerates, Kennedy was a nuisance who needed to be eradicated immediately.

Kennedy's economic policies were publicly ostracized by *Fortune* magazine editor Charles Murphy, New York governor Nelson Rockefeller, David Rockefeller, and the editors of the *Wall Street Journal*. In foreign policy, Kennedy attacked colonialism (overt control over a country's political and economic life) and neo-colonialism (covert control) and this made him many enemies, least of which the Rockefellers and Harrimans. Kennedy was also trying to eradicate the stranglehold of occult Freemasonry, which did not please the international bankers. The vote came in that Kennedy was to be ousted. Videos from the assassination, upon close inspection, clearly reveal that Kennedy was shot by his driver, William Greer.[7] Greer was not a Manchurian candidate like Lee Harvey Oswald, but he was well paid. Oswald was

---

[7] Before he was killed by the Illuminati, Milton Cooper possessed a video showing Kennedy being shot by his limo driver Greer. The video has since disappeared.

there in case something went wrong and to pose as a suspect. Witnesses report that there were more than one shot. Also, many people on street level close to the vehicle saw Greer shoot Kennedy. Over two hundred of these people have mysteriously died over the past forty years. It should also be noted that Martin Luther King, Jr. was assassinated in 1968 only after he began protesting the Vietnam War.

Assassination of Robert F. Kennedy

Shortly after midnight on June 5, 1968, California United States Senator Robert Kennedy was assassinated in a hotel after winning the Democratic nomination for President of the United States. It seemed the Jewish Freemasons were continuing their decimation of the Kennedy family, as we now know that occult Freemasonry is largely Jewish (Kabbalistic) and the Roman Catholic Church utterly opposes Judaism. John Kennedy and his brother were inserted into American politics by the Roman Church to undermine the role of the powerful Jewish bankers, but alas they both went down in smoke. Kennedy's killer was twenty-four year old Palestinian immigrant Sirhan Sirhan and he was clearly revealed to be a Manchurian candidate after repeated testimony and interrogation. Moreover, from closely studied video and audio tapes, there was another shooter just like in the John Kennedy assassination. Sirhan and Oswald were merely patsies to take the blame.

Assassination of Martin Luther King, Jr.

On April 4, 1968, Martin Luther King, Jr. was shot and killed by a slug from a high-powered rifle while he was standing on the balcony of his room at the Lorraine Motel. Two months later, James Earl Ray, a lifelong felon who had escaped from Missouri state prison a year before, was arrested for the murder at Heathrow Airport in London and extradited to Tennessee. Although he pleaded guilty in return for a ninety-nine-year sentence, he did not serve his time in silence. Almost immediately after being taken to prison he recanted his confession and petitioned for a new trial. In 1977, he escaped from prison and led authorities on a three-day manhunt. When he was captured the second time, he told a most unusual story. He spoke about a secretive figure name Raoul who recruited him as a smuggler when he was a fugitive in Canada and who later paid him to acquire (but not fire) the rifle that killed Martin Luther King. When he later produced an autobiography entitled *Tennessee Waltz: The Making of a Political Prisoner*, it was expanded and rereleased five years later as *Who Killed Martin Luther King Jr: The True Story by the Alleged Assassin*.

Along with the book, Ray gained a powerful ally in the King family, which was Martin Luther's son Dexter. When Dexter met Ray in prison and asked him if he had killed his father, Ray replied that he hadn't. Ray's lawyer William Pepper, author of *Orders to Kill: The Truth Behind the Murder of Martin Luther King*, helped bring a civil suit against Loyd Jowers on behalf of the King family. Jowers was the owner of Jim's Grill, a restaurant on the ground floor of the rooming house from which Ray had allegedly fired the fatal shot. Jowers claimed to have been offered 100,000 dollars to open his grill to the real murderers. Those who offered the money and actually participated in King's assassination were the government (including President Lyndon Johnson), the military (including the C.I.A.) and the Mafia. King was killed because he was outspoken about the atrocities in Vietnam, he was the leader of the civil rights movement and he was a bitter enemy of J. Edgar Hoover and the White House.[8]

Assassination of John Lennon

On December 8, 1980, Lennon and his wife Yoko Ono were emerging from their limousine outside their home at the Dakota apartment building on Central Park West when twenty-five-year-old Mark Chapman fired five shots at Lennon with a Charter Arms .38 pistol, four of them hitting their mark. Mae Brussell, the daughter of Edgar Magnin (the "Rabbi to the Stars") was a conspiracy theorist who focused on the activities of unregenerate Nazis operating within the U.S. government. Lennon was the person who subsidized the issue of *The Realist* that published Brussell's theories on Watergate in 1972, and during that time Lennon told its publisher Paul Krassner, "Listen, if anything happens to Yoko

---

[8] Jon Lewis, *The Mammoth Book of Cover-Ups: The 100 Most Disturbing Conspiracies of All Time* (Philadelphia: Running Press, 2007), 282-290.

and me, it was not an accident." After his assassination, Brussell was interviewed by Alex Constantine and she told him how Lennon's killing was just one of many and how the "federal government has maintained active programs to eliminate rock musicians and disrupt rock concerts." At the height of the Vietnam War protests between 1971 and 1972, the F.B.I. kept close tabs on Lennon and harassed him relentlessly because of his calumnious words against the war and the government. His killer, Mark Chapman, was most likely a Manchurian Candidate has he was a heavy drug user and a manic depressant.

The 1993 World Trade Center Bombing

Since at least the early 1990's, the World Trade Center complex has been a target for the federal government and the enacting of Hegelian dialectic. On October 28, 1993 the New York Times ran an article headlined, "Tapes Depict Proposal to Thwart Bomb Used in Trade Center Blast." The federal government had actually been caught on tape ordering their informants to let the bombing of the World Trade Center commence and to cook the bomb used. The government was also caught giving the terrorists the detonators. The ultimate goal of all of this was to create a national police state and a war upon the American people. Unlike the Operation Northwoods plan, the F.B.I. actually carried out the attack on the World Trade Center in 1993. To accomplish this, they paid a 43-year-old former Egyptian army officer named Emad Salem one million dollars and gave him real explosives and a detonator. Mr. Salem was told to build the bomb and give it to some stupid people so that they might blow up the World Trade Center. Mr. Salem soon became concerned about the fact that he had been given real explosives during a supposed "sting operation."

Mr. Salem recorded John Anticev, head of the New York office of the FBI, ordering him to let the bombing take place. The pretexts for World War I, World War II, the Cuban Missile Crisis, and the war in Vietnam were all chance attacks and promptings by the United States federal government and the military. The Persian Gulf War, the World Trade Center bombing, and the War in Iraq were directly financed and concocted by the United States. The goal of the attacks on the World Trade Center was to place a homeland security system on the American people. The only problem incurred was that the truck drivers did not park against the main support column as they had been ordered to do by Mr. Salem and the F.B.I. They had parked it a dozen feet away and the building had not fallen. Since the federal government did not get the massive death toll it needed to create a system of martial law suspending people's rights, the job was finished on September 11, 2001.

Oklahoma City Bombing

President Bill Clinton, under the duress of the Illuminati, needed a crisis to push plans for a socialized America and gun control agenda through Congress. This is only one of many instances where rights given to the people by the Constitution and the Bill of Rights were deceitfully manipulated into non-existence. On April 19, 1995 multiple bombs exploded through the Alfred P. Murrah Federal Building in downtown Oklahoma City, and of course, federal fingerprints were all over the crime scene. The Antiterrorist and Effective Death Penalty Acts had failed to reach initiation a year before, so the pictures of mangled and crippled children most certainly did the job. With the passing of these bills, enormous sections of the Constitution and Bill of Rights were torn to pieces as many freedoms were suppressed. The University of Oklahoma's seismographic reports, as well as the U.S. Geological Survey reports, showed that multiple explosions did in fact occur, however, the official statement issued by the government incurred that only one bomb erupted. Press reports said the building was blown in by a truck bomb, but upon closer inspection of the crime scene, it is obvious that the building was blown from the inside out. Also, the level of detonation used was highly sophisticated, and even though Timothy McVeigh was the only suspect, witnesses reported that many others were spotted with McVeigh and that they acted in accordance with McVeigh. The supposed bomb used by McVeigh, his level of expertise and his truck location are impossible factors when considering not only how this plan was carried out but how the devastation actually transpired. Also, isn't it strange that immediately after the bombing the feds had a perfect lone suspect willing to take all the credit?

Dr. Bill Deagle was the exit examining doctor for the Special-Op forensic team that came back from the Murrah Building, the site of the bombing. One of them broke down and told Deagle in great detail how the forensic team had removed two unexploded fourth-generation U.S. Army Corp. Engineer micro-nukes, thermate, R.D.X., and high explosive cores from the building. This is high-level, totally above what McVeigh would have been capable of with his simple tools. And another thing, the Special-Op who broke down also said that the buildings were brought down by the F.B.I. and A.T.F.

Stock Market Crisis of 1907

In 1907, J.P. Morgan used his massive influence in publishing a statement announcing that a prominent bank in New York was going bankrupt, knowing full well that implications. The public went into a fervor and started withdrawing their deposits. The smaller regional banks were all forced to call in their loans, resulting in many denizens selling their stock and bonds. A landslide of bankruptcies and repossessions followed. Senator Nelson Aldrich was appointed to solve this dilemma, but you already know how this story goes. Aldrich had intimate ties with the international bankers and he proposed a central bank so that this crisis could never happen again. A meeting was convened at a Morgan estate on Jekyll Island, and it was here that the Federal Reserve Act was written and agreed upon. The meeting was so secret the attendees used pseudonyms. President Woodrow Wilson agreed to pass this bill in exchange for campaign support after Aldrich pushed the bill through Congress.

Stock Market Crash of 1929

From 1914 to 1919 the Federal Reserve Banking fraud doubled the money supply in the midst of giving extensive loans to small banks, which in turn gave loans to the public. In 1920 the Fed called in all loans, and the small banks had to follow suite in order to keep up. 1500 banks collapsed as a result of bankruptcy. From 1921 to 1929 there was another 62 percent increase in the money supply, and a new loan was created. It was called the Margin Loan and its premise was such that the investor only had to put down 10 percent in order to own 100 percent of the stock, the drawback of which was that the loan could be called in at any time and it had to be paid off within 24 hours. This procedure was called a Margin Call. Prominent businessmen like J.D. Rockefeller and Bernard Barack quietly exited the market a few months before October, and as planned on October 24, the New York financiers called in Margin Loans in mass. 16,000 banks met their demise and the international bankers bought small banks and corporations at pennies on the dollar.

In contrast to before, after this crash the Fed actually decreased the money supply, forcing the 'Great Depression.' Senator Luis McFadden spoke out against the bankers and their plan for world economic control, and as usual he was poisoned at a banquet days before his impeachment bill was pushed. After this atrocity, the gold standard was abolished. The 1933 gold seizure called for every citizen to turn in all gold pieces and certificates into the Treasury, robbing the public of the only wealth they had left. Next, the Federal Income Tax was brought into existence. It is technically unconstitutional because it is not apportioned, the Constitution calling for all taxes to be apportioned. Also, the number of states required to ratify the amendment was never met (according to the 16th Amendment). Not only is 35 percent of your hard-earned money taken every year by the Fed, but there is no law in existence forcing you to pay this tax, even though it is generally accepted and implied that you must. Joe Turner and Sherry Jackson are two retired I.R.S. agents who have not filed a federal income tax report for many years on the basis that it is not required and that it is unconstitutional. They have asked many questions and are still waiting for answers that will never come.

Thomas Jefferson once said: "I believe that banking institution are more dangerous than standing armies . . . If the American people ever allow private banks to control the issue of currency, the banks and corporations that will grow up around them will deprive the people of their property until their children wake up homeless on the continent their fathers conquered." This is very fatidic and foreshadowing. The obvious case of intentional war prompting during 9-11 has been set aside as a whole new chapter in *Part 4* of this book. Short summaries of previous examples from history are written above so the gist is comprehended. In *Part 4*, Section 1 ("9-11"), I will look more at the mechanics of such schemes. The September 11 terrorist attacks are no different than all the other instigations perpetrated by the international bankers and the United States Federal government, and I would even go so far as to say that the 9-11 attacks were orchestrated in a much more malign fashion using much more organization. They truly are a course in big business and bad government, the atrocities afflicted costing many more innocent lives. How many more falsities and belligerence will we allow? They started it, yes, but we must end it. We have acknowledged so many fabrications as truth that the truth has come to bear bruises and scars and is barely even recognizable anymore. If you wonder how so few people can control the world, just look at what they do. They cause disasters so they can profit and further reduce the people to a low standard of living.

They have schematically robbed the people of the real wealth, which is love, wisdom, and precious metals, in exchange for a massive reduction of freedoms and total dependence on a fraudulent fractional banking system. What is worse, the amount of innocent people killed by these greedy men has only increased throughout the past two centuries. The main reason the colonies went to war with King George III and England was because they were not allowed the freedom to issue their own currency and that they were forced under the yoke of the central bank of England. It is a good thing the people do not keep up on their history, for if they did, those in charge would not be able to do what they do. It would be too obvious. They just do the same things they have been doing this whole time, and the people are none the wiser. Furthermore, the treasonous organizations that funded the war machines in Russia and Germany are the same organizations that funded the Obama administration and National Socialism in the United States. OBAMA IS A CARBON COPY OF HITLER. He uses fascism in the guise of Marxist socialism to trick the people into thinking that he is here to save them, when he is really here to bail out the banks. The brokerage firms and banks which financed Obama's campaign make a long list with the top ones being Goldman Sachs (1 million dollars in funds), Citigroup Inc. (700,000 dollars), JPMorgan Chase & Co. (700,000 dollars), and Morgan Stanley (500,000 dollars). Just like Hitler, Obama has tried to raise an army of youths and hypnotize the children of America.

What is worse is that the people of the world have not a clue of what is going on and they praise Obama like he's Jesus. That is exactly the adoration Hitler received when he promised to free the German people. And what happened after that? Well, you know the story. If you want to know what Obama is all about just look at the life and works of his political advisor, Zbigniew Kazimierz Brzezinski, the man who has been delegating U.S. affairs since the Carter administration. He is also good friends with Paul Wolfowitz, former president of the World Bank and former U.S. Deputy Secretary of Defense during the reign of Bush, Jr. He helped plan the September 11 attacks as well as the Plan 2000, the Globalists plan to instigate a third world war and reduce the world's population to 500 million. Brzezinski called for a more controlled society in his book and Obama plans to enact this policy with a swift ease. He even wants to build a civilian army. One of Obama's controllers' prime targets is the youth, just like with Hitler. Just watch the little children singing for Obama in his campaign commercials and then watch the children singing for Hitler during the 1933 election . . . . eerily similar. After Obama got elected, the WorldNetDaily website reported:

> The official website of President-Elect Barack Obama, Change. gov, originally announced that Obama would "require" all middle school through college students to participate in community service programs; but after a flurry of blogs protested children being drafted into Obama's proposed youth corps, the website's wording was softened.
>
> Originally, under the tab "America Serves", Change.gov read, "President-Elect Obama will expand national service programs like AmeriCorps and Peace Corps and will create a new Classroom Corps to help teachers in under-served schools, as well as a new Health Corps, Clean Energy Corps, and Veterans Corps. Obama will call on citizens of all ages to serve America, by developing a plan to require 50 hours of community service in middle school and high school and 100 hours of community service in college *every year* [my emphasis].

In a speech in July of 2008 in Colorado Springs, Obama stated that he wanted to see a "civilian national security force" that would be as powerful and well-funded as the Marines, Navy, and Air Force. Do you really want to fight and die for rich men connected to secret societies who do not care about you?

OPPOSE WAR AND GENOCIDE

MAKE LOVE . . . . NOT HATE

Bibliography

Ackerman, Diane. *An Alchemy of Mind*. New York: Scribner, 2005.

Astucia, Salvador. *Opium Lords: Israel, the Golden Triangle, and the Kennedy Assassination*. N.p.: Dsharpwriter, 2002.

Audesirk, Teresa et al. *Biology: Life on Earth*. San Francisco: Pearson Education, Inc., 2008.

Baigent, Michael et al. *Holy Blood, Holy Grail*. United Kingdom: Jonathan Cape, 1982.

Barrett, David. *A Brief History of Secret Societies*. Philadelphia: Running Press, 2007.

Blumenfeld, Samuel. *NEA: Trojan Horse in American Education*. Boise, ID: The Paradigm Company, 1984.

Booth, Mark. *The Secret History of the World*. New York: The Overlook Press, 2008.

Braden, Gregg. *The Divine Matrix: Bridging Time, Space, Miracles, and Belief*. Carlsbad, CA: Hay House, 2007.

Braden, Gregg. *The Spontaneous Healing of Belief: Shattering the Paradigm of False Limits*. Hay House, 2008.

Branton. *The Omega Files: Greys, Nazis, Underground Bases and the New World Order*. N.p.: Inner Light—Global Communications, 2000.

Burgermeister, Jane. Interview by Kerry Cassidy and Bill Ryan. *Project Camelot*. Vienna, 2009. http://www.youtube.com/watch?v=PelTWCUmTsU.

Burisch, Dan. Interview by Kerry Cassidy and Bill Ryan. *Project Camelot*. Las Vegas, July 2006. http://www.youtube.com/watch?v=KhK3Os_eE4g.

Cannon, Dolores. *The Convoluted Universe: Book One*. Huntsville, AZ: Ozark Mountain Publishing, 2001.

Carroll, Lee, Tom Kenyon, and Patricia Cori. *The Great Shift: Co-Creating a New World for 2012 and Beyond*. San Francisco, CA: Weiser Books, 2009.

Chopra, Deepak. *The Seven Spiritual Laws of Success: A Practical Guide to the Fulfillment of Your Dreams*. San Rafael, CA: Amber-Allen, 1994.

Chopra, Deepak. *The Higher Self*. Audio Book. Nightingale-Conant, 2001.

Chopra, Deepak. *The Book of Secrets: Unlocking the Hidden Dimensions of Your Life*. Audio Book. Random House Audio Dimensions, 2004.

Chopra, Deepak. *The Spontaneous Fulfillment of Desire: Harnessing the Infinite Power of Coincidence*. Audio Book. Random House Audio Dimensions, 2003.

Christi, Nicolya. *2012 A Clarion Call: Your Soul's Purpose in Conscious Evolution*. Rochester: Bear & Company, 2011.

Clow, Barbara. *The Pleiadian Agenda: A New Cosmology for the Age of Light*. Rochester, VT: Bear & Company, 1995.

Clow, Barbara. *Alchemy of Nine Dimensions: Decoding the Vertical Axis, Crop Circles, and the Mayan Calendar*. Charlottesville, VA: Hampton Roads, 2004.

Collier, Alex. Interview by Rick Keefe. *Under-Appreciated Science Productions*. 1994. http://www.youtube.com/watch?v=f2ubrA3X7rM.

Collier, Alex. "Moon and Mars Lecture." 1998. http://www.youtube.com/watch?v=5Ls7lcturUQ.

Collier, Alex. "Earth Transformation Conference." Lecture. Hawaii, 2010. http://www.youtube.com/watch?v=0vqGRFTmANI.

Coogan, Gertrude. *Money Creators*. N.p.: Noontide, 1986.

Cooper, Milton. *Behold a Pale Horse*. Flagstaff, AZ: Light Technology Publications, 1991.

Cooper, Milton. "The Secret Government." Lecture. 1998. http://www.youtube.com/watch?v=O3B4hBAEj7Q.

Deagle, Bill. "The New World Disorder." Lecture, The Grananda Forum. 2005. http://www.youtube.com/watch?v=oNJWF_JpIyA.

Deagle, Bill. Interview by Kerry Cassidy and Bill Ryan. *Project Camelot*. Vista, California, 2007. http://www.youtube.com/watch?v=5W_3aneRPOg.

Dean, Bob. Interview by Kerry Cassidy and Bill Ryan. *Project Camelot*. Phoenix, AZ, 2007. http://www.youtube.com/watch?v=AbgHyrmgRZM.

Eisen, Johathan. *Suppressed Inventions and Other Discoveries: True Stories of Suppression, Scientific Cover-Ups, Misinformation, and*

Brilliant Breakthroughs (revealing the world's greatest secrets of science and medicine). New York: Perigee Trade, 2001.

Clancy, Joseph, trans. *Odes and Epodes* (Horace). Chicago: University of Chicago Press, 1960.

Frissell, Bob. *Nothing in this Book is True, But it's Exactly How Things Are*. Berkeley, CA: Frog Books, 1994.

Fulford, Benjamin. Interview with Kerry Cassidy and Bill Ryan. *Project Camelot*. Tokyo, 2008. http://www.youtube.com/watch?v=NKl3mZG6KzM.

Goldberg, Bruce. *New Age Hypnosis*. Woodbury, MN: Llewellyn, 1998.

Goldwag, Arthur. *Cults, Conspiracies, & Secret Societies: The Straight Scoop on Freemasons, the Illuminati, Skull & Bones, Black Helicopters, the New World Order, and many, many more*. New York: Vintage Books, 2009.

Goswani, Amit. *The Self-Aware Universe: how Consciousness creates the material world*. New York: Penguin Putnam, 1995.

Graves, Debbie. "Arcturian Commentary on a Major Energy Shift and Answers to Questions." *The Arcturian Circle*. July 27, 2010. www.ourreturnhome.com.

Graves, Debbie. "Using Your Vibration and Thoughts to Create Flow." *The Arcturian Circle*. July 27, 2010. www.ourreturnhome.com.

Green, George. Interview by Kerry Cassidy and Billy Ryan. *Project Camelot*. Washington, April 2008. http://www.youtube.com/watch?v=sSYXrWIA618.

Greer, Steven. Interview by Kerry Cassidy and Bill Ryan. *Project Camelot*. Barcelona, July 2009. http://www.youtube.com/watch?v=hzqDVOjtNhg.

Hall, Manly. *The Secret Teachings of All Ages: An Encyclopedic Outline of Masonic, Hermetic, Qabbalistic & Rosicrucian Symbolical Philosophy*. Los Angeles, CA: Philosophical Research Society, 1978.

Hancock, Graham. *Fingerprints of the Gods*. New York: Three Rivers Press, 1996.

Hancock, Graham. Interview by Kerry Cassidy and Bill Ryan. *Project Camelot*. Los Angeles, November 2010. http://www.youtube.com/watch?v=UkCnE8YdFP0.

Helsing, Jan van. *Secret Societies and Their Power in the 20th Century*. Germany: Ewertverlag, 1995.

Hoagland, Richard. *Dark Mission: The Secret History of NASA*. Feral House, 2007.

Hoagland, Richard. Interview by Kerry Cassidy and Bill Ryan. *Project Camelot*. Albuquerque, December 2007. http://www.youtube.com/watch?v=GDEcfohz8xE.

Hock, Ronald, trans. *The Infancy Gospels of James and Thomas*. Santa Rosa, CA: Polebridge Press, 1995.

Cook, Albert, trans. *The Odyssey* (Homer). New York: W. W. Norton & Company, 1967.

Icke, David . . . . *And the Truth Shall Set You Free*. Escondido, CA: Truth Seeker, 1997.

Icke, David. *The Biggest Secret: The Book that Will Change the World*. Scottsdale, AZ: Bridge of Love, 1999.

Icke, David. *Alice in Wonderland and the World Trade Center Disaster: Why the Official Story of 9-11 is a Monumental Lie.* Wildwood, MO: Bridge of Love, 2002.

Icke, David. *Tales from the Time Loop.* Wildwood, MO: Bridge of Love, 2003.

Icke, David. *The David Icke Guide to the Global Conspiracy (and how to end it).* Isle of Wight, UK: David Icke Books, 2007.

Icke, David. "The Secret History of the USA." Online posting. David Icke's Telling the Truth Archives. http://www.4shared.com/document/aRSLy3r1/The_Secret_History_of_the_USA_.html.

Icke, David. "Federal Reserve System Fraud." Online posting. David Icke's Telling the Truth Archives. http://prernalal.com/banned%20books/David%20Icke%20%20Federal%20Reserve%20System%20Fraud.pdf.

Icke, David. Interview by Kerry Cassidy and Bill Ryan. *Project Camelot.* Sedona, 2009. http://www.youtube.com/watch?v=y4UyEUldOLQ.

Ingerman, Sandra and Hank Wesselman. *Awakening to the Spirit World: The Shamanic Path of Direct Revelation.* Boulder, Co: Sounds True, Inc., 2010.

Jang, Hwee-Yong. *The Gaia Project 2012: Earth's Coming Great Changes.* Trans. Mira Tyson. Woodbury, MN: Llewellyn, 2007.

Jones, Alex. *9-11: Descent into Tyranny.* Oklahoma City: Hearthstone Publishing, 2002.

Judge, Edward and John Langdon. *Connections: A World History.* New Jersey: Pearson Education, Inc., 2009.

Kavassilas, George. "Our Journey and the Grand Deception." Lecture. June 2, 2009. http://www.youtube.com/watch?v=IZDcn-LJNIo.

Keith, Jim. *Mass Control: Engineering Human Consciousness*. Kempton, IL: Adventures Unlimited Press, 2003.

Kennedy, William. *Lucifer's Lodge: Satanic Ritual Abuse in the Catholic Church*. N.p.: Reviviscimus, 2004.

Key, Wilson. *Media Sexploitation: The Hidden Implants in America's Mass Media—And How They Program and Condition Your Subconscious Mind*. Boston: Prentice Hall Trade, 1976.

Knight-Jadczyk, Laura. *The Secret History of the World: And How to Get Out Alive*. Canada: Red Pill Press, 2005.

Layton, Bentley. *The Gnostic Scriptures*. New York: Doubleday, 1987.

Lewis, Jon. *The Mammoth Book of Cover-Ups: The 100 Most Disturbing Conspiracies of All Time*. Philadelphia: Running Press, 2007.

Lipton, Bruce. *The Biology of Belief: Unleashing the Power of Consciousness, Matter and Miracles*. San Rafael, CA: Mountain of Love Productions, 2005.

Lipton, Bruce, and Steve Bhaerman. *Spontaneous Evolution: Our Positive Future (and a way to get there from here)*. San Rafael, CA: Mountain of Love Productions, 2009.

Marciniak, Barbara. *Bringers of the Dawn: Teachings from the Pleiadians*. Rochester, VT: Bear & Company, 1992.

Marrs, Jim. *Crossfire: The Plot that Killed Kennedy*. Basic Books, 1993.

Marrs, Jim. *Alien Agenda: Investigating the Alien Presence Among Us*. New York: HarperPaperbacks, 1997.

Marrs, Jim. *Rule By Secrecy: The Hidden History that Connects the Trilateral Commission, the Freemasons, and the Great Pyramids*. New York: HarperCollins, 2000.

Marrs, Jim. *The Trillion Dollar Conspiracy: How the New World Order, Man-Made Diseases, and Zombie Banks are Destroying America*. New York: HarperCollins, 2010.

Marrs, Jim. *The Rise of the Fourth Reich: The Secret Societies that Threaten to Take Over America*. New York: HarperCollins, 2008.

Marrs, Jim. *Above Top Secret: Uncover the Mysteries of the Digital Age*. New York: HarperCollins, 2008.

Marrs, Jim. Interview by Kerry Cassidy and Bill Ryan. *Project Camelot*. Texas, 2009. http://www.youtube.com/watch?v=g2v0cu8pQOc.

Marrs, Texe. *Codex Magica: Secret Signs, Mysterious Symbols, and Hidden Codes of the Illuminati*. N.p.: RiverCrest, 2005.

Marrs, Texe. *Mysterious Monuments: Encyclopedia of Secret Illuminati Designs, Masonic Architecture, and Occult Places*. N.p.: RiverCrest, 2008.

Maxwell, Jordan. *Matrix of Power: How the World Has Been Controlled By Powerful People Without Your Knowledge*. Daly City, CA: The Book Tree, 2003.

Maxwell, Jordan. *That Old-Time Religion: The Story of Religious Foundations*. Daly, CA: The Book Tree, 2003.

Maxwell, Jordan. Interview by Kerry Cassidy and Bill Ryan. *Project Camelot*. October 8, 2009. http://www.youtube.com/watch?v=5jJKue2Ff6o.

McCollum, Aaron. Interview by Kerry Cassidy and Bill Ryan. *Project Camelot*. January 2010. http://www.youtube.com/watch?v=22S2TNMf8v4.

McLaren, Karla. *Your Aura & Your Chakras: The Owner's Manual*. San Francisco: Weiser Books, 1998.

Millanovich, Norma. *We, the Arcturians*. Scottsdale, AZ: Athena Publishing, 1990.

Humphries, Rolfe, trans. *Metamorphoses* (Ovid). Bloomington, IN: Indiana University Press, 1955.

Pearson, Birger. *Ancient Gnosticism: Traditions and Literature*. Minneapolis: Fortress Press, 2007.

Penczak, Christopher. *Ascenson Magick: Ritual, Myth & Healing for the New Aeon*. Woodbury, MN: Llewellyn Publications, 2007.

Perkins, John. *Confessions of an Economic Hitman*. San Francisco: Berrett-Koehler Publishers, 2004.

Rachele, Sal. "The Founders on Earth History." Article. Last modified October 2010. www.salrachele.com/channelings.htm.

Rachele, Sal. "The Arcturians on Conspiracy." Article. Last modified October 2010. http://www.salrachele.com/webchannelings/arcturiansonconspiracy.htm.

Rachele, sal. "The Arcturians on Space Travel." Article. Last modified November 2010. http://www.salrachele.com/webchannelings/arcturiansonspacetravel.htm.

Robinson, John. *Born in Blood: The Lost Secrets of Freemasonry*. M. Evans & Company, 1989.

Rodwell, J.M., trans. *The Koran*. Mineola, NY: Dover Publications, 2005.

Rudolph, Kurt. *Gnosis: The Nature & History of Gnosticism*. San Francisco: HarperCollins, 1987.

Sanders, Pete. *You Are Psychic!* New York: Simon and Schuster, 1999.

Sitchin, Zecharia. *The 12th Planet*. New York: HarperCollins, 1976.

Sitchin, Zecharia. *The Stairway to Heaven*. New York: HarperCollins, 1980.

Smith, Huston. *Cleansing the Doors of Perception: The Religious Significance of Entheogenic Plants and Chemicals*. New York: J.P. Tarcher/Putnam, 2000.

Springmeier, Fritz. *Bloodlines of the Illuminati*. Austin, TX: Ambassador House, 1998.

Springmeier, Fritz. *Be Wise as Serpents*. N.p.: Self-published, 2001.

Starr, Jelaila. *We are the Nibiruans: Return of the 12th Planet*. Lenexa, KS: The Nibiruan Council, 1996.

Starr, Jelaila. *The Mission Remembered*. Lenexa, KS: The Nibiruan Council, 2007.

Starr, Jelaila. *Bridge of Reunion*. Lenexa, KS: The Nibiruan Council, 1998.

Stone, Clifford. Interview by Kerry Cassidy and Bill Ryan. *Project Camelot*. Roswell, NM, 2007. http://www.youtube.com/watch?v=5W_3aneRPOg.

Stone, Joshua. *Hidden Mysteries: ET's, Ancient Mystery Schools and Ascension*. Flagstaff, AZ: Light Technology Publishing, 1995.

Stone, Joshua, and Rev. Janna Shelley Parker. *A Beginner's Guide to the Path of Ascension*. Flagstaff, AZ: Light Technology Publishing, 1998.

Strassman, Rick. *DMT The Spirit Molecule: A Doctor's Revolutionary Research into the Biology of Near-Death and Mystical Experiences*. Rochester, Vermont: Park Street Press, 2011.

Sutton, Antony. *Wall Street and the Rise of Hitler*. N.p.: G S G and Associates Publications, 1976.

Sutton, Antony. *America's Secret Establishment: An Introduction to the Order of Skull & Bones*. Walterville, OR: Trine Day Publishers, 2002 (reprint).

Sweeney, Patrick. *RFID For Dummies*. Hoboken, NJ: Wiley Publishing, 2005.

Trull, D. *Tesla: The Electric Magician*. N.p.: ParaScope, Inc., 1996.

Tsarion, Michael. *Atlantis, Alien Visitation, and Genetic Manipulation*. Santa Clara, CA: Angels at Work Publishing, 2002.

Weiss, Brian. *Through Time Into Healing: Discovering the Power of Regression Therapy to Erase Trauma and Transform Mind, Body, and Relationships*. New York: Simon and Schuster, 1992.

Wilcock, David. "Project Camelot Awake and Aware Conference." Lecture. September, 2009. http://www.youtube.com/watch?v=scym0WH3Jww.

Wilson, Robert. *Prometheus Rising*. Reno, NV: New Falcon Publications, 2004 (original publishing 1983).

2012. Directed by Ben Stewart. 2010. DVD.

Endgame. Directed by Alex Jones. Prisonplanet.tv., 2007.

Esoteric Agenda. Directed by Ben Stewart. 2010. DVD.

Fabled Enemies. Directed by Jason Bermas. Produced by Alex Jones and Korey Rowe. Prisonplanet.tv., 2009.

Fall of the Republic: The Presidency of Barack H. Obama. Directed by Alex Jones. Prisonplanet.tv., 2009.

Kymatica. Directed by Ben Stewart. 2009. DVD.

Libra Rising. "Politics and the Underground." 4 Feb. 2003. Web. http://www.librarising.com.

Libra Rising. "Secret Covenant." 4 Feb. 2003. Web. http://www.librarising.com.

Masonic Symbols of Power in Their Seat of Power. Online posting. http://www.cuttingedge.org/n1040.html.

"Mystery Babylon." Produced by Texe Marrs. Short video. 2008. http://www.youtube.com/watch?v=P-po-Qhs2K8.

Police State 4: The Rise of F.E.M.A. Narrated by Alex Jones. Directed by Alex Jones, Rob Dew, and Jason Douglass. Prisonplanet.tv., 2010.

"Satan in the Vatican." Produced by Texe Marrs. Short video. 2007. http://www.youtube.com/watch?v=knmL2ODvJPw.

Terrorstorm: A History of Government-Sponsored Terrorism. Directed by Alex Jones. Prisonplanet.tv., 2007.

"The Blind and the Dead." Produced by Texe Marrs. Short video. 2008. http://www.youtube.com/watch?v=4xQp1UolKPU.

The Holy Bible: Revised Standard Version. New York: Penguin Group, 1962.

The Reptilian Agenda. Directed by David Icke. 2001. http://www.youtube.com/watch?v=ctIpUmJjkAs.

Zeitgeist: The Movie. Directed by Peter Joseph. 2007. DVD.

Zeitgeist: Addendum. Directed by Peter Joseph. 2008. DVD.

END OF VOLUME 1

Index

A

Alpha Draconis 45, 52, 55, 65, 100, 173, 242, 363
Andromedans 17, 46, 57-8, 85, 240, 363
Angelic Hierarchy 178
Arcturians 17, 26, 28, 46, 57, 59, 61-3, 122, 142, 234-5, 239-41, 243, 329, 363
Ascended Masters 8, 26, 28, 90-1, 124, 128, 143, 240, 363
aura 28, 30, 63, 65, 172, 239, 329, 363

B

Bilderberg 270, 301, 304, 363
Bill Deagle 164, 316, 363
Bush 109, 233, 261, 304, 308-10, 320, 363

C

chakras 16, 19, 21, 27-8, 32, 34, 38, 40, 42, 62-3, 92, 99, 107, 154, 159, 240
channeling 12, 107, 121-2, 175, 206, 221, 226, 234, 302, 310, 363
Club of Rome 296, 301, 363
Colombus 245-6, 363
Communism 156, 305, 363
Council on Foreign Relations xii, 171, 301, 305, 363

D

Da Vinci 225, 246, 260, 274
Density xvi, 9, 18, 25-7, 31, 33-4, 40, 43, 48-55, 60-3, 121-3, 126-7, 145-6, 179, 242, 291
Dimension xii, 5, 8-19, 22, 25, 27, 31-3, 36-40, 50, 72, 75-6, 100-1, 143-5, 177-9, 215, 239-44
dopamine 191, 363

E

Earth 9-11, 34-7, 42, 44-7, 49-55, 57-69, 73-6, 78-86, 89-91, 93-4, 101-4, 122-9, 148-9, 174-5, 239-45, 289-91
Elementals 11, 126

F

Fascism 163, 260-1, 299, 319
Federal Reserve 104, 158, 267, 277-9, 281, 296, 300, 306, 312, 317, 326, 363
Freemasons 120, 157, 160, 172, 205-6, 208, 261-7, 271, 300, 313, 324, 328, 363

G

Galactic Federation of Light   28, 67, 174, 364
Greys   57, 60, 67, 110, 148, 242, 321, 364

H

Hand Clow   9, 16, 59, 123, 127, 243, 364
Hasan   191-2, 196, 364
Hitler   154, 206, 302-3, 319-20, 331, 364

I

Icke   95, 109, 170, 261, 325-6, 333, 364

K

Knights of Malta   154, 205, 208, 251-2, 254, 258, 273-4, 364

M

Marciniak   40, 59, 327, 364
Maxwell   157, 275, 282, 328, 364
Merkabah   8, 19, 122, 143-4, 159, 164, 215, 364

N

New World Order   xii, 67, 87, 125, 166, 177, 180, 207-8, 260, 264, 269-70, 277, 296, 307, 310, 321

O

Orion   17, 41, 44-5, 52-8, 65, 77, 79-80, 100, 111, 136, 148, 242, 364

P

Pilgrims   196-7, 254-7, 364
Pleiadians   9-10, 17, 27, 46, 52-3, 57-9, 71, 78, 85, 91, 122, 144, 177, 239, 241, 243-4
Pope   112, 127, 131, 145, 156, 172, 188, 195-200, 203-5, 207, 220, 223, 229, 232, 273, 364

R

Reptilians   xi-xii, 45, 51-2, 55-8, 65, 67, 78-80, 82, 98-100, 109, 111-12, 148-9, 179, 242, 260-1, 291
Rockefeller   280, 285, 301, 303-4, 308, 312, 318, 364
Rome   127, 161-2, 170, 172-3, 181, 184, 205, 217-20, 229, 232, 241, 273-5, 295-7, 301, 363-4
Roosevelt   264, 276-7, 290, 297, 300, 303, 364
Rosicrucians   200-1, 205, 208, 262, 264-8, 274, 298, 364
Rothschild   xii, 98, 171, 206, 263, 267-8, 281, 296, 298-300, 364
Round Table   296-7, 301, 364
Royal Institute of International Affairs   171, 364

S

Secret government   64, 103, 306, 323
Sirius   17, 28, 46, 65, 70, 77, 84, 91, 100, 136, 148, 242, 364
Socialism   297, 304, 319, 364

T

Templars   131, 192, 197-205, 227, 230,
    245-6, 251, 254, 261, 271, 273-4, 365
Tesla   v, 287-93, 331, 365
Trilateral Commission   xii, 171, 296, 301,
    304, 328, 365

V

Vatican   139, 160, 184, 188, 204, 207-8,
    213, 229, 241, 251, 258, 273-4, 311,
    332, 365
vibrational frequency   25, 27, 36, 56,
    108, 365
Vietnam   304-8, 313-15, 365

W

Watchers   233-4, 365
Windsor   274, 365
Wolfowitz   320, 365
World Bank   276, 305, 320, 365
World War I   154, 290, 301-3, 305, 308,
    315, 365
World War II   133, 154, 174, 282, 303-5,
    307, 315, 365

Y

Yahweh   146, 160, 204, 365

Z

Zoroastrianism   130-1, 180, 186, 188, 365

Made in the USA
Las Vegas, NV
13 November 2021